International Financial Flows

A Statistical Handbook

International Financial Flows
A Statistical Handbook

Geoffrey E. J. Dennis

Senior Economist, W. Greenwell & Co.

formerly

Economist, Bank for International
Settlements, Basle

Lexington Books

D. C. Heath and Company
Lexington, Massachusetts
Toronto

First published in 1984 by

Lexington Books
D. C. Heath and Company
125 Spring Street
Lexington, Massachusetts 02173

Library of Congress Cataloging in Publication Data

Dennis, Geoffrey E. J. (Geoffrey Edwin James)
   International financial flows.

   Bibliography: p.
   1. Capital movements — Statistical services.
   2. International finance — Statistical services.
   I. Title.
HG3891.D46   1984   332'.042   83-25557
ISBN 0-669-07788-7

ISBN 0-669-07788-7

Typeset in Great Britain by Herts Typesetting Services, Hertford
Printed and bound in Great Britain by The Chanctonbury Press, Sussex

Contents

Acknowledgements

In nearly all respects, this book has taken a considerable time to complete. It may be said that it had its origins in early 1977, at Loughborough University, when Professor David Llewellyn and I began to write a consultancy report entitled *Trends in International Banking and Capital Markets* which was published by the Banker Research Unit. Inevitably, in undertaking the work for this report, which ran until the end of 1980, I became increasingly familiar and greatly interested in the available statistical information on international financial flows of funds. Further valuable experience for this work was gained through a lecture presentation on this statistical information that I made from 1978 at the annual Summer School for international bankers held at the University of Surrey. These schools were organised by Philip Thorn Associates Ltd. Indeed the original suggestion to write this book came from Philip Thorn, himself, and therefore I owe a special debt of gratitude to him for his encouragement.

The book has greatly benefited from the work undertaken while I was a visitor in the Financial Studies Division of the World Bank, Washington DC during the summer of 1981. I wish to express my gratitude to the World Bank for their courtesy and for the use of office and library facilities while I was there. In particular, I would like to thank Alex Fleming and Ami Fullerton for helping to organise my visit to the Bank and for their encouragement of, and interest in, my work. Many other people in the World Bank gave of their time to speak to me on one or more of the statistical areas in which they have expertise and I wish to thank in this respect Nicholas Hope, Jo Saxe, Tom Klein, Alisa Sarel, Alan Roe and Sally Chua for their help. I would also like to thank a number of other people whom I met while in the USA and who discussed various aspects of international financial statistics with me, including Rodney Mills at the Federal Reserve Board, Patrick Paradiso and Norman Klath of Morgan Guaranty Trust Company and Gerry Johnson, Richard Walton and, in particular, John O'Connor at the International Monetary Fund. The visit to the World Bank was financed by the Academic Initiatives and Development (AID)

Fund of Loughborough University and I express my sincere gratitude to my former employers for enabling me to pursue my research in this way. I would also like to thank Christopher Johnson of Lloyds Bank, David Ashby of Grindlays Bank and Werner Danneman of the IMF for assistance with various parts of my work.

My greatest intellectual debt is, however, to my friend, and former colleague at Loughborough University, David Llewellyn. It was he who first interested me in the field of international banking and I benefited greatly from his expertise during our work together on this subject. He has also been an enthusiastic supporter of this book and of the visit to Washington, which was such an advantage to the work. Finally, I wish to give particular thanks to Su Spencer for her very efficient preparation of the final manuscript which eventually had to be completed in considerable haste.

The basic work for this book was completed while I was Midland Bank Lecturer in Economics at Loughborough University, with minor updating of the statistical material immediately prior to publication being done since then. The views expressed are mine alone, therefore, and should not, in any way, be attributed to my new employers or to the Bank for International Settlements. I also accept all responsibility for any remaining errors and omissions.

Geoffrey E. J. Dennis

Basle, July 1983

Section 1
Introduction

Chapter 1

Background and Scope of the Book

During the 1970s international flows of funds increased in size greatly. Much of this rise may be broadly explained by the substantial balance of payents disequilibria which followed the two phases of sharp, upward movements in oil prices in 1973 and 1979. In addition, however, the seeds of increasing external disequilibria, and therefore the need to recycle funds from surplus to deficit countries, had been sown even earlier than 1973 as a result of the diverging economic performances of many industrialised countries, which led among other things to huge US balance of payments deficits in 1969–71 and the final collapse of fixed exchange rates in 1973. With the *de facto* abandonment of this constraint on economic policy and the first oil 'crisis' (which by being a novel experience for the world economy was potentially and, in practice, more disruptive than the subsequent oil price rises), inflation rose throughout the world economy. With certain countries, notably Germany, allowing a much less significant increase in their rates of inflation than others, further divergences of economic performance occurred. At the same time, structural factors began to affect balance of payments performance in many countries to a greater extent than previously. This was most obviously seen the the almost total dependence of certain industrialised countries, such as Japan and Germany, on a vital commodity (oil) that was both high in price and uncertain in supply, while other countries, for example the UK, gained a major structural balance of payments support through the discovery of huge petroleum resources within their borders.

While most non-oil exporting developing countries were faced with similar increases in their import bills, these countries also suffered severely from the decline in the value of their exports as recession in the industrialised world in 1974–5, and less buoyant growth for much of the 1970s than had been experienced previously, reduced the demand for those primary products which frequently constituted a major segment of the exports of developing countries. The enormous balance of payments deficits of both the industrialised world and the non-oil developing countries plus, in the latter case, the long term nature of those deficits, posed a severe problem of recycling funds from the surplus oil-producers to these deficit units. The growth of the external debt of developing countries is a testament to the strength of these forces and the attempts of many developing countries to borrow funds both simply to finance these deficits and to invest in revenue-raising projects.

With the second round of substantial oil price increases in 1979, the OPEC balance of payments surplus reappeared in dramatic fashion, while the current deficit and cumulative debt problems of the non-oil developing countries, having been only partially alleviated in the adjustment period after the first oil shock, worsened again. In this period, however, a more concerted and determined effort was made by the industrial nations to restrict the inflationary consequences of the oil price increases. In this they were generally successful, although the world recession of 1980–2 was probably both longer and deeper as a result. The interrelation of such factors as weak commodity prices and low demand for developing country exports with high interest-rates, as the fight against inflation continued, culminated in the serious debt difficulties faced by many developing countries, in particular Mexico, Brazil and Argentina, in the second half of 1982.

While this combination of circumstances led to sharp increases in international flows of funds in this whole period, there has also, in recent years, been a rise in the number of statistical systems that report such flows. It is the objective of this book to provide a comprehensive guide to the meaning, scope, methods of use and problems of certain of these reporting systems. In a sense, therefore, this book seeks to provide a different perspective on the international financial turmoil of the 1970s. As such, minimal comment will be made in the book on the main trends and events of the period under study. Given the much more modest objective of the book, considerable emphasis is placed on the statistical series themselves and their meaning.

Following this introductory chapter the book has five main sections. Each of the first four of these sections considers a particular type of international financial data, which may, nevertheless, be derived from more than one source within a given section. In Section

2, on international banking flows, the main focus is the data published by the Bank of International Settlements (BIS). In addition, however the rapidly growing activity of the International Monetary Fund (IMF) in publishing such data is discussed while other sources of such banking data are also noted. The alternative concepts of 'external bank lending' and the 'international lending market' are defined and there is a study of the available data on the global 'eurocurrency market' (Chapter 6). In addition, Chapter 7 considers some of the published information on the maturity transformation of international banks.

Section 3 covers data on borrowing on the world's capital markets through the negotiation of eurocurrency credits (Chapter 9) and the floating of external bonds (Chapter 10). The main source of statistical material for this section is the Organisation for Economic Cooperation and Development (OECD), although reference is also made to the now-defunct Capital Market System (CMS) of the World Bank and to data published by Morgan Guaranty Trust Company.

Section 4 covers data on the external debt of developing countries published by the World Bank (Chapter 11) and the Development Assistance Committee (DAC) of the OECD (Chapter 12). In addition, Chapter 12 describes the flow data on transfers of funds of all types to developing countries published by the DAC. While there is considerable overlap between Sections 2, 3 and 4 in terms, in particular, of flows from international banks, Section 5 is independent of all other sections. This describes the information published by the IMF on its own activity of raising funds from and lending to member countries. Chapter 14 is crucial in the work of this section in that it seeks to explain the very complex 'Fund Accounts' (published on a monthly basis in *International Financial Statistics*) that summarise the borrowing and lending activities of the IMF.

The final section consisting of one chapter is rather different and is intended to act in part as an overall conclusion, but mainly to provide some empirical evidence on the comparability of the sources surveyed in the book. Through graphical inspection and the estimation of simple regression equations, it considers the question of whether these sources provide similar estimates of new borrowing for a sample of eleven countries. Given the disparate sources and their conceptual differences, the result that only limited positive association between the series is found should not be surprising. However this neither devalues the empirical evidence itself nor questions the validity of any of the statistical sources, given that they each have a different set of objectives and a role to play in the provision of information concerning international financial flows.

In this book, data for the statistical series being described are taken to the end of 1981 (the latest date, at the time of writing for which figures are available for all the series in the book). In general, flow data are presented in annual form and stock data on an end-year basis. This both simplifies the treatment of the series and allows the main focus to be placed on the constituents of the series themselves rather than a commentary on what trends may be indicated in the figures for a particular time-period.

These sections therefore establish the scope of the book. In concentrating on a survey of published statistical sources on international flows of funds, mainly emanating from international organisations and other parts of the public sector, it is inevitable that certain areas of interest are omitted. Perhaps the most notable exclusion from this book is a treatment of the rapidly growing activity of country risk assessment. This is justified given that most of the leading banks in the international lending business possess their own country risk 'systems' of greater or lesser degrees of sophistication and that there is as yet no central public sector source of information of this type.

Increasing interest is being shown in reporting systems of international financial flows. Certain very brief surveys of some of them have been published recently.[1] The source of information that has had most influence on the structure and contents of this book is the manual of international financial statistics published by the BIS.[2] However the uniqueness of this volume lies in the way the statistical series are presented and the inclusion of some empirical evidence.

Many purposes are served by writing a handbook on international financial statistics. Apart from the general objective of providing a broad picture of the scale and direction of international flows of funds in recent years, the book is intended to serve a number of purposes both for individual banks and central monetary authorities.[3] At the level of the individual bank, it would seem that at least five purposes may be served both by having the statistics available AND, even more crucially, of ensuring that economists and other members of the bank's staff are familiar with the data and their advantages and drawbacks. Firstly, the international banking data are themselves the 'raw material' of an international bank's activities. In a sense they are a global 'snapshot' of the business which an international banker is completing at an individual level. Secondly, such data

[1] See IMF Survey (1976), Holsen (1978), Baer (1981), Economist (1982).

[2] See BIS (1979).

[3] See Bank of England (1981).

on bank lending, capital market borrowing and external debt provide an indication of the indebtedness of countries to which a bank may be lending or may be contemplating extending a credit line. As such, these data should form part of an up-to-date and rigorous risk analysis of individual debtor countries. Thirdly, and reversing the previous argument, international banking data provide an indication of the rate of growth of external lending both at a global level and by banks in an individual country. As a result, a bank will be able to compare the rate of growth of its overall international lending operations with such figures covering all banks. This point leads on to a fourth, and in recent years, crucial purpose of these data, namely that of allowing a bank to estimate the movement of its market share of total lending and deposits. Finally, an individual bank may wish to use such figures for internal forecasting and analysis (Bank of England, 1981). To attain such an objective, it is clear that a deep understanding of the figures is required.

International financial data are of considerable importance to central banks for many reasons, some of which overlap with those relating to individual private banks set out above. While a central bank will be interested in a reliable measure of international financial flows, its major concern, on which evidence may be derived from the data systems surveyed in this book, is likely to be the exposure of the banks under its jurisdiction to individual countries and in total. This would lead on naturally to a consideration of the possible regulation and supervision of international banking activity and of capital adequacy. International banking data also provide an estimate of the eurocurrency market in the currency of the country where a particular central bank is located. For example, it is likely that a major purpose served by international banking data for the Bank of England is to provide a reliable estimate of the size of the eurosterling market.

Unfortunately, the picture of international financial flows that may be derived from the statistical systems surveyed in this book and the successful attainment of the objectives of certain groups in studying such systems, are hampered by certain problems that afflict these data series. Many problems exist at the level of individual series and will be discussed at the appropriate points later in the book. However, certain general problems should be briefly noted at this stage. Firstly, the figures are imperfect in the sense that information on certain flows – in particular short-term financing and non-guaranteed private sector debt – are not complete. Secondly, as will be apparent at certain points in the text, comparability of the series is handicapped by a lack of consistency over certain definitional issues (*The Economist,* 1982). These include the definitions of a eurocurrency credit and oil exporting country, whether or not an estimate of the eurocurrency market should include data on bank's foreign currency positions *vis-à-vis* residents and many others. Thirdly, to be of maximum usage, statistical information has to be as up-to-date as possible. However given the enormous scope of the data collection processes for many of these series, adequate timeliness is difficult to achieve. Fourthly, confidentiality between lender and borrower and over the external debt of a particular country may restrict the amount of available information on certain flows of funds. While such confidentiality is understandable and has to be respected the effect may be to provide a somewhat distorted picture of financial flows to and from certain countries. Fifthly, the data systems surveyed in this book provide information on the quantity of financial flows. Added information of considerable value to an individual bank is the quality of such flows; this is the point where the aggregate data systems of this book and the country risk analysis of individual banks may be used in their most effective combination.

Finally, no one data system covers all financial flows. As a result, it may be necessary to aggregate data from individual systems, with the elimination where possible of overlaps. To enable this to be done most effectively even more collaboration between the organisations producing the disparate data sources is probably needed. An alternative path which may be followed to improve the quality of information on international financial flows has recently been proposed by the Group of Thirty.[4] This panel of international bankers and academics recommended firstly the establishment of a central statistical unit to collect and process full information on international bank lending. The doubts over this proposal are that the international bank lending data already being published byt the BIS are of a high standard, that much of the information to be collected by this unit is likely to be highly confidential and that flows from non-banks are ignored. A second proposal of the Group argues for the establishment of a consultative group of international bankers to improve the flow of information on all aspects of financial intermediation. It remains to be seen whether the Institute of International Finance which was established in Washington in 1983 will fulful either of these objectives successfully.

It should be clear from this brief introductory chapter that the provision of statistics on international financial flows and the volume of the flow themselves are growing rapidly. As the number of countries involved in international lending and the number of resche-

[4] Group of Thirty (1982).

duling rise, considerable pressure will exist for continuous statistical improvements. It should be left to the reader to judge the quality of the series as they are available at present and to identify where improvements could be made in the reporting of international financial flows.

Section 2
International Banking Statistics

Chapter 2

Statistical Methodology

Before undertaking any discussion of publicised statistics on international banking flows, the methodology underlying the survey should be set out clearly. Such statistics may be defined within any one data series according to certain procedures on the principles of currency, residency, geography and by sector. Many of the observed differences in figures from alternative sources are a result of the adoption of different procedures on these principles or the fact that series use different principles to define their data. These principles will be explained in this chapter (see Dennis, 1983).

The application of the first two of these principles is illustrated in

TABLE 2.1
The Currency/Residency Structure of Banks' Claims

	Currency of Claim		
	DOMESTIC (Funded in domestic markets)	*DOMESTIC* (Funded in eurocurrency markets) (e.g. Dollars)	*FOREIGN*
HEAD OFFICE Claim on: Domestic Resident Non-Resident[1]	A B	A B	C D
OVERSEAS BRANCH Claim on: Domestic Resident Non-Resident[2]	(e.g. Sterling) A B	[1] B	[2] D

[1] Including claims against overseas branches of the parent bank.
[2] That is, non-residents of the country in which the branch itself is located.

Table 2.1, in which each cell corresponds to a certain type of bank claim. The table is in two parts to show the different statistical treatments of the claims of a bank's head office and one of its overseas branches. In this section, the examples of a US bank with its head office in New York and a branch in London will be used. The distinction is also made in Table 2.1 between a domestic currency loan funded through domestic money markets and one funded in the eurocurrency markets outside the country in which the lending bank is located. It is assumed that all foreign currency loans are funded in the euromarkets. Given that most banks having some international business also have some asset and liability positions in domestic currencies and against domestic residents of the country where the bank is located,[1] there is generally no such thing as a *purely* international bank. Element A in Table 2.1 covers such domestic banking and as such activity is not part of international banking it is beyond the scope of this survey. Turning to the 'international' elements of the balance-sheet and considering initially lending by the head office of the US parent bank, Type B assets in Table 2.1 are frequently termed 'traditional bank claims' that is cross-border (i.e. against non-residents including banks and overseas branches of the parent bank) claims in the domestic currency of the country in which the bank is located. A dollar loan by a US bank to Brazil for example would be included in this category. The source of the dollar funds for the Brazilian loan in question is immaterial to its inclusion in this category of cross-border bank claim (although it is, of course, likely to be of vital importance to the bank making the loan). However, this distinction is of considerable importance in figures for new eurocurrency credits, as will be clarified in Section 3 where data on these credits are presented. Element C reflects the existence of a foreign currency claim of a bank against a resident of the same country. An example in this case would be a dollar loan by a German bank to a company in that country. Although not part of that bank's 'external' banking activity, such a cross-currency position is a part of the broad concept of the 'eurocurrency' market (the critical characteristic of which is the existence of a bank asset denominated in a currency foreign to the country in which the bank is located). Finally, element D corresponds to the narrow definition of the eurocurrency market where a bank claim is both of the cross-border and cross-currency type. A dollar loan by a German bank to a firm in France would be an example of such a claim.

---

[1] The key exceptions to this rule are likely to be banks in an offshore financial centre (e.g. the Bahamas, Cayman Islands) where local law may prohibit such domestic business.

Turning briefly to the second half of Table 2.1, in which the lending is assumed to be undertaken by a US bank branch in London, the analysis of the last two paragraphs should be repeated with the crucial differences (in comparison to head office loans) that the domestic currency of this branch is now considered, for statistical purposes, to be sterling and the category of non-residents includes all borrowers outside the United Kingdom. It is clear from this table that, for the purposes of quantifying certain types of international banking flow, the location of the bank or branch is of paramount importance and not the country of incorporation of the parent bank. One interesting implication of this procedure is that a dollar loan by an overseas branch of a US bank to a US company is included in international banking statistics as a eurocurrency claim on non-residents (a Type D asset in Table 2.1) as, although the flow of funds is ultimately between two sectors in the same economy, the loan is indicative of the operation of financial intermediation at the international level. As a result, the second half of Table 2.1 covers a much broader concept of offshore lending than that undertaken by 'shell' branches in offshore centres such as those in the Bahamas and Singapore (see Chapter 3). Such offshore lending is included in Table 2.1, alongside the lending activity by fully-staffed overseas operations of a parent bank.

Returning briefly to banks' claims in domestic currency against residents (Element A). Such activity is excluded from international lending data even if the funds used are raised in the euromarkets. Despite this procedure, the interplay between domestic monetary policy and the euromarkets may be seen even in this case. Although the use of the euromarkets as a source of funds for dollar lending to US residents, for example, is not reflected in international banking data, such a practice may be consequent upon the shortage or high cost of domestic dollar funds, with nominal demand and the success of domestic monetary policy being influenced accordingly (Frydl, 1982). In summary, the importance of principles of residency and currency in the labelling of assets should be immediately clear from Table 2.1, with residency referring to whether the asset or liability position of a bank is against a resident or non-resident and the currency principle referring to whether the position is denominated in domestic or foreign currency.

Data published by various sources estimating the extent of bank business covering elements B, C and D will be surveyed in this section. The combination of elements B and D are defined as 'external bank lending' in that all claims are of the cross-border type (i.e. against non-residents). Here the residency principle is used to define the asset figures. Secondly, elements C and D are cross-currency assets, and are termed *'the eurocurrency market'*. As noted above the key characteristics of such assets is their denomination in foreign currency and therefore this illustrates the use of the currency principle. Finally, the composite total of elements B, C and D includes any asset satisfying the criterion of residency (cross-border) or currency (cross-currency). This concept will be referred to as *'the international lending market'* which is a useful, but by no means unanimously-adopted, label for this amalgam of bank claims.

An important consideration in the analysis of any banking data is the group of countries whose banks are included in the survey. This collection of countries is conventionally known as the 'Reporting Group' or 'Reporting Area' and will be referred to in this way, here. This is the operation of the principle of geography in defining a data series in international banking. Clearly, if two series have Reporting Areas that differ in size, this will be an important source of variation in the data from these series, demonstrating the importance of this geographical principle.

Statistics for the international banking assets included in Table 2.1 may be reported in 'gross' or 'net' forms and it is in this sense that the data may be defined on a sectoral principle. In this interpretation, gross figures include all banks' assets and liabilities whether these positions are against other banks or non-banks. Therefore, they are inflated by any inter-bank flows that occur which do not add to the volume of credit created in the international banking sector. In contrast a 'net' series is derived by adjusting the gross figures for such inter-bank activity according to certain estimating procedures. Given that it is a gross figure that is actually reported by banks, and that the necessary adjustments for inter-bank activity may be difficult to estimate accurately, the resultant net series are likely to be subject to higher margins of error than the gross figures.[2]

The data to be surveyed are derived, as is clear from Table 2.1, from the *asset* sides of international banks' balance-sheets and in this volume the concept of international banking will be defined accordingly. It may be argued[3] that, in particular to do with the eurocurrency market, measurement should be based on bank liabilities. Given that, although total assets and liabilities of a bank will be equal, there is no certainty that foreign currency or external positions

---

[2] These interpretations of 'gross' and 'net' positions should be distinguished from the alternative interpretation of gross claims on a country (that is without considering banks' liabilities to that country) and claims 'net' of liabilities.

[3] For example, Duffy and Giddy (1978).

will be equivalent, this is an important issue. The argument for making use of liabilities data is based on their homogeneous character (compared to assets which may include physical items) and the fact that the advantages of the euromarkets over domestic money markets (for example, the absence of reserve requirements) impinge more directly on this side of a bank's balance-sheet. However the alternative procedure of concentrating on bank assets is followed in this volume to allow emphasis to be placed on outstanding bank lending.[4] Accordingly, no specification of the data is made on the principle of the source of funds. However, at certain points in the text, a figure for assets minus liabilities (the 'net'[5] position of a bank) will be calculated for banks in a certain country or for all banks against a particular borrowing or lending country or country group.

All major sources of international banking data present them in *stock* form, i.e. the total of outstanding bank assets and liabilities at one point in time. This procedure will, in general, be followed in this text so that data for the fourth quarter of 1981, for example, should be interpreted as the outstanding stock of assets at the end of that quarter. Nevertheless, at times, the *flow* change in assets or liabilities will be presented to define the change in outstanding bank positions over a particular time-period. Combining the principles in the last two paragraphs, it is therefore possible to define the flow change in net bank assets (or liabilities) over a particular time-period. In Chapter 3, this will be defined as the 'absorption' of funds by borrowing countries (a rise in net bank assets) or the 'supply' of funds by borrowing countries (a rise in net bank liabilities). All data included in this section are denominated in dollars.

Two major conceptual problems in the interpretation of banking data should be noted at this stage. These problems of 'valuation effects' and 'end of year inter-bank operations' both have the potential effect of distorting the reported data on international banking. In any particular time-period if these influences on the series are considered to be significant they should be allowed for by adjustment of the data themselves.

[4] In fact, this is a very common procedure in commentaries on international banking and the eurocurrency market (e.g. Ashby, 1981, Sterling 1980a, 1980b, Griffith-Jones, 1980).

[5] This should not be confused with the 'net' size of external bank lending. See Footnote 2.

VALUATION EFFECTS

Valuation effects arise when exchange rates between the dollar and any other currency in which any international bank activity is denominated fluctuate during a particular data period. All tertiary sources publish banking data denominated in US dollar values. In principle both the BIS and IMF convert non-dollar banking statistics into dollar values at the market rate ruling at the end of the data period.[6] Therefore, any fall in the dollar exchange rate against a local currency within a reporting period will artificially increase the dollar value of that country's international banking activity. Conversely, any rise in the dollar's value will reduce the end-period dollar value of banks' outstanding assets and liabilities.[7]

With the advent of floating exchange rates in the 1970s, this problem of data distortion has become potentially very serious. Although such effects cannot be predicted due to the uncertainty over future exchange rate movements, ex-post estimates may be made. Formerly these were reported on an annual basis in the BIS *Annual Report,* while they have frequently been reported in an *ad hoc* way in the text of the BIS quarterly survey of international banking developments (see Chapter 3). More recently, BIS publicity, although reporting stock data in unadjusted form, has published flow data which have been adjusted for exchange-rate effects. Comparison of the two series enables an estimate of these effects to be made. Estimates of the valution effects affecting external bank lending in 1978–81 are given in Table 2.2. In 1981, for example, the rise in the

TABLE 2.2
Valuation effects[1] affecting series for external bank lending (BIS data; $ billion)

1978	+ 20.0
1979	+ 5.0
1980	– 20.0
1981	– 37.1

[1] A positive (negative) figure indicates that a fall (rise) in the dollar's exchange rate has artificially raised (lowered) the dollar value of bank positions. Therefore to derive the valuation-adjusted change in external bank lending, the valuation effects should be subtracted from (added to) the unadjusted data.

[6] Individual central banks collect their own figures in local currency and report them in this form to these two organisations.

[7] Obviously if there are no changes in end-period exchange rate values the data are unaffected, even if intra-period fluctuations have occurred.

dollar led to an artificial reduction of the dollar value of external bank lending. To derive the valuation-adjusted change in external bank lending, therefore, the exchange-rate effects ($37.1 billion) should, in this case, be added to the unadjusted figures.

However, such annual figures may mask the offsetting valuation effects that arise from sharp and opposing quarterly exchange rate fluctuations. For example, in the second half of 1981, a fall in the dollar led to *positive* valuation effects of $31.2 billion which were more than offset by negative valuation effects in the first half of the year. Therefore, the use of quarterly data that is unadjusted for valuation effects is particularly hazardous, due to the potential for greater distortion compared to annual data for new bank lending.

In his own study (see below) Jay Sterling (Sterling 1980a) calculated valuation effects for his reporting group of fifty-eight countries. Given the smaller scope of the BIS reporting group of fifteen countries plus US bank branches in certain offshore centres (see Chapter 3), Sterling's estimates of valuation effects will be higher than those of the BIS. Between 1964 and 1978 Sterling estimated cumulative net valuation effects to be $122 billion, reducing the size of his estimate of the true international lending market by around 9%.[8]

WINDOW-DRESSING EFFECTS

A second source of possible data distortion is the result of the regular build-up of asset and liability positions between international banks towards 'make-up day'. Such operations, which typically occur at the end of calendar years are often termed 'window-dressing' effects and are generally unwound in the first quarter of the following year so that their effect on the published data is generally confined to these two quarters. This growth of inter-bank activity at such times affects any international banking data to the extent that it involves reporting banks.[9]

A number of procedures may be followed to adjust for such operations, which are difficult to estimate directly and accurately. A first alternative is to undertake a seasonal adjustment of the basic

[8] The main periods of negative valuation effects were 1967–70 (some devaluations against the dollar) and 1974–5 and of positive effects were 1971–4 and 1976–8.

[9] There is a separate source of distortion of the data from the inter-bank flows and funds which occur at all times of the year as funds are 'churned' or redistributed through the markets. The derivation of a 'net' series to adjust for these permanent effects is explained in Chapters 3 and 6.

series. Given the seasonal pattern of 'window-dressing' effects, such a procedure would enable them to be allowed for in a reasonably reliable way. Secondly, the actual data for the previous two quarters may be extrapolated into the final quarter of the relevant year. The problem with this procedure is the imposition of the same average rate of growth to all three quarterly periods, which is likely to be invalid. Finally, and similar to the previous procedure, the December figure may be estimated by interpolation, i.e. the imposition of a trend line between the observations for the end of the third quarter of one year and the first quarter of the following year. In similar vein to the last point, this imposes – perhaps unjustifiably – a similar rate of growth onto the two quarters covered by the interpolation. It is therefore justifiable to argue that – in the absence of reliable estimates of such end-year inter-bank operations – seasonal adjustment is the optimum strategy to allow for these effects.

While it is important to be aware of the twin problems of valuation effects and 'window-dressing' when international banking statistics are discussed, in the chapters to follow raw unadjusted data published by the various sources will in general be quoted, due to the limited amount of adjusted data available. In addition, most attention is paid to annual data in which valuation effects are likely to cancel out in part and in which window-dressing operations will affect all observations equally.

DATA SOURCES

As in many other fields of economics, international banking statistics may be reported at three levels. Primary sources represent the collection of data on international banking at the level of the individual bank or bank branch. Alternatively, secondary data sources refer to the aggregation by individual central banks of relevant data on international banking activity of banks within that particular country, perhaps including overseas branches of banks whose parent offices are located at home. Finally, in tertiary sources, data are compiled across a certain group of countries to reflect as wide as possible a concept of global international financial intermediation. In this section four main tertiary sources of data are used. These are the Bank for International Settlements (BIS), the International Monetary Fund (IMF), and Morgan Guaranty Trust Company, with reference to a series compiled within the confines of an individual research project by Jay Sterling.

It should also be made clear, that with the basic statistical raw material provided by any of these sources, in particular the first two noted above, it is possible to derive a series on an individual basis to cover as broad a concept of international banking activity as the scope of the above series allows. This has been done by the author and reference is made to this in Chapter 5. No reference is made (except in Chapter 7 on maturity transformation) to data from secondary sources. This procedure was followed for two main reasons. Firstly, the subject area of the volume aims to cover external financial intermediation at the international level rather than in one country alone while, secondly, the large number and wide variety of statistical presentations at the national or secondary source level would permit at best only a limited – and therefore perhaps unrepresentative — survey.[10]

---

[10] National banking statistics are presented in as much detail as is available in a series of central bank publications such as the *Federal Reserve Bulletin, Bank of England Quarterly Bulletin, Statistische Beihefte zu den Monatsberichten der Deutschen Bundesbank* (Bundesbank Statistical Supplements) and the *Singapore Monetary Authority Quarterly Statistical Bulletin.*

Chapter 3

BIS International Banking Statistics

INTRODUCTION

The BIS, as the international organisation that represents the central banks of the industrialised world, began collecting statistics on certain aspects of international financial intermediation in the early 1960s. Its original purpose, and one that is equally applicable today, was to monitor the development of the eurodollar market [1] 'from a macroeconomic and balance of payments point of view' (Mayer 1979a). This was particulary important given the possibility that medium- and long-term international banking activity would develop alongside the existing short-term trade credit activities of banks. By 1963, the BIS had achieved the position of receiving from the central banks of the major European countries information on the outstanding eurocurrency assets and liabilities of resident banks. The data were first published in the *Annual Report* of the BIS in 1964. In the following year the collection of data on banks' external positions in domestic currency enabled the BIS to produce estimates of overall external bank lending whatever the currency of denomination. Since 1974, these statistics combined with a commentary have been published in increasing detail in a quarterly *Press Release* originally entitled 'Eurocurrency and other international banking developments' and more recently simply 'International banking developments'.

As this information has been refined and become more widely publicised over the period since 1963, the BIS has gained the reputation of providing high quality, detailed statistics on banking activity in the major financial centres of the world. However it does not

[1] In the early 1960s the eurocurrency market was almost exclusively in dollars.

provide a fully comprehensive 'global' figure in the sense that not all financial centres are included in the BIS data.

Over time, it became clear that other objectives too were served by these figures (Mayer, 1979a). For central banks, the data gave an indication of the exposure of banks under their jurisdiction to individual countries or country groups in the rest of the world and also allow a comparison between the rate of growth of external assets of such domestic banks with those in other countries. Although only aggregate figures, such data provide a clear indicator of these developments. On the liabilities side, the data permit an analysis of the dependence of banks on certain countries — in particular since 1973 the oil-exporters — for new inflows of funds.

Finally, for an individual bank the data facilitate a comparison between its own portfolio and the overall position of the international banking sector. Such information would allow a bank to make a general judgement as to whether exposure to a particular country borrower should be increased or reduced and also provide information on the overall external position, *vis-à-vis* the bank of a particular borrowing country.

DATA PRINCIPLES

When the BIS first collected these data in 1963, the Reporting Area consisted of nine [2] European countries (Belgium, France, Germany, Italy, Luxembourg, Netherlands, Sweden, Switzerland and the United Kingdom), with Canada and Japan joining the Group later that year. US banks were added to the Reporting Group in 1973. In addition, US bank branches in various offshore centres began to report to the BIS and were included in these figures at certain points during the 1970s, namely the Bahamas, Cayman Islands and Panama (data for 1973), Hong Kong and Singapore (1975) and Lebanon (in December 1977 and from September 1979 to September 1981). The European segment of the Reporting Group was extended to twelve countries at the end of 1977 with the inclusion of Austria, Denmark and Ireland. Finally in the *Press Release* for the fourth quarter of 1980, a memorandum series with data for non-US bank branches in the offshore centres specified above and for all bank branches in two new centres — Bahrain and Netherlands Antilles — was published for

---

[2] Technically Belgium and Luxembourg are treated as one country in the series with Belgian bank positions against residents of Luxembourg being netted out of BIS data and vice-versa. Therefore, the European Reporting Area is sometimes said to consist of *eight* countries only.

the first time. Therefore the scope of BIS data is restricted with respect to this 'geographical' principle so that a 'worldwide' measure of banking activity is not presented. However, as will be seen in Chapter 5, the small Reporting Area in terms of the *number* of countries includes a very large proportion of the *volume* of international banking activity, so in effect reducing the disadvantage of the restricted number of reporting countries.

In this chapter, emphasis will be placed on data published by the BIS on 'external bank lending' and the 'international lending market'. There will be little explicit discussion of the 'eurocurrency market' until Chapter 6. This is for three main reasons. Firstly, the main series of gross bank activity (i.e. without netting out inter-bank positions) are organised by the BIS under the residency principle. Secondly, given the similar concentration of IMF banking data (Chapter 4) on the residency principle, an initial comparison between these two major public sector sources of data on international banking may be made on these terms. This is undertaken in Chapter 5. Finally, it is more fashionable to produce estimates of the eurocurrency market than to make use of the residency principle. Therefore, a separate chapter is devoted to such estimates with the introduction of certain new data sources at that time.

In order to publish these data, the BIS makes use of a two-stage reporting process. Firstly, individual national central banks obtain the required information from as broad a range of institutions as possible. In fact,

> 'most reporting countries include all financial institutions that have foreign and domestic currency positions *vis-à-vis* non-residents' [3]

The objective is therefore to capture all external business undertaken by all types of financial institutions. To the extent that an incomplete intra-Reporting Group coverage exists, the fault is therefore more likely to lie with inadequate reporting by individual countries rather than a less than comprehensive definition of that set of institutions that should report. Secondly, these figures are reported to the BIS and then aggregated across countries. This reporting procedure is undertaken on a quarterly basis to provide the information for each successive *Press Release*.

[3] BIS (1979).

TABLE 3.1

Components of the International Lending Market
(BIS Data; $ Billion; End-Year)

	External Bank Lending (Cross-Border Claims)					Domestic: Cross-Currency Claims		The International Lending Market	Memorandum Item	
	European Reporting Area		Full Reporting Area			European Reporting Area	Full Reporting Area[1]		External Bank Lending[2]	The International Lending Market[2]
	Foreign Currency	Domestic Currency	Foreign Currency	Domestic Currency	Total					
	(1)	(2)	(3)	(4)	(5)	(6)	(7)	(8)	(9)	(10)
1971	100	12	114	12	126			126	126	126
1972	132	13	150	13	163			163	163	163
1973	187	21	247	49	296			296	296	296
1974	215	32	282	79	361	24[3]		384	361	384
1975	258	39	343	99	442	89		532	442	532
1976	305	48	418	130	548	102		650	548	650
1977	385	81	514	176	690	129		819	767	896
1978	502	109	659	233	893	156		1049	1000	1156
1979	640	136	829	281	1111	196	242	1353	1246	1488
1980	751	152	981	342	1323	255	319	1642	1498	1817
1981	840	152	1117	425	1542	282	380	1922	1778	2158
Key	d	b	d	b	b+d	c	c	b+c+d	b+d	b+c+d

Column (5) = Column (3) + Column (4).
Column (8) = Column (5) + Column (7).

[1] Excluding banks in the US.
[2] Including estimates of claims of non-US bank branches in the specified offshore centres and all banks in Bahrain and Netherlands Antilles.
[3] Against non-banks only.

THE INTERNATIONAL LENDING MARKET BY BANKING COUNTRY

Table 3.1 sets out the main aggregates of BIS data in US dollars [4] on an annual basis from 1971 to 1981. The table enables all three concepts of international banking activity defined in Chapter 2 to be evaluated. Specifically, *external bank lending* is calculated for the European and full Reporting Areas in columns 1–5. The *eurocurrency market* is defined as the aggregation of Columns 1, 3, 6 and 7 as will be discussed in Chapter 6. Finally, the *international lending market* is evaluated in column 8. The key in Table 3.1 and the tables to follow refers to the particular types of asset identified in Table 2.1. In addition, in two other series (columns 9 and 10) use is made of the recently published memorandum items (noted above) specifying a wider coverage of international banking in offshore centres. These figures are only available from 1977. One further constraint should be noted. Statistics for foreign currency claims against domestic residents are available for the European Reporting Area from 1974 (against non-banks only until 1975) but only since 1979 for banks in Canada and Japan and not at all for banks in the US.

Some broad conclusions may be drawn from these aggregate figures. The broadest measure of international banking activity available from BIS series indicates an asset total of $2,158 billion at the end of 1981, an increase of 86.7% over the previous three years. Concentrating on the international lending market (but without the new estimates of offshore banking activity), a total asset figure of £1,922 billion was recorded for 1981 of which 66.3% was accounted for by bank lending from Europe (including foreign currency claims on domestic residents). Of the European Reporting Group total for the international lending market of £1,274 billion at the end of 1981, 11.9% comprised cross-border domestic currency claims but this is substantially raised to 22.1% for the full Reporting Area to reflect the inclusion of US banks, the bulk of whose assets are denominated in dollars. Foreign currency claims on domestic residents amounted to 22.1% of the European total for the international lending market and 19.7% for the full Reporting Area. The broadest concept of international banking for which a full data span is available is that of external bank lending. This has grown tenfold to $1,542 billion during the 1970s and in 1981, the European Reporting Area accounted for

[4] Non-dollar figures are converted into US dollar values and the end-quarter market exchange-rate. The one exception to this rule is the data from France which are converted at the average rate applicable for the last month of the relevant quarter (BIS, 1979).

64.3% of total assets defined in this way. Of this total, domestic currency claims amounted to 15.3% ($152 billion) for the European Reporting Area and 27.6% ($475 billion) for the full Reporting Area.

Table 3.2 disaggregates the information in Table 3.1 to provide a breakdown of the figures by banking country.[5] This is done for cross-border eurocurrency claims in the full Reporting Area (Columns 1–13 and 17–20). Although a full breakdown of cross-border claims in domestic currency is published, this is not included until Chapter 5 when these figures are compared to IMF data. Only aggregate figures for the European Reporting Area and the full Reporting Area (Columns 15 and 22) are set out in Table 3.2. No disaggregation by banking country of foreign currency positions against domestic residents is published by the BIS. Data on these are included in Table 3.2 for the European Reporting Area (Column 14) and for Canada and Japan (Column 21). [6]

From Table 3.2, it may be seen that the figures for cross-border eurocurrency assets of European banks are dominated by banks in the UK. The proportion of UK bank assets in the total has remained relatively steady at just under 50% over the data period. This is a much larger share than that of the next biggest banking centre (France) the assets of which constituted 14.3% of the total in 1981. Of course the other centres, Denmark and Ireland, which joined the Reporting Group in 1977, and Sweden are very small together constituting only 1.5% of the 1981 total. In the non-European segment, US banks' external assets accounted for 13.3% of the overall 1981 total for the international lending market, nearly all of which were denominated in domestic currency (97.9%: see Table 5.1). The activity of US branches in offshore centres accounted for 8.9% of the total international lending market in 1981 (a drop from 11.1% in 1977) but if the wider definition of offshore centres is utilised the proportion rises to 21.2% for 1981. (See also Bank of England, 1982)

These stock figures in Tables 3.2 mask many variations in growth rates both between countries and between years for any one

---

[5] In this as in other disaggregated series the data span used is shorter, in this case from 1975 to 1981.

[6] Since 1977 this series has been split into dollar and other foreign currency components. The proportion of domestic foreign currency positions denominated in dollars rose from 72.4% in 1977 to 75% in 1981.

(BIS Data; $Billion; End-Year)

EUROPEAN REPORTING AREA (continued below)

CROSS-BORDER FOREIGN CURRENCY CLAIMS

	Austria	Belgium	Luxem-bourg	Den-mark	France	Ger-many	Ireland	Italy	Nether-lands	Sweden	Switzer-land	UK	Total
	(1)	(2)	(3)	(4)	(5)	(6)	(7)	(8)	(9)	(10)	(11)	(12)	(13)
1975		14.5	24.6		39.0	10.6		15.0	17.3	2.6	16.3	118.2	258.1
1976		17.4	32.0		48.0	14.3		12.3	22.0	2.9	18.4	138.0	305.3
1977	7.4	22.9	44.0	2.1	62.2	17.3	1.5	14.8	27.2	3.2	23.0	159.2	384.8
1978	9.6	31.8	58.3	2.8	80.8	20.8	1.5	22.2	36.6	3.4	31.4	202.8	502.0
1979	13.7	39.7	79.4	3.8	100.4	21.7	1.5	28.3	44.5	4.8	31.9	270.0	639.7
1980	15.0	52.4	87.3	3.6	118.8	21.5	2.0	29.7	50.8	6.4	30.1	333.6	751.2
1981	15.6	58.8	87.1	4.2	120.4	23.8	2.1	35.6	53.3	6.5	31.4	401.2	840.0

Key: d.

	EUROPEAN REPORTING AREA			OTHER REPORTING COUNTRIES								
	Domestic Foreign Currency Claims	Cross-Border Domestic Currency Claims	Inter-national Lending Market	Cross-Border Foreign Currency Claims				Domestic Foreign Currency Claims	Cross-Border Domestic Currency Claims[1]	Total Inter-national Lending Market[2]	Non-Reporting Banks in Offshore Centres[3]	Grand Total
				USA	Canada	Japan	Offshore Centres[1]					
	(14)	(15)	(16)	(17)	(18)	(19)	(20)	(21)	(22)	(23)	(24)	(25)
1975	89.4	39.2	386.7	1.5	13.3	18.9	51.1		60.3	531.8		
1976	101.7	47.7	454.7	1.8	16.8	19.6	74.9		81.9	649.7		
1977	129.2	81.4	595.4	2.4	17.7	18.1	91.1		94.2	818.9	77	896
1978	156.1	109.4	767.5	3.5	21.9	25.7	106.5		124.2	1049.2	107	1156
1979	196.2	136.3	972.2	2.4	25.0	34.1	127.6	45.8	145.6	1352.7	135	1488
1980	255.0	151.7	1157.9	4.2	34.1	48.7	142.1	64.0	190.3	1642.0	175	1817
1981	282.1	152.3	1274.4	5.3	36.8	63.6	171.8	98.2	272.2	1922.3	236	2158
Key	c	b	b + c + d	d				c	b	b + c + d	d	b + c + d

[1] US bank branches in the Bahamas, Cayman Islands, Hong Kong, Lebanon (1977 and 1979–80), Panama and Singapore.
[2] Banks in Canada and Japan only.
[3] Including estimates of assets of non-US bank branches in the six centres specified in Footnote 1 and all banks in Bahrain and Netherlands Antilles.

country.[7] Many alternative arguments may help to explain these variations in rates of growth. Factors leading to an above-average increase in a country's international banking activity include weak domestic demand for credit, the existence of credit controls in the domestic economy and of outward exchange controls (e.g. in the UK before October 1979) and the increased profitability of international, compared to domestic, lending. Factors which may help to explain a slowdown in the rates of growth of external bank lending in a particular centre include increased competition as new banks enter the market and the introduction or tightening of prudential controls on banks' lending activities. This latter argument was likely to have been significant in the reduction of external lending by banks in Germany and Switzerland in 1980. Finally, and of major significance, interest-rate relationships particularly between domestic and euro-currency markets for an individual currency and between different eurocurrency markets will contribute to these variable growth-rates. Therefore, in the second quarter of 1980 for example, the decline in US interestrates encouraged non-residents to increase their borrowing from US banks. It is clear, therefore, that many and varied factors come into play to explain movements in the share of any particular banking country in the international lending market over time. (See IMF, 1981, Llewellyn 1980.)

BORROWER GEOGRAPHICAL BREAKDOWN (EXTERNAL BANK LENDING)

By inverting the data in Table 3.2, information may be derived on the positions of individual borrowing and lending countries and country groups *vis-à-vis* the banking sector as a whole. This is currently published in Tables 3 and 4 of the BIS *Press Release* and much of the data is reproduced here in a variety of forms in Tables 3.3–3.5. The scope of these tables is however narrower than Table 3.2 as the data cover external bank lending only.[8] Table 3.3 presents a time-series of the Reporting Group's gross claims and liabilities and therefore their net position against geographical regions. Table 3.4 presents individual country details for the major outstanding borrowers from and lenders to the international banking system while Table 3.5 summar-

[7] These growth rates of *external* bank claims of banking centres are calculated in an IMF International Capital Markets Paper (IMF 1981), Table 12.

[8] No country breakdown of positions in foreign currencies against domestic residents is published by the BIS.

ises the information in the two previous tables by providing data on net positions by geographical region and for some important country borrowers and lenders.

Unfortunately, the country breakdown in the Press Release (Table 4) from which Table 3.4 is derived is, at the time of writing, not complete in a number of senses. The oil-exporting countries in the Middle East are not identified separately being grouped into low absorbers and high absorbers while there is no information on German bank positions *vis-à-vis* the GDR. More crucially, full country breakdowns are unavailable for the reporting banks in Switzerland and the USA. In particular, for Switzerland country breakdowns are available for the Reporting Group itself and Singapore only. For other countries against which Swiss banks have external positions, the figures are included in the residual item for that particular geographical area. Full breakdowns are given by US banks for the Reporting Group, other developed countries and Eastern Europe. These omissions reduce the value of these figures to some extent. One further point to note in the construction of Tables 3.3–3.5 is that when the Reporting Area is referred to the offshore centres are omitted. This follows the BIS convention in the publication of such information and is likely to be due to the fact that the six centres whose banking data are included in the main series are scattered across the geographical areas in these tables. In addition to this aggregate information for all external bank positions a full breakdown by geographical region is available for external foreign currency positions of the European Reporting Area only (Table 6 of the *Press Release*, but not set out here). This table also includes a non-bank versus bank sectoral data split.

Some care is needed in the interpretation of the figures in Tables 3.3–3.5 with respect to the positions against the Reporting Group and the offshore centres. In the data in these tables, 'external' positions of banks include:

(i) Assets and liabilities against residents of other Reporting Group countries.

(ii) Assets and liabilities against residents of non-Reporting Group countries.

Given that positions against residents of the country where the bank is located are by definition excluded from the series, category (i) above is the total of what may be termed '*intra-group positions*'. An example would be the claim of a French bank against a resident in the UK or Italy but not in France itself. Before giving some examples of intra-group transactions, a distinction should be drawn between the

TABLE 3.3
External Bank Positions Against Country Groups
(BIS Data; $Billion; End-Year)

Banks Claims	Full Reporting Area[1]	Offshore Centres[2]	Other Developed Countries[3]	Eastern Europe	OPEC Countries[4]	Other Developing Countries				Unallocated[6]	TOTAL
						Latin America[5]	Middle East	Asia	Africa		
1975	235.1	61.9	40.8	21.6	14.3	43.5	3.3	12.9	3.3	5.0	441.7
1976	269.5	83.5	54.5	28.8	24.1	57.4	4.4	14.7	4.4	.1	547.4
1977	349.9	98.9	55.5	38.3	39.1	65.9	5.2	20.5	7.1	9.3	689.7
1978	466.9	123.5	63.9	47.5	56.4	79.9	6.5	23.1	11.3	14.1	893.1
1979	587.7	155.6	72.4	55.9	64.1	103.5	8.2	31.1	14.3	17.9	1110.7
1980	704.0	187.5	85.6	59.8	70.0	130.2	9.8	38.9	16.1	21.2	1323.1
1981	819.9	237.5	98.9	60.8	72.0	158.5	11.5	43.1	17.0	22.8	1542.0
Banks' Liabilities											
1975	270.1	40.8	33.2	6.3	51.8	16.3	6.0	10.6	4.1	7.9	447.1
1976	319.6	56.0	35.0	7.6	64.2	22.3	7.3	14.9	5.3	11.3	543.5
1977	408.5	71.5	28.1	8.4	77.9	25.2	10.0	20.1	6.7	15.6	672.0
1978	533.5	96.9	38.1	10.6	82.5	33.2	13.8	22.2	7.4	18.1	856.3
1979	685.7	139.2	46.1	15.4	120.3	38.4	15.9	26.0	9.3	23.0	1119.3
1980	823.7	164.6	50.1	15.6	159.7	36.3	18.9	27.5	10.0	28.2	1334.6
1981	948.4	219.5	51.1	14.8	156.8	39.8	19.3	29.2	10.0	34.1	1523.0

Banks' Net Position[7]										
1975	− 35.0	+ 21.1	+ 7.6	+ 15.3	− 37.5	+ 27.2	− 2.7	+ 2.3	− 0.8	− 2.9	− 5.4
1976	− 50.1	+ 27.5	+ 19.5	+ 21.2	− 40.1	+ 35.1	− 2.9	− 0.2	− 0.9	− 5.2	+ 3.9
1977	− 58.6	+ 27.4	+ 27.4	+ 29.9	− 38.8	+ 40.7	− 4.8	+ 0.4	+ 0.4	− 6.3	+ 17.7
1978	− 66.6	+ 26.6	+ 25.8	+ 36.9	− 26.1	+ 46.7	− 7.3	+ 0.9	+ 3.9	− 4.0	+ 36.8
1979	− 98.0	+ 16.4	+ 26.3	+ 40.5	− 56.2	+ 65.1	− 7.7	+ 5.1	+ 5.0	− 5.1	+ 8.6
1980	− 119.7	+ 22.9	+ 35.5	+ 44.2	− 89.7	+ 93.9	− 9.1	+ 11.4	+ 6.1	− 7.0	− 11.5
1981	− 128.5	+ 18.0	+ 47.8	+ 46.0	− 84.8	+ 118.7	− 7.8	+ 13.9	+ 7.0	− 11.3	+ 19.0

Key: b + d

[1] Excluding the offshore centres.

[2] The offshore centres group in this table is not completely equivalent to those centres included in the Reporting Group. It includes in addition Barbados, Bermuda, Liberia, Netherland Antilles, Vanuatu and other British West Indies.

[3] Other countries in Western Europe and Australia, New Zealand and South Africa.

[4] Including Bahrain, Brunei, Oman and Trinidad and Tobago.

[5] Including those countries in the Caribbean not classified as offshore centres.

[6] Including international institutions, except the BIS.

[7] + = Net Bank Claims; − = Net Bank Liabilities.

TABLE 3.4
External Bank Positon Against Individual Countries
(BIS Data; $ Billion; End-Year)

	Claims			Liabilities			Net Position		
	1979	1980	1981	1979	1980	1981	1979	1980	1981
Inter-Reporting Group									
Austria	15.3	16.9	16.4	12.3	12.7	11.6	+ 3.0	+ 4.2	+ 4.8
Belgium–Luxembourg	73.1	89.6	92.2	59.2	67.8	72.5	+ 13.9	+ 21.8	+ 19.7
Denmark	14.6	14.8	14.6	5.2	5.5	5.2	+ 9.4	+ 9.3	+ 9.4
France	63.5	72.5	83.7	70.3	78.2	69.9	- 6.8	- 5.7	+ 13.8
Germany	60.4	65.7	70.5	33.4	37.1	37.8	+ 27.0	+ 28.6	+ 32.7
Ireland	4.3	5.4	5.9	1.8	2.5	2.8	+ 2.5	+ 2.9	+ 3.1
Italy	34.1	43.7	54.0	29.7	30.9	36.3	+ 4.4	+ 12.8	+ 17.7
Netherlands	28.7	28.5	26.4	40.3	47.1	48.0	- 11.6	- 18.6	- 21.6
Sweden	11.4	15.3	16.5	3.8	5.2	4.6	+ 7.6	+ 10.1	+ 11.9
Switzerland	26.2	33.5	34.2	122.5	144.9	162.3	- 96.3	- 111.4	- 128.1
UK	105.8	136.4	154.0	149.8	181.5	207.6	- 44.0	- 45.1	- 53.6
Sub Total: European Area	437.3	522.3	568.4	528.1	613.6	658.6	- 90.8	- 91.3	- 90.2
Canada	19.2	23.5	36.8	17.8	23.1	27.4	+ 1.4	+ 0.4	+ 9.4
Japan	49.3	69.1	81.2	16.0	26.9	34.3	+ 33.3	+ 42.2	+ 46.9
USA	81.9	89.1	133.6	123.8	160.1	228.1	- 41.9	- 71.0	- 94.5
Sub Total	587.7	704.0	819.9	685.7	823.7	948.4	- 98.0	- 119.7	- 128.5

Bahamas	+ 6.2	+ 10.5	+ 13.5	71.9	50.2	39.2	78.1	60.7	52.7
Cayman Islands	– 0.3	– 0.6	– 1.5	49.7	39.7	32.7	49.4	39.1	31.2
Hong Kong	+ 5.5	+ 4.9	+ 3.5	23.0	17.7	12.2	28.5	22.6	15.7
Lebanon	– 5.3	+ 4.7	+ 4.2	6.7	6.0	5.1	1.4	1.3	0.9
Panama	+ 10.4	+ 8.0	+ 3.3	15.2	13.6	17.8	25.6	21.6	21.1
Singapore	+ 3.1	+ 3.3	+ 1.3	29.1	18.5	14.0	32.2	21.8	15.3
Total: Full Area	– 108.9	– 98.3	– 82.1	1144.0	969.4	806.7	1035.1	871.1	724.6
Others									
Norway	+ 4.3	+ 5.5	+ 5.3	6.1	5.0	4.0	10.4	10.5	9.3
Spain	+ 4.3	+ 0.6	– 2.0	17.5	17.6	17.5	21.8	18.2	15.5
Yugoslavia	+ 7.1	+ 6.9	+ 5.5	2.6	2.7	2.0	9.7	9.6	7.5
South Africa	+ 8.3	+ 4.8	+ 5.1	1.6	2.0	1.3	9.9	6.8	6.4
GDR	+ 8.0	+ 7.5	+ 5.8	2.1	2.0	1.9	10.1	9.5	7.7
Poland	+ 14.0	+ 14.5	+ 13.9	0.7	0.6	1.1	14.7	15.1	15.0
USSR	+ 7.5	+ 4.8	+ 4.3	8.4	8.6	8.6	15.9	13.4	12.9
Bermuda	+ 6.3	+ 5.5	– 4.5	8.4	7.8	6.9	2.1	2.3	2.4
Netherlands Antilles	– 1.9	+ 0.2	– 0.6	8.9	5.7	5.3	7.0	5.9	4.7
Argentina	+ 16.3	+ 12.3	+ 5.4	6.6	6.6	7.7	22.9	18.9	13.1
Brazil	+ 44.9	+ 38.6	+ 28.8	4.8	4.7	8.1	49.7	43.3	36.9
Mexico	+ 43.2	+ 32.6	+ 22.5	12.1	9.4	8.2	55.3	41.0	30.7
Venezuela	+ 3.8	+ 5.5	+ 5.2	18.5	15.8	13.4	22.3	21.3	18.6
Oil-Exporting Countries[1]	– 88.6	– 85.3	– 58.8	111.9	108.9	81.3	23.3	23.6	22.5
Israel	– 3.3	+ 3.5	– 2.3	9.0	8.2	6.9	5.7	4.7	4.6
Algeria	+ 2.7	+ 2.8	+ 3.7	4.2	4.6	3.4	6.9	7.4	7.1
Liberia	+ 4.6	+ 4.9	+ 4.5	2.7	2.4	2.3	7.3	7.3	6.8
Nigeria	+ 2.9	+ 2.2	+ 0.3	1.8	5.6	2.2	4.7	3.4	2.5
Indonesia	– 1.5	– 2.4	– 0.1	6.1	6.7	4.3	4.6	4.3	4.2
Korea, South	+ 13.7	+ 10.7	+ 7.2	3.2	3.3	3.1	16.9	14.0	10.3
Philippines	+ 4.3	+ 3.5	+ 2.7	2.9	3.4	2.7	7.2	6.9	5.4

TABLE 3.5(a)
Summary of Banks' Main External Positions Against Geographical Areas [1,2]
(BIS Data; $ Billion; End-Year)

	1979	1980	1981
INTRA-GROUP			
Main Depositors:			
Switzerland	– 96.3	– 111.4	– 128.1
USA	– 41.9	– 71.0	– 94.5
UK	– 44.0	– 45.1	– 53.6
Main Borrowers:			
Japan	+ 33.3	+ 42.2	+ 46.9
Germany	+ 27.0	+ 28.6	+ 32.7
Belgium–Luxembourg	+ 13.9	+ 21.8	+ 19.7
TOTAL	– 98.0	– 119.7	– 128.5
OUTSIDE GROUP: TOTAL	+ 89.4	+ 108.2	+ 147.5
GRAND TOTAL	+ 8.6	– 11.5	+ 19.0

Key: b + d
[1] Excluding the offshore centres.
[2] + = Bank Claim on Geographical Area.
    – = Bank Liability against Geographical Area.

position of the reporting banks against the countries of the Reporting Group and vice versa, i.e. the position of the countries making up the Reporting Area against the reporting banks. The former will be termed the positions of the Reporting Group against reporting countries and the latter the position of reporting countries against the reporting banks. This seemingly confusing terminological issue will be seen to be of considerable significance. In addition, the position of the Reporting Group (of banks) as a whole, i.e. against all countries both inside and outside the reporting countries, will enter the discussion.

The interpretation of intra-group positions will be aided by a series of examples. [9]

1. *Reporting Banks in Country A have liabilities of 100 against Reporting Banks in Country B and vice versa.*

    These inter-bank transactions cancel out so that Country A has a zero net position against Country B and vice versa. There are no net external transactions for the group as a whole.

[9] See Llewellyn and Dennis (1979).

TABLE 3.5(b)
Summaries of Bank Positions Against Regions Outside the Reporting Area
(BIS Data; $Billion; End-Year)

	1979	1980	1981
Offshore centres	+ 16.4	+ 22.9	+ 18.0
Other Developed Countries[1]	+ 26.3	+ 35.5	+ 47.8
Eastern Europe	+ 40.5	+ 44.2	+ 46.0
OPEC Countries	− 56.2	− 89.7	− 84.8
Developing Countries:	(+ 67.5)	(+ 102.3)	(+ 131.8)
Latin America	+ 65.1	+ 93.9	+ 118.7
Middle East	− 7.7	− 9.1	− 7.8
Asia	+ 5.1	+ 11.4	+ 13.9
Africa	+ 5.0	+ 6.1	+ 7.0
Other	− 5.1	− 7.0	− 11.3
TOTAL	+ 89.4	+ 108.2	+ 147.5
Other Western Europe	+ 16.2	+ 23.8	+ 29.4
Other Developed Countries	+ 10.1	+ 11.7	+ 18.4
Eastern Europe	+ 40.4	+ 44.2	+ 46.0
Caribbean Area	+ 11.7	+ 14.1	+ 10.1
Latin America	+ 70.3	+ 99.9	+ 124.1
Middle East	− 79.5	− 108.2	− 108.9
Other Africa	+ 14.0	+ 11.7	+ 17.3
Other Asia	+ 10.0	+ 16.9	+ 21.4
International Institutions	− 0.7	+ 1.1	+ 2.3
Other	− 3.6	− 6.9	− 12.4
TOTAL	+ 89.4	+ 108.2	+ 147.5

Key: b + d

[1] Including Other Western European Countries (See second part of the table).

2. *Reporting Banks in Country A have liabilities of 100 against Reporting Banks in Country B.*

(It may be assumed that the asset counterpart of this external liability is a domestic loan.)

Country A has a net external liability of 100 matched by Country's B's net external claim. The effect of the lack of an external asset counterpart to Country A's external liability is that the net external position of the Reporting Group against reporting countries (intra-group position) is − 100. The net external position of the Reporting Group against the rest of the world is zero.

3. *Reporting Banks in Country A have liabilities of 100 to non-banks in Country B and lend the funds to non-banks outside the Reporting Area.*

   Country A has a net external liability of 100 matched by an external asset outside the Reporting Group. These transactions leave the Reporting Group with a net intra-group liability of 100 and a claim of 100 on a non-reporting country. The net external position of the Group is therefore zero, while that of the reporting countries is + 100 and that of countires outside the group is − 100.

4. *Reporting Banks in Country A have liabilities of 100 to non-banks in Country B and of 80 to non-banks in a non-reporting country C. Of these funds 70 are lent to non-banks at home and 110 to non-banks in a non-reporting country (Country D)*

   Country A has a net intra-group liability of 100 to Country B and a liability of 80 outside the Reporting Group. Only part (110) of these external liabilities is matched by external claims. The reporting countries have a net asset position against the Group of 100 and the non-reporting countries a net liability position of 30 to the Group. The net external position of the Reporting Group is − 70 reflecting the use of external funds for domestic lending.

   This may be summarised:

Reporting Countries (Country B) have net claims against the Group	+ 100
Non-reporting countries (Countries C & D) have net liabilities against the Group	− 30
Net claim position against the Group	+ 70
Net external liabilities position of the Group (Counterpart of domestic lending)	− 70
TOTAL	0

Given that overall assets and liabilities must be equal, this last example specifically implies that when the Reporting Group has a net external liability (asset) position, the counterpart is a switching of funds into (out of) domestic lending.

In the light of these examples, the intra-group positions in Tables 3.4 and 3.5 may be explained more clearly. The main net depositers of funds at the Reporting Banks are Switzerland ($128.1 billion at the end of 1981),[10] the USA ($94.5 billion) and the UK ($53.6 billion). These substantial inflows from reporting countries are not balanced by outflows of similar magnitude with the only major net borrowers being Japan ($46.9 billion at the end of 1981), Germany ($32.7 billion) and Belgium/Luxembourg ($19.7 billion). Therefore the reporting countries as a whole had a net claims position of $128.5 billion against the Reporting Banks or alternatively bank liabilities to the Reporting Area countries arising from such intra-group transactions totalled $128.5 billion (Tables 3.4 and 3.5).

Before considering the data for bank positions against non-reporting counries in detail, the situation of the offshore centres must be discussed. Offshore banking may be defined as that which takes place within a country's borders but effectively outside its banking system. The banking figures for those countries that have developed as offshore centres have been 'grossly inflated by their intermediary function' and 'tell very little about these countries' role as ultimate borrowers of banking funds' (Mayer 1979a). Therefore a different interpretation of the data is required for such centres.[11]

Offshore centres have grown in importance very rapidly in the 1970s. The main characteristic of their activity is that financial intermediation is performed virtually exclusively for non-residents. Banks resident in major banking centres have been induced by a variety of factors to establish branches in offshore centres the most important of which have become the Bahamas, Cayman Islands, Hong Kong, Panama and Singapore (Mills and Short, 1979). These factors include the absence of official regulations (e.g. reserve requirements) on business completed in these centres, tax advantages and a reduction in costs if the branch's operations are co-ordinated from the bank's head office. Where the latter occurs, these operations are referred to as 'shell' branches. An added factor has been the situation of the Caribbean centres in the same time-zone as New York which has aided communications between banks' head offices and their offshore branches. An initial impetus to the development of offshore centres was the capital controls programme established by

[10] There is an added complication in the interpretation of intra-group positions data for Switzerland. Swiss banks do not report to the BIS their sizeable trustee business in foreign currencies. Hence the large total of banks' liabilities to Switzerland (as these funds are redeposited by Swiss banks in other market centres) will in part reflect the receipt of funds from outside Switzerland (e.g. from oil-exporting countries) rather than from Switzerland itself as the figures suggest.

[11] This will also be true for the figure for Caribbean Area — where the offshore centres dominate the data — in the second half of the Table 3.5(b).

the US government in 1965.[12] Although abandoned in 1974, thus removing this crucial initial motivation for the establishment of offshore branches, the controls were a vital early factor in their development. A greater potential threat to the market share of the offshore centres in the Caribbean may be the decision of the US Federal Reserve Board to allow US banks to operate 'International Banking Facilities' (IBFs) in New York and certain other states (such as Florida) from December 3, 1981 (Ashby, 1981, Morgan Guaranty, 1981). Essentially an IBF is a bookkeeping device that separates a bank's international business from its domestic operations. The IBF itself is able to accept deposits from and make loans to internatioanl customers free from domestic regulations such as reserve requirements and interest rate ceilings (Key, 1982). The objective in setting up IBFs is to attract more international banking business to the US, by increasing the competitiveness of US banks, and as a result enhance the role of New York as an international banking centre. It is likely that the US will increase its share of euromarket activity at the expense, in particular, although not the total demise, of the shell branches in the Caribbean. However, although business in the new IBFs began at a brisk pace, the rate of growth of IBF assets levelled off fairly quickly. By the end of June 1982, their assets had reached $117 billion, with the number of separate IBF operations totalling over 300 at that time. Despite such impressive figures it is likely that the future growth of IBFs will be effectively restrained by uncertainty over the tax status of IBs political uncertainty in the wake of the freeze on Iranian assets and, given the FED's concern with preventing any loss of control over monetary policy, the maintenance of a number of limits on IBF operation such as the prohibition of any issues by them of negotiable instruments such as CDs or acceptance credits (Walmsley, 1982, Koenig, 1982). Further competition for the existing offshore banks and the established on-shore centres is likely to come, in the future, from the creation of other new offshore centres. The most likely in the immediate future is Tokyo with certain regulatory chances possibly encouraging an increase in banking activity in Hong Kong.

[12] The programme consisted of three measures all designed to restrict the outflow of capital (see Duffy and Giddy, 1978). The Foreign Direct Investment Regulations forced multinational companies based in the USA to finance additional expenditure by raising funds outside the country. The Voluntary Foreign Credit Restraint Programme limited the growth of bank loans to foreign borrowers and the Interest Equalisation Tax effectively closed the US foreign bond market to overseas borrowers.

Referring to the data for the end of 1981 (Table 3.3), the gross figures for bank claims ($237.5 billion) and liabilities ($219.5 billion) against offshore centres have been inflated by the practice of head offices booking out loans to external borrowers through their offshore branches. However such intermediation activity is washed out of the 'net' figures. Therefore the net borrowing by offshore centres of $18.0 billion at the end of 1981 is either ultimate borrowing by such countries for development purposes for example, or funds booked out by head offices to offshore centres that do not report to the main BIS series (e.g. Netherlands Antilles), as in this case the accompanying liability would not be recorded in the BIS figures.

Referring once more to Tables 3.4 and 3.5, the net liabilities of the Reporting banks to the Reporting Group of countries at the end of 1981 of $128.5 billion noted above it more than offset by net external claims on non-reporting countries of $147.5 billion. The regional distribution of this figure is set out according to two alternative geographical conventions in Table 3.5 (b). The clear conclusions from this table are the dominance of Latin America as a net borrower — Brazil and Mexico alone were net borrowers of $78.1 billion at the end of 1981 (Table 3.4) — and the net depositing of funds, as expected, by, in one presentation, the oil-exporting countries and, in the second version, the Middle East. Eastern Europe is another major net borrower while the limited extent to which banks have accumulated net claims on Asia and Africa is also particularly notable.

Given these two aggregates for the external positions of Reporting banks against countries both inside and outside the Reporting Area, the residual $19 billion reflects the switching of funds from domestic liabilities into international lending. This in itself is a dramatic change from the end of the previous year when $11.5 billion was switched *into* the domestic market. These figures will be referred to below when the flow changes in bank positions (supply and absorption) are evaluated for recent years.

'NET' INTERNATIONAL BANK CLAIMS

It is well known that many international banking flows that make up the statistics reported so far in this chapter are simply between banks. Although such inter-bank 'churning' of funds (Johnston, 1983) enhances the allocation of eurocurrency funds through the redistribution of liquidity, it does not add to the creation of credit for final borrowers. Therefore, reliable series that adjust for such inter-bank flows and so distinguish between the roles of the international

banking system as a global inter-bank market and a financial intermediary for non-bank end-users are of considerable value in assessing
the credit-creating potential of the international banking system and
the true size of the eurocurrency market (Chapter 6).

The process of identifying 'net' international bank claims may
be completed in either of two ways. Firstly, total claims may be
divided into two seprate series of claims on banks and non-banks
respectively, or, secondly, inter-bank activity may be netted out to
obtain a 'net' series of bank lending to ultimate borrowers.

The BIS publishes series that divide total claims into those on banks
(including official monetary authorities) and non-banks for all types
of international banking assets set out in Table 2.1 for the European
Reporting Area only to the end of 1978, and for the full Reporting
Area (except that no data are available on US banks' positions in
foreign currency against domestic residents and there is no sectoral
split of this information for banks in Japan) since then. Table 3.6 sets
out this information. For external positions in foreign currencies, the
porportion of non-bank claims in the total has remained very stable at
around 25%, while for such claims on domestic residents the figures
have been slightly higher at just under 30%. However, the situation is
markedly different when positons in domestic currency against non-
residents are considered. The non-bank proportion in this total was
over 50% in 1978 and has been consistently higher than for the other
types of asset. However, the extension of the reporting area in 1979
has been accompanied by a decline of this non-bank share in the total
of 37.4% by 1981. Aggregating all three types of asset the proportion
of claims on non-banks in total assets is still only at an average of
around 30% reflecting the minor influence of domestic currency
assets. Such figures illustrate very well the extent of inter-bank flows
in international banking and therefore the need to extract 'net'
data.[13]

A partial breakdown of claims on non-banks by geographical
region is published by the BIS for the external foreign currency
positions of European Reporting Banks (Table 6 of the *Press Release*).
This indicates that the proportion of claims on non-banks in total
claims on a particular geographical area varies from only 5.8% for
claims on Canada and Japan to 57.3% for the rest of the world
(defined as countries outside the Reporting Area except Eastern

---

[13] The dominance of inter-bank flows is even more significant on the liabilities
side where the proportion of non-bank liabilities in the broadest total was as
low as 18.1% at the end of 1981.

TABLE 3.6
Claims of Reporting Banks¹ by Sector
(BIS Data; $ Billion; End-Year)

	External Foreign Currency Claims			Domestic Foreign Currency Claims			External Domestic Currency Claims			Total Claims		
	Total	On Non-Banks	(2) As % of (1)	Total	On Non-Banks	(5) As % of (4)	Total	On Non-Banks²	(8) As % of (7)	Total	On Non-Banks	(11) As % of (10)
	(1)	(2)	(3)	(4)	(5)	(6)	(7)	(8)	(9)	(10)	(11)	(12)
1975	258	61	23.1	89	24	27.0	39			387		
1976	305	74	24.3	102	29	28.7	48			455		
1977	385	97	25.2	129	41	31.8	81	40	49.4	595	178	29.9
1978	502	127	25.3	156	46	29.5	109	57	52.3	767	230	30.0
1979	829	215	25.9	242	65	26.9	281	121	43.1	1353	401	29.6
1980	981	257	26.2	319	84	26.3	342	138	40.4	1642	479	29.2
1981	1117	297	26.6	380	100	26.3	425	159	37.4	1922	556	28.9
Key:		d			c			b			b + c + d	

¹ Data is for the European Reporting Banks only until 1979. In addition, column (4) excludes positions of banks in the US and Column 5 positions of banks in the US and Japan.

² The bank versus non-bank division of domestic currency claims on non-residents is available from 1977 only. Therefore, the aggregates in Columns 11 and 12 are not calculated before this date.

Europe) at the end of 1981. [14]

More detail is now available on intra-group positions *vis-à-vis* non-banks in a newly-published table that provides this information for countries in the full Reporting Area for all three types of asset and liability identified in Table 3.6. This information is summarised in Table 3.7 using data for the end of 1981, and is interesting for a number of reasons. Firstly, it confirms the small totals that apply when claims on non-banks are considered albeit, in this case, for a restricted country breakdown. For example, given the size of the international lending market for the full Reporting Area of $1,922 billion at the end of 1981, only $251 billion (13.1%) of the total are intra-group claims on non-banks. Secondly, it is apparent that much of the general pattern of major country borrowers and depositors observed in Tables 3.4 and 3.5 (a) is confirmed here, despite the slightly different conceptual bases on which the two tables are constructed (given that Table 3.7 includes foregin currency claims on domestic residents). In Table 3.7, the only net sources of funds for the Reporting Banks at the end of 1981 were the non-bank sectors in the US ($66.6 billion), Switzerland ($13.5 billion) and the Netherlands ($0.9 billion). The major net borrowers of funds were non-banks in Germany ($30.1 billion — particularly in Deutschemarks from over-seas banks), Italy ($28 billion), Canada ($16.1 billion), Sweden ($13.5 billion) and France ($11.7 billion). Of all the reporting countries, only the UK has changed from being a net depositor in Table 3.4 to being a net borrower in the alternative coverage of Table 3.7, a development explained by the substantial volume of foreign currency claims on domestic residents which are excluded from Table 3.4. [15]

The BIS adopts the alternative methodolgy of calculating 'net' size concepts for external bank lending and the European eurocurrency area (including foreign currency claims on domestic residents). Although the two series are therefore conceptually different a similar set of principles is used to derive the 'net' series. These will be described more fully in Chapter 6 when the 'net' eurocurrency market series is set out, as the principles involved in deriving such a series are typically explained in BIS literature with respect to the

---

[14] The breakdown by region is very restricted being limited to the European Reporting Area, the USA, Canada and Japan, the offshore centres, Eastern Europe and the rest of the world.

[15] Similarly, the large volume of foreign currency claims of Italian banks on domestic residents explains the significant rise in net intra-group claims with respect to that country in Table 3.7 compared to Table 3.4

TABLE 3.7
Country Breakdown of Intra-Group Positions Against Non-Banks of Reporting Countries
(BIS Data; $Billion; End-1981)

Position Against:	Claims				Liabilities				Net Position
	External Domestic Currency Claims	Foreign Currency External Claims	Foreign Currency Domestic Claims	Total	External Domestic Currency Liabilities	Foreign Currency External Liabilities	Foreign Currency Domestic Liabilities	Total	
Austria		2.3	1.6	3.9		0.6	0.6	1.2	+ 2.7
Belgium–Luxembourg	0.2	7.8	11.5	19.5	2.1	5.3	7.2	14.6	+ 4.9
Denmark		9.8	—	9.8		0.4	0.1	0.5	+ 9.3
France	0.4	8.5	8.7	17.6	0.3	3.8	1.8	5.9	+ 11.7
Germany	29.6	7.6	1.5	38.7	3.7	3.6	1.3	8.6	+ 30.1
Ireland		3.9	1.4	5.3		1.0	0.4	1.4	+ 3.9
Italy	0.1	17.4	14.5	32.0	—	2.8	1.2	4.0	+ 28.0
Netherlands	0.6	4.1	2.6	7.3	0.4	4.7	3.1	8.2	− 0.9
Sweden		7.6	7.0	14.6		0.6	0.5	1.1	+ 13.5
Switzerland	1.1	4.9	3.2	9.2	1.9	17.0	3.8	22.7	− 13.5
UK	1.3	7.1	27.0	35.4	1.9	6.2	18.5	26.6	+ 8.8
Canada		7.3	21.1	28.4		6.7	5.6	12.3	+ 16.1
Japan	0.5	8.6		9.1	0.1	0.8		0.9	+ 8.2
USA	15.8	4.4		20.2	82.2	4.6		86.8	− 66.6
TOTAL	49.7	101.3	100.2	251.2	92.6	58.1	44.1	194.8	+ 56.4
Key:	b	d	c	b+c+d	b	d	c	b+c+d	

eurocurrency market (e.g. Mayer 1976, 1979a). However in the 'net' figures for external bank lending set out in Table 3.8, the same basic procedure is adopted of 'netting out' from gross figures all inter-bank flows between reporting banks. This is due to the double-counting that would occur as such flows are reported to the BIS by more than one bank. In effect, no 'new' credit is created by such inter-bank transactions and therefore to derive a logical estimate of credit creation through external bank lending netting-out should occur.

In Table 3.8, Column 9 sets out the estimates of net international bank credit outstanding as reported by the BIS (Table 1 of the *Press Release*). The difference between this total and the conceptually equivalent series in Table 3.6 (that is external claims on non-banks which stood at the end of 1981 at $456 billion — Columns 2 and 8) may be explained in the following way. Once the procedure of netting-out all inter-bank transactions is completed, *certain* interbank transactions are then reincorporated into the series to yield the totals in Column 9 of Table 3.8. These reincorporated transactions are described in full in Chapter 6 but basically involve banks outside the Reporting Area, non-Reporting banks within the Reporting Area, trustee funds at Swiss banks, the switching of funds into or out of domestic currency and the placement of domestic currency funds in the euromarkets.

Therefore, the explanation for the net concept of external bank lending being larger than the series for claims on non-banks is that the former includes certain categories of interbank transaction. This is easily justified as

> 'netting out all interbank positions would not even leave behind the skeleton of the market but simply a conglomeration of bits and pieces', (Mayer 1979a).

A second point that may explain a small part of the discrepancy between 'net' series and the claims on non-banks is that reliable estimates of the extent of the switching of funds into and out of domestic currency are difficult to obtain and rely to a large extent on 'informed guesswork'. The regional breakdown of the figures in Table 3.8 is not published in this form and is derived on the basis of a procedure adopted by the IMF (see IMF, 1981). Given the gross claims of Reporting banks on the Reporting Group itself (including offshore centres) in Column 1 (which are taken directly from Table 3.3), inter-bank flows are removed to derive an estimate in Column 3 of net

TABLE 3.8
'Net' External Bank Lending
(BIS Data; $ Billion; End-Year)

| | Gross External Claims on Reporting Area[1] | Inter-Bank Flows | 'Net' External Claims on | | | | | | Total 'Net' External Claims |
| | | | Reporting Area[1] | Other Developed Countries[2] | Eastern Europe | OPEC Countries | Other Developing Countries | Other Unallocated[2] | |
	(1)	(2)	(3)	(4)	(5)	(6)	(7)	(8)	(9)
1975	297.0	182.4	114.6	40.8	21.6	14.3	63.0	5.0	260
1976	353.0	218.0	135.0	54.5	28.8	24.1	80.9	6.1	330
1977	448.8	259.7	189.1	55.5	38.3	39.1	98.7	9.3	430
1978	590.4	358.1	232.3	63.9	47.5	56.4	120.8	14.1	535
1979	743.3	445.7	297.6	72.4	55.9	64.1	157.1	17.9	665
1980	891.0	513.1	378.4	85.6	59.8	70.0	195.0	21.2	810
1981	1057.4	602.0	455.4	98.9	60.8	72.0	230.1	22.8	940

Key: b + d

Column (3) = Column (1) – Column (2); Column (9) = Columns (3) + (4) + (5) + (6) + (7) + (8).

[1] Includes offshore centres specified in Table 3.3 (see footnote 2) and so is not exactly equivalent to the offshore centres in the Reporting Group.
[2] See footnotes to Table 3.3

intra-Reporting Group claims.[16] As data on external bank claims on non-reporting countries should not be distorted by inter-bank flows, the data in the remainder of Table 3.8 are equivalent to that in the table of gross claims (Table 3.3). Therefore intra-group claims alone have been scaled down to allow for inter-bank activity.

SUPPLY/ABSORPTION OF BANK FUNDS (FLOW ANALYSIS)

So far in this chapter all figures for international banking positions have been presented in *stock* form, i.e. an outstanding volume of bank assets or liabilities. To conclude the chapter, this emphasis will be altered with the specification of some of these figures in the form of *flows*. This will allow the calculation of the increase in gross lending to, or borrowing from, a particular geographical area by the reporting banks. In addition, to take into account changes in both claims and liabilities against a particular region or country, figures for the change in the net position will be calculated. Therefore, for example, in Table 3.3 when Eastern Europe moved from being a net borrower of $44.2 billion from the banks at the end of 1980 to one of $46 billion at the end of 1981, that area would be defined as a net *absorber* of $1.8 billion during 1981. In more detail, the rise in gross claims on Eastern Europe of $1.0 billion in 1981 was augmented by a fall in gross liabilities of $0.8 billion leaving Eastern Europe as a net absorber of $1.0 + $0.8 = $1.8 billion. Conversely, the Reporting countries themselves increased their net deposits at the Reporting banks from $119.7 billion at the end of 1980 to $128.5 billion at the end of 1981, due to a larger rise in gross bank liabilities to these countries ($124.7 billion) than in gross claims ($115.9 billion). In such a case, the group is defined as a net *supplier* of funds amounting, in this case, to $8.8 billion during 1981. Therefore a country or region is defined as an absorber of funds when, over a particular period time, net bank claims on that geographical area rise or net bank liabilities fall. Similarly, an area is a net supplier of funds when net bank liabilities to it rise or net bank claims fall.

Although in principle flow figures may be calculated for any of the

[16] The estimate of inter-bank flows and therefore double-counting is derived by subtracting the figure for net external bank lending (Column 9 of Table 3.8) from its equivalent in gross terms (Column 5 of Table 3.1). For example at the end of 1981, the inter-bank flows equalled 1,542 – 940 = 602 ($ billion). No country breakdown of these intra-group net claims is possible as the inter-bank flows information is only available in aggregate form.

tables presented so far in this chapter, concentration is placed in this section on the external bank positions data with respect to countries both inside and outside the Reporting Area in Tables 3.3–3.5. This is based on the possibility of calculating from these tables, the supply and absorption of funds by geographical regions with respect to the Reporting Group of banks.

Table 3.9 calculates the supply and absorption of funds from reporting banks by geographical region on an annual basis since 1975. This exercise is repeated for intra-group supplies and absorptions in Table 3.10.[17] Some interesting conclusions emerge from these figures. In the period covered by these tables, the major net suppliers of funds to the Reporting banks have been the Reporting Countries themselves (an aggregate net supply of $101.6 billion). Within this total, major country suppliers have been Switzerland ($89.9 billion), the USA ($88.4 billion), the UK ($45.3 billion) and the Netherlands ($18.6 billion). These figures were partly offset by the net absorption of countries such as Germany ($27.9 billion), Japan ($26.6 billion), Belgium-Luxembourg ($17.5 billion) and France ($17.3 billion). Among the non-reporting countries, the major role of OPEC nations and other countries in the Middle East as suppliers of funds to international banks is clearly seen from Table 3.9. The net supply of $3.7 billion from the Middle East in 1975 was followed by a period of net absorption by the combination of OPEC and Middle East countries in 1976–8. The dramatic return of the oil exporters' external payments accounts into surplus in 1979–80, as oil prices moved up rapidly again, is reflected in the new net supplies of $63.6 billion of funds to the banks in those two years. Finally the dramatic fall in the OPEC external surplus in 1981 is reflected in the net absorption by this group of countries of $4.9 billion, comprising a $2.9 billion fall in banks' liabilities and a $2 billion increase in banks' claims on OPEC in that year.

The major net absorber was Latin America (an aggregate of $93 billion between 1975 and 1981), with other net absorbing regions being well behind this figure. These included the non-reporting developed countries ($44.2 billion), Eastern Europe ($36.4 billion) and, from the 1975–81 data period only, Asia ($11.6 billion) and Africa ($7.8 billion). These figures confirm the general impressions gained from Tables 3.4 and 3.5 that banks' claims on developing

---

[17] In both tables, while the data from 1976 onwards are for all external bank lending, the figures for 1975 are for external bank lending in foreign currency only. In the regional table (3.9) this necessitates a redefinition of geographical areas in 1976.

TABLE 3.9
Supply and Absorption of External Bank Funds by Region
(BIS Data; $ Billion; End-Year)

	Full Reporting Area[1]	Offshore[2] Centres	Other Developed Countries[2]	Eastern Europe	Middle-East	Latin America	Caribbean Area	Singapore	Others	Unallocated[2]	Total Group
	(1)	(2)	(3)	(4)	(5)	(6)	(7)	(8)	(9)	(10)	(11)
1975[3]	− 8.1		+ 4.0	+ 5.7	− 3.7	+ 1.5	+ 3.5	+ 1.0	+ 1.1		+ 5.0

	Full Reporting Area[1]	Offshore[2] Centres	Other Developed Countries	Eastern Europe	OPEC Countries	Other Developing Countries				Unallocated[2]	Total Group
						Latin America	Middle East	Asia	Africa		
1976	− 15.1	+ 6.4	+ 11.9	+ 5.9	− 2.6	+ 7.9	− 0.2	− 2.5	− 0.1	− 2.3	+ 9.3
1977	− 8.5	− 0.1	+ 7.9	+ 8.7	+ 1.3	+ 5.6	− 1.9	+ 0.6	+ 1.3	− 11	+ 13.8
1978	− 8.0	− 0.8	− 1.6	+ 7.0	+ 12.7	+ 6.0	− 2.5	+ 0.5	+ 3.5	+ 2.3	+ 19.1
1979	− 31.4	− 10.2	+ 0.5	+ 3.6	− 30.1	+ 18.4	− 0.4	+ 4.2	+ 1.1	− 1.1	− 45.4
1980	− 21.7	+ 6.5	+ 9.2	+ 3.7	− 33.5	+ 28.8	− 1.4	+ 6.3	+ 1.1	− 1.9	− 2.9
1981	− 8.8	− 4.9	+ 12.3	+ 1.8	+ 4.9	+ 24.8	+ 1.3	+ 2.5	+ 0.9	− 4.3	+ 30.5

Key: b + d
− = Net supply of funds by region.
+ = Net absorption of funds by region.

[1] Except offshore centres. Bank positions vis-à-vis such centres are included in the appropriate regional totals.
[2] See footnotes to Table 3.3
[3] Data for 1975 are for external foreign currency positions only and are from a different BIS series generating, therefore, a slightly different regional breakdown for that year.

TABLE 3.10

Supply and Absorption of External Bank Funds (Intra-Group Positions)
(BIS Data; $Billion; End-Year)

	Austria	Belgium-Luxembourg	Denmark	France	Germany	Ireland	Italy	Nether-lands	Sweden	Swit-zerland	UK	Canada	Japan	USA	Total Intra-Group
	(1)	(2)	(3)	(4)	(5)	(6)	(7)	(8)	(9)	(10)	(11)	(12)	(13)	(14)	(15)
1975¹	—	+1.8	—	+0.5	-1.5	—	-1.3	-0.7	+0.7	-4.1	-0.5	-0.2	+2.5	-5.3	-8.1
1976	—	+0.3	—	-1.0	+2.7	—	+2.5	-1.7	+1.2	-4.1	-4.2	-0.4	+1.1	-11.6	-15.1
1977²	+0.9	+6.0	+5.6	-1.1	+5.3	+0.9	+1.0	-1.9	+2.1	-13.9	-2.6	+2.5	-1.6	-11.3	-8.5
1978	+0.6	+5.1	+1.8	+0.3	+10.9	+0.2	-1.6	-0.4	+1.3	-11.7	-4.6	+0.8	+4.3	-14.5	-8.0
1979	+1.5	-1.7	+2.0	-2.0	+4.8	+1.4	-1.5	-3.9	+1.4	-24.3	-23.8	+1.3	+6.7	+6.9	-31.4
1980	+1.2	+7.9	-0.1	+1.1	+1.6	+0.4	+8.4	-7.0	+2.5	-15.1	-1.1	-1.0	+8.9	-29.1	-21.7
1981	+0.6	-1.9	+0.1	+19.5	+4.1	+0.2	+4.9	-3.0	+1.8	-16.7	-8.5	+9.0	+4.7	-23.5	-8.8

Key: b + d

¹ Data for 1975 are for external foreign currency positions only.
² Due to the extension of the Reporting Group, the supply and absorption of funds by Austria, Denmark and Ireland is calculated from 1977 on the assumption that a net position of zero applied in the previous year.

countries are concentrated on Latin America, with Asian and African borrowers having limited recourse to international bank credit. The importance of bank credit to Eastern Europe is also confirmed.

This flow information is condensed and summarised in Table 3.11 which divides the overall position of the Reporting Group of banks into intra-group positions and those against non-reporting countries. For the Reporting Group of banks as a whole, a figure of zero for any one year against all countries (Column 3 of Table 3.11 and Column 11 of Table 3.9) would imply that, for that year, all funds supplied to the banks from external sources were re-lent or 'recycled' to external borrowers. In fact, the external financial intermediation process would be operating in full. A negative total figure indicates that the Reporting Banks receive more funds from net external suppliers than they lend out abroad implying that funds of that amount are switched into domestic lending. Conversely, a positive total figure is indicative of a switch of funds from domestic to external lending.

It is clear from Table 3.11 that the aggregate Group position against all countries has fluctuated considerably over the years from 1975 to 1981. Over the period as a whole the Group has supplied $29.4 billion to all external borrowers, by implication switching this amount from domestic lending. It is also clear from Table 3.11 that the variations in the Group's aggregate position may be traced largely to the fluctuations in intra-Group supplies of funds as the absorption of funds by countries outside the Group has been remarkably stable

TABLE 3.11
Summary of the Supply and Absorption of Funds Inside and Outside the Reporting Group
(BIS Data; $Billion; End-Year)

	INTRA-GROUP Supply (+)/ Absorption (−)	OUTSIDE GROUP Supply (+)/ Absorption (−)	AGGREGATE absorption from external sector (−)/ supply to external sector (+) by Reporting Banks
	(1)	(2)	(3)
1975	− 8.1	+ 13.1	+ 5.0
1976	− 15.1	+ 24.4	+ 9.3
1977	− 8.5	+ 22.3	+ 13.8
1978	− 8.0	+ 27.1	+ 19.1
1979	− 31.4	− 14.0	− 45.4
1980	− 21.7	+ 18.8	− 2.9
1981	− 8.8	+ 39.3	+ 30.5

Key: b + d

apart from 1979, when there were large net supplies of funds from both reporting and non-reporting countries, and 1981, when there was a substantial increase in lending to countries outside the Reporting Group. Combined with a smaller supply of funds from the Reporting Area, this led to a sharp switch from the position in which reporting banks absorbed $2.9 billion in 1980 to one where they supplied in net terms $30.5 billion to all borrowers in the following year.

SUMMARY

The interpretations that have been placed on international banking data towards the end of this chapter — in particular with respect to the supply and absorption of funds — must be treated with care due to temptation to derive 'too much' from the figures. While the aggregate figures and the data on the positions of non-reporting countries as borrowers from or lenders to international banks are considered to be of very high quality, any imperfections in the data will become potentially more important as the figures are used in increasingly refined ways. The interpretation of intra-group positions is particularly difficult. This is due in large part to the indistinct dividing-line between the Reporting Group and the rest of the world due to the positions of the offshore centres and also to the situation of Swiss banks' trustee accounts which do not appear in their balance-sheets. Therefore for intra-group positions, and the supply and absorption calculations in Tables 3.9–3.11 which are based on these, the data are indicative of broad magnitudes only. However, in other respects, the information provided by the BIS and surveyed here is a remarkably accurate statistical summary of international banking activity.

Chapter 4

IMF International Banking Statistics

INTRODUCTION

The International Monetary Fund (IMF) publishes a certain amount of information on international banking flows but in a radically different form and for different reasons compared to the BIS. The IMF see their statistics on the external business of banks as a crucial adjunct to the data that they publish on countries' domestic monetary situations. Therefore the complete balance-sheet data received by the IMF on the overall activities of financial institutions in a particular country are used to compile the information in the 'Money and Banking' section of *International Financial Statistics* (IFS). From these figures which cover lines 20–49 of a typical country page in *IFS*, the external activities of included financial institutions are condensed for presentation in a standard unit of account (the US dollar) in the 'International Liquidity' section of a country page in *IFS*. This information is given in Line 7. Given that both the Money and Banking section and that part of the International Liquidity section that is relevant are based on the same institutional breakdown, the data on the external business of financial institutions permit a connection to be established in statistical terms between the international activities of banks and ultimately the whole international monetary system and the domestic financial situation within an economy. [1]

Therefore for the compilation of the IMF's international banking data, there is no separate reporting by individual countries of such activity. Much of the information used as the basis of these figures is derived by the IMF from officially published reports from individual

[1] See O'Connor (1980), Walton (1981).

52

countries (e.g. central bank bulletins) although some is obtained from specific submissions by the central banks of these countries. Given this background, it is clear that the processes and objectives of presenting these figures are very different from those of the BIS where the reporting of external bank positions is a separate activity in its own right. It follows from these factors and the global responsibility that the IMF holds (compared to the main role of the BIS within the industrialised world) that the objective of the IMF is to produce a truly 'global' figure of international banking. As a result, the IMF seeks estimates of internationaly banking activity in all countries — however small — and, as will be seen below, they have been very successful in collecting data from a wide range of countries. Given that *IFS* is a monthly publication, the IMF's banking data are available on a monthly basis. However to achieve this, given the wide variety and large number of countries surveyed, many variations in reporting procedures, such as the availability of data on annual or quarterly bases only in some instances, have to be overcome. The necessary standardisation and estimation techniques such as the distribution of quarterly or annual observations across intervening months eliminate the majority of these variations, however (O'Connor, 1980).

DATA PRINCIPLES

The main principle that governs the presentation of IMF international banking data is that of *residency*. While this is equivalent to much of the BIS data, the reasoning behind this decision by these two organisations is very different. While the BIS is concerned with the scale and development of international financial intermediation, the IMF uses the residency principle for consistency with its domestic money and banking series but primarily because the distinction between the domestic and overseas sectors is the most relevant one for the IMF's standard balance of payments presentations.[2]

The importance of the residency principle in defining IMF data has led to the absence of any presentation of the data according to the currency principle, with the sole exception of banks in the UK. While

[2] Over such a broad range of countries that make up the IMF series, consistent application of this principle is difficult due to the variations in national reporting methods. At times therefore the basic residency principle has to be amended to one based on nationality (nationals versus foreigners) or currency, compared to the ideal of residents versus non-residents. (O'Connor, 1980). This may not be too serious a problem however for certain countries where these principles may virtually coincide (especially nationality and residency).

this procedure is a logical result of the IMF philosophy in publishing these data, it does prevent the calculation of a measure of the eurocurrency market from IMF data, this being particularly true given the lack of segregation of domestic and foreign currency components of domestic assets too. As a result, it is not possible to derive money supply statistics which distinguish between domestic and foreign currency components (e.g. Sterling M_3). However, for many of the smaller countries included in IMF data, virtually all of the banks' external positions will be denominated in foreign currencies anyway, so that the differences between external bank lending and eurocurrency claims on non-residents will be very small. Given the aim of the IMF to provide a 'global' figure of international banking activity, the principle of geography in defining the data is redundant. Finally as is explained later, the objective of achieving a bank versus non-bank sectoral division of the data is being rapidly advanced in *IFS*.

INSTITUTIONAL COVERAGE

The institutional coverage of IMF data is established by defining the institutions the external accounts of which constitute the aggregate series for any one country. For many years, the IMF has published data on the external positions of 'deposit money banks' defined as:

> 'commercial banks and other banks that have large demand deposits'.[3]

However, to recognise the existence of external business in other types of financial institution, this series was broadened from the May 1980 issue of *IFS* onwards to include the external accounts of 'other financial institutions' and 'international licence banks'. The category of 'other financial institutions' includes such institutions as:

> 'savings and mortgage loan associations, development banks, buildings and loan associations and life insurance companies.'[4]

A problem with this category is the rather indistinct line between those institutions of this type that incur financial liabilities in the form of deposits and those that do not. In general, the latter are excluded from the series where they can be clearly identified (e.g. pension funds, bond-issuing companies).

[3] For example, *IFS*, August 1981, p.8.
[4] See footnote (3).

'International licence banks' are banks that, in general, are not permitted to take deposits from the general public of the country in which they are located. In effect, they have a licence to accept deposits from and make loans to the overseas sector only and as such are not covered elsewhere in the 'Money and Banking' section of *IFS*. This category primarily captures the activities of banks in offshore centres.

There have been a number of problems in obtaining adequate statistical information on the activities of such 'international licence banks'. Firstly, it is often the case that such offshore banks are not subject to the reporting requirements faced by the more conventional banks. This is related to a second problem namely a possible divergence of treatment on the 'residency' of such offshore banks. Many national monetary authorities in countries where these banks operate treat them as resident banks for reporting purposes while others treat them as non-residents. These factors and the lack of relevance for such offshore banks of the residency principle with respect to their assets and liabilities (given that, theoretically, all positions are against non-residents) led to the creation of this new category of institution in *IFS* to deal with these analytical confusions and reporting variations.

In May 1980, *IFS* coverage of external bank lending was extended by the addition to the 'deposit money banks' data, of figures in US dollars for the foreign accounts of other financial institutions and international licence banks.[5] The series are now aggregated to derive asset and liability totals for 'deposit banks' for each country and then aggregated across countries in a world table in which the major banking counties are separately identified. In this table, a world total of deposit banks' foreign assets and liabilities is now calculated, a feature that was absent in the previous coverage of deposit money banks only.

EXTERNAL BANK LENDING

The data in Table 4.1 correspond to the concept of external bank lending which, given the overwhelming importance in IMF data of the residency principle, is the broadest concept of international banking, as defined in Chapter 2, that is derivable from IMF statistics.

[5] The external positions data for deposit money banks are presented in Lines 7a (assets) and 7b (liabilities), for other financial institutions in Lines 7e (assets) and 7f (liabilities) and for international licence banks in 7k (assets) and 7m (liabilities).

TABLE 4.1
External Bank Lending
(IMF Data: $ Billion; End-Year)

	Claims of:		(2) As % of (1)
	Deposit Banks	Deposit Money Banks	
	(1)	(2)	(3)
1971	192	179	93.2
1972	246	227	92.3
1973	361	328	90.9
1974	465	417	89.7
1975	560	490	87.5
1976	688	594	86.3
1977	863	727	84.2
1978	1134	966	85.2
1979	1432	1221	85.3
1980	1740	1476	84.8
1981	2098	1763	84.0

Key: b + d

It also identifies separately the former narrow series of the external positions of 'deposit money banks' only and the broader recently-introduced series for 'deposit banks'.

The world total for external bank lending at the end of 1981 was derived from data for 146 countries. In many of the countries included in the series international banking activity is negligible but the objective of the IMF in achieving a truly 'global' summary of external bank lending is facilitated by such a comprehensive coverage. To explore these figures more deeply, Table 4.2 presents a regional distribution of the totals in Table 4.1 and specifies at the foot of the table the number of countries in each region.

It is immediately clear from Table 4.2 that despite the large number of countries in the IMF version of the Reporting Group, the banking activities of the industrial countries are dominant, although the proportion in the total accounted for by this group fell from 88% in 1971 to 76.4% in 1981. Of the other regions, banks in the Western Hemisphere accounted for 11.9% of the world total in 1981 compared to only 7.3% in 1971. External bank lending from Asia accounted for 6.2% of the total in 1981 with the figures for the Middle-East and the oil-exporting countries being 2.8% and 2.1% respectively of the world total. International banking activity in the non-industrialised countries in Europe and in Africa is very small.

TABLE 4.2
External Bank Lending of Deposit Banks by Region
(IMF Data; $ Billion; End-Year)

	Industrial Countries	Oil-Exporting Countries	Developing Countries							World Total
			Non-Oil Exporting Countries							
			Total	Africa	Asia	Europe	Middle East	Western Hemisphere		
1971	169	2	21	1	4	1	2	14		192
1972	212	3	31	1	6	1	3	21		246
1973	307	4	50	1	10	1	4	34		361
1974	380	6	78	1	18	1	5	53		465
1975	446	8	105	1	23	2	7	73		560
1976	525	11	150	1	30	2	11	106		688
1977	656	13	190	2	40	3	21	126		863
1978	875	16	236	2	50	3	29	152		1134
1979	1112	22	290	3	68	4	34	183		1432
1980	1346	35	353	3	92	5	45	207		1740
1981	1603	45	447	3	131	6	58	250		2098
Number of reporting Countries	21	12	(113)	38	21	7	8	39		146

Key: b + d

The *IFS* presentation of the world totals from which Tables 4.1 and 4.2 have been drawn does not list separately all the countries included in the aggregates.[6] However, given that the aim is to identify the major banking countries, about half are separately listed in the world table, including in the case of the industrial countries all components except Iceland. Similarly, the listed coverage is almost complete for the Middle-East (only the Peoples' Democratic Republic of Yemen is omitted) and nine out of twelve countries in the oil-exporting group are separately identified. At the opposite end of the scale, there is scant separate listing of centres in Africa (14 out of 40) and Asia (15 out of 39). For most other countries included in the world totals, the figures on resident banks' external assets and liabilities are included in that country's individual page alone.

Of the 146 countries that make up the Reporting Group, as many as fifteen are not members of the IMF. The motives for including the data of such countries in the world total vary. In the cases of Switzerland as a major banking centre, and Cayman Islands, Hong Kong and Netherlands Antilles as major offshore centres, the arguments for their inclusion are overwhelming. Eleven smaller non-member countries who either have or have had dependency status (e.g. Bermuda, Macao and Reunion) are also included in the totals.[7] Conversely, fifteen members of the IMF are not included in the world total for a variety of reasons of which the most important are likely to be related to the availability and quality of these figures. Not all member countries whose external banking activity is included in the world totals have separate country pages in *IFS*. This is primarily due to the lack of sufficient data of a high enough quality to justify a separate page. Yet because, for many countries, external bank lending is one of the earliest available macroeconomic series, such figures are included in the IMF world totals. However, this lack of a country page does lead to the disadvantage that some components of the world total cannot be separately identified either in the country pages or the world tables in *IFS*.

It can be seen from Table 4.1 that data for the former 'deposit

[6] A full list of the countries included in the global total and its regional components is published inside the back cover of each issue of *IFS*. In Chapter 5, when a comparison of BIS and IMF banking data is made, more emphasis will be placed on the individual country figures.

[7] These are Bhutan, Cape Verde, China, Djibouti, Equatorial Guinea, Guinea, Guinea-Bisseau, Hungary, India, Kampuchea, Laos, Madagascar, Sao Tome and Principe, Tanzania and Western Samoa. For some of the countries, however, (e.g. Madagascar and Tanzania) data may be absent for the most recent year in the series (1981).

money banks' specification dominates the world totals despite the much wider institutional coverage in the new 'deposit banks' series. However the proportion accounted for by the deposit money banks is steadily declining at an average rate of around one percentage point per annum primarily due to the expansion of banking activity in the offshore centres covered under the 'international licence banks'.

At present, the IMF series contains significant foreign assets of 'other financial institutions' for three countries only — Ireland, Italy and Venezuela — and for nine countries — all offshore centres — in the category of international licence banks.[8] Table 4.3 sets out the asset figures for these non-deposit money bank institutional categories in the 12 countries concerned. The procedure for calculating the assets of deposit money banks in Table 4.1 was therefore to subtract these figures from the full series (deposit banks) total. This is valid assuming that the country coverage of the assets of other financial institutions and international licence banks in Table 4.3 includes all significant entries.

A cursory study of Table 4.3 indicates that the major function fulfilled by the extension of the old 'deposit money banks' series into a 'deposit banks' series is the inclusion of the banking activities in offshore centres — in particular, the Bahamas. The external assets of the only three significant entries in the 'other financial institutions' category totalled only $4.9 billion in 1981. This amounts to less than 0.3% of the world total of external bank lending and only 10% of the total for the three countries concerned. It is clear therefore that for the 'other financial institutions' category, the addition to the world total for external bank lending is, as yet, more important in principle than in substance. Following on from this point, however, it is believed that significant foreign assets exist but are not yet included by IMF in their series for Kuwait ('other financial institutions') and Egypt, Greece, Sri Lanka, Tunisia and Vanuatu ('international licence banks') (O'Connor, 1980). Once these figures are available, the quantitative importance of the wider institutional coverage will increase more significantly given that, as reported above, this is occurring steadily at present anyway due to the rapid growth of the external assets of banks in the offshore centres.

---

[8] On the liabilities side, significant entries exist for around twenty countries in the 'other financial institutions' category while the country coverage is virtually identical to that for assets with respect to the international licence banks. Other countries may report assets of these 'other financial institutions' and 'international licence banks' but they are too small to be included in the series.

TABLE 4.3
External Assets of 'Other Financial Institutions' and 'International Licence Banks' in certain countries
(IMF Data; $ Billion; End-Year)

	Other Financial Institutions			International Licence Banks									Grand Total
	Ireland	Italy	Venezuela	Bahamas	Bahrain	Cayman Islands[1]	Hong Kong	Netherlands Antilles	Panama	Philippines	Singapore	UAE	
1971	0.4	1.5	—	8.2	—	—	1.8	—	—	—	0.9	—	12.8
1972	0.4	1.4	0.1	12.6	—	—	2.2	—	—	—	2.2	—	18.9
1973	0.7	1.6	0.1	20.7	—	3.1	2.5	—	—	—	4.2	—	32.9
1974	1.0	1.6	—	27.3	—	4.4	4.6	—	1.1	—	7.7	—	47.9
1975	0.8	1.9	—	38.3	1.7	6.9	8.7	—	1.7	—	9.6	—	69.5
1976	0.7	2.0	—	54.8	5.6	12.0	12.7	1.2	2.7	—	13.3	—	94.2
1977	1.1	2.3	0.1	62.8	13.5	16.3	16.8	1.8	4.1	0.4	16.4	0.1	135.6
1978	1.4	2.5	0.2	73.4	20.4	18.3	20.9	2.3	6.1	0.7	21.6	0.3	168.0
1979	1.8	2.7	0.2	82.3	23.1	26.6	27.6	3.6	12.3	0.8	29.5	0.3	210.7
1980	1.9	3.0	0.2	92.0	30.6	33.0	38.0	4.5	15.2	1.0	40.9	0.4	263.8
1981	1.7	3.0	0.2	107.0	41.8	42.1	49.8	7.7	16.4	1.0	64.6	0.3	335.4

Key: b + d

[1] As no deposit money banks' data are published for the Cayman Islands, this is the only series available for this centre.

SECTORAL DIVISION OF EXTERNAL BANK CLAIMS

In an attempt to secure a picture of the true credit-creating potential of the international banking system the IMF is gradually gathering information on the division of overall external bank lending in its global Reporting Group into claims on banks and on non-banks.[9] At present these figures are published for around one-third of the countries in the IMF 'world', although unpublished data (which are currently being refined) is believed to exist in IMF data files for as many as 75% of the reporting countries. One particular problem in generating consistent data of this type is the possible existence of different national criteria for defining a non-bank. The major concern is over the treatment of official monetary authorities. However, an increasingly common procedure seems to exist of allocating this sector to the 'bank' category (Walton, 1981). One unfortunate outcome of this convention is, however, an assymmetry between the definition of monetary authorities as being non-banks for reporting purposes but as banks when considered as end-users or end-suppliers of funds. The published IMF figures for the end of 1981 are set out in Table 4.4 by geographical region. No distribution of this lending total into domestic and foreign currency claims is available (as is the case in BIS data) so that the figures in Table 4.4 are for external bank lending in aggregate.

It is clear from this table that enormous geographical variations exist in the proportions of non-bank claims in the regional totals. Combined with the inclusion of a only a small sample of the full Reporting Area, this makes any firm conclusions from these figures difficult and the calculation of an overall figure rather meaningless, except to say that for all areas (except Africa), claims on non-banks account for less than 50%, and in most cases significantly so, of total assets.

The share of claims on non-banks in total claims of 41.9 per cent., derived from a small sample of countries in the BIS Group, contrasts sharply with that of 29.6% for the full Reporting Area, using BIS data themselves (Table 3.6). However, it is logical to conclude that the former figure is distorted by its derivation from only *five* reporting countries. This conclusion is given credence by a figure of 31.6% for the proportion of claims on non-banks in total assets for *ten* European

---

[9] With reference to Chapter 3, the alternative procedure of calculating a 'net' series of international bank lending is not adopted in *IFS*.

TABLE 4.4
External Claims on Non-Banks of Reporting Countries by Region
(IMF Data; $ Billion: End-1981)

Reporting Areas[1]	Total[2] Claims	Claims on: Non-Banks	Banks[3]	(2) as % of (1)
	(1)	(2)	(3)	(4)
BIS Group (5)	809.7	339.6	470.1	41.9
Other Europe (4)	16.9	1.1	15.8	6.5
Oil-Exporting Countries (6)	18.0	4.0	14.0	22.2
Western Hemisphere (10)	72.2	27.3	44.9	37.8
Middle East (5)	6.2	0.5	5.7	8.1
Asia (9)	70.7	21.2	49.5	30.0
Africa (8)	0.5	0.4	0.1	80.0

Key: b + d.

[1] Where figures in brackets refer to the number of countries included in each category, i.e.
BIS Group — France, Germany, Luxembourg, Switzerland, USA.
Other Europe — Cyprus, Malta, Norway, Spain.
Oil-exporting countries — Algeria, Kuwait, Oman, Qatar, UAE, Venezuela.
Western Hemisphere — Bahamas, Barbados, Colombia, Costa Rica, Guyana, Jamaica, Netherlands Antilles, Panama, Trinidad and Tobago, Uruguay.
Middle East — Bahrain, Jordan, Lebanon, Arab Republic of Yemen, People's Republic of Yemen.
Asia — Bangladesh, Malaysia, Nepal, Pakistan, Papua New Guinea, Philippines, Singapore, Sri Lanka, Thailand.
Africa — Ethiopia, Ivory Coast, Kenya, Malawi, Mali, Mauritius, Morocco, Tunisia.
[2] For Bahamas, Bahrain, Netherlands Antilles, Panama, United Arab Emirates and Venezuela, these data cover only commercial banks as the non-bank versus bank division is unavailable for international licence banks while the reverse is true for Singapore for which the data therefore covers lending by international licence banks only.
[3] Including official monetary authorities.

Reporting countries, using data for the end of 1978, reported by Walton (1981), compared to a BIS figure for the full European Reporting Area of 30.1%.

Therefore despite a different methodological approach, and once variations in the Reporting Group are taken into account, the estimates of non-bank claims in total assets published by the two sources of this proportion are broadly comparable. This conclusion is in many ways a valid one for the IMF data as a whole. The differences in the objectives, scope and details between the BIS and IMF series are enormous but the similarities of outcome that may be derived from the alternative sources are notable. However it is important having described the two series individually to compare them more rigorously and it is with this that the next chapter is concerned.

Chapter 5

External Bank Lending and the International Lending Market: A Comparison of Sources

INTRODUCTION

In this chapter, the surveys of BIS and IMF banking statistics undertaken in the previous two chapters are pulled together through a comparison of available statistics on external bank lending and the international lending market. Emphasis will be placed on statistical discrepancies arising from variations in the Reporting Group and in the figures of banking activity in countries which are included in both Reporting Groups. At the same time, another new series[1] will be introduced, which although formulated by the author concerned from published sources for *individual* banking countries, is remarkably consistent with IMF data. Finally other differences between the BIS and IMF series and their presentation will be discussed.

EXTERNAL BANK LENDING

As noted in Chapter 4, IMF data are based on the residency principle and therefore a comparison between them and BIS data is undertaken here for external bank lending only. Variations in the aggregate data on external bank lending published by these two sources may be considered at two levels.

Firstly, as was made clear in the two previous chapters, differences

[1] J. Sterling (1980a, 1980b).

exist in the definitions of the Reporting Group, which arise from the differing objectives of the two organisations in compiling these figures. Secondly, even within the lowest common denominator of the two Reporting Groups, statistical differences emerge primarily due to variations in institutional coverage.

Table 5.1 sets out data (for the end of 1981) for external assets of banks in the BIS Reporting countries – divided into domestic and

TABLE 5.1
Reporting Group Comparisons
(BIS and IMF Data; $ Billion; End-1981)

	BIS data			IMF data	BIS data as % of IMF data −(3) as % of (4)
	External claims			Total external claims	
	Foreign currency	Domestic currency	Total		
	(1)	(2)	(3)	(4)	(5)
Austria	15.6	5.3	20.9	22.5	92.9
Belgium	58.8	2.7	61.5	69.9	88.0
Denmark	4.2	0.1	4.3	5.3	81.1
France	120.4	23.1	143.5	141.8	101.2
Germany	23.8	51.1	74.9	84.5	88.6
Ireland	2.1	0.1	2.2	8.6	25.6
Italy	35.6	0.7	36.3	39.7	91.4
Luxembourg	87.1	1.3	88.4	114.5	77.2
Netherlands	53.3	12.3	65.6	66.1	99.2
Sweden	6.5	0.7	7.2	7.5	96.0
Switzerland	31.4	31.7	63.1	162.4	39.9
UK	401.2	23.2	424.4	430.9	98.5
European reporting group total	840.0	152.3	992.3	1153.7	86.0
USA	5.3	250.1	255.4	306.3	83.4
Canada	36.8	1.1	37.9	37.8	100.3
Japan	63.6	21.0	84.6	84.6	100.0
Offshore centres[1]	171.8 (407.8)	—	171.8 (407.8)	353.5 (406.9)	48.6 (100.2)
BIS reporting group total	1117.5 (1353.5)	424.5	1542.0 (1778.0)	1935.9 (1989.3)	79.7 (89.4)
IMF world total				2098.4	
Key:	d	b	b + d	b + d	

[1] Data for the offshore banking operations covered by the main BIS series (i.e. US bank branches in the Bahamas, Cayman Islands, Hong Kong, Panama and Singapore) are outside parentheses. The figures inside parentheses include the extended BIS coverage (i.e. all bank branches in the above centres, Bahrain and the Netherlands Antilles). See Table 5.2.

foreign currency assets – and, includes for comparison, *IFS* figures for these countries.[2] Despite the limits of the BIS Reporting Group compared to the 'global' total of external bank lending in *IFS* data, the BIS total of $1542 billion amounted to 73.5% of the *IFS* figure ($2098.4 billion). However, around two thirds of this discrepancy is accounted for by intra-Reporting Group differences. Therefore, as a proportion of the IFS figure for the BIS Reporting Group itself ($1935.9 billion) the BIS figure amounts to 79.7%. The discrepancy between the two overall totals is therefore made up of three elements:

(i) Intra-Reporting Group treatment of offshore centres.
(ii) Intra-Reporting Group variations in reported external assets of non-offshore centres.
(iii) The inclusion in IMF data of more reporting countries.

Firstly, therefore, the main BIS data series includes only five offshore centres and then only the positions of US bank branches in those centres. The relevant figure from the BIS series for the end of 1981 of $171.8 billion was only 48.6% of the IMF figure for these same centres of $353.5 billion (including the assets of non-US bank branches). The details are set out in Table 5.2. However, with the addition of the memorandum item in BIS data, which includes non-US bank branches' assets in the centres plus all banks' assets in two new centres – Bahrain and Netherlands Antilles – any discrepancy with the IMF figures for the five years for which a comparison is possible is virtually eliminated. With this broader coverage of banking activity in offshore centres, the total external assets of the BIS Reporting Group rise to $1778 billion or 89.4% of the IMF figure that includes the two additional centres ($1989.3 billion, Table 5.1). A fuller comparison of data for banking activity in offshore centres is set out in Table 5.3.

Secondly, variations in the recorded figures for external lending by banks in particular reporting countries appear to be primarily due to differences in institutional coverage between the two sources. Table 5.4 sets out such information[3] as is known on these institutional differences between the two series, using data for the end of 1981. It

[2] A notable feature of this table is the variation in the proportion of total external bank claims that is denominated in a country's domestic currency from 97.9% for the USA and 68.2% for Germany to less than 2% for Canada and Italy. All reported assets of banks in the included offshore centres are assumed to be denominated in foreign currencies.

[3] Much of this part of the chapter is greatly reliant on the work of Richard Walton (1981).

TABLE 5.2
External assets in Offshore Banking Centres
(BIS and IMF Data; $ Billion; End-Year)

End-1981	BIS data		IMF data[2,3]
	Main Series – 5 centres[1]	Main Series Plus Memorandum Item – 7 centres[2]	
Bahamas			150.3
Cayman Islands			42.1
Hong Kong			49.8
Panama			41.1
Singapore			70.2
SUB-TOTAL	171.8		353.5
Bahrain			42.7
Netherlands Antilles			10.7
		407.8	406.9
All Centres			
1977		168	173
1978		214	212
1979		263	263
1980		317	317
1981		408	407

Key: b + d

[1] US banks' branches only

[2] All banks' branches.

[3] Drawn from IMF data so that the list of centres coincides exactly with the BIS offshore centres coverage.

is clear from this table and from the calculations in Column 5 of Table 5.1 that for most of the reporting countries the inter-series discrepancies are low (less than 20% for all but three countries – Ireland, Luxembourg and Switzerland). Two further points should be noted from Table 5.4. Firstly, in all cases, except Canada, Denmark and Sweden (for which no confident explanations of the discrepancies are advanced) and France, the factors set out in the table are consistent with the direction of variation in the two series. A certain degree of confidence may be justifiably be attached to this information, therefore. Secondly, despite the previous point, no presumption should be made that the identified arguments necessarily exhaust the sources of variations between the two series, such that, if these particular factors were allowed for, the data would automatically

TABLE 5.3
External Assets of Banks in Certain Offshore Centres[1]
(BIS and IMF Data; $ Billion; End-Year)

	BIS data			IMF data	
	Main series – 5 centres[2]	Memorandum item – 7 centres[3]	Total	Series for 5 centres	Series for 7 centres
1971				16	16
1972				24	24
1973	24.9			39	39
1974	33.2			63	63
1975	51.1			89	92
1976	74.9			128	136
1977	91.1	77	168	157	173
1978	106.5	107	214	188	212
1979	127.6	135	263	234	263
1980	142.1	175	317	279	317
1981	171.8	236	408	354	407

Key: b + d

[1] See Table 5.2 for listing of the components of each series.

[2] US banks' branches only.

[3] All banks' branches.

coincide. This is obviously true for Ireland and Switzerland (foot-notes 2 and 3 in Table 5.4) and may be so for other countries.

A similar pattern of consistency between the expected and actual direction of variation between the two series as noted for 1981 figures in Table 5.4 was reported by Walton[4] using data for the end of 1978. He also noted that, excluding the offshore centres, the proportion of the BIS Reporting Area total in the equivalent *IFS* figure was relatively stable at between 91% and 94% from 1973 to 1979. (The 1981 figure was 86.6% – Table 5.1.) The relative stability of this proportion tends to confirm the general impression of Table 5.4 that intra-Reporting Group discrepancies between the two series are more likely to be due to differences in institutional coverage rather than any other factor such as uneven data quality.

The third source of variation between BIS and IMF data for external bank lending is the concentration of BIS data on the Reporting Group

[4] As with the data for 1981 in Table 5.4, the only exception found by Walton was for banks in France. At the end of 1978, as three years later, the external assets of these banks were higher in the BIS series, in contrast to the expected variation between these and IMF figures.

TABLE 5.4
Identification of Intra-Reporting Group Differences in
BIS/IMF Assets Series
(BIS and IMF Data; $ Billion; End-1981)

	Data of:	
	BIS	*IMF*
1. *BIS Figure Lower*		
(a) *BIS has narrower institutional coverage:*		
AUSTRIA — BIS does not include external accounts of smaller banks	20.9	22.5
ITALY — in addition, BIS does not include bills sent abroad for collection or Specialised Credit Institutions (SC1)	36.3	39.7
NETHERLANDS — in addition, IMF data is likely to cover a wider range of balance-sheet items including capital accounts *vis-à-vis* foreign affiliates	65.6	66.1
SWEDEN —	7.2	7.5
USA — BIS excludes accounts of Ex-Im Bank[1] and all custody items	255.4	306.3
(b) *BIS excludes certain types of asets:*		
GERMANY — long-term development loans excluded by BIS	74.9	84.5
IRELAND — domestic currency external assets excluded by BIS (until June 1980)[2]	2.2	8.6
SWITZERLAND — trustee business in foreign currencies excluded by BIS[3]	63.1	162.4
UK — overseas investments and working capital and gold assets balanced partly by broader BIS institutional coverage	424.4	430.9
USA — See)a)		
(c) *BIS excludes claims against certain countries:*		
BELGIUM — claims against residents in Luxembourg excluded by BIS	61.5	69.9
LUXEMBOURG — claims against residents in Belgium excluded by BIS	88.4	114.5
(d) *Unknown:*		
DENMARK —	4.3	5.3
2. *BIS Figure Higher*		
(a) *Unknown:*		
CANADA[4] —	37.9	37.8
FRANCE — also, BIS excludes accounts of Banque Fancaise du Commerce Exterieur[1]	143.5	141.8
3. *BIS/IMF Figures Identical*		
JAPAN[5]	84.6	84.6

Key: b + d

[1] Institutions such as these that specialise in granting export credits may be excluded from BIS data for other countries too.

[2] A huge difference exists between the two series for Ireland. Given that for end-1981, the split of IMF data is $6.9 billion (commercial banks) and $1.7 billion (other financial institutions) the source of the discrepancy is unclear.

[3] Given that the IMF estimated trustee accounts at $92.8 billion at the end of 1981, the whole of the discrepancy is not explained by this factor.

Table 5.4 cont.
[4] The explanation may be a different institutional coverage.

[5] For earlier years, the BIS figure has typically been higher than that of the
IMF. This is likely to be explained by the BIS inclusion and IMF exclusion
of long-term accounts.

of fifteen countries plus offshore centres. With the IMF objective of
calculating as broad a figure for international bank activity as possible, the centres omitted by the BIS are, where reliable data are
available, included in *IFS*. Certainly, for many of these non-BIS group
countries external bank lending is negligible but there are some
important and developing centres that should be noted. Table 5.5
lists those countries which, according to IMF figures, had external
bank assets of $1 billion or more at the end of 1981. External lending
from such non-BIS reporters totalled $109 billion at the end of
1981.[5] This information on such a broad range of centres is ex-

TABLE 5.5
External Claims of Banks in Certain Non-BIS Reporting Group Countries
(IMF Data; $ Billion; End-1981)

Saudi Arabia	15.6
Spain	14.8
UAE	8.2
Kuwait	8.0
Israel	6.3
Indonesia	5.1
Lebanon	4.3
Korea	4.2
Egypt	3.4
Philippines	3.4
Finland	3.2
Iran[1]	2.9
Brazil	2.6
Yugoslavia	2.2
Bermuda[1]	2.0
Norway	1.9
Greece	1.7
Portugal	1.6
Qatar	1.2
Thailand	1.1
Argentina	1.0
Libya	1.0

Key: b + d
[1] End-1980.

[5] From Table 5.1 the IMF 'World' total of $2098.4 billion minus its total for the
broadest BIS Reporting Area of $1989.3 billion.

tremely valuable but the conclusion remains that, although covering a small number of centres, BIS data include the bulk of external bank lending in volume terms.

This general conclusion is also indicated by data from two other series to be introduced at this point. These are set out alongside the BIS and IMF aggregates for 1971 to 1981 in Table 5.6, to facilitate comparisons of all four series. Firstly, the author has extracted from the IMF 'World' of 146 countries all those countries whose banks had, within the observation period, outstanding external assets of at least $200 million in any one year. From this series it can be seen that, in the period as a whole, over 99% of all international banking activity, according to IMF data, is accounted for by banks in 62 countries with the remaining 86 countries accounting for less than 1% of the total. This indicates that by defining a reporting group that, although much larger in the number of countries covered than the BIS group, is still half of the number included in the IMF series, virtually all of the international banking activity in the world may be captured. Secondly, Jay Sterling has compiled a series for the years from 1964 to 1978 for all three types of bank claim in Table 2.1 using national official publications such as central bank bulletins (Sterling 1980a, 1980b). Therefore Sterling made use of secondary data sources in comparison to this author's use of information already compiled by the IMF (Chapter 2).[6] The condition for the inclusion of a country in Sterling's Reporting Group was that the aggregate volume of claims, of all three types, of banks in a particular country should exceed $300 billion in any one year or $200 billion in any three years during his data period. Column (4) of Table 5.6 extracts from this series the figures for external bank lending (i.e. foreign currency claims on domestic residents are excluded). His figures confirm the validity of his approach to deriving these data and also of the conclusion from this author's series that a Reporting Area of less than half the number of countries for which banking data are available includes virtually all international banking activity.

THE INTERNATIONAL LENDING MARKET

Only a brief comparison of estimates of the international lending

[6] This conceptual difference in the construction of the two series may partly explain the lack of complete overlapping between the Reporting Areas. Fifty-three reporting countries are common to both series. In addition Sterling includes Colombia, India, Iraq, Mexico and Taiwan, in his Reporting Area, while this author has included Bangladesh, Dominican Republic, Jordan, Morocco, Oman, Romania, Sudan, Turkey and Uruguay.

TABLE 5.6
External Bank Lending
(Various Series; $ Billion; End-Year)

	BIS series 15 reporting countries and offshore centres[1]	IMF world total	Author's Data — 62 countries[2]	Sterling — 58 countries[3]
	(1)	(2)	(3)	(4)
1971	126	194	193	185
1972	163	247	246	245
1973	296	355	352	350
1974	361	460	455	445
1975	442	556	553	539
1976	548	684	681	669
1977	690 (767)	859	852	829
1978	893 (1000)	1123	1112	1086
1979	1111 (1246)	1413	1402	
1980	1323 (1498)	1711	1702	
1981	1542 (1778)	2098	2904	

Key: b + d.

[1] From 1977 with the memorandum item, which includes non-US banks' branches external assets in the specified offshore centres and all banks' branches in Bahrain and Netherlands Antilles, in parentheses.

[2] The countries included (with the number in each area and total area external assets at the end of 1981 — except Bermuda and Iran which are end-1980 — in parentheses) are:
BIS Reporting Group (15 countries — $1582.4 billion plus 7 offshore centres — $406.9 billion).
Other Europe (8 — $26.3 billion) — Finland, Greece, Norway, Portugal, Romania, Spain, Turkey, Yugoslavia.
Other Developed (3 — $1.3 billion) — Australia, New Zealand, South Africa.
Oil-Exporting Countries (11 — $44.7 billion) Alergia, Indonesia, Iran, Kuwait, Libya, Nigeria, Oman, Qatar, Saudi Arabia, UAE, Venezuela.
Middle-East (4 — $14.7 billion) — Egypt, Israel, Jordan, Lebanon.
Western Hemisphere (6 — $7.4 billion) — Argentina, Bermuda, Brazil, Chile, Dominican Republic, Uruguay.
Asia (6 — $10.0 billion) — Bangladesh, Korea, Malaysia, Pakistan, Philippines, Thailand.
Africa (2 — $0.6 billion) — Morocco, Sudan.

[3] The countries included (with the number in each area in parentheses) are:
BIS Reporting Group (15 countries plus 8 offshore centres).
Other Europe (6) — Finland, Greece, Norway, Portugal, Spain, Yugoslavia.
Other Developed (3) — Australia, New Zealand, South Africa.
Oil Exporting Countries (11) — Algeria, Indonesia, Iran, Iraq, Kuwait, Libya, Nigeria, Qatar, Saudi Arabia, UAE, Venezuela.
Middle-East (2) — Egypt, Israel.
Western Hemisphere (6) — Argentina, Bermuda, Brazil, Chile, Coloumbia, Mexico.
Asia (7) — India, Korea, Malaysia, Pakistan, Philippines, Taiwan, Thailand.

market is possible due to the lack of information on this very broad concept of international banking. Table 3.1 sets out BIS series for the 'international lending market' for alternative definitions of the Reporting Group. Sterling (1980a) estimated from his series that at the end of 1978, the international lending market totalled $1301 billion, 12.5% higher than the broadest BIS figure (i.e. including all banks' activity in seven offshore centres). No published data are available from Sterling's series for 1979–81, but applying a similar rate of increase as occurred in BIS figures from 1978 to 1981 (86.7%) generates an estimate for the international lending market for Sterling's series of $2429 billion at the end of 1981.[7] This estimate for the international lending market in 58 countries is the broadest concept of international bank lending included in this survey. Given the *ad hoc* nature in which it was derived, this figure should only be treated as an approximation. However it is clear that a figure of around $2500 billion for the international lending market at the end of 1981 is broadly correct.

BIS AND IMF SERIES: OTHER AREAS OF COMPARISON

This section concentrates on two other areas of difference between the BIS and IMF data series, namely the degree of detail with respect to country breakdowns and secondly technical variations in the presentation of the series. (Two other crucial factors – the lack of a division between foreign and domestic currency positions in IMF data and the procedures adopted by the two sources to deal with inter-bank flows and therefore double-counting – have been considered in detail in Chapter 3 and 4 and are not therefore discussed again here.)

In Chapter 3, the extent of the geographical breakdown of reporting banks' external assets and liabilities in BIS data was discussed in detail. In contrast to this situation, at present, the IMF publishes no borrower country breakdown at all. However, this information is gradually being accumulated by the IMF with a view to future publication. For example Walton (1981) reported that for banks in Hong Kong, the UK and US, fairly detailed up-to-date country breakdowns are available, while in addition some information is available for Belgium, Canada, France, Germany, Israel and Switzer-

---

[7] Sterling himself stated that 'a reasonable order of magnitude estimate for December 1979 would be $1700 billion' (Sterling 1980a, p 77).

land. The key advantage of the data for these nine countries (which at the end of 1981 accounted for approximately 61% of the *IFS* 'World' assets total and 57% on the liabilities side) is the existence of a bank versus non-bank division of these figures. In addition, a geographical breakdown is available without this bank versus non-bank division for banks in Bahrain, Italy, Luxembourg, the Netherlands and the UAE.[8] The addition of these countries raises the coverage of the *IFS* 'World' total to 74% for external assets and 70% for liabilities. Walton also provides a statiscial comparison of the breakdown by geographical area of IMF and BIS data, to the extent that this is feasible given the limitations of both series.

However as the number of banking centres from which this information is obtained increases, the problems of deriving a consistent country breakdown for the expanding Reporting Area become more serious. Two of these problems should be noted. Firstly, reporting variations exist in particular with respect to the depth of the data i.e. the identification of separate countries or regions. Not all centres may provide a breakdown of external positions that specifies an exhaustive list of countries. Secondly, as the degree of detail in this respect increases, it becomes more likely that problems of confidentiality will be encountered leading inevitably to a decline in the quality of the data.

As this information is accumulated by the IMF, it will eventually become possible to 'invert' the data by reporting country, to derive a full geographical breakdown by end-user and end-supplier. When this information is obtained it will facilitate the evaluation of the external asset or liability position of each borrowing country against the international banking system as symbolised by the IMF 'World' representing therefore a broader picture than is currently available in BIS figures. In addition, new information may be gained from this process on the banking activities of non-reporting countries in the following way. The full country breakdown of the banks in the IMF 'World' total would enable an estimate of Country A's external claims and liabilities *vis-à-vis* the world's banks to be made. If this is different from that country's own national estimates of its position *vis-à-vis* international banks', the difference in theory should consist of positions of non-reporting banks against Country A. In this way, an estimate of international banking activity in countries outside the IMF 'World' total (e.g. COMECON countries) may be possible.

Certain technical variations between BIS and IMF series in the

---

[8] A limited amount of this type of information is also available for banks in Panama, the Philippines and Singapore.

collection and presentation of these figures should be noted. BIS data are published quarterly usually about three to four months in arrears (the main part of the lag being due to late reporting not slow publication by the BIS) while in general *IFS* data are obtained and published on a monthly basis. The length of the reporting lag in IMF data varies considerably due to the number of countries being covered but it may be as short as a two-month period although for the world total the lag is typically slightly longer. However unlike BIS data, IMF figures are published on a piecemeal basis when they become available.[9]

IMF data also encounter the problem — due primarily to the very wide reporting group — of certain countries only providing data on an annual or quarterly basis. (This is less of a problem to the BIS due to the smaller reporting area and the fact that it publishes on a quarterly basis anyway.) Such differences in periodicity (Sterling 1980b) are dealt with by the IMF through the distribution of the quarterly or annual observations across the intervening months, a procedure that, when used, is noted in *IFS* (O'Connor 1980).

An interesting difference in procedure relates to the problem of certain components of the BIS and IMF aggregates having different starting dates. The BIS resolves this simply by having breaks in the series. Four have occurred in the 1970s — three corresponding to the successive extensions of the reporting area in 1973, 1975 and 1977[10] and a fourth at the end of 1978 when custody items began to be excluded from US banks' external assets. Additions have therefore been made, at various times, to the BIS series without the restatement of prior figures. It is therefore rather complex to derive a complete, unbroken run of BIS data and this makes the calculation of annual growth rates for certain years extremely hazardous.[11] Sterling states that:

'while the BIS has done an admirable job in continually improving its statistics, it has done so at the expense of continuity and comparability in its data series' (Sterling 1980b, p33).

In contrast, the IMF — which is faced by considerable problems of

[9] Although where necessary such problems of currentness are tackled by extrapolation of previous observations (O'Connor, 1980). This may also be done in the case of a total interruption of reporting (e.g. Iraq since 1976).

[10] Further causes of the break at this time were the inclusion of buyers' credits and of commercial bills and acceptances into the external domestic currency accounts of France and the UK respectively.

[11] This is a point that should be noted with respect to all BIS data in this survey.

different starting dates for the numerous components of its world figures — has attempted to obtain continuous and constant data runs over a period of many years through regular backward revisions of its data.

SUMMARY

It is clear from the material presented in Chapters 3–5 that many differences exist between the international bank lending data published by the BIS and IMF. Some of these differences lead to variations in aggregate and single country figures. However, it is apparent that a surprisingly large proportion of the discrepancies in the aggregate series are caused by the different definitions of the Reporting Group in use and variations in institutional coverage. Other differences between BIS and IMF data relate to the degree of detail available within the series and to variations of presentation and procedure. It is suggested that these variations should not be a source of surprise given the different methodologies underlying the figures and the objectives of each organization in collecting, processing and publishing them. Although it is important to be aware of the sources of these discrepancies, each set of data (and Sterling's series introduced in this chapter) provides a wealth of high-quality information on the activity of international banking as it has expanded rapidly during the 1970s and early 1980s.

Chapter 6
Measures of the Eurocurrency Market

INTRODUCTION

So far in this survey of banking data, no attempt has been made to identify and compare measures of the eurocurrency market itself (i.e. the market in foreign currency claims or deposits). A separate chapter is devoted to these measures at this point due primarily to the fact that as a concept it is more frequently referred to than the concepts of external bank lending and the international lending market discussed to date. In addition two new data series are available when the eurocurrency market is measured and these are introduced here.

The importance of the eurocurrency market in the international monetary system by the end of the 1970s was considerable. Helmut Mayer identifies five major economic 'dimensions' of the market to symbolise its importance. The market

  (i) serves as an international inter-bank money market
 (ii) acts as a source of credit to private firms and public entities
(iii) serves as an outlet for official reserves,
 (iv) acts as a source of credit and as a reserve outlet for Eastern European countries,
  (v) allows a large amount of dealing between the reporting banks themselves associated with various kinds of arbitrage operations, maturity transformation, geographical diversification etc.' (Mayer 1979a)

Given these factors and the frequent references to the eurocurrency market, it is crucial to have an understanding of the available statistical series that aim to measure its size.

To move from a measure of external bank lending to one of the eurocurrency market, external lending in domestic currencies (item b in Table 2.1) should be removed and lending in foreign currency to domestic residents (item c) should be added (Johnston, 1983). Therefore the eurocurrency market is defined as the sum of items c and d in Table 2.1, demonstrating the switch of the series from the use of the principle of residency to that of currency. It should also be noted that the narrower term of the eurodollar market is not generally used in this chapter. This reflects the widespread existence of non-dollar-denominated deposits in the modern eurocurrency market, despite the dominance of the dollar during the market's early history, i.e. up to the mid-1960s. In addition the 'euro' label, again as a result of the market's initial developments, is a misnomer given that much of the market is now located outside Europe.

EUROCURRENCY MARKET ESTIMATES

Table 6.1 sets out estimates of the size of the eurocurrency market on an annual basis since 1971. Columns (1) and (2) are the BIS estimates of the European-based and full eurocurrency markets respectively. Specifically, Column (1) is the aggregation of Columns (1) and (6) of Table 3.1 so that foreign currency positions against domestic residents are included, but from 1974 only. The figures outside parentheses in Column (2) are the sum of Columns (3) and (7) of Table 3.1 with data on domestic positions in foreign currency of the non-European Reporting Area being available since 1979 only and then only for banks in Canada and Japan. The figures in parentheses add the extended treatment of offshore centres noted in Chapter 3 to the basic series.

Column (3) is a minor variation on the BIS published figures compiled by Johnston (1983). Two differences exist between his figures and those in Column 2. Firstly, he excludes all US banks' external lending although, at the end of 1981, 2.1 per cent of this total ($5.3 billion) was denominated in foreign currencies (Table 5.1) and should therefore remain in a measure of the eurocurrency market. Secondly, Johnston includes data on the eurocurrency claims on domestic residents of banks in the European Reporting Area, Canada and Japan for the full data period. In contrast, as noted above the published BIS statistics include these positions for the European reporting banks since 1974 only and for banks in Canada and Japan since 1979. Therefore, prior to 1979, Johnston's measure of the eurocurrency market exceeds the published BIS total, while from that date onwards the BIS total is larger. The discrepancy in 1980 ($5

TABLE 6.1
The Eurocurrency Market — Various Series
($ Billion: End-Year)

	BIS Series				
	European Reporting Area (Claims)	Full[1,2] Reporting Area (Claims)	Johnston[2,3] Series (Claims)	Morgan Guaranty Series (Liabilities)	Ashby Series (Claims)
	(1)	(2)	(3)	(4)	(5)
1971	100	114	125	150	157
1972	132	150	164	210	212
1973	187	247	264	315	317
1974	239	282	323	395	384
1975	347	432	451	485	483[4]
1976	407	520	540	595	594
1977	514	643 (720)	663 (740)	740	739
1978	658	805 (912)	845 (952)	950	945
1979	836	1071 (1206)	1069 (1204)	1220	1196
1980	1006	1300 (1475)	1295 (1470)	1515	1464[5]
1981	1122	1497 (1734)		1800	

Key: c + d[6]

[1] Including positions against domestic residents (Table 3.1) since 1974 for the European Reporting Area and since 1979 for banks in Canada and Japan (Column 2).
[2] Figures in parentheses refer to the extended offshore centres coverage (Chapter 3).
[3] Including positions against doemtic residents in Canada and Japan as well as the European Reporting Area throughout and excluding all US banks' external assets.
[4] From 1975, an extended reporting area is used.
[5] Reported as aggregate only in Ashby, 1972.
[6] With variations across the series concerning positions against domestic residents (see text).

billion) is a rounded estimate of foreign currency claims by US banks that were outstanding at the end of 1980.

The first new series to be introduced here is that published by Morgan Guaranty Trust Company of New York in the monthly journal *World Financial Markets* (Column (4) of Table 6.1). This series, which goes back to 1964, was originally published to provide information on the growth of this market for the bank's clients and staff. However, it has also become a major source of exposure for the bank given the widespread publicity that the series and other information in the journal receives. Given that Morgan Guaranty does not publish information on external lending in domestic currencies and therefore concentrates on the eurocurrency market alone, the data are defined exclusively in terms of the currency principle.

However, the major conceptual difference to note in the case of this series is the measurement of the eurocurrency market on the liabilities side of banks' balance-sheets. Certain theoretical reasons may be advanced for this procedure including the greater homogeneity of eurocurrency deposits compared to assets and the fact that the source of one of the competitive advantages of the euromarkets over domestic money markets, namely the absence of reserve reqirements, affects the liabilities side of bank's balance sheet more directly (Duffy and Giddy, 1978).[1] More practically, Morgan Guaranty believes that, at least in gross terms, it is more important to know to whom the reporting banks have liabilities.

The other new series to introduce is that compiled in recent years by David Ashby of Grindlays Bank (Column (5) in Table 6.1) and publicised in a series of articles (Ashby 1974, 1978, 1979a, 1979b, 1981). Given his use of claims data the series is conceptually compatible with BIS data although as explained below, Ashby includes a greater number of banking centres in his Reporting Area and for non-European centres has, at times, a different institutional coverage.

Despite the differences in the make-up of the three series to be noted below, the overall totals for the eurocurrency market recorded in Table 6.1 are very similar, if the full BIS Reporting Area including the extended treatment of the offshore centres, is referred to. Therefore, for 1980 (the latest year for which estimates are published for all series), the claims figures varied from $1464 billion to $1475 billion (a discrepancy of 0.8 per cent), while the difference between the BIS liabilities figure of $1479 billion (Table 6.2) and that of Morgan Guaranty ($1515 billion) was slightly higher at 2.4 per cent.

Three sources of discrepancy between the series in Table 6.1 should be noted. Firstly, the scope of the Reporting Area differs in all three series. This is illustrated in Table 6.2 using data for the end of 1979 (the last full year for which full published data from Ashby's series are available) and for 1980–1. Ashby's Reporting Group is the largest as, in comparison to the BIS area, he includes eurocurrency claims of banks in Spain, Kuwait, the Philippines and the UAE and excludes positions of banks in the Lebanon and the USA.[2] The

---

[1] However, despite these theoretical arguments and the case put by Duffy and Giddy, it is still far more usual to define all these measures of international banking on the assets side of balance-sheets.

[2] As noted above, the omission of the USA from Ashby's Reporting Group and that of Morgan Guaranty is neither unusual nor particularly inappropriate given the very small volume of US banks' external claims that are denominated in non-dollar currencies. Lebanon is also excluded from BIS data for end-1981.

The Eurocurrency Market — Alternative Definitions of the Reporting Group
($Billion; End-Year)

	1979				1980			1981		
	BIS Series		Morgan Guaranty Series	Asby Series	BIS Series		Morgan Guaranty Series	BIS Series		Morgan Guaranty Series
	Claims	Liabilities	Liabilities	Claims	Claims	Liabilities	Liabilities	Claims	Liabilities	Liabilities
	(1)	(2)	(3)	(4)	(5)	(6)	(7)	(8)	(9)	(10)
European Reporting Area (BIS)	836	839		836	1006	1015		1122	1137	
Canada (External Positions)	25	30		26	35	41		37	57	
Japan (External Positions)	34	47		45	49	68		64	87	
Canada, Japan (Domestic Positions)	46	32		x	64	45		98	61	
USA	2	2	x	x	4	3	x	5	4	x
Bahamas }	✓			139						
Cayman Islands }	✓	As in (1)		25	As in (1)	As in (1)		As in (1)[1]	As in (1)	
Hong Kong	✓			x						
Lebanon	✓		x	32			x			x
Panama	✓			38						
Singapore	✓									
SUB TOTAL (US BANKS ONLY)	128	129			142	144		172	176	
Bahrain	✓			28						
Netherlands Antilles	✓			5						
SUB-TOTAL (ALL BANKS IN ALL CENTRES)	(263)	(254)			(317)	(308)		(408)	(400)	
Spain			x	11			x			x
Kuwait			x	5			x			x
Philippines			x	2			x			x
UAE			x	4			x			x
TOTAL	1071 (1206)	1078 (1203)	1220	1196	1300 (1475)	1315 (1479)	1515	1497 (1734)	1522 (1746)	1800

Key: c + d.

[1] Except Lebanon, which is excluded from BIS data for end 1981.

Morgan Guaranty series omits all of these six countries included by Ashby and the BIS. Table 6.3 estimates the size of these discrepancies with the comparison between Ashby's data and that of the BIS (for 1979) being made on the assets side and that between the data of the BIS and Morgan Guaranty on the liabilities side of banks' balance sheets (for 1979–1981). The net discrepancy between the BIS series and that of Ashby due to the different components of the Reporting Group was $16.7 billion ($22–$5.3 billion) in 1979. If this variation in the components of the Reporting Group is taken into account, BIS estimates exceed those of Ashby even further. This discrepancy will be explained below in terms of the treatment of eurocurrency claims on domestic residents in the two series. Similarly, in a comparision of BIS and Morgan Guaranty liabilities data, should statistics for Lebanon (for 1979–80 only) and the United States be added to the Morgan Guaranty figures, the discrepancies between the series would be widened to 2.8 per cent for 1980 and from 3.1 per cent to 3.3 per cent for 1981.[3] Moreover, the extent to which all these series omit other

TABLE 6.3
Eurocurrency Positions of Banks in Certain Countries
($Billion; End-Year)

Comparison — BIS and Ashby		Comparison — BIS and Morgan Guaranty			
Claims		Liabilities			
	1979		1979	1980	1981
Kuwait	5	Lebanon	1.2[1]	1.5[1]	×[2]
Philippines	2	USA	1.9	3.8	3.7
Spain	11				
UAE	4				
	22	Net Discrepancy	3.1	5.3	3.7
Lebanon	2.4[1]				
USA	2.4				
Net Discrepancy	16.7				

Key:c + d.

[1] Taken from *IFS*.

[2] Excluded from BIS data too for end-1981.

[3] Strictly speaking, given that the data source for the Lebanon is *IFS*, the figures for this country are for external (not foreign currency) liabilities and therefore the comparison is not completely valid. However, as the Lebanon is an offshore centre, the concepts are likely to coincide particularly using the rounded figures of Table 6.3.

centres of eurocurrency activity is indicated by Sterling's (1980a) estimate of the size of the eurocurrency market — generated from his Reporting Area of 58 countries — in 1978 which exceeded $1050 billion, virtually 10 per cent higher than any measure in Table 6.1.

The second variation between the series in Table 6.1 is the extent to which foreign currency positions against domestic residents are included in the totals. While Ashby includes eurocurrency claims against domestic residents of the European Reporting Area only, the BIS, as noted above, has included domestic positions of banks in Canada and Japan since 1979. (Domestic eurocurrency claims of these latter banks had reached $46 billion by the end of 1979.) The principle adopted by Morgan Guaranty in this respect is that it includes such data on domestic positions where it is available and of good quality. For the European centres, Canada and Japan, use is made of the aggregate BIS information, but for other non-European centres good quality domestic positions data are available for Hong Kong and Singapore only. For other centres, where little reliable information on such positions is available to Morgan Guaranty, this information is excluded. However, given the offshore centre status of many of the non-European countries, the omission of foreign currency positions against domestic residents is not serious in such cases. Given the inclusion of these domestic positions for a wider range of reporting countries in Morgan Guaranty data this is likely to explain a small part of the discrepancy between the BIS and Morgan Guaranty estimates of eurocurrency liabilities.

However there is a third source of variation — namely a difference in the institutional coverage between series within any particular common reporting country — which may be relevant in the comparison between the BIS and Morgan Guaranty series. Whether this is the case is, unfortunately, impossible to tell given the published information. However, in the comparison between the series of Ashby and the BIS such a variation in institutional coverage appears to exist. Given that Ashby's data for the BIS European Reporting Group is reconciled with BIS totals, any variation that exists applies to the coverage of institutions in Canada, Japan and the common group of offshore centres. Reference to Table 6.2 will help at this point. For example, Ashby quotes 1979 figures for eurocurrency claims against overseas residents in Japan and Canada of $45 and $26 billion, respectively, compared to BIS estimates of $34 and $25 billion. Clearly, it is likely that the significant difference in the case of Japan is due to the inclusion by Ashby — using separate sources of information — of a wider range of banks in that country. A similar variation is likely to exist in the case of the offshore centres category too.

Unfortunately, a more definite conclusion on the explanation of such institutional variations is not possible given the extent of the published information on the construction of the two series.

Despite these discrepancies there is considerable conceptual overlap and statistical correspondence between the series being surveyed in this chapter. This enables an observer to derive a reliable estimate of the size of the eurocurrency market which ever series is used.

Table 6.4 provides information on the volume of eurocurrency activity in the main banking centres for 1975–81. The list of centres used in the table covers all those included in one or other of the Reporting Groups specified in Table 6.2. (Despite including all the main centres, it does not therefore exhaust the list of countries conducting eurocurrency lending.) The table is constructed in the following way. For the BIS area, including domestic positions, BIS data are used. For all other centres, Ashby's figures are used for 1975–79 and then updated for 1980–1 using IMF data. (This assumes that all external lending by non-BIS reporting banks included in Table 6.4 is in foreign currencies, which is not wholly valid but is a reasonably close approximation to reality, given the rounded numbers in this table.)

The shares of particular countries in the eurocurrency market, as defined in Table 6.4, have fluctuated considerably over the 1975–81 period (see Fig. 6.1). The European segment of the market has fallen from 71.4 per cent of the total (including domestic positions) in 1975 to only 63.4 per cent in 1981, reflecting, in the main, the growth of the offshore centres. Since 1975, these centres have seen the most rapid growth of eurocurrency lending with their share of the total having risen from 19.3 per cent in 1975 to 23.6 per cent two years later, although this had levelled off to 23 per cent at the end of 1981. Within this offshore centres category, the share of the Bahamas and Cayman Islands fell from 12.8 per cent in 1975 to 10.9 per cent in 1981, having peaked at 14.2 per cent in 1977. It is likely that this decline will continue as a result of the recent decision to allow American banks to introduce International Banking Facilities (IBFs) in New York (Chapter 3). However, notable share increases over the 1975–81 period were recorded for banks in Singapore (2.7 per cent to 4.0 per cent of the total), Panama (1.6 per cent to 2.3 per cent), Bahrain (0.4 per cent to 2.4 per cent) and Hong Kong (1.9 per cent to 2.8 per cent).

Within the European area the United Kingdom share of the market, having fallen sharply early in the 1970s, remained fairly steady over the data period in Table 6.4. Eurocurrency assets of banks in the

TABLE 6.4
Eurocurrency Claims by Banking Country
(BIS, IMF and Ashby Data, $Billion, End-Year)

	1975	1976	1977	1978	1979	1980	1981	Share in Total (1981)
BIS Europe								
External Positions:								
Austria			7	10	14	15	16	0.9
Belgium	15	17	23	32	40	52	59	3.3
Denmark			2	3	4	4	4	0.2
France	39	48	62	81	100	119	120	6.8
Germany	11	14	17	21	22	22	24	1.3
Ireland			2	2	2	2	2	0.1
Italy	15	12	15	22	28	30	36	2.0
Luxembourg	25	32	44	58	79	87	87	4.9
Netherlands	17	22	27	37	45	51	53	3.0
Sweden	3	3	3	3	5	6	7	0.4
Switzerland	16	18	23	31	32	30	31	1.8
UK	118	138	159	203	270	334	401	22.6
Domestic Positions:	89	102	129	156	196	255	282	15.9
Sub-Total	347	407	514	659	836	1006	1122	63.4
Other Centres								
External Positions:								
Canada	14	17	18	22	25	35	37	2.1
Japan	20	22	22	34	34	49	64	3.6
USA	1	2	2	4	2	4	5	0.3
Bahamas	55	79	90	105	112	125	150	8.5
Bahrain	2	6	16	23	28	31	43	2.4
Cayman Islands	7	12	16	18	27	33	42	2.4
Hong Kong	9	13	17	20	25	38	50	2.8
Netherlands Antilles	—	1	2	3	5	7	11	0.6
Panama	8	10	14	19	32	34	41	2.3
Singapore	13	17	21	27	38	45	70	4.0
Kuwait	2	3	4	5	6	7	8	0.5
Lebanon	2	2	2	2	3	4	4	0.2
Philippines	1	1	2	2	2	3	3	0.2
Spain	3	4	5	7	11	13	15	0.8
UAE	2	3	2	3	4	6	8	0.5
Domestic Positions:								
Canada/Japan					46	64	98	5.5
Total	486	662	747	953	1229	1504	1771	—

United Kingdom accounted for 35.7 per cent of the European market in 1981 (34 per cent in 1975) and 22.6 per cent of the overall total (24.3 per cent). Banks in Belgium–Luxembourg have retained their position in the market with their share having risen from 8 per cent in 1975 to 9.7 per cent in 1979 before declining again to only 8.2 per

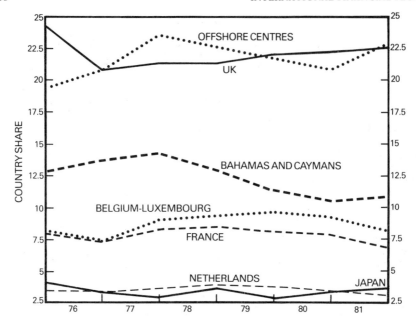

FIGURE 6.1
Country shares in total eurocurrency market

cent at the end of 1981. Similarly, the share of eurocurrency lending by banks in France in the total fell from 8 per cent to 6.8 per cent over the data period. It is notable that the strong currency countries of the Netherlands, Switzerland and Germany have experienced slower growth and sharply declining shares of the total market, mainly due to institutional restrictions consequent upon the desire to limit the role of these currencies as international reserve assets. As was the case with external bank lending the eurocurrency claims of banks in Denmark, Ireland and Sweden are very small.

Finally, the shares in the total market of eurocurrency lending by banks in Canada and Japan have fallen quite sharply to 2.1 per cent and 3.6 per cent respectively by the end of 1981, while the shares of other non-European centres listed in Table 6.4, although growing rapidly (particularly Kuwait, Spain and the United Arab Emirates), remained below 1 per cent of the total market at the end of 1981.

TABLE 6.5
Geographical Breakdown of European Banks' External Eurocurrency Positions
(BIS Data; $Billion; End-Year)

	Reporting[1] European Countries	Other Western Europe	Eastern Europe	USA	Canada	Japan	Middle East	Caribbean Area	Latin America	Singapore	Australia, New Zealand & South Africa	Others	Total
Banks' Assets													
1975	114.8	20.9	15.9	17.8	2.5	17.7	4.9	25.9	12.9	4.5	4.9	15.4	258.1
1976	131.4	26.5	20.8	19.5	3.5	18.1	8.7	28.6	17.4	6.8	6.5	17.5	305.3
1977	191.7	23.7	25.7	22.6	4.6	14.2	13.6	29.8	21.5	7.3	7.1	23.0	384.8
1978	260.5	29.3	31.3	25.9	5.4	19.2	19.2	37.9	29.6	8.3	54	30.0	502.0
1979	322.3	35.5	36.0	40.6	8.2	26.3	21.3	52.4	43.2	9.9	5.0	39.0	639.7
1980	370.1		38.9	41.4	52.4[2]			84.4[2]				164.0[3]	751.2
1981	393.4		39.9	56.4	65.6			96.5[2]				188.2[3]	840.0
Banks' Liabilities													
1975	132.0	19.4	5.4	16.6	4.7	3.6	35.2	14.1	9.6	1.6	0.5	16.0	258.7
1976	149.1	20.5	6.4	20.1	6.1	4.4	44.4	20.7	11.7	1.8	0.8	24.7	310.7
1977	209.4	18.1	7.0	26.6	5.7	2.7	55.4	23.0	14.0	2.4	0.7	31.2	396.2
1978	275.0	25.4	8.7	38.3	7.3	5.7	60.2	32.5	18.1	3.9	0.8	34.9	510.8
1979	348.0	30.4	13.0	54.6	7.0	9.5	83.5	40.9	23.3	5.6	1.3	48.7	665.8
1980	411.2		12.8	61.5	29.4			78.6[2]				207.0[3]	800.5
1981	442.6		11.9	89.7	40.9			91.3[2]				215.1[3]	891.5
Banks' Net Position													
1975	−17.2	+1.5	+10.5	+1.2	−2.2	+14.1	−30.3	+11.8	+3.3	+2.9	+4.4	−0.6	−0.6
1976	−17.7	+6.0	+14.4	−0.6	−2.6	+13.7	−35.7	+8.1	+5.7	+5.0	+5.7	−7.2	−5.4
1977	−17.7	+5.6	+18.7	−4.0	−1.1	+11.5	−41.8	+6.8	+7.5	+4.9	+6.4	−8.2	−11.4
1978	−14.5	+3.9	+22.6	−12.4	−1.9	+13.5	−41.0	+5.4	+11.5	+4.4	+4.6	−4.9	−8.8
1979	−25.7	+5.1	+23.0	−14.0	+1.2	+16.8	−62.2	+11.8	+19.9	+4.3	+37	−9.7	−26.1
1980	−41.1		+26.1	−20.1	+23.0			+5.8[2]				−43.0[3]	−49.3
1981	−49.2		+28.0	−33.3	+24.7			+5.2[2]				−26.9[3]	−51.5

Key: d.

[1] From 1977, this column includes Austria, Denmark and Ireland as borrowers from and lenders to reporting banks, to reflect their inclusion in the Reporting Group itself in that year.
[2] Offshore centres only in 1980–1.
[3] In 1980–1, a much broader figure due to the narrower geographical breakdown published since the end of 1979.

BORROWER GEOGRAPHICAL BREAKDOWN

The BIS alone publishes a geographical breakdown by borrower of banks's foreign currency positions. However a less detailed breakdown ia available in comparison to that published for external bank lending (Tables 3.3–3.5). Table 6.5 sets out this information which applies to positions of European Reporting banks only, against nonresidents. In addition, in the *Press Release* for 1980 (Quarter 4), the presentation of these data was altered significantly. Prior to the change, individual country detail was available for the USA, Canada and Japan outside the Reporting Area, with, in addition, a full country breakdown of the intra (European Reporting)-group positions (Table 3a of the *Press Release*).[4] Following the change in the presentation of the these figures a less comprehensive regional breakdown of foreign currency positions is now published with separate country detail available for the USA only (see the data for 1980–1 in Table 6.5) while the country breakdown of intra-group positions is no longer included. However, to compensate, a breakdown of the claims into those on banks and on non-banks in the specified geographical regions is now published.

The pattern of net borrowers and net lenders is similar in Table 6.5 to that recorded in Table 3.3. The major net lender to the European banks since 1975 has been the Middle-East (defined in this case to include many of the OPEC nations) with a net supply of funds from 1975 to 1979 of $31.9 billion ($62.2–$30.3 billion) reflecting the rise in the external surpluses of these countries particularly in 1979. Other major net suppliers have been the European Reporting Area ($32 million between 1975 and 1981) and the USA ($34.5 billion), the latter having converted a net borrower position into one net lending to the European banks. Major net absorbers have been Eastern Europe ($17.5 billion) and Latin America ($16.6 billion), the latter figure being from 1975–9 only. The position of other areas is considerably obscured by the broad category — particularly for 1980–1 — of 'other countries'.

Despite the similar pattern of results to those recorded in Tables 3.3

---

[4] This information on intra-group positions is not given here due to the similarity in results to those intra-group positions reported in Table 3.4. In addition the principles used in interpreting the figures are identical to those described in Chapter 3. Reference should be made to that description which is not repeated here. This also applies to the calculation of the changes in net positions (the supply and absorption of funds) which may be made from Table 6.5 and was also described in Chapter 3.

and 3.4, certain important differences should be noted. Most importantly the magnitudes are much smaller, reflecting the narrower concept of bank positions in Table 6.5. This is reflected most notably in the lower net intra-group positons and in the lower net borrowing by Eastern Europe. The significantly lower absorption by Latin America between 1975 and 1979 ($16.6 billion compared to $37.9 billion) is not purely a result of the smaller scale of total eurocurrency lending from Europe however, but also reflects the great volume of borrowing by countries in that area from US banks, excluded from Table 6.5.

CURRENCY BREAKDOWN OF EUROCURRENCY CLAIMS

It is important to have information on the currency components of the eurocurrency market for many reasons, including an awareness of the extent of possible valuation effects as non-dollar positions are converted into dollar values. Table 6.6 sets out the information published by the BIS on this breakdown. It includes a fairly wide currency breakdown for the external claims of the European Reporting Area and a breakdown of domestic eurocurrency claims into dollar and non-dollar components. The shares of the major currencies in external claims are graphed in Fig. 6.2.

The dollar continues to dominate eurocurrency business with its share of external claims standing at 75.5 per cent at the end of 1981. This represents a peak share for the period since 1975 and follows a relative slump in the dollar's share to below 70 per cent in the late 1970s. The share of the dollar in domestic eurocurrency lending is similar to that in external claims. It fell from 72.4 per cent in 1977 to 68.2 per cent one year later before rising to 75.5 per cent (an identical share to that for external claims) at the end of 1981. Overall, therefore the dollar's share in total eurocurrency lending has actually increased from 70.4 per cent in 1977 to just over 75 per cent in 1981.

The share of DM-denominated claims in the total of European banks' external assets rose from 16.1 per cent in 1975 to 19.4 per cent in 1978 but dropped back again to only 11.2 per cent in 1981. Similarly, the small fall in the Swiss franc share from 6.0 per cent in 1975 to 5.6 per cent in 1981 masks some intra-period fluctuation around the 5–6 per cent level. Claims denominated in these three currencies totally dominate the eurocurrency market with less than 8 per cent of the volume of total external assets denominated in

TABLE 6.6
Currency breakdown of Reporting Banks'¹ Eurocurrency Claims
(BIS Data; $Billion; End-Year)

	External Claims										Domestic Claims			Grand Total
	Dollars	Deutsche-mark	Swiss Francs	Sterling	Guilders	French Francs	Yen	Belgian Francs	Others	Total	Dollars	Others	Total	
	(1)	(2)	(3)	(4)	(5)	(6)	(7)	(8)	(9)	(10)	(11)	(12)	(13)	(14)
1975	190.2	41.6	15.4	2.0	2.1	2.6			4.2	258.1			89.4	347.5
1976	224.0	48.7	17.9	2.2	3.8	2.6			6.1	305.3			101.7	407.0
1977	268.4	70.4	23.6	5.3	4.3	3.3	1.7	2.4	5.4	384.8	93.5	35.7	129.2	514.0
1978	339.5	97.4	27.9	7.3	6.9	5.7	5.4	3.2	8.7	502.0	106.5	49.6	156.1	658.1
1979	599.3	127.4	39.4	11.6	8.6	8.1	6.3	28.2		828.9	169.8	72.2	242.0	1070.9
1980	724.9	126.3	51.2	13.7	7.7	11.9	10.6	33.7		979.0	227.7	91.3	319.0	1298.0
1981	843.2	125.0	62.6	14.6	8.2	8.2	16.4	39.3		1117.5	287.3	93.0	380.3	1497.8
Key				d						c				c + d

¹ European Reporting Area until 1979.

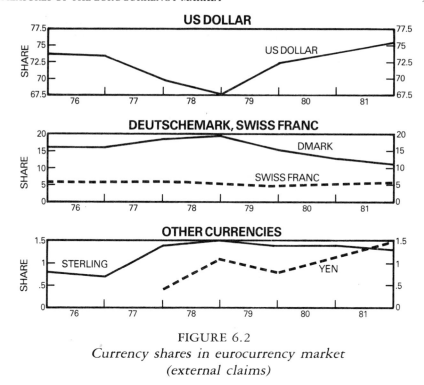

FIGURE 6.2
Currency shares in eurocurrency market
(external claims)

currencies other than these three at the end of 1981. Of the other currencies, the share of sterling has risen considerably from 0.8 per cent in 1975 to 1.3 per cent in 1981 as has that of the Japanese yen (0.4 per cent in 1977 to 1.5 per cent). The share of French franc denominated claims in the total rose from 1 per cent in 1975 to 1.2 per cent in 1980 before declining sharply to 0.7 per cent at the end of 1981. However, these are relatively minor movements given the huge size of the market and of dollar-denominated claims. Any fluctuations in the value of the dollar in the 1970s and any concern over its stability and future value have as yet done little to reduce its overwhelming importance in the eurocurrency market (Bank of England 1982).

NET SIZE OF THE EUROCURRENCY MARKET

Following the pattern of Chapter 3, this section describes the available measures of the 'net' eurocurrency market, while the principles

TABLE 6.7
'Net' Size Estimates of the Eurocurrency Market
(Various Series; $Billion; End-Year)

	BIS Data: European Area	Morgan Guaranty Data	Ashby Data
1971	71	85	80
1972	85	110	105
1973	132	160	162
1974	177	220	217
1975	205	255	259
1976	247	320	321
1977	300	390	387
1978	377	495	487
1979	475	615	611
1980	575	760	692[1]
1981	661	890	

Key: c + d.

[1] June. Provisional figure.

involved in the derivation of the net series are described in full. No reference is made in this chapter to the alternative procedure for identifying the actual creation of credit for end-users namely that of presenting series of eurocurrency claims on banks and non-banks. These series were described in Chapter 3 with reference to eurocurrency positions as well as for external bank lending. In addition, such series are only published by the BIS while the three sources being compared in this chapter all publish net size estimates of the eurocurrency market which will be the focus of attention in this section.

Table 6.7 presents the next size estimates of the eurocurrency market according to the three sources being surveyed. Three points should be noted about this table. Firstly, all series include eurocurrency claims on domestic residents. Secondly, while Morgan Guaranty and Ashby are measuring the net size of the eurocurrency market on a global basis, the BIS series refers to the European Reporting Area only. Thirdly, while the Morgan Guaranty gross series was defined in terms of liabilities, the net series is in terms of claims. This is based on the greater importance of being aware of which sectors *owe* the funds to the reporting banks when the series is in net form. Considering the

TABLE 6.8
The 'Net' Size of the Eurocurrency Market Sources and Uses of Eurocurrency Funds[1]
(BIS Data; $Billion; End-Year)

	European Report-ing Area	USA	Canada and Japan	Other Devel-oped Countries	Eastern Europe	Offshore Banking Centres	Oil-Export-ing Countries	Other Devel-oping Countries	Unallo-cated	Total
				USES						
1975	63.0	16.5	20.2	25.8	15.9	35.6	5.3	19.5	3.2	205.0
1976	74.4	18.2	21.6	33.0	20.8	40.8	9.6	24.7	3.9	247.0
1977	110.4	21.3	18.7	30.8	25.7	43.9	15.7	30.3	3.2	300.0
1978	139.5	24.6	24.6	34.7	31.4	55.0	24.3	40.1	2.8	377.0
1979	171.3	36.7	33.0	40.5	36.0	67.5	30.4	55.1	4.5	475.0
1980	216.4	39.7	45.1	52.1	38.9	73.0	33.8	71.0	5.0	575.0
1981	248.5	51.1	52.2	61.4	39.8	83.1	35.6	83.3	6.0	661.0
				SOURCES						
1975	79.5	15.4	8.3	19.9	5.4	21.8	34.6	16.2	3.9	205.0
1976	86.7	18.8	10.5	21.3	6.4	30.1	45.2	21.3	6.7	247.0
1977	117.3	25.4	8.4	18.8	7.0	33.4	54.5	29.6	5.6	300.0
1978	144.5	37.0	13.0	26.2	8.8	45.4	54.7	39.8	7.6	377.0
1979	174.0	50.5	15.2	31.7	13.0	52.8	81.0	47.8	9.0	475.0
1980	211.0	59.7	22.1	33.5	12.8	68.0	109.8	46.6	11.5	575.0
1981	252.5	84.5	27.9	34.8	11.9	77.9	109.4	46.2	15.9	661.0
				NET POSITIONS[2]						
1975	− 16.5	+ 1.1	+ 11.9	+ 5.9	+ 10.5	+ 13.8	− 29.3	+ 3.3	− 0.7	—
1976	− 12.3	− 0.6	+ 11.1	+ 11.7	+ 14.4	+ 10.7	− 35.6	+ 3.4	− 2.8	—
1977	− 6.9	− 4.1	+ 10.3	+ 12.0	+ 18.7	+ 10.5	− 38.8	+ 0.7	− 2.4	—
1978	− 5.0	− 12.4	+ 11.6	+ 8.5	+ 22.6	+ 9.6	− 30.4	+ 0.3	− 4.8	—
1979	− 2.7	− 13.8	+ 17.8	+ 8.8	+ 23.0	+ 14.7	− 50.6	+ 7.3	− 4.5	—
1980	+ 5.4	− 20.0	+ 23.0	+ 18.6	+ 26.1	+ 5.0	− 76.0	+ 24.4	− 6.5	—
1981	− 4.0	− 33.4	+ 24.3	+ 26.6	+ 27.9	+ 5.2	− 73.8	+ 37.1	− 9.9	—

Key: c + d.

[1] For full details of geographical areas, see footnotes to Table 3.3.
[2] − = NET SOURCE; + = NET USE.

figures themselves, the effect of the smaller Reporting Group on the BIS eurocurrency market net figure (Column 1) is clearly seen in comparison with the other two conceptually compatible series. It is encouraging however that despite small differences in the Reporting Group, the net series of Ashby and Morgan Guaranty have very close correspondence.

The BIS publishes a borrower breakdown by geographical region of the net eurocurrency market. (Table 7 of the *Press Release*). It is labelled by the BIS as the 'sources and uses of eurocurrency funds' to clarify its status as a table of 'net' positions, i.e. against end-users and end-suppliers. This breakdown is set out in Table 6.8. The figures should be interpreted in a similar way to the borrower breakdown details presented earlier in this chapter for the gross eurocurrency market (Table 6.5) and also to the equivalent tables for external bank lending in Chapter 3 (Tables 3.3–3.5). Major net absorbers of funds from the eurocurrency market between 1975 and 1981 were the group of developing countries ($33.8 billion), other developed countries ($20.7 billion), Eastern Europe ($17.4 billion), the European Reporting Area ($12.5 billion) and Canada and Japan ($12.4 billion). The figure for the European Reporting Area is considerably out of line with the equivalent gross figures (Table 6.5) reflecting the extent to which the supply of funds in gross terms is accounted for by inter-bank depositing. The only major net suppliers of funds were the oil-exporting countries ($44.5 billion between 1975 and 1981 and the USA ($34.5 billion). In general, therefore, the broad conclusions on the geographical breakdown of the supply and absorption of eurocurrency funds in net terms are similar to those that are applicable to the gross market.

To derive an estimate of the net size of the eurocurrency market a set of well-defined principles should be followed.[5] Essentially, all inter-bank transactions between banks within the Reporting Area should be 'netted' out of the gross figure. An example of such an inter-bank flow is given in Figure 6.3.

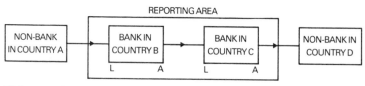

FIGURE 6.3

The symbols L and A refer to banks' liabilities and assets. This flow of funds from a non-bank surplus sector in Country A to a non-bank deficit sector in Country D is double-counted due to the inter-bank transaction between the banks in Countries B and C. Specifically, the liability of the bank in Country C to the bank in Country B is counted as well as the latter's liability to the non-bank in Country A. A similar double-counting occurs on the claims side. No 'new' credit is created by the inter-bank transaction and therefore it should be netted out of the figures.[6]

[5] See Mayer (1976, 1979a) and Johnston (1983) for a detailed description and analysis of these principles which, although specified by these authors with reference to BIS figures, are generally applicable too. See also Ellis (1981).
[6] The economic function of these inter-bank flows is not in question however. By redistributing funds between international banks, such transactions serve to enhance the allocation of liquidity. In addition, if such transactions involve a significant degree of maturity transformation, liquidity-creating effects may follow (Johnston, 1983).

This rule and the example in Figure 6.3 apply whether the Countries A and D, in which the end-supplier and end-user of the funds are located, are inside or outside the Reporting Area. However, should one of the banks in the transaction in Figure 6.3 be outside the Reporting Area, double-counting does not occur. For example let Country B be outside the Reporting Area. Then the liability of the bank in Country B to the non-bank sector in Country A and the claim of the bank in B on the bank in C would not be reported. Due to the status of the bank in Country B as a non-reporter, it is as if that bank were the end-supplier of funds. No double-counting occurs and therefore the inter-bank transaction should not be netted out. This is illustrated in Figure 6.4.

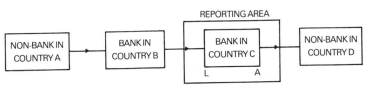

FIGURE 6.4

One problem with this procedure is that double-counting would still occur if a reporting bank (e.g. in Country C) lent funds to a non-reporting bank (in Country E, perhaps) which then re-deposited the funds in the eurocurrency market. There is no provision to net out such inter-bank transactions despite the double-counting that has occurred. Such activity is difficult to estimate although it is likely to be small given the cost of borrowing funds from the eurocurrency market relative to the return obtained by re-depositing funds in the market and given the large amount of world banking captured in the BIS area.

The general rule demonstrated in Figure 6.4 of netting out all intra-Reporting Areas, inter-bank transactions does not apply, however, in four cases. Firstly, any transactions between reporting banks and financial institutions which do not themselves 'report' are not, of course, double-counted, nor therefore netted out of the figures. This is illustrated in Figure 6.5.

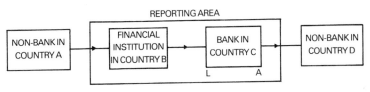

FIGURE 6.5

This example applies to non-reporting financial institutions such as official monetary institutions (e.g. central banks), and certain non-bank financial institutions (e.g. specialised credit institutions and savings and loan associations). Although within the Reporting Area in Country B, the financial institution in Figure 6.5 is a non-reporter and so is, in effect, treated as an end-supplier of funds to the bank in Country C.

Secondly, large quantities of funds are placed in the international markets by Swiss banks on behalf of their customers. Such 'trustee funds' are not recorded as assets by the Swiss banks that hold them but appear as liabilities to Switzerland in the reports of the banks receiving the funds. Given the ultimate non-bank status and direction of these funds, they are considered to be from a non-bank source and are therefore included in the 'net' size figures.

Thirdly, any *domestic* currency funds placed by a reporting bank with a bank in another country are not netted out in any measure of the eurocurrency market. For example, French franc funds placed by a French bank in Germany would not be recorded as a foreign currency asset of that French bank. An example is given in Figure 6.6.

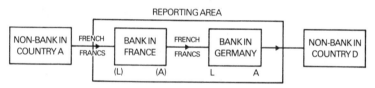

FIGURE 6.6

In Figure 6.6, the reporting bank in France receives the French franc funds from a non-bank depositer which may be in France or elsewhere (e.g. Country A), and then on-lends these funds to a bank in Germany. Neither the liability nor the claim of the French bank are included in any measure of the eurocurrency market due to these positions being denominated in domestic currency. The liability of the German bank to the bank in France and its claim on the non-bank sector in Country D alone are reported with the result that no double-counting occurs. Therefore, no netting out procedure is observed in such cases with, in effect, the French bank being considered to be the end-supplier of eurocurrency funds.[7]

[7] Notwithstanding this, some reduction in the 'net' size figures of the eurocurrency market is made to account for the holding of foreign currency working balances by banks, a practice unrelated to eurocurrency market lending activity. (See Mayer 1976, 1979a.)

Alternatively, should the objective be a measure of external bank lending rather than the eurocurrency market, the currency of the inter-bank transaction is irrelevant and the franc claim of the French bank on the overseas bank would be reported. Therefore, double-counting would occur in this case, and so netting-out should still take place. Conversely, the netting-out procedure should not be undertaken when the net figure for international bank lending is derived in the case of a foreign currency, inter-bank transaction within one reporting country. In that case, the domestic inter-bank flow of funds would be excluded from the 'gross' figure anyway and so no double-counting occurs.

Finally, and in similar vein to the previous point, the netting out of inter-bank flows should not take place for any measure of the net eurocurrency market when funds are switched from domestic currency and placed in the euromarkets or alternatively are borrowed in the markets, switched into domestic currency and lent at home. An example is given in Figure 6.7.

REPORTING AREA

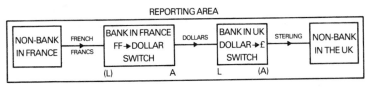

FIGURE 6.7

In Figure 6.7, the bank in France having received a French franc deposit switches the funds into dollars and on-lends them to a bank in the UK. This bank then switches them back into domestic currency and lends them to a non-bank at home. No double counting occurs as neither the liability of the bank in France (in francs) nor the claim of the UK bank (in sterling) would be reported. The inter-bank transaction must not be netted out therefore given that in effect the ultimate end-supplier of the eurocurrency (dollar) funds is the bank in France and the ultimate end-user the UK bank.

It may be argued however that this complete transaction should be excluded from data on the eurocurrency market (i.e. netting-out should occur) given that the transactions between banks and non-banks are in both cases completed in domestic currency and within one country. However to do this ignores the vital intermediary role played by the eurocurrency market, through the inter-bank flow in dollars, between the non-bank sectors in France and the UK. Therefore, an estimate of the type of transaction in Figure 6.7 should logically be included in the figures for the size of the eurocurrency market. In the example in Figure 6.7 no added complication exists when a net figure for external bank lending is required as the French franc deposit and the sterling claim would not be counted in this case, either, albeit for a different reason namely that the source and use of funds were both the domestic economy.

Of the three series of the net size of the eurocurrency market included in Table 6.7, Morgan Guaranty alone attempts a breakdown of the aggregates allowing an estimation of these adjustments to be made. Table 6.9 seeks to quantify this breakdown. The importance of not eliminating all inter-bank positions from a 'net' size figure is clear from this table given that in the early 1970s, claims on non-reporting financial institutions were similar in size to claims on non-banks, while the proportion of claims on non-banks in the net size figures only reached 50 per cent in the second half of the 1970s. The extent of the switching of eurocurrency funds into domestic currency is limited, at around 10 per cent of the net size figures.

The principles for deriving a net figure of bank lending are very general in two senses. Firstly, they are applicable to estimates of both the eurocurrency market and external bank lending (notwithstanding

TABLE 6.9
Sectoral Breakdown of Bank's Net Eurocurrency Claims (Morgan Guaranty Data; $Billion; End-Year)

	Claims on:		Switching of Eurocurrency Funds into Domestic Currencies in European Reporting Area	Total 'Net' Claims
	Non-Banks	Central[1] Banks & Banks outside the Reporting Area		
1971	35	35	15	85
1972	45	45	20	110
1973	70	70	20	160
1974	105	95	20	220
1975	130	105	20	255
1976	165	130	25	320
1977	210	150	30	390
1978	265	185	45	495
1979	325	230	60	615
1980	400	285	75	760
1981	485	325	80	890

Key: c + d.

[1] Including unallocated claims.

slight variations in the netting-out procedures noted above). Secondly, although reference has frequently been made in this section to the construction of a net series by the BIS, similar principles are employed by Morgan Guaranty[8] for example and are applicable generally. In addition, a general listing of bank positions either to be included in a net series or excluded from it may be drawn up that is applicable to any data on international bank lending.[9]

However, despite its generality, this methodology of deriving net size estimates of bank lending and the whole concept of a net figure itself have not been free from criticism. Firstly, while it may be argued that the gross figures overstate the significance of the eurocurrency market and international bank lending due to the inclusion of a large volume of inter-bank flows, it has also been pointed out that the 'net' figures may be too narrow (e.g. Ashby, 1974). It is said that these figures represent the 'economist's' view of the market due to the emphasis on end-use and end-source involving non-banks. In contrast, for many bankers it may be important to have an estimate of the total volume of bank lending so that the 'gross' figures are more relevant. Secondly, a major problem is the quality of the estimates themselves. For example, reliable estimates of the amount of switching into and out of domestic currency and of the extent of re-depositing by non-reporting banks in the eurocurrency markets are particularly difficult to obtain. Therefore, any 'net' size figure relies to a large extent on 'guesswork' (Mayer, 1976) with the quality being particularly uncertain as the Reporting Area is expanded to encompass an increasing number of banking centres. For example, Mayer notes that the 'guesstimating' involved in the net figure of outstanding international bank credit (see Chapter 3), involving lending by non-European reporting banks including those in offshore centres, is much greater than that needed to derive a net estimate of the European eurocurrency market (Mayer 1979a).

SUMMARY

It is important to have as reliable an estimate as possible of the sizes of both the gross and net eurocurrency markets. Fortunately it is clear

[8] See Morgan Guaranty (1978).
[9] See Duffy and Giddy (1978), p. 26. These authors also note that *intra*-bank flows (i.e. between sister branches of one bank or between the parent branch and any sister branch) should be separately identified, although the suggested procedure of including such flows in a 'gross' figure but excluding them from a 'net' figure of bank lending is the same as that for *inter*-bank flows.

from the data described in this chapter that, notwithstanding the difficulty of obtaining a net size figure of good quality, considerable correspondence exists between the published series for both gross and net eurocurrency lending. This is partly due to the reliance by most sources on BIS figures for the core European centres and on similar publicity — in particular central bank bulletins and *IFS* — for other centres. This correspondence indicates that, despite the enormous scale of the modern eurocurrency market, it is possible to derive a good estimate of the market's size and its distribution across the world's financial centres.

Chapter 7

Maturity Analysis in International Banking

INTRODUCTION

None of the statistical series described to date in this book has included information on the maturity profile of international banks' assets and liabilities. In recent years, the BIS has begun to publish data that seek to fill this important gap in the statistical summary of international banking. The collection by the BIS of data on the maturity breakdown of banks' external claims began in late-1976. Regular publication of a six-monthly *Press Release* entitled 'The maturity distribution of international bank lending' started in July 1978 with data for the end of 1977.

The objectives of the BIS in furnishing this information are numerous. With the rapid growth of commercial bank lending in the 1970s (in the wake of increased balance of payments disequilibria) the proportion of the outstanding debt of developing countries owed to international banks has been increasing. Therefore, to augment the information on countries' external debt published by the World Bank and the OECD (see Chapters 11 and 12), greater detail on the maturity distribution of countries' indebtedness to banks was considered to be necessary. In addition, such information is useful to both central and commercial banks as the risks of lending to the developing world, as a whole, and to individual countries, in particular, have increased. Another advantage that the BIS maturity figures have is that despite a publication lag of, on average, five to six months (BIS, 1979), this information is available on a more complete and up-to-date basis than is the external debt information published by the World Bank and the OECD (Campbell, 1978).

DATA PRINCIPLES

Under this statistical system, individual banks report to their central
bank data on the maturity profile of their external claims plus
aggregate data for external liabilities and unused credit commitments. Conversion of non-dollar figures into dollar values is completed at the market exchange rate ruling at the end of the relevant six-
month period.[1] These figures are then reported by central banks to
the BIS.

Given that this data system is defined in terms of the residency
principle, the appropriate concept being quantified is that of *external
bank lending*. This covers items b and d in Table 2.1, includng
external claims in both domestic and foreign currencies. The figures
to be set out in this chapter should not therefore be taken as
necessarily representative of the maturity profile of assets in the
eurocurrency market, although a high proportion of the bank positions that make up these tables will be denominated in foreign
currencies.

The maturity of bank claims is measured in terms of the time-period
remaining before maturity (i.e. *residual* not original maturity) and
claims are allocated to the following categories:

   (i) up to including one year.[2]
  (ii) over one year up to and including two years and
 (iii) over two years.

Claims arising out of rollover credits are allocated according to the
latest date on which repayment may be made by the borrower. For
example, a loan with five years to final maturity is allocated to the
long-term maturity category even though, in effect, it is 'rolled-over'
every six months.

In principle, this half-yearly reporting system is, with respect to the
scope of the Reporting Area and the degree of detail included in the
borrower country breakdown, more comprehensive than the quarterly system. With the number of 'onshore' banking countries included in the Reporting Area being identical to that in the quarterly

---

[1] The exception to this rule is that banking data from France is converted to
dollar values at the *average* market rate for each data period. All these reporting
procedures are the same as those under the quarterly BIS system (Chapter 3).

[2] This category includes in addition to longer-term credits nearing maturity,
certain short-term assets such as bills of exchange and any working balances
held with banks and other financial institutions.

system — namely the European Group of twelve countries plus Canada, Japan and the USA — the differences lie in the coverage of banking activity in the offshore centres. The data reported to the BIS by the Federal Reserve Board under this system include the positions of US banks' overseas branches throughout the world. For other reporting countries, figures are included for banking activity in the eight offshore centres that comprise the extended (memorandum) treatment of these centres in the quarterly system (The Bahamas, Bahrain, Cayman Islands, Hong Kong, Lebanon, Netherlands Overseas Territories (mainly Netherlands Antilles), Panama, and Singapore). In addition, the data include banking activity in Barbados, Bermuda, Liberia, Vanutu and the British West Indies.

However the coverage within this extended Reporting Area is not complete in a number of respects and this weakens the above conclusion that the comprehensiveness of the half-yearly statistical system is greater. Firstly, no asset or liability data of overseas affiliates of banks in Luxembourg are included, while the same is true, with respect to liabilities only, of overseas branches of banks with parent offices in Italy and the UK. Secondly, no date are available on the undisbursed credit commitments of Irish, Italian, Dutch and Swiss banks of their overseas branches. However, this should not be of particular concern with the series being a relatively recent innovation, as accurate information on undisbursed credit commitments is difficult to obtain and such figures as are available are of great value. Finally within the reporting countries themselves the number of banks that actually report these data does not exhaust the list of those engaged in external lending, while, in some cases, those banks that do report do not include all categories of external assets and liabilities.

The country breakdown in the half-yearly system does not include any positions against other reporting countries (i.e. intra-group positions). This is due to the distorted view of the maturity structure of banks' claims on these countries that would arise from such figures given the intermediary role of the reporting banks (i.e. the extent of inter-bank flows). Despite this, positions against the offshore centres are included as a memorandum item. The effect of inter-bank flows in distorting the maturity structure of claims on such centres is clear and is noted below. Although less complete than the quarterly system in this respect, in certain other senses the degree of country detail included in this system is a considerable improvement. The country breakdown is virtually complete for all countries outside the Reporting Area with the one major exception being, as in the quarterly system, positions of banks in Germany *vis-à-vis* the GDR. Despite the fact that some of the individual country information with respect to

US banks is included in the residual categories, the breakdown is complete and represents the first time that an international, statistical system has achieved this degree of comprehensiveness (Mayer 1976). In addition, an improvement over the quarterly system is also apparent in the fully country breakdowns published in this system for banks in Switzerland. Finally, however, the number of countries that appear as borrowers and lenders from the international banking system is lower in the maturity data than the quarterly press release[3] although an offset is that data are published of positions against individual oil-exporting countries rather than against groupings of low- and high-absorbers as in the quarterly system.

BIS MATURITY DATA

Table 7.1 sets out annual data from 1977 to 1981 on external bank lending to geographical areas and includes bank liabilities to these areas and their unused credit commitments. The conclusions from this table are remarkably similar to those which were drawn from Table 3.3, something to be expected given the similarity of the Reporting Group coverage. Therefore total claims on the rest of the world (i.e. outside the Reporting Area and excluding the offshore centres) were $434.6 billion in Table 3.3. A similar correspondence exists in other years, while the liabilities data from the two tables are also close although slightly less so than the claims data.[4]

The main results in terms of banks' net positions in Table 7.1 are similar to those that have been described before and do not need to be set out in detail here. The major net borrowing areas are Latin America (absorption of $92.3 billion between 1977 and 1981), leading to net bank claims of $130.2 billion at the end of 1981,

---

[3] The countries included in the half-yearly maturity series but excluded from the quarterly data are Equatorial Guinea and New Caledonia, while the reverse applies for the Canary Islands, Falkland Islands, French West Indies, St Helena and the Solomon Islands.

[4] The full figures are ($ billion):

	Claims		Liabilities	
	Table 3.3	Table 7.1	Table 3.3	Table 7.1
1977	240.9	217.0	192.0	171.7
1978	302.7	284.9	225.9	210.8
1979	367.4	366.1	294.4	275.0
1980	431.6	426.4	346.3	314.3
1981	484.6	489.4	355.1	327.7

TABLE 7.1
External Bank Positions and Undisbursed Credit Commitments by Borrower Country Groups
(BIS Data; $ Billion; End-Year)

	Developed Countries	Eastern Europe	Latin America	Middle East	Other Africa	Other Asia	Total	Offshore Centres	Grand Total
Banks' Claims:									
1977	52.7	36.6	74.5	18.1	12.5	22.6	217.0	n/a	
1978	63.2	47.6	94.9	27.4	22.7	29.2	284.9	117.8	402.7
1979	74.4	56.1	131.3	33.7	28.7	41.9	366.1	166.4	532.5
1980	87.0	59.7	162.9	34.1	30.9	51.6	426.4	198.1	624.5
1981	101.5	60.8	196.6	36.3	32.8	61.2	489.4	240.8	730.2
Banks' Liabilities									
1977	26.8	8.3	36.6	66.0	9.9	24.0	171.7	n/a	
1978	37.3	10.4	45.0	82.9	10.1	25.1	210.8	111.4	322.2
1979	46.4	15.3	54.9	110.0	16.1	32.2	275.0	157.6	432.6
1980	49.7	15.2	56.9	136.7	20.0	35.9	314.3	188.1	502.4
1981	51.2	14.6	66.4	139.2	16.9	39.3	327.7	247.3	575.0
Net Position									
1977	+25.9	+28.3	+37.9	−47.9	+2.6	−1.4	+45.3	n/a	
1978	+25.9	+37.2	+49.9	−55.5	+12.6	+4.1	+74.1	+6.4	+80.5
1979	+28.0	+40.8	+76.4	−76.3	+12.6	+9.7	+91.1	+8.8	+99.9
1980	+37.3	+44.5	+106.0	−102.6	+10.9	+15.7	+112.1	+10.0	+122.1
1981	+50.3	+46.2	+130.2	−102.9	+15.9	+21.9	+161.7	−6.5	+155.2
Undisbursed Credit Commitments									
1977	13.6	9.6	15.1	8.4	5.4	9.0	61.2	n/a	
1978	16.9	12.1	24.8	9.6	8.1	14.0	85.6	7.2	92.8
1979	18.0	9.9	26.2	8.6	9.1	18.4	90.3	9.3	99.6
1980	25.7	9.6	28.3	7.7	8.6	19.9	99.7	10.6	110.3
1981	27.6	7.1	28.2	8.3	8.8	22.8	102.9	13.1	116.0

Key: b + d

developed countries outside the Reporting Area (absorption of $24.4 billion from 1977 to 1981), Asia ($23.3 billion), Eastern Europe ($17.9 billion) and Africa ($13.3 billion). The only net lenders to the international banking system at the end of 1981 were the Middle East (net bank liabilities of $102.9 billion), this area having supplied funds totalling $55 billion since the end of 1977, and the offshore centres (net supply of $12.9 billion between 1978 and 1981).

The figures for undisclosed credit commitments indicate that in addition to outstanding net bank claims against the rest of the world (excluding the offshore centres) of $161.7 billion at the end of 1981, a further $102.9 billion of funds have been committed but not yet drawn. For borrowers in Asia the volume of undrawn bank funds exceeded the volume of net claims at that time while the developed countries outside the Reporting Area were also fairly favourably placed in this respect at the end of 1981. The Latin American area had the largest absolute volume of committed but undrawn funds at its disposal at the end of 1981 ($28.2 billion), but they amounted to only a small proportion of its gross and net debt to the banking system. Similary, the volume of undisbursed funds committed to Eastern Europe at $7.1 billion was low in relation to outstanding claims. Finally, despite being net lenders to the banking system, countries in the Middle East held $8.3 billion of undrawn funds in the banks at the end of 1981.

To explore the position of individual countries and to make use of the published maturity profile, Table 7.2 sets out the asset/liability positions of banks against those countries that, at the end of 1981, owed over $5 billion (in gross terms) to the banking system. This table clearly illustrates the concentration of external lending on a small number of countries. Of total external claims, excluding those on the offshore centres, 22.4% was owed by two countries (Brazil and Mexico) and 52% by only ten countries. This latter figure had been relatively steady at around the 50% level in the period since this information has been made available by the BIS.

Of the total external claims, 61.4% were due to mature within one year. However, this proportion is distorted somewhat as the figures for claims against the offshore centres are heavily influenced by inter-bank business due to the practice of major banks of 'booking out' many external loans through such centres (see Chapter 3). Therefore at the end of 1981, 90.7% of total bank claims against these centres were due to mature in one year and of all the claims with a maturity of one year or less, 48.7% were against offshore centres. For an undistorted picture of the maturity profile of claims against non-

Reporting Group countries therefore, the figures for offshore centres should be excluded (reducing the percentage of total claims to mature within one year to 47%) and concentration placed on the sub-totals in Table 7.2.

The figure of claims maturing within one year should not be considered in isolation even now, however. Any pressure that a country may be under to repay loans that are close to maturity may be partially alleviated by the existence of both undisbursed credit commitments and funds held on deposit by that country in the international banking system. To illustrate how these concepts are linked, Table 7.3 sets out the net position of banks against a series of countries defined as claims to mature within one year once both deposits and unused credit facilities have been taken into account.

This table identifies the ten countries with the heaviest gross short-term repayment obligations at the end of 1981. Undrawn credit facilities do not cover these short-term claims for any of these ten major borrowers. However, for three countries (Spain, Venezuela and the USSR), the volume of funds held by them on deposit at reporting banks more than offsets these short-term obligations. In contrast, when both these sources of funds to finance repayments are included, as many as six countries (Brazil, Mexico, Argentina, Korea, South Africa and Poland) are unable to cover their short-term obligations.

Table 7.3 also lists those countries (except offshore centres) with total obligations to banks, at the end of 1981, of $1 billion or more, of which 50% or more mature within one year. The extent to which differing situations with respect to unused credit commitments and bank deposits affect the conclusions for individual countries is very clear. A geographical pattern is also vaguely detectable. Specifically, the Middle-Eastern countries have significant bank deposits which in all cases exceed short-term bank claims on them (particularly for Saudi Arabia), with the unused credit commitments adding to the conclusion that such countries have adequate funds to repay these loans. In general, Latin American countries have sizeable short-term obligations which are not covered by funds on deposit. In addition, even when unused credit facilities are considered too, the net positions of Cuba and Ecuador remain in favour of the banks. Overall, however, only these two countries in this sample (in contrast to the ten major borrowers) are unable to cover their short-term liabilities to the banks with funds on deposit and undisbursed commitments combined. Finally, certain countries such as Finland, Taiwan and India have sizeable unused credit facilities, which have the effect of

TABLE 7.2
External Liabilities, the Maturity Distribution of External Claims and Unused Credits Commitments of Banks against Individual Countries
(BIS Data; $ Billion; End-1981)

| | Liabilities | Assets | | | | | Undisbursed Credit Commitments[3] |
| | | Total | Maturity Distribution | | | | |
			Up to and including one year[1]	Over one year, up to and including two years	Over two years	Unallocated[2]	
Developed Countries	51.2	101.5	42.0	6.1	43.8	9.6	27.6
Australia	1.3	9.9	4.0	0.5	4.8	0.5	6.9
Finland	2.9	7.3	4.1	0.4	2.6	0.3	2.6
Greece	5.9	9.8	3.6	0.7	4.5	1.0	2.6
Norway	6.5	10.7	3.9	0.9	5.1	0.7	2.9
Portugal	1.9	7.5	2.8	0.3	3.0	1.4	1.4
South Africa	1.9	11.2	6.0	0.8	2.8	1.5	3.4
Spain	18.3	23.2	9.3	0.9	11.2	1.8	4.1
Yugoslavia	2.8	10.7	3.0	0.8	5.1	1.8	1.3
Eastern Europe	14.6	60.8	25.6	6.1	20.0	9.2	7.1
GDR	2.2	10.7	4.6	1.6	2.9	1.6	1.7
Hungary	0.9	7.7	3.1	0.6	3.5	0.6	0.4
Poland	0.8	15.3	5.5	1.9	5.3	2.6	1.8
Rumania	0.3	5.1	1.8	0.5	1.5	1.4	0.5
USSR	8.7	16.3	8.2	0.9	4.8	2.5	2.0
Latin America	66.4	196.6	91.4	16.6	78.4	10.3	28.2
Argentina	6.7	24.8	11.6	3.0	9.5	0.8	3.9
Brazil	5.2	52.7	18.3	4.3	25.0	5.1	6.1
Chile	4.1	10.5	4.2	0.9	5.1	0.3	1.8
Columbia	4.3	5.4	2.7	0.3	2.3	0.2	1.6
Mexico	12.4	50.9	27.7	4.8	22.6	1.9	7.3
Venezuela	19.7	26.2	16.1	1.7	7.5	0.9	3.2

East	139.2	36.3	28.6	1.4	4.4	2.0	8.3
Israel	9.5	6.0	4.3	0.3	1.3	0.1	0.6
Kuwait[4]	10.7	5.1	4.7	0.1	0.2	0.1	0.6
Saudi Arabia[4]	43.3	5.6	4.6	0.3	0.5	0.2	2.1
Other Africa	16.9	32.8	9.8	2.2	11.3	9.5	8.8
Algeria[4]	3.8	8.4	1.5	0.8	3.9	2.1	2.0
Nigeria[4]	1.7	6.0	2.0	0.4	2.8	0.9	3.6
Other Asia	39.3	61.2	32.8	4.0	21.2	3.3	22.8
Indonesia	7.6	7.2	3.0	0.6	3.2	0.5	2.6
Korea	3.6	19.9	11.5	1.3	6.5	0.5	5.1
Philippines	3.6	10.2	5.8	0.5	3.7	0.5	2.8
Taiwan	6.8	6.6	4.1	0.4	2.0	0.3	2.5
Thailand	1.8	5.1	3.1	0.3	1.6	0.1	1.3
SUB TOTAL	327.7	489.4	230.1	36.3	179.1	43.8	102.9
Offshore Centres	247.3	240.8	218.3	3.4	15.8	3.2	13.1
Bahamas	75.4	71.0	68.7	0.2	1.7	0.3	0.6
Bahrain[5]	11.4	9.0	8.7	—	0.1	0.1	0.1
Cayman Islands	49.3	46.6	44.5	0.3	1.2	0.7	0.6
Hong Kong	28.6	31.3	27.8	0.7	2.3	0.5	4.5
Liberia	2.7	6.9	1.8	0.6	4.2	0.3	1.2
Netherlands Antilles	9.9	7.0	5.4	0.2	1.2	0.2	0.8
Panama	16.6	26.9	22.6	0.8	3.0	0.5	1.2
Singapore	36.7	36.6	34.4	0.5	1.4	0.3	2.0
GRAND TOTAL	575.0	730.2	448.5	39.8	194.9	47.1	116.0

Key: b + d

1 Including all external assets of Italian banks as such banks are not permitted to lend at long term and no maturity distribution is available.

2 Including positions of banks in France of one year and over or as no separate division of such assets into the less than and more than two year category is published.

3 Excluding banks in Ireland, Italy, the Netherlands and Switzerland.

4 For these countries, the liabilities figure excludes the positions of US banks and their overseas branches so that the assets and liabilities figures are not comparable.

5 Excluding the positions of US banks which are included in the totals for the Middle East.

improving the liquidity positions of these countries.[5]

The changes in the maturity profile of banks' claims against certain countries and geographical areas and also in banks' liabilities and undisbursed credit commitments from 1978 to 1981 are illustrated in Table 7.4, and certain ratios relating to these figures are set out in Table 7.5. Overall, the maturities of banks' claims shortened considerably with the proportion maturing within one year rising from 41.8 per cent of the total at the end of 1978 to 47 per cent three years later, although part of this change only reverses the trend of rising maturities that was established in the second half of 1978 (the relevant figure in the middle of 1978 being 45.3 per cent.). The share of total claims maturing in over two years rose from 34.1 per cent. in the middle of 1978 to a peak of 38.5 per cent. in mid-1980 before falling to 36.6 per cent. by the end of the following year. Therefore, in the most recent period, there is confirmation in the banking figures of the observed decline in the average maturity on syndicated eurocurrency credits (Chapter 9). In addition, in the three years following the end of 1978, the ratio of unused credit commitments to short-term bank claims fell sharply from 0.718 to 0.447 indicating a substantial reduction in this liquidity cushion for borrowers as a whole.

The position of Latin American borrowers has worsened most noticeably between 1978 and 1981. From Table 7.4, the proportion of total claims to mature inside one year rose from 38.1% to 46.5% for this region with the proportion maturing in over two years falling from 44.4% to 39.9%. Most dramatically, however, the ratio of unused credit commitments to short-term claims fell from 0.685 in 1978 to 0.309 at the end of 1981 while that of bank deposits to short-term claims fell from 1.243 to 0.726 over the same period. This evidence of an increasingly difficult financial position for Latin America is matched to a certain extent for Asian borrowers. For this group the ratios of, firstly, unused credit commitments and, secondly, bank deposits to short-term claims fell from 1.000 to 0.695, and from 1.793 to 1.198, respectively, between 1978 and 1981.

The position of African borrowers remains relatively favourable

[5] Clearly the figures in Table 7.3 cover major borrowers in absolute terms. Some other countries may have large outstanding short-term obligations relative to the size of their deposits, unused credit commitments, foreign exchange reserves and other macro-economic variables. Such countries may have disproportionately large repayment burdens therefore despite their exclusion from Table 7.3.

TABLE 7.3
External Positions of Banks against Individual Countries
(BIS Data; $Billion; End-1981)

Major Borrowers	Bank claims maturing within one year	Bank liablities	Net short-term claims minus liabilities	Undisbursed credit commitments	Net position
	(1)	(2)	(3)	(4)	(5)
Mexico	27.7	12.4	15.3	7.3	8.0
Brazil	18.3	5.2	13.1	6.1	7.0
Venezeula	16.1	19.7	− 3.6	3.2	− 6.8
Argentina	11.6	6.7	4.9	3.9	1.0
Korea	11.5	3.6	7.9	4.1	3.8
Spain	9.3	18.3	− 9.0	4.1	− 13.1
USSR	8.2	8.7	− 0.5	2.0	− 2.5
South Africa	6.0	1.9	4.1	3.4	0.7
Philippines	5.8	3.6	2.2	2.8	− 0.6
Poland	5.5	0.8	4.7	1.8	2.9
Other Borrowers					
Finland	4.1	2.9	1.2	2.6	− 1.4
Liechtenstein	1.7	2.8	− 1.1	—	− 1.1
Cuba	0.8	0.1	0.7	0.1	0.6
Ecuador	2.3	0.8	1.5	0.9	0.6
Peru	2.7	1.8	0.9	1.4	− 0.5
Egypt	3.0	5.6	− 2.6	1.5	− 4.1
Iran	1.5	6.3	− 4.8	0.4	− 5.2
Israel	4.3	9.5	− 5.2	0.6	− 5.8
Kuwait	4.7	10.7	− 6.0	0.6	− 6.6
Libya	1.0	5.0	− 4.0	0.4	− 4.4
Saudi Arabia	4.6	43.3	− 38.7	2.1	− 40.8
UAE	3.3	7.9	− 4.6	1.0	− 5.6
Sudan	0.8	0.8	—	0.1	− 0.1
India	0.7	2.9	− 2.2	2.0	− 4.2
Pakistan	0.9	1.6	− 0.7	0.3	− 1.0
Taiwan	4.1	6.8	− 2.7	2.5	− 5.2
Thailand	3.1	1.8	1.3	1.3	—

Key: b + d

+ = bank claim on individual country.
Column (3) = Column (1) − Column (2);
(5) = (3) − (4) = (1) − (2) − (4).

although after rising to 2.35 at the end of 1980, the ratio of bank deposits to short-term claims fell back to 1.724 at the end of the following year. The share of total claims maturing in one year or less stood at 29.9% at the end of 1981 (27.8% in 1978) and those maturing in over two years was at 34.5% (35.7% in 1978). A

TABLE 7.4
Developments in the Maturity Profile of Banks' External Positions against Geographical Areas and Industrial Countries
(BIS Data; $ Billion; End-Year)

| | | | Assets | | | | | |
| | | | | Maturity Distribution | | | | |
		Liabilities	Total	Up to and including one year	Over one year, up to and including two years	Over two years	Unal-located	Undis-bursed Credit commit-ments
Developed	1978	37.3	63.2	25.4	5.5	25.1	7.2	16.9
Countries	1979	46.4	74.4	28.3	5.5	32.6	8.0	18.0
	1980	49.7	87.0	33.8	5.6	38.9	8.7	25.7
	1981	51.2	101.5	42.0	6.1	43.8	9.6	27.6
Norway	1978	3.0	9.1	2.5	0.6	4.7	1.3	1.9
	1979	4.4	9.7	2.8	0.7	5.2	1.1	2.2
	1980	5.4	10.8	3.7	0.9	5.3	1.0	2.6
	1981	6.5	10.7	3.9	0.9	5.1	0.7	2.9
Spain	1978	15.4	13.2	5.1	1.2	5.6	1.3	1.9
	1979	18.5	16.9	7.1	1.3	7.3	1.2	2.7
	1980	18.4	19.7	8.0	1.2	9.1	1.3	3.8
	1981	18.3	23.2	9.3	0.9	11.2	1.8	4.1
Yugoslavia	1978	3.1	6.1	1.2	0.7	2.9	1.3	1.9
	1979	2.1	8.2	1.9	0.8	4.1	1.6	2.0
	1980	2.8	10.4	2.9	0.7	5.0	1.8	2.0
	1981	2.8	10.7	3.0	0.8	5.1	1.8	1.3
Eastern	1978	10.4	47.6	20.6	5.4	15.1	6.5	12.1
Europe	1979	15.3	56.1	23.6	6.0	18.9	7.6	9.9
	1980	15.2	59.7	23.3	7.2	20.1	9.1	9.6
	1981	14.6	60.8	25.6	6.1	20.0	9.2	7.1
Poland	1978	0.8	12.4	4.2	2.1	3.9	2.2	4.4
	1979	1.2	15.8	6.2	2.3	5.0	2.4	3.9
	1980	0.6	16.2	5.4	2.7	5.5	2.6	3.9
	1981	0.8	15.3	5.5	1.9	5.3	2.6	1.8
USSR	1978	6.0	13.1	5.4	0.9	4.9	1.9	4.1
	1979	8.8	13.0	5.0	0.8	4.8	2.4	2.8
	1980	8.5	13.4	5.6	0.9	4.3	2.6	1.7
	1981	8.7	16.3	8.2	0.9	4.8	2.5	2.0
Latin	1978	45.0	94.9	36.2	11.4	42.1	5.3	24.8
America	1979	54.9	131.3	56.7	12.6	55.0	7.0	26.2
	1980	56.9	162.9	75.2	13.4	65.8	8.6	28.3
	1981	66.4	196.6	91.4	16.6	78.4	10.3	28.2
Argentina	1978	4.9	6.7	3.2	1.0	2.3	0.2	2.5
	1979	8.1	13.4	6.9	1.1	5.0	0.4	2.9
	1980	6.5	19.9	10.4	1.6	7.3	0.6	4.0
	1981	6.7	24.8	11.6	3.0	9.5	0.8	3.9
Brazil	1978	11.2	31.7	8.1	3.7	17.3	2.6	7.4
	1979	8.5	38.6	11.3	4.0	20.1	3.2	6.7
	1980	5.2	45.7	16.2	4.1	21.7	3.7	6.4
	1981	5.2	52.7	18.3	4.3	25.0	5.1	6.1
Mexico	1978	7.0	23.3	7.3	3.1	11.6	1.2	4.7
	1979	8.0	30.9	10.7	3.4	15.0	1.9	6.1
	1980	9.2	42.5	18.8	3.6	18.0	2.0	6.7
	1981	12.4	56.9	27.7	4.8	22.6	1.9	7.3
Venezuela	1978	10.2	14.0	7.6	1.3	4.7	0.4	3.6
	1979	14.2	20.8	12.7	1.5	6.1	0.5	4.1
	1980	17.4	24.3	14.3	1.7	7.6	0.8	3.7
	1981	19.7	26.2	16.1	1.7	7.5	0.9	3.2

			Assets				
			Maturity Distribution				Undis-bursed Credit commit-ments
		Liabilities	Total	Up to and including one year	Over one year, up to and including two years	Over two years	Unal-located	
Middle	1978	82.9	27.4	16.7	1.8	7.4	1.5	9.6
East	1979	110.0	33.7	22.8	1.8	7.0	2.1	8.6
	1980	136.7	34.1	25.0	1.7	5.3	2.2	7.7
	1981	139.2	36.3	28.6	1.4	4.4	2.0	8.3
Other	1978	10.1	22.7	6.3	1.7	8.1	6.6	8.1
Africa	1979	16.1	28.7	7.6	2.2	10.8	8.2	9.1
	1980	20.0	30.9	8.5	2.0	11.4	9.0	8.6
	1981	16.9	32.8	9.8	2.2	11.3	9.5	8.8
Other	1978	25.1	29.2	14.0	2.5	9.8	2.8	14.0
Asia	1979	32.2	41.9	21.9	2.6	14.1	3.3	18.4
	1980	35.9	51.6	28.3	3.1	17.1	3.1	19.9
	1981	39.3	61.2	32.8	4.0	21.2	3.3	22.8
Korea	1978	2.3	6.9	3.7	0.5	2.2	0.5	3.6
	1979	3.2	12.0	6.7	0.7	3.9	0.6	4.0
	1980	3.5	16.7	10.4	0.9	4.8	0.5	4.3
	1981	3.6	19.9	11.5	1.3	6.5	0.5	4.1
TOTAL	1978	210.8	284.9	119.2	28.3	107.5	29.9	85.6
	1979	275.00	366.1	160.9	30.6	138.3	36.2	90.3
	1980	314.3	426.4	194.2	32.9	158.6	40.7	99.7
	1981	327.7	489.4	230.1	36.3	179.1	43.8	102.9

Key: b + d

lengthening of maturities of claims on Eastern Europe occurred between 1978 and 1981 although with low unused credit commitments (27.7% of short-term claims) and deposits (57% of short-term claims) at the end of 1981, the figures signify the difficult financial position of such countries. Despite a relatively short-term profile of obligations to banks and low unused credit facilities, the large volume of funds on deposit at banks of Middle-Eastern countries indicates, as expected, a sound financial position. Finally, the position of developed countries outside the Reporting Area has been relatively stable with the ratio of unused credit commitments to short-term claims remaining at around 0.66 from 1978 to 1981. However, the ratio of deposits to short-term claims fell from 1.468 in 1978 to 1.219 three years later, while the share of total claims to mature in over two years increased from 39.7% to 43.2% over the same period.

The objective of the BIS in publishing a statistical system that details the maturity profile of banks' assets (and estimates the undrawn credit facilities) has been matched in part by similar developments in national data. For example, a maturity breakdown of the foreign claims of US banks and their overseas affiliates may be derived by combining data published by the Federal Reserve and the

TABLE 7.5
Key Asset/Liability Ratios for Geographical Areas and Certain Countries
(BIS Data; End-year)

	Ratio of short-term claims[1] to total claims		Ratio of long-term claims[2] to total claims		Ratio of unused credit commitments to short-term claims[1]		Ratio of liabilities to short-term claims[1]	
	1978	1981	1978	1981	1979	1981	1978	1981
Developed Countries	0.402	0.414	0.397	0.432	0.665	0.657	1.469	1.219
Norway	0.275	0.364	0.516	0.477	0.760	0.744	1.200	1.667
Spain	0.386	0.401	0.424	0.483	0.373	0.441	3.020	1.68
Yugoslavia	0.197	0.280	0.475	0.477	1.583	0.433	2.583	0.933
Eastern Europe	0.433	0.421	0.317	0.329	0.587	0.277	0.505	0.570
Poland	0.339	0.359	0.315	0.346	1.048	0.327	0.190	0.145
USSR	0.412	0.503	0.374	0.294	0.759	0.244	1.111	1.061
Latin America	0.381	0.465	0.444	0.399	0.685	0.309	1.243	0.726
Argentina	0.478	0.468	0.343	0.383	0.781	0.336	1.531	0.578
Brazil	0.256	0.347	0.546	0.474	0.914	0.333	1.383	0.284
Mexico	0.313	0.487	0.498	0.397	0.644	0.264	0.959	0.448
Venezuela	0.543	0.615	0.336	0.286	0.474	0.199	1.342	1.224
Middle East	0.609	0.788	0.270	0.121	0.575	0.290	4.964	4.7
Other Africa	0.278	0.299	0.357	0.345	1.286	0.898	1.603	1.724
Other Asia	0.479	0.536	0.336	0.346	1.000	0.695	1.793	1.198
Korea	0.536	0.578	0.319	0.327	0.973	0.357	0.622	0.313
TOTAL	0.418	0.470	0.377	0.366	0.718	0.447	1.768	1.424

[1] Banks' claims of up to and including one year to maturity.
[2] Banks' claims of over two years to maturity.

US Treasury. In addition, the newly released 'Country Exposure Lending Survey' (CELs) published by the Federal Reserve Board has, since December 1977, provided an additional maturity analysis of the foreign claims of US banks and their affiliates (Short and White, 1978). Similarly, the Deutsche Bundesbank provides a breakdown of foreign claims of German banks into short- and long-term categories.

Such information is provided in a number of forms for UK and UK-based banks in the *Bank of England Quarterly Bulletin*. Two separate series are noted at this stage. Firstly, a maturity distribution of external claims in foreign currencies and sterling is published for all banks operating in the UK. A second series is the same in concept but covers UK banks including their overseas affiliates only.[6] For both series, the degree of detail is slighly greater than in the BIS series in that more separate maturity categories are identified although with the inclusion of data on unused credit commitments and a country breakdown of all this information, the figures follow the general format of the BIS series. [7]

The initiative made by the BIS to obtain on a formal basis details of the maturity breakdown of banks' external assets clearly represents a major improvement in the amount of information available on the internatonal banking system. However, certain limitations — in addition to the reporting omissions mentioned earlier — should be noted. Firstly as an estimate of the repayment obligations of individual countries to banks such figures are only a partial picture of a country's total debt position. This is due to their exclusion of repayment obligations to all other creditors, in particular governments and official agencies.[8] Secondly, a country's short-term repayment obligations should be viewed alongside other economic conditions in that country. In particular, a high level of foreign exchange reserves may indicate the existence of adequate resources to repay a larger volume of short-term debt than is the case for a country that is short of reserves. Other important factors are a country's growth potential, the level and stability of its exports and whether it has

---

[6] See Tables 14.2, 14.3 and 15 in recent issues of the *Bank of England Quarterly Bulletin*.

[7] No liabilities figures are included in these tables. In addition. Table 14.1 in the *Bank of England Quarterly Bulletin* includes a country breakdown (without any maturity analysis) of UK-based banks' external positions in foreign currency on a monthly basis. Such a detailed analysis of banks' *eurocurrency* claims is not available even in BIS published data.

[8] In addition, any obligations, to banks outside the Reporting Group are, of course, excluded from these figures.

indigenous energy resources. In fact, the logical conclusion of this argument is that a full analysis of a country's economic, social and political conditions is liable to be more representative of the creditworthiness of a country than a consideration of these maturity figures in isolation. Thirdly, the BIS data in certain situations may over-dramatise the liquidity difficulties of some countries. In particular, many short-term obligations may be rolled over by creditors so that, in effect, they are self-financing. Other credits will be repaid and then renegotiated, a process that leads effectively to a rise in the average maturity of an individual country's liabilities to banks. Fourthly, with respect to all countries, not merely the offshore centres, a division of claims into those on banks and non-banks with the accompanying maturity analysis would allow more meaningful conclusions to be drawn from these figures.

MATURITY TRANSFORMATION

In this section, an attempt is made to assess the extent of maturity transformation of banks based in London. To date in this chapter, the discussion has been confined to the maturity profile of banks' assets. With the addition of information on banks' liabilities, an estimate may be made of the degree of mismatching in particular maturity categories of banks' balance-sheets. These data are not published on a global basis by the BIS and therefore the data on UK-based banks from the *Bank of England Quarterly Bulletin* are used here as an example of high quality national source data on this issue. The positions quantified in the tables to follow, are denominated in foreign currencies and are against both domestic and external sectors. Therefore the data provide an indication of the extent of maturity transformation in the UK segment of the eurocurrency market (items c and d in Table 2.1).

Maturity transformation is the activity of a bank in transforming a short-term liability into a long-term asset and is the essence of financial intermediation. In fact

'The phenomenon itself is not disturbing, since maturity transformation is the essence of banking; without it, bankers would be acting simply as cloakroom attendants for money' (Mendelsohn 1979, p.58).

Despite this, concern is often expressed at the extent of maturity transformation in all forms of financial intermediation, but in particular in international banking. Therefore the data presented in this chapter are considered to provide very important information and, in the future, the development of new series that estimate, on an increasingly reliable basis, the extent of this process is to be anticipated.

There are several reasons why international banks engage in maturity transformation. Most crucially, the preferences of a depositer are for a short-term arrangement while a borrower typically prefers to negotiate a longer-term loan. Therefore the maturity preferences of both groups are generally satisfied in this way. A bank is able to offer this maturity transformation as a result of the economies of scale that exist in banking, not least to do with risk-pooling. In addition, if there is a rising yield curve (where short-term rates are lower than long-term rates), a bank may earn a considerable profit from maturity transformation.[9] Finally, a bank may in a sense be 'forced' to engage in maturity transformation under certain circumstances. If a bank has received a deposit, it may make little or no profit by on-lending these funds in the inter-bank market should a non-bank borrower be absent from the market at a particular point in time. To gain a profit therefore, the bank may have to actively seek lending business so its efforts are automatically channelled into achieving this maturity transformation.

The arguments over whether maturity transformation in the euro-currency market is excessive and an evaluation of its dangers are finely balanced. The usual doubts expressed over this activity in these markets have been the absence of a clearly defined lender of last resort (in comparison to domestic banking), the possibility of funds leaking from the markets and into domestic money markets leaving euro-banks short of liquidity and the possibility that rises in short-term interest-rates above long-term rates may cause the banks to be 'locked into' losses on such long-term contracts.

However, all these may be answered in a satisfactory way. Firstly, the lender of last resort function has increasingly been accepted by the parent offices of individual bank branches through the 1970s. In fact, since the collapse of Herstatt Bank in 1974, the concept of parental responsibility for individual bank branches, with the central bank of the country in which the parent office is located having ultimate responsibility as the lender of last resort with respect to parent banks, has become much more widely accepted than pre-

[9] However, a rising yield curve will not always exist. If short-term rates rise but are expected to fall back in the future, a reverse yield gap emerges between short- and long-term rates. In this situation, no profit is available from this element of maturity transformation.

viously. Notwithstanding this, the absence of support from the Italian central bank at the time of the collapse of Banco Ambrosiano Holding in Luxembourg during 1982 has led to some renewed concern over the strength of the so-called 'Basle Concordat'. Secondly, any leakage of funds into the domestic markets is not a loss to the banking system as a whole. Such funds may be transferred back, if needed, from the domestic markets to the euro-banks perhaps through the parent offices of such euro-banks. Finally, the problems that may accompany adverse interest-rate developments and the short-term nature of banks' liabilities relative to the longer-run maturity of banks' claims have both been alleviated by the introduction of the 'rollover' credit. Deposits which are *de jure* short-term are often *de facto* long-term. A rollover credit implies that a seven-year eurocurrency credit, for example, is effectively refinanced or 'rolled-over' every six months. This involves a redefinition of the interest-rate paid by the borrower on the basis of the cost to the bank of six-month deposits at the end of each rollover period. Such a procedure facilitates a high degree of effective maturity transformation while reducing considerably the risk to banks of adverse interest-rate movements during the life of the loan. Of course, the interest risk is not completely removed in that adverse movements may occur within the six-month rollover period itself (Bank of England, 1982).

In the data presented below, liabilities are allocated to maturity categories according to the period remaining to the earliest possible repayment date. The fact that most lending is in the form of 'rollover' credits is ignored in the classification of banks' claims. All assets are classified according to the period remaining to the ultimate maturity date of the loan and not to the next six-month rollover date where this is appropriate.[10]

Table 7.6 presents an annual time-series from 1975 to 1981 of the maturity distribution of UK-based banks' foreign currency claims and liabilities and also their net positions.[11] This table demonstrates, as expected, that, in general, UK-based banks have net assets in the maturity range of one year and over and net liabilities in the short-term maturity categories. Therefore, in November, 1981, 19.9% of eurocurrency claims carried a maturity of one year and over compared to only 4.4% of liabilities. Likewise, 20.7% of foreign currency liabilities had a maturity of less than eight days compared to 16.6% of assets. The mismatching in the one year and over maturity ranges was

---

[10] See additional notes to Table 14.2 in the *Bank of England Quarterly Bulletin*.

[11] 1975 was chosen as the starting date for these series as during that year the composition of bank groups that constitute this series was changed.

TABLE 7.6
Maturity Analysis of UK-Based Banks' Positions in Foreign Currencies
(Bank of England Data; $ Billion; End-November)

	1975	1976	1977	1978	1979	1980	1981
Assets							
Less than 8 days	26.7	32.6	35.9	42.1	61.5	75.1	92.8
8 days–1 month	26.6	28.2	31.5	39.6	57.1	72.0	93.3
1–3 months	40.7	43.9	51.5	64.6	87.8	100.7	134.4
3–6 months	28.8	28.8	36.7	44.0	63.7	80.9	90.2
6–12 months	10.9	13.9	16.9	22.9	25.5	30.7	36.1
One year and over	41.2	46.5	52.3	64.9	74.6	94.5	111.1
Total	175.0	193.9	224.7	278.0	370.2	453.9	557.8
Liabilities							
Less than 8 days	33.2	42.1	49.5	55.8	78.5	95.8	116.8
8 days–1month	31.5	35.7	39.0	49.6	70.0	85.1	112.7
1–3 months	49.8	54.1	64.0	80.4	106.8	126.2	168.2
3–6 months	36.3	34.0	42.1	52.7	72.2	96.3	106.9
6–12 months	12.1	14.6	16.8	23.2	27.5	30.7	34.2
One year and over	11.9	13.0	14.1	16.0	18.8	22.8	25.0
Total	174.9	193.5	225.4	277.6	373.8	456.9	563.8
Net Position							
Less than 8 days	− 6.5	− 9.5	− 13.6	− 13.7	− 17.0	− 20.7	− 24.0
8 days–1 month	− 4.9	− 7.5	− 7.5	− 10.0	− 12.9	− 13.1	− 19.4
1–3 months	− 9.1	− 10.2	− 12.5	− 15.8	− 19.0	− 25.5	− 33.8
3–6 months	− 7.5	− 5.3	− 5.4	− 8.7	− 8.5	− 15.4	− 16.7
6–12 months	− 1.2	− 0.7	+ 0.1	− 0.3	− 2.0	—	+ 1.9
One year and over	+ 29.3	+ 33.5	+ 38.2	+ 48.9	+ 55.8	+ 71.7	+ 86.1
Total	+ 0.1	+ 0.4	− 0.7	+ 0.4	− 3.6	− 3.0	− 6.0

Key: c + d.

balanced virtually in full by the total of net liabilities of less than six months. Net liabilities in the six to twelve months category were low. It is clear that the extent of mismatching has not increased greatly relative to the size of banks' balance-sheets between 1975 and 1981.

This may be investigated further by allowing for the absolute increase in total assets and liabilities over the data period. This is done in Table 7.7 through the calculation of transformation ratios for each maturity category. A transformation ratio is derived by deflating the net position figures by the sum of total assets and liabilities.[12] The

[12] A ratio that would generate equivalent conclusions may be calculated, alternatively, by dividing the net position in each maturity category by total assets *or* liabilities (and not the sum of them as in Table 7.7). The general issue of whether mismatching should be measured in absolute terms or relative to the balance sheet of the banking system was recently discussed in Duncan (1981), Ashby (1982).

TABLE 7.7
Transformation Ratios[1] for UK-Based Banks Foreign Currency
Position by Maturity
(Bank of England Data; End-November)

	1975	1976	1977	1978	1979	1980	1981
Less than 8 days	− 1.86	− 2.45	− 3.02	− 2.47	− 2.28	− 2.27	− 2.14
8 days–1 month	− 1.40	− 1.94	− 1.67	− 1.80	− 1.73	− 1.44	− 1.72
1–3 months	− 2.60	− 2.63	− 2.78	− 2.84	− 2.56	− 2.80	− 3.01
3–6 months	− 2.14	− 1.37	− 1.20	− 1.57	− 1.14	− 1.69	− 1.49
6–12 months	− 0.34	− 0.18	—	− 0.05	− 0.27	—	+ 0.17
One year and over	+ 8.37	+ 8.65	+ 8.49	+ 8.80	+ 7.50	+ 7.87	+ 7.68

Key: c + d.

[1] The net position in each maturity category as a percentage of the sum of assets and liabilities.

higher is this figure the greater the degree of mismatching of assets and liabilities in any particular maturity category, such that a set of high figures for any one year is indicative of a high degree of maturity transformation. The figures in Table 7.7 indicate that the maturity transformation has indeed increased since 1975 but the pattern is neither very clear nor consistent over individual maturity categories. The proportion of net liabilities with maturities of less than eight days to the total balance-sheet has risen from 1.86% in 1975 to 2.14% in 1981 and with maturities of three months and under has risen from 5.86% in 1975 to 6.87% six years later. However to offset this conclusion the proportion of net liabilities of between 3 to 12 months has fallen significantly while maturity transformation in the range of one year and over has also declined with the transformation ratio falling from 8.37% in 1975 to 7.68% in 1981. It appears that within this data period the maximum extent of maturity transformation occurred between 1976 and 1978 since when it has declined significantly.

A further indicator of the degree of maturity transformation is set out in Table 7.8 (Sandeman, 1979). This table indicates the proportion of foreign currency liabilities in a particular maturity category that is covered by foreign currency assets of equivalent maturity. The general conclusion from Table 7.8 is that the position of UK-based banks with respect to maturity transformation has changed little between 1975 and 1981. The major exception to this conclusion is in the maturity category of one year and over where the proportion of liabilities to assets fell from 28.9% in 1975 to 22.5% in 1981,

TABLE 7.8
Coverage of Foreign Currency Liabilities by Foreign Currency
Assets in each Maturity Category for UK-Based Banks
(Bank of England Data; Liabilities/Assets; End-November)

	1975	1976	1977	1978	1979	1980	1981
Less than 8 days	1.24	1.29	1.38	1.33	1.28	1.28	1.26
8 days–1 month	1.19	1.27	1.24	1.25	1.22	1.18	1.21
1–3 months	1.22	1.23	1.24	1.25	1.22	1.25	1.25
3–6 months	1.26	1.18	1.15	1.20	1.13	1.19	1.19
6–12 months	1.11	1.05	0.99	1.01	1.08	1.00	0.95
1 year and over	0.29	0.28	0.27	0.25	0.25	0.24	0.23

Key c + d.

representing a significant increase in bank exposure over this period. In the maturity category of six months and over (which is very relevant due to the rolling-over of many eurocurrency claims every six months), the figure has fallen from 46.1% of liabilities in 1975 to 40.2% in 1981. At the short end of the maturity spectrum the concern of banks is rather different in that they would seek to be able to 'cover' a rapid outflow of liabilities through the liquidation of short-term assets. From Table 7.8, the proportion of liabilities to assets in the maturity range of less than eight days, rose from 1.244 in 1975 to 1.259 in 1981 indicating that this asset coverage of short-term liabilities fell from 80.4% to 79.5% over this period. Although this represents only a minor change over the whole period, the coverage did fall as low as 72.5% in 1977. In general, nevertheless, the asset coverage of very short-term liabilities remains adequate.

The information in Table 7.9 allows a judgement to be made on the degree of maturity transformation that exists with respect to particular borrowing/lending sectors. However, in the form that this table is designed no conclusion is possible on this for the London inter-bank market.[13] Net liabilities or assets of UK-based banks against other banks in the UK should sum to zero in each maturity category.[14] Therefore, the recorded mismatching in Table 7.9 is, in fact, a statistical error (Johnston, 1983). To gauge the extent of maturity transformation in the London inter-bank market it is necessary to identify the positions of individual groups of banks (see Tables 7.10–7.12).

[13] See the recent study by Ellis (1981).

[14] This assumes that the list of reporting banks is equivalent to that which makes up the category of UK banks as borrowers and lenders of funds in Table 7.9.

TABLE 7.9
Maturity Analysis by Sector of UK-Based Banks' Positions
in Foreign Currencies
(Bank of England Data; $ Billion; End-November)

	Less than 8 days	8 days– 1 month	1–3 months	3–6 months	6 months –1 year	1 year and over	Total
Claims on:							
UK Banks	26.6	28.5	40.9	27.3	9.2	4.6	136.9
UK Non-Banks	4.6	3.1	4.0	2.8	1.5	10.2	26.0
Overseas Banks	53.3	52.4	77.7	50.4	18.1	32.3	284.3
Overseas Non-Banks[1]	8.2	8.9	11.2	8.8	7.1	60.3	104.8
Other[2]	0.2	0.4	0.5	0.5	0.3	3.7	5.5
Total	92.8	93.3	134.4	90.2	36.1	111.1	557.8
Liabilities to:							
UK Banks	25.3	28.0	39.8	26.4	7.1	3.3	129.8
UK Non-Banks	9.1	4.5	3.9	1.8	0.5	0.6	20.3
Overseas Banks	57.2	48.0	75.3	50.6	16.2	9.4	257.0
Overseas Non-Banks[1]	21.5	18.1	22.4	10.6	5.4	3.5	81.1
Other[3]	3.9	14.2	26.8	17.5	5.1	7.8	75.5
Total	116.8	112.7	168.2	106.9	34.2	25.0	563.8
Net position against:							
UK Banks	+ 1.3	+ 0.5	+ 1.1	+ 0.9	+ 2.1	+ 1.3	7.1
UK Non-Banks	− 4.5	− 1.4	+ 0.1	+ 1.0	+ 1.0	+ 9.6	+ 5.7
Overseas Banks	− 3.9	+ 4.4	+ 2.4	− 0.2	+ 1.9	+ 22.9	+ 27.3
Overseas Non-Banks[1]	− 13.3	− 9.2	− 11.2	− 1.8	+ 1.7	+ 56.8	+ 23.7
Other	− 3.7	− 13.8	− 26.3	− 17.0	− 4.8	− 4.1	− 70.0
Total	− 24.0	− 19.4	− 33.8	− 16.7	+ 1.9	+ 76.1	− 6.0

[1] Including official monetary institutions.
[2] Commercial bills and other negotiable paper.
[3] Foreign currency certificates of deposit and other negotiable paper issued.

With respect to other sectors, however, a judgement on the degree of maturity transformation may be made. Net claims on non-banks abroad totalled $23.7 billion at the end of November 1981, with significant maturity transformation indicated by net claims of one year and over of $56.8 billion. In that maturity class, total liabilities amounted to only 5.8% of claims. Banks based in the UK provided a considerable amount of maturity transformation for domestic non-banks, with positive net claims in all maturity categories. Overseas banks were major net borrowers from the London eurocurrency market at the end of 1981 ($27.3 billion). Most of these net claims were concentrated in the maturity category of one year and over, with liabilities in this category amounting to less than 30% of assets. Therefore, overseas banks were not only net borrowers from UK-based banks but also used the London eurocurrency market to achieve significant maturity transformation. Finally, the last line of the liabilities section of Table 7.9 indicates the substantial net borrowing of funds by UK-based banks through the issue of foreign currency certificates of deposits and other short-term paper.

To study the differences in behaviour with respect to maturity transformation of different categories of UK-based banks, Table 7.10 indicates the extent of mismatching across maturity classes by evaluating net positions and transformation ratios from data for 1975 and 1981. Considerable differences do exist between these groups as would be expected given that while UK and consortium banks complete most of their maturity transformation in London, much of that undertaken by other banks is completed elsewhere. In particular, many overseas-owned banks may channel funds on a matched basis to their parent offices.

Of the groups identified in Table 7.10, US banks had the highest net liabilities of up to eight days in 1981, indicating that these banks can apparently afford to be less liquid than other categories of banks. This arises from the ability of overseas branches of US banks to obtain dollard funds from parent offices in New York, in general without much difficulty. Therefore, the transformation ratio of US banks in London in the up to eight days category was −3.6% in 1981 (compared to −2.6% in 1975) and was far ahead of any other bank group.This conclusion is confirmed by Table 7.11 which shows the proportion of net foreign currency liabilities of less than eight days to maturity to total liabilities. The figure for US banks in 1981 was −7.2% representing a significant absolute rise from −5.2% in 1975. The equivalent figure for all UK-based banks was −4.2% in 1981 or −3.3% if US banks are omitted.

The picture is very different for Japanese banks who traditionally have had net claims in the shortest maturity range. This was true in 1975, when the net claims figure in the less than eight days maturity range stood at $1.4 billion, and also in 1976. However by 1981, this had turned into a net liability position of $4.1 billion. In general, the pattern of Japense banks' liabilities is longer-term due to the official requirement that claims of over one year should be matched by liabilities of similar maturity. Therefore the demand for long-term certificates of deposit by Japanese banks is substantial. In November

TABLE 7.10
Net Position and Transformation Ratios in Foreign Currencies for Categories of UK-Based Banks (Bank of England Data; $ Billion; End-November)

	British Banks		US Banks		Japanese Banks		Other Overseas Banks		Consortium Banks		All Banks	
	1975	1981	1975	1981	1975	1981	1975	1981	1975	1981	1975	1981
Net Position:												
Less than 8 days	− 1.6	− 5.1	− 3.5	− 10.0	+ 1.4	− 4.1	− 2.3	− 3.7	− 0.5	− 1.0	− 6.5	− 24.0
8 days–1 month	− 1.8	− 6.2	− 1.3	− 3.8	− 1.0	− 2.3	− 0.2	− 4.6	− 0.6	− 2.4	− 4.9	− 19.4
1–3 months	− 2.5	− 12.6	− 2.3	− 5.3	− 1.9	− 4.6	− 1.1	− 7.9	− 1.4	− 3.6	− 9.1	− 33.8
3–6 months	− 2.5	− 6.8	− 1.1	− 1.5	− 1.1	− 1.7	− 1.6	− 3.9	− 1.2	− 2.9	− 7.5	− 16.7
6–12 months	− 0.8	+ 1.5	+ 0.4	− 0.8	− 0.4	− 1.0	− 0.3	− .16	− 0.1	+ 0.6	− 1.2	+ 1.9
Over 1 year	+ 9.3	+ 29.8	+ 7.6	+ 18.5	+ 2.8	+ 10.7	+ 5.5	+ 17.8	+ 4.2	+ 9.3	+ 29.3	+ 86.1
Total	+ 0.2	+ 0.5	− 0.2	− 2.9	− 0.1	− 2.9	—	− 0.7	+ 0.3	− 0.1	+ 0.1	− 6.0
Transformation Ratio:												
Less than 8 days	− 2.30	− 2.04	− 2.61	− 3.64	+ 2.90	− 1.60	− 2.94	− 1.23	− 2.51	− 2.35	− 1.86	− 2.14
8 days–1 month	− 2.59	− 2.48	− 0.97	− 1.38	− 2.07	− 0.90	− 0.26	− 1.54	− 3.01	− 5.63	− 1.40	− 1.72
1–3 months	− 3.59	− 5.04	− 1.72	− 1.93	− 3.93	− 1.80	− 1.41	− 2.64	− 7.03	− 8.45	− 2.60	− 3.01
3–6 months	− 3.59	− 2.72	− 0.82	− 0.55	− 2.28	− 0.66	− 2.05	− 1.30	− 6.03	− 6.81	− 2.14	− 1.49
6–12 months	− 1.15	+ 0.60	+ 0.30	− 0.29	− 0.83	− 0.39	− 0.38	− 0.54	− 0.50	+ 1.41	+ 0.34	+ 0.17
Over 1 year	+ 13.36	+ 11.92	+ 5.68	+ 6.74	+ 5.80	+ 4.18	+ 7.04	+ 5.96	+ 21.11	+ 21.68	+ 8.37	+ 7.68

Key: c ÷ d

1981, 7.2% of the liabilities of Japanese banks had a maturity of one year or more compared to 3.6% for all the UK-based banks. In fact, the liabilities of Japanese banks in this maturity range covered 46.1% of assets of the same maturity at the end of 1981, compared to 14.4% for all other banks. The differences in the behaviour of Japanese banks are also illustrated in the second part of Table 7.10. The transformation ratio for the one year and over to maturity category fell from 5.8% in 1975 to 4.2% in 1981, significantly below the ratio for all banks in 1981 of 7.7%.

Of all the different banking groups in London, the consortium banks undertake the greatest amount of maturity transformation. The transformation ratio of these banks in the one year and over maturity category was as high as 21.7% in November 1981, while they covered only 3.2% of their claims in this maturity category with equivalent liabilities. The differences compared to other banks are much less marked at the short end where, in 1981, the proportion of net liabilities to total liabilities stood at – 4.8% compared to – 4.2% for all banks (Table 7.11).

Finally, in this section, Table 7.12 sets out the net position of the different UK-based banking groups with respect to the domestic inter-bank market (i.e. other banks in London). It is notable from this table that no one banking group was undertaking significant maturity transformation with the inter-bank market at the end of 1981. US and other overseas banks were net suppliers to the UK interbank market in all maturity ranges (except the shortest maturity category in the case of US banks). A slight hint of maturity transformation is indicated for Japanese and consortium banks whose short-term net liability positions were converted into a virtually matched book for the maturity range of six months and over. Meanwhile, the British banks were lending short and borrowing 1–6 month funds from other banks. The lack of any significant maturity transformation in the inter-bank market, even when different banking groups are separately identified, confirms that the process of netting out such transactions will not bias the estimates of the maturity transformation and liquidity-creating effects of the eurocurrency market (Johnston, 1983).

Many attempts have been made to estimate the contribution that maturity transformation makes to liquidity creation in the euromarkets. Conventionally, this has been done by assigning weights to assets and liabilities according to their maturity so that the quantitative effect of the maturity transformation process on liquidity crea-

TABLE 7.11

Proportion of Net Foreign Currency Liabilities of less than
eight days in Total Liabilities of UK-Based Banks
(Bank of England Data; %; End-November)

	British Banks	US Banks	Japanese Banks	Other Overseas Banks	Consortium Banks	All Banks	All (except US) Banks
1975	− 4.6	− 5.2	+ 5.8	− 5.9	− 51	− 3.7	− 2.8
1976	− 5.2	− 6.1	+ 1.1	− 5.8	− 6.0	− 4.9	− 4.2
1977	− 5.8	− 8.0	− 0.2	− 6.1	− 5.8	− 6.0	− 4.9
1978	− 4.0	− 7.3	− 2.3	− 3.8	− 6.1	− 4.9	− 3.8
1979	− 2.1	− 6.6	− 2.1	− 5.6	− 5.0	− 4.5	− 3.6
1980	− 2.9	− 7.7	− 1.5	− 3.7	− 5.2	− 4.5	− 3.3
1981	− 4.1	− 7.2	− 3.2	− 2.5	− 4.8	− 4.2	− 3.3

Key: c + d.

tion may be estimated.[15] The major problem with the results of these studies is the arbitrary nature of the weights. There are no clear rules for determining them and the estimates of liquidity creation for any given degree of mismatching depend on those selected.

A further point follows from Table 7.12. It is clear from the time-series of this information over a number of years reported by Ellis (1981) and Johnson (1983) that significant fluctuations in these net positions against the inter-bank market occur on a yearly basis. Therefore it is crucial to remember that all the data reported in this section are merely a 'snapshot'[16] of the maturity structure of banks' assets and liabilities at one point in time. Little may be known about intra-period shifts in maturity profiles that are simply not part of the quarterly data published by the Bank of England. However concentration on a run of end-period data rather than one set of figures (as in Table 7.12) would reduce the likelihood of drawing invalid conclusions should significant shifts in these maturity profiles occur over successive observation periods.

SUMMARY

The recent developments in the reporting of the maturity profile of internatonal bank' assets and liabilities described in this chapter are

[15] Studies of this sort include Niehans and Hewson (1976), Little (1979). See also Mayer (1979b), Thornton (1980).

[16] See the additional notes to Table 14.2 in the *Bank of England Quarterly Bulletin*.

TABLE 7.12
Maturity Transformation in Inter-Bank Market
of UK-Based Bank Groups
(Bank of England Data; $ Billion; End-November 1981)

	British Banks	US Banks	Other Japanese Banks	Over-seas Banks	Consortium Banks
Net position against other banks:					
Less than 8 days	+ 2.4	− 1.7	− 2.6	+ 3.4	− 0.2
8 days–1 month	+ 0.9	+ 1.1	− 2.1	+ 2.0	− 1.3
1–3 months	− 0.5	+ 3.6	− 1.1	+ 1.1	− 2.2
3–6 months	− 0.3	+ 2.3	—	+ 1.1	− 2.0
6 months–1 year	+ 0.1	+ 0.1	+ 0.4	+ 1.5	− 0.1
1 year and over	+ 0.3	+ 0.7	− 0.3	+ 0.3	+ 0.2
Total	+ 2.8	+ 6.1	− 5.6	+ 9.5	− 5.6

Key: c + d.

very welcome. However, as yet, these data are relatively raw and certain improvements in BIS's data in particular are expected in the future (Mayer 1979a). These include inprovements in the timeliness of the statistics and the extension of the maturity analysis to the liabilities side of the banks' balance-sheets, such that conclusions on maturity transformation itself may be generated at the global level. At this stage, certain national source statistics, such as those published by the Bank of England for UK-based banks, are more comprehensive in scope. However in time it is likely that improvements to the BIS series will allow their integration with such national data to provide a fuller picture of the maturity profile of banks' external positions *vis-à-vis* individual countries.

Section 3

Capital Market Statistics

Chapter 8

Sources of Data and Aggregate Capital Market Borrowing

INTRODUCTION

In this chapter, a survey is made of some of the published information on the flows of new borrowing in international capital markets. This survey covers new international bank loan arrangments (eurocurrency credits) and new issues of external bonds. The number of international organisations and private financial institutions that compiles information on such borrowing is considerable although this survey concentrates on three sources which have as a common factor their wide availability. These are, in the public sector the OECD and the World Bank and, in the private sector Morgan Guaranty Trust Company. In general these sources are the most widely quoted in the financial press, when an estimate of new borrowing in international capital markets is given. Unfortunately, the statistical series compiled and made available in this area by the World Bank were discontinued towards the end of 1981, although this will not prevent the use of some of this data on a historical basis, in this section. Apart from these three, little further mention is made of other sources even though a number of very detailed (and sometimes computerised) statistical systems are available in the private sector such as the *Caploan Euromarkets Information System* and the *Euromoney Syndication Service*. Although, in general, providing more detail than the three sources to be surveyed here, such sophisticated systems are likely to be less widely available to the general observer of the markets, if only due to their expense.

SOURCES

Given the close contact between the OECD and the World Bank in the compilation of international capital markets data and their similar status as public sector institutions, the history and data-collection procedures in the two organisations are considered side-by-side at the start of this section. Statistics on new capital market borrowing published by the OECD are compiled in the organisation's Directorate of Financial and Fiscal Affairs. This process was begun as a result of the publication of a General Report on the 'Improvement of Capital Markets' by the OECD in 1967. In that year, the OECD concluded arrangements with the World Bank, whereby the Bank's staff would compile statistics on new external bond issues[1] which would be verified and supplemented, where necessary, by the OECD. This cross-checked information was then to be published by both sources.[2] The publication by the OECD of *Financial Statistics* followed by 1970, which contained from its first issue, data on new external bond issues. Since 1974, data on new eurocurrency credit arrangements have also been included. Initially, *Financial Statistics* was published as an annual document (in two parts — the first one containing the statistics themselves and the second one the explanatory and methodological notes) with updating supplements being issued every two months. However, from October 1980, that part of *Financial Statistics* which included issues of external bonds and domestic securities, international bank loans and interest rates began to be published on a monthly basis in a much smaller document entitled *Financial Statistics Monthly* (although other data included in the former annual document such as the financial accounts of OECD countries continued to be made available on a less frequent basis than every month). The methodological supplement relating to all series previously included in the annual *Financial Statistics* document is still published once a year only.

In addition to this basic source the OECD's Committee on Financial Markets has since 1975 produced a report entitled *Financial Market Trends* which includes data and analysis of the eurocurrency credit and external bond markets and also of other financial developments at the domestic and international levels. Although initially the circu-

---

[1] The label 'external' bonds covers both 'foreign' bonds and 'international' or 'euro' bonds. These different types of bonds are defined in Chapter 10.

[2] Despite this, discrepancies in the annual estimate of new bond issues published by the two sources have occurred and this was increasingly so after the mid-1970s.

lation of *Financial Market Trends* was restricted it has been made more widely available on a commercial basis since early 1977. This document is now published five times each year. Essentially, while *Financial Statistics* provides significant statistical detail on these capital markets, *Financial Market Trends* provides more summary information and market commentary.

World Bank data on new eurocurrency credits and external bonds have been compiled over time by the Financial Studies Division of the Financial Analysis and Policy Department in the Capital Markets System (CMS). The CMS originated in 1946, soon after the Bank's establishment, when information on new 'foreign' bond issues was compiled for internal use; these figures were made available publicly from 1955. In 1967 the CMS was extended to include data on issues of 'international' or 'euro' bonds and this was followed in the same year by the completion of the data-provision and verification arrangements with the OECD noted above. In 1972, statistics on the flows of new eurocurrency credits began to be compiled by the CMS for internal use initially; these were publicised from 1974 when the quarterly report *Borrowing in International Capital Markets* was first published including both bond issues and new credit commitments.[3]

In order to cope with the rapid expansion of international capital markets and therefore the enormous increase in information on new bond and credit issues, the CMS was computerised in 1976 with a data base that went back to 1972. The last three issues of *Borrowing in International Capital Markets* were published on a less-frequent (six-monthly) basis, covering 1980 and the first half of 1981. In addition, a series of monthly articles on new capital market activity, drawn from CMS data and written by World Bank staff, began to be included in the *International Monetary Fund (IMF) Survey* in June 1981. With the abandonment of the CMS, these articles themselves were discontinued in January 1982. In summary, therefore, detailed CMS data as contained in *Borrowing in International Capital Markets* are available to the middle of 1981, with summary figures, allowing the main series to be extended to the end of 1981, being included in the *IMF Survey*.

The precise procedures and lists of sources used for the compilation of the OECD's statistics in this area vary slightly between bonds and credits. For bonds the sources used are:

'The World Bank, in co-operation with other international organisations and various national administrations, from published information and other reliable sources.'[4]

[3] This document carried the code EC-181. The first issue contained information for the third quarter of 1974.

[4] OECD, *Financial Statistics*.

The close relationship between the OECD and World Bank in the compilation of data on bond issues is clear from this quotation. The other sources include financial journals and press reports (including tombstone announcements of individual agreements) and other statistical compilations such as Salomon Brothers' *International Bond Market Round-Up*. Both the OECD and World Bank have extensive cross-checking or verification procedures, which include an annual listing of new issues sent to member countries of the OECD Group of Financial Statisticians. This enables each individual national authority to verify the list of external bonds issued in their own national market and issued by borrowers from that country in other markets. A listing may also be sent to international organisations (such as the EEC) and regional development banks (such as the European Investment Bank) to verify borrowing by such organisations in the bond market, while verification is also completed via the listings of certain commercial banks such as Chemical Bank (USA), Orion Bank (UK), Société Generale de France (France) and Banca Commerciale Italiana (Italy). Finally, supplementary information on publicly-issued bonds may be drawn from the bond prospectuses themselves.

In the case of eurocurrency credits, the relationship between OECD data and the World Bank was much less formal. OECD data on such credits are compiled.

'in liaison with other international organisations, from published information and other reliable sources'.[5]

However, the processes of information-gathering and verification for such eurocredits in the two organisations do still overlap to a considerable degree. Verification is undertaken through a variety of statistical compilations, for example, Blyth Eastman's *Financing in International Capital Markets,* William Low's *International Insider,* Christian Hemain's *International Bondletter and Eurocurrency Financing Review* (AGEFI), the *Caploan Euromarkets Information System* and the *Euromoney Syndication Service.*

Clearly this process of information gathering and cross-checking is very comprehensive. The main result is that the coverage of the data published by the OECD and World Bank is considerable, while for each particular type of credit market instrument it is likely to be similar within the two organisations. In particular, with respect to publicly-issued bonds, the OECD and CMS listings are virtually complete. This is particularly true of bonds floated on markets in OECD countries as, by law, such issues must be announced and registered with the appropriate national authorities. Therefore for

[5] OECD, *Financial Statistics.*

this class of financing instrument, the verification procedures involve genuine cross-checking with little, if any, supplementation of information. In other words, few bonds of this type escape inclusion in these series. For privately-placed bonds and publicly-issued bonds in non-OECD countries (the latter being a very small figure), the coverage is marginally less complete. With no legal requirement for such issues to be registered or announced, the coverage varies betwen borrowing and market countries and also from one time period to another. For such bonds, the verification procedures, while allowing the cross-checking of already-accumulated information, also supplements this information substantially raising therefore the overall coverage or 'capture' rate.

For eurocurrency credits, it is believed that around 80% of the *number* of new credit deals are included in the OECD series and the CMS. The key omissions are, by definition, unpublicised loans many of which are likely to be small (often less than $10 million). Given this, the capture rate of the *volume* of new funds arranged in a particular period is likely to be significantly higher than 80%. The average varies across countries given that a small and infrequent country borrower may seek maximum publicity for a particular deal to demonstrate its credit-worthiness, while a heavy borrower may have little interest in announcing small credits. Finally, with the increasing sophistication of financing methods in the eurocurrency market it is unfortunately more likely that the coverage will decline in the future than become more comprehensive. In a sense, the OECD data system may in the future be partly overtaken by the rapid innovations in methods of financial intermediation.

During its existence, the CMS gained the justifiable reputation of being the most authoritative public sector statistical information service for these markets. This was based on, notwithstanding the comments made above, the high capture rate of bond issues and credit arrangements, the comprehensiveness of the information and most notably on the degree of published detail. This was particularly so given the individual listing of new bond issues and credit arrangements in the most recent data period with certain essential information. However, the major drawback of the CMS was its timeliness. The document *Borrowing in International Capital Markets* was usually published around four to five months after the end of the period to which the data referred. As a result, the CMS did not gain the publicity and accepted authority in the financial press that the standard of the service warranted and which was received instead by other sources where the delay in publication is shorter. This situation may have been one of the reasons behind the 'winding-up' of the CMS operation, although the practice of publishing preliminary information in the *IMF Survey* represented a belated attempt to rectify this disadvantage.

In contrast, a general advantage of the OECD's service is in fact its timeliness. The information in *Financial Market Trends* is particularly up-to-date as it covers figures and commentary on the period up to the end of the month that precedes publication. Information on new eurocurrency credits is available in *Financial Statistics* with a delay of around two months only, although in the case of bonds the time-lag is longer. Information on such new issues is usually published two to five months after the end of the quarter to which the data refer. Clearly, therefore, given the greater aggregation of the data included in *Financial Market Trends* there appears to be a general trade-off between the degree of published detail and timeliness which the OECD are seeking to avoid with their two publications. A further general attribute of the OECD's *Financial Market Trends* is the depth of analysis of the international capital markets contained therein, while it also includes credits under active negotiation and a broad range of summary tables.

In contrast to the official sources of capital markets data surveyed so far in this section, the information provided by Morgan Guaranty Trust Company on such borrowing is much less detailed and, in general, the whole operation of compiling this information is smaller in scope. Data on new bond issues and medium-term eurocurrency credits have been published by Morgan Guaranty for a number of years in their monthly journal *World Financial Markets*. This information is compiled by the bank's staff from a similar range but smaller *number* of sources to that used by the OECD and the World Bank. In addition, the close links between the World Bank and Morgan Guaranty in this respect have, over time, provided efficient verification for both organisations. Despite the lower scale of its data compilation operation, Morgan Guaranty believes its coverage of new borrowing in international capital markets is very high and broadly comparable with that attained by the OECD and the World Bank.

The main advantage of the Morgan Guaranty information in this area (and the reason that it achieves such wide publicity) is the rapidity with which data are published on a regular monthly basis. Therefore, the issue of *World Financial Markets* for any particular month will include new bonds and credits actually announced in that month of publication. With such timeliness and the fact that Morgan Guaranty records these new agreements earlier in their negotiation process (a point of crucial importance that is developed in the next chapter) this means that these figures are widely quoted as virtual 'leading' indicators of the international capital markets. Such rapid and preliminary information is then backed up by a six-monthly assessment and survey of the market. However as would be expected from such a rapid indicator, the chief drawback of the Morgan Guaranty series is the lack of detail. In general, market commentary is limited to the six-monthly surveys, while only a limited country breakdown is given in the statistical series, with no listing of individual credit arrangements or bond issues.

All of these three series are secondary sources of information on new borrowing in international capital markets. It should be noted, however, that with the increasing spread of information on activity in these markets it is possible to construct a series on an individual basis from the press and financial journals (including tombstone announcements). This statement is not intended to belittle and large and sophisticated compilation procedures of many international organisations and private banks throughout the world but to suggest that a substantial part of the volume of new commitments of funds may be 'captured' from regular consultation of a small number of published sources.[6] The value of the large-scale compilation procedures of major organisations is that they increase capture rates from levels that may be fairly high to ones for public bonds, for example, that are virtually complete.

In the section to follow and in Chapters 9 and 10 the basic statistical information used will be drawn from OECD publicity. Certain historical data from the CMS will also be quoted, where appropriate, but complete reliance on these latter data was rejected due to the now defunct status of the CMS. The aggregate data will cover the period from 1970 to 1981 with much of the detailed information beginning only in 1973 or later.

AGGREGATE DATA

During the 1970s and early 1980s the provision of finance through eurocurrency credits and external bond issues grew very rapidly. Table 8.1 sets out the aggregate borrowing totals in these markets on an annual basis from 1970 to 1981. The annual volume of new capital

[6] This was done, for example, for part of the period from 1977 to 1980 by the author and D. T. Llewellyn in the information service *Trends in International Banking and Capital Markets* published by the Banker Research Unit of Financial Times Ltd.

market borrowing in 1981 was $194.7 billion,[7] nearly twenty times greater than the volume recorded in 1970. Considering the decade as a whole, the volume of eurocurrency credits at $517.7 billion amounted to 63.1% of total capital market borrowing, with external bonds at $303.2 billion accounting for 36.9 per cent of the total. However, these proportions have fluctuated considerably from year to year. In general, the growth of external bonds has been reasonably steady with only one year (1973) when new issues were lower than in the previous year. Therefore, the fluctuations in the shares of these two financing instruments in total capital market borrowing are predominantly explained by the considerable volatility of the volume of new eurocurrency credits. The years when the proportion of credits in the total exceeded 60% were generally periods of extremely rapid expansion of eurocurrency credits, specifically 1973 and 1974 and from 1978 onwards. However, after a 94.7% increase in the volume of credits in 1978, a certain degree of stability followed in 1979–80 before the explosion of new activity in 1981. After being relatively stable at around $35–40 billion in 1976–80, bond issues also jumped in 1981. Overall, new capital market borrowing rose by 63.2% in 1981.

Many factors explain the overall growth in capital market borrowing in the 1970s (Llewellyn, 1978, 1980). These may be divided into those factors affecting the supply of international liquidity and those influencing demand and these are very briefly noted here. On the supply side, the major growth influence has been the structure of balance of payments disequilibria in the 1970s in the wake, in particular, of the increases in the price of oil and the accompanying portfolio preferences of surplus sectors. Other supply side factors have been the long periods of low domestic demand for funds (particularly in 1974–5 and 1978–81) due to recession, which have 'released' funds for external lending by banks, the liberalisation of controls on international flows of funds (particularly the abolition of US capital controls in 1974 — see Chapter 3 — and the ending of UK exchange control in 1979) which has led to a once-for-all increase in world liquidity and the effect of the regular US balance of payments deficits in increasing the volume of dollar liquidity in the world economy.

The number of separate factors influencing the demand for exter-

[7] This figure was artificially increased by a total of $50.4 billion worth of financing by US corporations in dollars during the second half of 1981, which, as the operations were completed abroad, were included in the OECD series. Many of the conclusions for 1981 concerning capital market activity to be drawn below are distorted slightly by these financing operations.

TABLE 8.1
Borrowing in International Capital Markets
(OECD Data; $ Billion)

	1970	1971	1972	1973	1974	1975	1976	1977	1978	1979	1980	1981	Total (1970–81)
Eurocurrency credits[1]	4.7	4.0	6.6	20.9	28.5	20.6	27.9	33.8	65.8	79.1	79.9	145.9	517.7
External bonds	5.9	7.7	11.3	10.0	12.2	22.8	34.3	36.1	35.8	38.9	39.4	48.8	303.2
Total capital market borrowing	10.6	11.7	17.9	30.9	40.7	43.4	62.2	69.9	101.6	118.0	119.3	194.7	820.9
% of credits in total	44.3	34.2	36.9	67.6	70.0	47.5	44.9	48.4	64.8	67.0	67.0	74.9	63.1
% of bonds in total	55.7	65.8	63.1	32.4	30.0	52.5	55.1	51.6	35.2	33.0	33.0	25.1	36.9

[1] IBRD data for 1970–1972.

nal credit is considerable. In parallel with the supply side analysis, the major demand factor has been the need of many countries to borrow to finance balance of payments deficits. This applied to certain developed countries and in particular to the non-oil developing countries who suffered not only from the increases in the price of oil but also from the fall in primary product prices and the stagnation of world demand for their exports in the subsequent world recessions. Funds were also borrowed by developing countries for ambitious infrastructure investment projects, in particular in energy and transport, and to build up foreign exchange reserves (at a time in the late 1970s when borrowing conditions on eurocurrency credits were favourable). This argument leads on automatically to a further important demand factor namely the availability — at low cost and without conditions — of private finance for developing countries, in comparison to the conditional liquidity of smaller amounts from the official sector, in particular the IMF (Chapters 13 and 14). Finally, the huge totals of capital market borrowing in 1978–81 were accounted for, in part, by the refinancing of previously-negotiated credits as they matured or before maturity, to take advantage of the more favourable borrowing conditions in that period compared to those that existed in 1974–5 (see Chapter 9).

Table 8.2 sets out borrowing by country groups in the overall international capital markets and its two individual segments between 1973 and 1981. The shares of each group in the two segments varied considerably over this period and this is confirmed in Table 8.3 which depicts the share of borrowing accounted for by eurocurrency credits and external bonds for each individual country group. This latter table therefore estimates the 'reliance' of each group on each form of financing. From 1973 to 1981, borrowing by OECD countries[8] accounted for over half (57.4 per cent) of total borrowing, a figure that was remarkably steady over the data period until 1981. Borrowing by OECD countries dominated the external bond market (68.4%) much more so than that of eurocurrency credits (51.3%) and in one year borrowing by this group of countries in the eurocurrency credit market fell to as low as 30.1% of the total ($6.2 billion in 1975 – not shown in the table). The reliance of the OECD group on each type of financing was very similar with 57.5% of the total volume of funds raised being in the form of eurocurrency credits. However this dependence did fluctuate dramatically on an annual basis with bond issues accounting for only 26.2% of total

[8] This is a broader group than the former CMS category of industrialised countries as it includes Greece, Portugal, Spain and Turkey, all of which were categorised as developing countries by the World Bank.

TABLE 8.2
Capital Market Borrowing by Country Group (OECD Data; $ Billion and %)

	Average 1973–75	1976	1977	1978	1979	1980	1981	Total (1973–81)
Eurocurrency credits								
OECD countries	12.3	9.9	13.0	30.4	29.1	41.2	97.4	257.8
Developing countries	8.9	14.4	17.9	31.5	44.8	35.0	46.6	217.1
Eastern Europe	1.1	1.7	1.4	3.1	3.7	2.7	1.5	17.5
International Organisations	0.2	1.0	1.3	0.7	1.3	0.6	0.1	5.7
Other/unallocated	0.7	0.9	0.1	0.1	0.2	0.5	0.3	4.4
Total	23.3	27.9	33.8	65.8	79.1	79.9	145.9	502.4
External bonds								
OECD countries	9.1	23.8	24.4	23.2	26.6	28.5	36.7	190.4
Developing countries	1.0	2.0	4.1	5.1	3.1	1.7	3.3	22.2
Eastern Europe	0.1	0.1	0.2	—	—	0.1	—	0.6
International organisations	4.5	8.3	7.1	6.8	8.8	8.8	8.5	61.9
Other/unallocated	0.3	0.3	0.2	0.7	0.4	0.4	0.2	3.2
Total	15.0	34.3	36.1	35.8	38.9	39.4	48.8	278.3

Total borrowing								
OECD countries	21.3	33.7	37.4	53.6	55.7	69.6	134.1	448.2
Developing countries	9.9	16.4	22.0	36.6	47.8	36.7	50.0	239.3
Eastern Europe	1.2	1.8	1.6	3.1	3.8	2.7	1.5	18.1
International organisations	4.7	9.3	8.4	7.5	10.2	9.5	8.6	67.6
Other/unallocated	1.1	1.2	0.3	0.8	0.5	0.9	0.5	7.6
Total	38.3	62.2	69.9	101.6	118.0	119.3	194.7	780.7
Shares in total borrowing								
Eurocurrency credits								
OECD countries	52.8	35.5	38.5	46.2	36.8	51.6	66.8	51.3
Developing countries	38.2	51.6	53.0	47.9	56.6	43.8	31.9	43.2
Eastern Europe	4.7	6.1	4.1	4.7	4.7	3.4	1.0	3.5
International organisations	0.9	3.6	3.8	1.1	1.6	0.8	0.1	1.1
External bonds								
OECD countries	60.7	69.4	67.6	64.8	68.4	72.3	75.2	68.4
Developing countries	6.7	5.8	11.4	14.2	8.0	4.3	6.8	8.0
Eastern Europe	0.7	0.3	0.6	—	—	0.3	—	0.2
International organisations	30.0	24.2	19.7	19.0	22.6	22.3	17.4	22.2
Total borrowing								
OECD countries	55.6	54.2	53.5	52.8	47.2	58.3	68.9	57.4
Developing countries	25.8	26.4	31.5	36.0	40.5	30.8	25.7	30.7
Eastern Europe	3.1	2.9	2.3	3.1	3.2	2.3	0.8	2.3
International organisations	12.3	15.0	12.0	7.4	8.6	8.0	4.4	8.7

TABLE 8.3

Shares of Credit Instruments in Capital Market Borrowing by Country Group (OECD data; %)

	Average 1973–75	1976	1977	1978	1979	1980	1981	Total (1973–81)
OECD countries								
Eurocurrency credits	57.7	29.4	34.8	56.7	52.2	59.2	72.6	57.5
External bonds	42.3	70.6	65.2	43.3	47.8	40.1	27.4	42.5
Developing countries								
Eurocurrency credits	89.9	87.8	81.4	86.1	93.7	95.4	93.2	90.7
External bonds	10.1	12.2	18.6	13.9	6.3	4.6	6.8	9.3
Eastern Europe								
Eurocurrency credits	91.7	94.4	97.5	100.0	100.0	96.3	100.0	96.7
External bonds	8.3	5.6	12.5	—	—	3.7	—	3.3
International organisations								
Eurocurrency credits	4.3	10.8	15.5	9.3	12.7	6.3	1.2	8.4
External bonds	95.7	89.2	84.5	90.7	87.3	93.7	98.8	91.6

borrowing (73.8% being in the form of credits therefore) in 1974 rising to 71.9% (28.1%) in the following year.

The group of developing countries accounted for 30.7% of the volume of funds raised on international capital markets over the period included in Table 8.2. However, while the total of eurocurrency credits arranged for this group was only 15.8% below that of the OECD countries at $217.1 billion (43.2% of the total), only 8% of total bond issues were made on behalf of developing countries. These shares have fluctuated considerably with the proportion of total eurocurrency credits going to developing countries falling as low as 31.9% in 1981 and peaking at 56.6% in 1979, while the equivalent minimum and maximum proportions of funds raised by external bond issues were 4.3% in 1980 and 14.2% in 1978. What is notable however is the limited access through a small number of borrowers (see Chapter 10) of this group of countries to the external bond markets as a whole. Therefore between 1973 and 1981, only 9.3% of the total funds raised by this group were from external bond issues compared to 90.7% in the form of eurocurrency credits. Indeed, the reliance of developing countries on borrowing in the eurocurrency market relative to the external bond markets has actually increased since the end of 1978.

Borrowing by Eastern European countries (excluding the International Investment Bank) has been almost totally confined to the market for eurocurrency credits. Between 1973 and 1981, 96.7% of the volume of funds raised by this group was obtained in this way. This amounted to $17.5 billion or 3.5% of the total volume of eurocurrency credits during this period. This share peaked at 9.2% in 1975 when $1.9 billion was borrowed by this group, a figure which was nearly one-third of the volume of funds raised through eurocurrency credits by OECD countries in that year. In contrast, Eastern European countries raised only $0.6 billion through bond issues between 1973 and 1981 (0.2% of total issues). Finally, the international organisations borrowed $67.6 billion on the international capital markets between 1973 and 1981, 91.6% being in the form of external bond issues. In fact over this period, 22.2% of the total volume of funds raised by bond issues was borrowed by this group, a share that went as high as 43.4% in 1974. The international organisations raised only $5.7 billion through eurocurrency credits over the 1973–81 period, amounting to 1.1 per cent of the total for that market. Of the total borrowing by international organisations 44% was accounted for by the World Bank itself, all of which was raised in the external bond markets.

SUMMARY

It is clear from this chapter that activity in the international capital markets incresed dramatically during the 1970s and early 1980s with the number and range of sources of information on these markets expanding likewise. From the welter of information available from the three sources surveyed in this chapter, the following two chapters seek to distil and present a clear statistical picture of, firstly, the eurocurrency credit market and secondly the markets for external bond issues in many of their facets.

Chapter 9
Eurocurrency Credits

DEFINITIONS

The objective of this chapter is to describe and compare statistics on new eurocurrency credit arrangements published by the sources listed in the previous chapter. Unfortunately, although all three sources cover very similar types of credit or bank loan (with some variations, which are clarified in Fig. 9.1), the labels used by the sources differ slightly. In essence, however, they all concentrate on eurocurrency credits and this is the general term used in the analysis of this chapter.

The OECD data on 'international medium- and long-term loans' include two separate types of bank claims. These are:

'loans with an original maturity of more than one year which have been granted by commercial banks wholly or in part out of eurocurrency funds, irrespective of whether the counterpart is a resident or a non-resident of the country in question.'

and

'bank loans in domestic currency to both domestic and non-resident borrowers granted wholly or in part by foreign banks in the country concerned, which may be expected to fund their lending both from domestic sources and the eurocurrency markets.'[1]

Therefore the data exclude loans in the form of negotiable instruments, such as bonds, and loans by domestic banks (only) in domestic currency even though it is increasingly likely that these may be funded in part in the eurocurrency markets. The terminology used by

[1] OECD, *Financial Market Trends*, March 1982, pp 1–2 and *Financial Statistics*, 1982, p 13.

LOCATION OF LENDING BANK →	USA	UK
SOURCE OF ↓ FUNDING		
DOMESTIC MONEY MARKET		b
EUROCURRENCY MARKET	a	a,b

INCLUDED IN
a: OECD/World Bank Series
b: Morgan Guaranty Series

FIGURE 9.1
Definitions of eurocurrency credits
Example: $100 million loan to company in Brazil

the World Bank was similar, leading, in effect, to the inclusion in both data series of the same classes of bank loans. It defined eurocurrency credits as:

'credits granted by banks out of eurocurrency funds on deposit with them or borrowed by them in the eurocurrency market . . . The term "credit" is used to refer to loans, lines of credit and other forms of medium- and long-term credit.'[2]

For both sources, the term 'euro' includes offshore markets both inside and outside Europe. In contrast to these definitions, Morgan Guaranty approaches this issue in a rather different way. It defines eurocurrency credits as

'bank loans in currencies which are not native to the country in which the banks or bank offices making the loan are located.'[3]

Therefore emphasis is placed in the Morgan Guaranty definition on the currency in which the loan is denominated and by the OECD and World Bank on the source of funds.

In practice, however, the alternative definitions effectively overlap. Figure 9.1 should help to clarify the definitional variations. In it, the example of a dollar loan to a company in Brazil is used. The cell of the table corresponding to a dollar claim of a domestic bank located in the US itself is empty as this type of loan is excluded by all three sources. However, it is omitted on different grounds by Morgan

[2] *Borrowing in International Capital Markets*, 1980 (2nd half) p ii.

[3] Morgan Guaranty (1977), p 6 or, for example, *World Financial Markets* September, 1981, p 22.

Guaranty (claim in the domestic currency of lending bank) compared to the OECD and World Bank (loan assumed to be funded in the domestic market). The opposite case is that of a dollar loan being made from London and funded in the eurocurrency market — that is outside, in this case, the UK. This is included in all series as the euromarket funding presupposes the presence of foreign banks in the credit arrangement.

Some potential conflict between the sources arises in the cases of a dollar loan from London funded in the domestic money market (included by Morgan Guaranty only) and a dollar loan from a US bank which is funded in the eurocurrency market (included by the OECD and World Bank). However it is likely that both these cells will be fairly small in value so limiting the terminological discrepancies, in pracice.

Two problems do however present themselves in the application of these principles. Firstly, the source of funds may not always be clear for any particular credit, leading to possible variations in the treatment of individual credits. Secondly, most credits of this type are syndicated (i.e. granted by a number of banks) making the Morgan Guaranty definition difficult to apply; that is if one, only, of the banks involved in a dollar credit is based in the USA, should the whole credit be excluded? To resolve this, Morgan Guaranty generally adopts the procedure that if one or more banks or branches outside the USA are included in the lending group for a dollar loan for example, that credit is included in its series. This procedure was particularly useful for dealing with the huge volume of dollar credits (over $50 billion) arranged by US companies with US banks in 1981. (These were mainly in the form of stand-by credits, in association with merger activity, and may not have been used in full or even, in some cases, in part.) Both the OECD and Morgan Guaranty included these credits given that it was likely that some of the loans were booked out at foreign branches of US banks[4] or alternatively involved US branches of foreign banks.

A related point is that a useful rule of thumb to identify a eurocurrency loan, compared to other forms of bank credit, for the purposes of inclusion in the data series, is that any loan priced over the London Inter-Bank Offered Rate LIBOR,[5] the conventional interest rate on which eurocurrency credits are based, should be included in such a series. In contrast, any loan priced over a domestic rate (such as the

[4] *World Financial Markets*, December 1981, p 8.

[5] The normal LIBOR used is the six-month eurodollar rate. See late in this chapter.

US prime rate) should be excluded, unless an overseas branch is included in the lending group. Therefore as a significant part of the dollar borrowing by US companies in 1981 was priced against the US prime rate, such loans were included in the Morgan Guaranty and OECD series only if the loan:

(i) carried a LIBOR option as an alternative to the prime rate base alone,
(ii) was booked out overseas, or
(iii) had a non-US bank, based in the US, as part of the lending group.

Clearly the 'grey' area covering which arrangements should and should not be included in a time-series for eurocurrency credits is significant and is likely to increase as financing instruments become even more sophisticated.

Certain other statistical principles relating to characteristics of eurocurrency credits are adopted by all sources such that no inter-source discrepancies result from these. Most eurocurrencycredits are widely syndicated but, despite this, none of the three sources surveyed excludes non-syndicated or 'single bank' credits. In addition, all series include 'club loans' through which a credit is funded in full by a small group of lead banks and managers. Such loans are, by their nature, commonly small in volume. In 1980 only 4.8% of all eurocurrency credits included in the World Bank's listing were single bank credits demonstrating the importance of the syndication process.

A distinction is usually made in the eurocurrency credit market between 'revolving' and 'fixed-term' (often simply called 'term') loans, although both are conventionally included in statistical series. Revolving credits are essentially short-term facilities that include a specific rollover condition (often every six months) that effectively increases the maturity of the credit to a number of years. Such revolving credits are often negotiated in the form of stand-by credits, the funds from which may be needed for a short time-period only and may be repaid in a lump sum when the need for the funds has passed. Alternatively a 'term' loan carries a schedule of repayment for the full life of the loan. Once the drawdown period on such a term loan is complete and any grace period has elapsed, repayments begin on a schedule agreed when the loan was first negotiated. However repayment conditions vary enormously from loan to loan. Term loans are much the more common of the two types with 93.2% of those credits that were not classified as 'other and unknown' between 1974 and 1980 being of this type, with only 6.8% being revolving loans. The importance of the revolving loan has declined since 1974 when 19.8% of the total were of this type.[6]

All sources have restricted their series to include eurocurrency credits with a maturity of more than one year only, where this is defined as the time-period between the signature of the loan commitment and the final repayment date. many reasons are advanced for this procedure. Firstly this is a common and well-established convention for data on eurocurrency credits although for the World Bank, in particular, it has been of additional significance as it is consistent with the maturity convention of the World Bank's Debtor Reporting System (DRS) (see Chapter 11). Secondly, any loans of one year or less to maturity are considered to be of a distinctive and separate type and as such are not medium- or long-term arrangements. Finally, the whole area of short-term financing is a complex and confusing one. Although a cut-off at a shorter maturity is becoming increasingly desirable with the growth of short-term funding it is generally impractical. A particular problem with the measurement of maturities on eurocurrency credit commitments is the convention of using the *original* maturity, in contrast to the banking data (surveyed in Chapter 7) which, again according to common practice, use *residual* (i.e. remaining) maturity. This factor highlights one sense in which a comparison of banking and capital market data is difficult to achieve.

Finally, all three sources being surveyed in this chapter have excluded from their series acceptance credits (or facilities) and included tax-sparing credits. Acceptance credits are letters of credit which may be held by banks for a particular borrower. However if the bank for any reason decides to sell this credit, it may discount it with, for example, a non-bank financial institution. In this case, the credit has become equivalent to a negotiable, marketable instrument or short-term bill with the funds ultimately being provided by a non-bank. Therefore, given that in general there is no guarantee that such funds will ultimately be lent by a bank, these acceptance facilities are excluded from series of new eurocurrency credits. This is both sensible, *a priori,* and helpful for the interpretation of the data as a whole as some very large acceptance facilities (including one of $2.5 billion for Pemex of Mexico in 1979), have been arranged in recent years. One exception to this rule is that recently the OECD have included medium-term sterling acceptance facilities in their series, as these have begun to grow rapidly due to heavy involvement by banks outside the UK.

Tax-sparing credits (Euromoney, 1979) have allowed the exploit-

[6] World Bank data.

ation of a loop-hole in taxation agreements between certain developing countries and the British government. If a developing country in this particular category can prove that any given credit is crucial to its development, withholding tax on that credit may be waived. However, despite this, the British Government will consider that the withholding tax has been paid and will credit this against corporation tax to be paid by the lending banks. Therefore, the lending banks can charge lower spreads on these loans such that, in effect, the Inland Revenue of the UK is subsidising the developing country in question. Such tax-sparing loans have been fairly common in recent years, an example being a $50 million credit to Singapore Airlines for eight years at a spread of 1/16% over LIBOR completed in December 1980. However, proposals to limit the exploitation of double taxation in this way were included in the UK budget in March 1982 which will reduce to a certain extent the attraction of such tax-sparing credits to the banks. Despite their unique character such credits are included in the statistical series surveyed here, although they are in general excluded from any calculations of average spreads to avoid any distortion of these calculations from this source.

DISCREPANCIES BETWEEN STATISTICAL SERIES

Four potential sources of discrepancy between the treatment of eurocurrency credits by the series being surveyed are discussed in this section. Firstly, and of considerable importance, is the variation in the procedures for allocating certain credit agreements to particular time-periods. The procedures adopted by the OECD and World Bank are equivalent. Quoting from the OECD for example:

'The date of signature of the contract (where available) is the one used for the breakdown by period or, if not, the date of completion at which the final arrangements as regards the loan are concluded.'[7]

The time difference between completion and signature is usually around one week only, although it may be as long as six months if certain conditions attached to the loan are altered between completion and signature. If neither date is known, the date of press notification is used. The OECD and World Bank justify their procedures on the grounds that a loan may be altered in size or form

[7] *Financial Statistics*, 1982, p 13.

between commitment and signature and indeed may never be completed. In addition, to record completed loans is as consistent as is feasible with the DRS's emphasis on disbursed loans from banks, given that data on disbursed credits themselves are difficult to obtain, as will be explained towards the end of this chapter.

In contrast, Morgan Guaranty includes eurocurrency credits

'in the month in which the syndicating banks make the commitment to lend and agree on the final terms of the loan, even though the date of final signing of the loan documents and the eventual, if any, disbursement of the proceeds occur at a later date.'[8]

In fact, therefore, Morgan Guaranty measures eurocurrency credit *announcements* in contrast to the OECD and World Bank which measure credit *signatures*. Morgan Guaranty justify their procedure on the argument that the measurement of eurocurrency loan announcements is the objective of its data series so that it may act as a rapid, leading indicator of eurocurrency market lending. However, this procedure requires certain rules to be adopted by Morgan Guaranty. If a credit previously included as an announcement in its series is not completed, it is removed from the series at a later data. Similarly, if the size of a credit is altered between commitment and signature the data are amended accordingly. If the size of a non-dollar credit is changed, the dollar value of this credit is recalculated at the exchange rate ruling at the time of commitment. On the other hand, however, if the exchange rate between the dollar and the currency in which a particular eurocredit is denominated changes between commitment and signature no revaluation of the dollar value of this credit is calculated given that the dollar value of the loan at the commitment stage and its non-dollar value have remained constant.

The time difference between the commitment date used by Morgan Guaranty and the date of signature of the OECD and World Bank may only be a few days for a credit to a 'prime' borrower, but could be up to six months for a difficult loan to a 'non-prime' borrower. On average, a *two* month difference is likely to exist which is long enough to generate serious discrepancies between these series, particularly as the variation around this average may be considerable. Examples of such discrepancies are easy to locate. For example, credits of $500 million to the Kingdom of Denmark, $400 million to Peugeot-Citroen of France, $850 million to the Kingdom of Sweden and two loans of $300 million each to the Bank of Finland were recorded by Morgan Guaranty in its total for June 1980 but included

[8] Morgan Guaranty (1977), p 7.

by the OECD and World Bank in their figures for the second half of that year. In fact, in the case of these 'prime' credits, the timing discrepancies were small as all five loans were, according to the OECD and World Bank, signed in July. However, although small, the time-lags between the commitment dates and signature were sufficiently long to generate a discrepancy in quarterly or half-yearly totals between the alternative series. Many other examples (which cannot be identified from published information as Morgan Guaranty does not list individual credits separately) will undoubtedly exist and be hidden in the data.

Secondly, while the identification of the borrowing country[9] is clear for most eurocurrency credit arrangements, variations do exist between sources in the procedures adopted for borrowing by certain classes of subsidiary companies and by multinational companies. For all three sources under study, credits are classified by the nationality of the borrower except for loans to international organisations which are classified separately. The nationality of private and public enterprises is determined by their place of incorporation. However, while the OECD and Morgan Guaranty include borrowing by operating subsidiaries in the data for the country in which the subsidiary itself is incorporated, the World Bank considered the country where the parent company was incorporated to be the borrower. Treatment of borrowing by financial subsidiaries *is* consistent between sources in that the borrowing country is identified as that where the parent company is incorporated. This latter procedure is justified given that the obligations of a purely financial subsidiary will generally be guaranteed by the parent company.

However, these procedures may not be easy to put into practice in all circumstances. If a chain of inter-company relationships exists in which the parent of a financial subsidiary is itself a financial subsidiary, it may be difficult to identify the ultimate non-financial parent company. Even for certain subsidiaries, particularly in the Middle East, where a chain does not exist, it is not always clear of which the parent company and therefore its country of incorporation actually is. Finally, a financial subsidiary may have a number of parent companies in different countries. If this is the case the appropriate procedure is to include borrowing by such entities in the 'unallocated or unattributable' item.

For borrowing by multinational companies, Morgan Guaranty have a specific allocation procedure:

---

[9] This paragraph also applies to external bond issues, see Chapter 10.

'Where the borrower is a consortium entity whose ownership is multinational and its country of incorporation differs from those of its participants, the borrower is classified as a multinational entity rather than attributed to a particular country.'[10]

Therefore, Morgan Guaranty includes such borrowing in the international organisations category. In contrast, the OECD and World Bank seek to allocate these loans to borrowing countries on an *ad hoc* basis where possible, and include them in the 'unallocated' item only where a clear borrowing country is not identifiable. With the rapid growth of multinational consortia in the 1970s and the existence of numerous subsidiary companies that borrow on the international capital markets, these discrepancies of procedure are likely to lead to significant and increasing variations in individual country totals although not, of course, to the overall total itself.

Thirdly, any loans granted by international organisations, such as the World Bank itself and the IMF, regional development banks, such as the European Investment Bank and Asian Development Bank, and export-credit agencies such as the Export-Import Bank are automatically excluded from all series. However, while the OECD and World Bank also omit any loans *guaranteed* by these organisations, Morgan Guaranty only excludes these if they are denominated in domestic currencies or are fixed-rate foreign currency loans. The former organisations justify their procedure as they consider such loans are not true eurocurrency credits, an assumption disputed implicitly given the Morgan Guaranty procedure. In addition, the World Bank sees its procedure as being consistent with the DRS, while it may also be argued that the task of collecting information on export credits is undertaken in the official sector by the Development Assistance Committee (DAC) of the OECD (Chapter 12). These procedures do not prevent such organisations being included when they *borrow* from the international capital markets.

Finally, both the OECD and World Bank convert the value of non-dollar credits into dollars at the average daily spot exchange rate for the month in question. With Morgan Guaranty allocating loans to different time-periods as a rule anyway, the dollar value of non-dollar credits may be different in its series compared to the other two. Therefore it is likely that differences will arise between the sources due to such 'valuation effects'.

[10] Morgan Guaranty (1977), p 7.

THE DATA

The annual volume of new eurocurrency credits has fluctuated considerably in the period from 1973 to 1981 (Tables 8.1, 9.1). The threefold increase in eurocredit announcements in 1973 over the previous year was primarily due to the rise in both the demand for and supply of funds following the quadrupling of the price of oil in the autumn of 1973. In addition, the number of banks seeking to participate in eurocurrency syndications rose rapidly in 1972–3. These competitive pressures led to very favourable terms being available on eurocurrency credits as competition for business intensified.

However, confidence in the eurocurrency market collapsed dramatically in the middle of 1974 with a small number of bank failures (most notably Herstatt Bank of Cologne) and the announcement of some foreign exchange losses. Despite the lack of association between these crises and the activity of euromarket lending itself, a reappraisal of the latter occurred with the result that the volume of new eurocurrency credits fell from $28.5 billion in 1974 to only $20.6 billion in 1975. Borrowing conditions hardened drastically with the virtual disappearance until 1978 of the credit with a maturity of over ten years.[11] Under such conditions borrowers were less willing to conclude agreements, while banks themselves were more careful in their assessment of the risk on individual loans. In addition, with the rapid adjustment of the economies of the industrialised world to the oil price increase of two years earlier, the demand for euromarket funds by these countries fell dramatically. Total eurocurrency credits arranged by OECD borrowers declined from $18.3 billion in 1974 (64.2% of the total) to only $6.2 billion in 1975 which amounted to only 30.1% of the total in that year.

Gradually, through the remaining years of the decade confidence in the stability of the eurocurrency markets returned. Lending volumes increased quickly in the years after 1975 reaching $65.8 billion in 1978 (over three times higher than the total for 1975) and nearly $80 billion in both 1979 and 1980. Finally, aided by the unprecedented upsurge in dollar financing for US corporations, total eurocredits reached $145.9 billion in 1981, over thirty times greater than the volume recorded in 1970. After 1975, borrowing conditions also improved gradually, due primarily to the slack domestic demand for credit, the entry of new banks into this market and the resultant

[11] In 1973, 22.4% of total eurocredits carried a maturity of ten years or over compared to 11.4% in 1974 and only 1% in 1975 (World Bank data).

increase in competitive pressures between banks. However, despite some fears of a repeat of the 1974 banking crisis, as lending margins were trimmed and banks stood in danger of becoming over-exposed to certain developing countries, the market withstood well the shock of a second-round of substantial increases in the price of oil in 1979. At the time this led to some fears being expressed over whether the euromarket banks would be flexible enough to deal with a second phase of recycling of oil revenues. Accordingly, and combined with sharp increases in dollar interest-rates, the withdrawal of Japanese banks from the market and political worries over the crises in Iran and Afghanistan, there was some hardening of borrowing conditions in 1980, particularly with respect to the average maturity on loans. In addition, with spreads on credits to developing countries increasing somewhat, while those on loans to OECD countries continued to ease, there was a noticeable increase in the tiering of conditions for 'prime' compared to 'non-prime' borrowers. With the second phase of recycling passing with relative smoothness (the international banking crisis in the second half of 1982, which occurred after the end of the data period covered in this book, 'broke' at a time when the surpluses of the oil-exporting countries had virtually disappeared), spreads continued to ease up to the end of 1981 although there was a further slight shortening of average maturities. The only area experiencing unusual difficulty in raising funds in 1981 was Eastern Europe, due almost entirely to the rescheduling being arranged by Poland (to be followed much more seriously by a number of Latin American, and indeed many other developing, countries in 1982).

The extent to which borrowing through eurocurrency credits between 1973 and 1981 has been concentrated on a small number of countries is clear from Table 9.1 (which lists all countries which have borrowed $800 million or more in any one year) and Table 9.2. Amongst OECD countries, apart from the very high figure of $75 billion for the USA (77.8% of which was borrowed in 1981), the major borrowers over this period have been Italy ($27.6 billion), the UK (24.1 billion, concentrated in the earlier years included in Table 9.1), Spain ($21.4 billion) and Canada ($20.6 billion). Except for 1977 and 1979, over 40% of borrowing by the OECD group was accounted for by only three borrowers; apart from the five countries already noted only France made an appearance in the list of three major borrowers for any particular year. In the period from 1973 to 1981 as a whole, 49.1% of total borrowing by the OECD countries was accounted for by the USA, Italy and the UK.

TABLE 9.1
Eurocurrency Credits by Major Borrowing Country
(OECD Data; $ Million)

	1973–6	1977	1978	1979	1980	1981	Total (1973–1981)
OECD countries	(46783)	(13041)	(30368)	(29072)	(41163)	(97366)	(257793)
Australia	311	166	647	731	1693	3734	7282
Belgium	—	—	40	1000	3060	260	4360
Canada	1174	542	5694	926	6439	5792	20567
Denmark	1752	866	2385	1217	1566	1625	9411
Finland	1439	314	546	42	1134	492	3967
France	4656	1762	2365	2787	1922	3847	17339
Greece	1187	217	555	945	1191	941	5036
Ireland	1143	408	330	638	275	977	3771
Italy	7243	676	2811	3362	6483	6984	27559
New Zealand	803	527	450	515	715	982	3992
Norway	1145	182	1175	1246	1036	741	5525
Portugal	259	87	615	811	706	1756	4234
Spain	4482	1692	2219	3730	4524	4708	21355
Sweden	1024	1385	1846	1471	1324	2470	9520
Turkey	360	184	250	3171	—	—	3965
UK	10789	1720	4723	1990	1871	3019	24112
USA	3190	843	2637	3723	6387	58192	74972
Oil exporters	(10251)	(6356)	(9719)	(8772)	(6836)	(5737)	(47671)
Algeria	2438	489	2062	1800	343	—	7132
Ecuador	80	445	50	886	714	326	2501
Indonesia	2632	88	1592	695	967	1101	7075
Iran	2019	1710	1095	—	—	—	4824
Nigeria	25	—	1750	1212	668	1858	5513
UAE	652	1057	495	488	113	72	2877
Venezuela	1478	1648	1720	3035	2937	1333	12151

Other developing countries	(30941)	(11532)	(21844)	(36002)	(28162)	(40928)	(169409)
Argentina	1493	818	1298	2107	2390	2864	10970
Brazil	7855	2554	4938	6498	5279	7268	34392
Chile	125	327	1141	683	919	2305	5500
Columbia	405	43	75	888	662	1023	3096
Hong Kong	823	137	504	842	1335	2239	5880
Korea	1735	682	1582	2694	2037	3174	11904
Malaysia	765	130	932	197	1083	1475	4582
Mexico	6796	2657	5664	10438	5980	10571	42106
Peru	1773	144	—	550	344	909	3620
Philippines	2142	637	1463	1774	1277	1141	8434
Yugoslavia	979	343	748	1651	1832	564	6117
Eastern socialist countries	(5092)	(1409)	(3071)	(3719)	(2666)	(1509)	(17467)
Hungary	690	200	500	950	550	550	3440
Poland	1823	19	406	861	736	—	3845
International organisations/ development institutions	(1686)	(1297)	(675)	(1335)	(606)	(95)	(5694)
International Investment Bank	1070	1100	500	1025	—	—	3695
Unattributable and other countries[1]	(3154)	(146)	(130)	(182)	(485)	(278)	(4375)
Total	97908	33781	65806	79082	79919	145912	502408

[1] Liechtenstein, South Africa. In the earlier part of the data period, South Africa was classified as a non-OECD developed country and included in a separate category.

TABLE 9.2
Concentration of Eurocurrency Credit Amongst Country Borrowers
(OECD Data; %)

	1973-6	1977	1978	1979	1980	1981	Total (1973-81)
Proportion of total credits absorbed by:							
3 countries	26.4	20.6	24.8	26.1	24.2	52.1	30.1
5 countries	38.1	30.8	36.2	35.1	38.2	60.9	40.4
7 countries	46.0	40.7	43.8	42.9	47.7	66.7	48.9
10 countries	53.3	50.5	53.9	52.5	57.0	73.5	57.0
Proportion of credits to OECD countries absorbed by:							
3 countries	48.5	39.7	43.6	37.2	46.9	72.9	49.1
5 countries	64.9	56.9	60.2	57.7	65.3	81.6	65.4
7 countries	71.7	68.6	75.2	69.6	74.5	88.6	75.8
10 countries	79.2	79.9	87.3	81.5	85.7	94.6	84.4
Proportion of credits to developing countries absorbed by:							
3 countries	42.0	38.7	40.1	44.6	40.6	45.0	40.8
5 countries	53.1	53.8	51.1	55.3	53.2	56.1	51.4
7 countries	62.3	62.6	61.2	63.3	62.4	64.9	58.5
10 countries	73.7	72.7	73.5	71.7	71.9	73.3	67.3

The concentration of borrowing in the developing countries group was less marked, primarily due to the larger number of countries in that group that have entered this market. However, the total for 1973–1981 was dominated by Mexico ($42.1 billion) and Brazil ($34.4 billion) which accounted for 35.2% of borrowing by the developing countries over this period; in each year included in Table 9.2, these two countries were the leading developing country borrowers in the eurocredit market. Other major non-oil developing country borrowers between 1973 and 1981 were Korea ($11.9 billion), Argentina ($11 billion) and the Philippines ($8.4 billion). Amongst the oil-exporting countries, heavy borrowing has been completed by Venezuela ($12.2 billion), Algeria and Indonesia (both $7.1 billion), while in the Middle East, Iran borrowed $4.8 billion (all before the end of 1978) and the UAE $2.9 billion.

Borrowing by the Eastern European area has been much more evenly spread across the countries. The major borrowers between 1973 and 1981 were Poland ($3.8 billion, but none in 1981 itself) and Hungary ($3.4 billion). In addition, the International Investment Bank, an international organisation of COMECON contries, borrowed $3.7 billion over the same period.

Considering all countries together, the concentration is, as expected, less marked. However, it is still remarkable that 30.1% of funds raised in these markets between 1973 and 1981 went to only three countries — the USA, Mexico and Brazil — while the ten heaviest borrowers took 57% of the total. Once again, these concentration ratios have been distorted somewhat by the heavy US borrowing in 1981.

Both the OECD and World Bank have published figures on borrowing by the type and purpose (sector) of the borrower (Tables 9.3 and 9.4). The notable conclusion from Table 9.3 is the dominance of public sector borrowers. Between 1974 and 1981[12] over 60% of total funds raised in the eurocurrency credit markets went to public sector borrowers, in particular 'other public bodies' (mainly non-financial public enterprises — 24%) and central governments (22.7%). In contrast, borrowing by the private sector amounted to $181.6 billion (39.3% of the total), the bulk of which was accounted for by private non-financial enterprises. However, there is some evidence that the balance against private borrowers may have been corrected later in the data period. The share of private sector borrowing in the total doubled from 19.1% in 1977 to 39.6% in 1980

[12] The data in this table and many of those to follow in this chapter and in chapter 10 are available from 1974 onwards only.

TABLE 9.3
Eurocurrency Credits by Type of Borrower
(OECD Data; Shares in Total)

1976	1974–1976	1977	1978	1979	1980	(1981)	Total (1974–81)
Central governments	30.6	35.6	31.9	20.4	20.5	12.6	22.7
State and local governments	3.1	2.4	3.0	2.8	3.2	1.3	2.5
Public financial enterprises	15.2	17.4	10.3	15.8	9.8	7.0	11.4
Other public bodies	21.0	24.9	29.6	33.8	26.9	16.0	24.0
Private financial enterprises	29.6	19.1	2.7	2.0	4.2	3.7	39.3
Private non-financial enterprises			22.7	25.2	35.4	59.5	
Other	0.6	0.6	—	—	—	—	0.2
Memo							
Public sector	69.9	80.3	74.8	72.8	60.4	36.9	60.6
Private sector	29.6	19.1	25.4	27.2	39.6	63.2	39.3

before jumping to 63.2% in 1981. Clearly the influence of the large borrowing by US companies in these recent figures is again strong. However, the trend towards an increased share for private sector borrowers is not wholly accounted for by this factor, given that the volume of funds going to public sector borrowers has remained at around $50 billion per annum since 1978.

Within these aggregate figures, notable differences exist within the country groupings. The share of government borrowing in the total for OECD countries is generally much lower than in the oil-exporting countries. In OECD countries, governments borrow heavily in domestic markets forcing many would-be private borrowers onto the international markets. Much fund-raising is undertaken in developing countries by public enterprises of all types which may be involved in large energy and other infrastructure investment projects.

The breakdown of the figures according to purpose or borrowing sector (Table 9.4) indicates the relatively small share going to manufacturing industry. After remaining very stable at around 10% up to 1979, this figure did however double to 18.8% in 1981. The importance of eurocurrency finance to the energy sector is clear with 31% of total funds between 1974 and 1981 being used in this way. The very high figure of 44.5% in 1981 suggests that much of the large borrowing by US companies in the year was for energy projects. The share going to investment in transport and communications has remained low at between 5% and 10% of the total, while borrowing by financial institutions accounted for 14.5% of the total between 1974 and 1981. Once again, however, one of the major borrowing sectors has been governments (including central and local governments), which accounted for 25.2% of total borrowing over the data period, although this declined through the period to reflect the growth in shares of the energy and manufacturing sectors.

The overwhelming importance of dollar-denominated eurocurrency credits in the total is indicated by the data in Table 9.5. Between 1974 and 1981, 94.8% of all new eurocurrency credits were denominated in dollars. The only other currencies to reach a 1% share of the market in this period were the Deutschemark (1.7%) and sterling (1.4%). This high proportion of dollar-denominated credits has shown little sign of declining significantly despite the fluctuations in the market value of the currency during the 1970s and is based on the dollar's overwhelming importance as the leading vehicle currency for international payments. Notwithstanding this, a slight fall in the dollar's share to 93% occurred in 1981, compared to 95.5% a year earlier. Rising proportions of certain national currencies, in particular sterling (2.5%) and the Hong Kong dollar (1%), plus some

TABLE 9.4
Eurocurrency Credits by Borrowing Sector
(OECD Data; Shares in Total)

	1974–1976	1977	1978	1979	1980	1981	Total (1974–81)
Governments	33.7	38.0	34.9	23.2	23.7	13.9	25.2
Financial institutions	17.9	19.2	13.0	17.9	13.9	10.7	14.5
Energy	19.8	18.6	26.3	30.6	28.3	44.5	31.0
Transport	8.7	4.9	7.6	8.3	8.7	5.0	7.6
Communications	2.2	2.0					
Manufacturing	10.0	10.3	9.9	9.1	16.1	18.8	13.5
Others	7.8	7.0	8.6	11.3	9.4	7.1	8.4

growth in credits denominated in currency baskets or composite units such as SDRs or the European Currency Unit (ECU) were the counterweights to the slightly declining share of the dollar. One point concerning the interpretation of the figures in Table 9.5 should be noted. They only indicate the currency breakdown of eurocredit *announcements*. However with the inclusion in many credits of a multi-currency clause, a borrower is able actually to draw the funds in non-dollar currencies (OECD 1982c), this being increasingly likely as the time-period between signature and drawdown increases. Therefore it is expected that the share of the dollar in bank *drawings* will have been somewhat lower than the figures in Table 9.5 would indicate. Unfortunately, such information on the currency of bank drawings is very difficult to obtain.

BORROWING CONDITIONS

A statistical summary of borrowing conditions on eurocurrency credits may be presented in a variety of ways. Essentially, borrowing conditions in this market include:

(i) The original maturity of the credit.
(ii) The spread or margin charged on the loan over the base interest rate.
(iii) The base interest-rate itself.
(iv) The size of the credit.

Clearly, therefore, given this list, it is difficult to obtain an accurate and unambiguous index[13] of borrowing conditions either in the market as a whole or for individual borrowing countries. In addition many attempts — some of an econometric nature — have been made to explain movements in borrowing conditions over time and between countries at one point in time. (See, for example, Johnston 1979, Fleming and Howson 1980, Goodman 1980 and Inoue 1980.) Such a variety of information makes a clear judgement on this aspect of the statistical survey of eurocurrency credits very difficult. In this section, a combination of OECD (Figs 9.2, 9.3) and World Bank (Tables 9.6, 9.7) data are used. No information on borrowing conditions are published by Morgan Guaranty in *World Financial Markets*.

In general, the two factors seen to be the most important and certainly the most indicative of conditions in the eurocredit market are the maturity and spread attached to a eurocurrency credit. The maturity of the loan refers to the original maturity from the date of

[13] One such index is published regularly in *Euromoney*.

TABLE 9.5
Eurocurrency Credits by Currency of Denomination
(OECD and World Bank Data[1]; Shares in Total)

	1974–1976	1977	1978	1979	1980	1981	Total (1974–81)
US dollar	95.8	95.6	95.3	95.3	95.5	93.0	94.8
Deutschemark	2.6	2.6	1.9	2.4	1.1	1.1	1.7
Sterling	0.8	0.3	1.2	1.0	1.0	2.5	1.4
Hong Kong dollar	—	—	0.1	0.1	0.3	1.0	0.4
Opec currencies[2]	0.3	—	0.3	0.6	0.1	0.1	0.2
French franc	—	—	0.1	0.1	0.6	0.2	0.2
Yen	—	0.3	0.1	0.1	—	—	0.1
Others	0.5	1.2	1.0	0.3	1.4	2.4	1.3

[1] All data from the World Bank except 1981.
[2] Saudi-Arabian Riyal, Kuwaiti Dinar, Bahrain Dinar and UAE Dirham.

TABLE 9.6
Eurocurrency Credits by Maturity
(IBRD Data; Shares in Total[1])

	1974–1976	1977	1978	1979	1980	1981[2]	Total (1974–81[2])
Over 1–3 years	3.5	2.8	3.0	4.5	5.4	5.8	4.1
Over 3–5 years	39.3	16.6	5.2	9.2	7.2	10.1	15.2
Over 5–7 years	32.9	68.4	26.2	12.2	22.9	11.6	27.0
Over 7–10 years	19.7	12.3	59.7	56.7	56.9	64.8	46.0
Over 10 years	4.5	—	5.9	17.3	7.4	7.6	7.6

[1] Excluding credits of unknown maturity.
[2] First half only.

completion of the credit to the final repayment date, with any rollover feature (every three or six months for example) being ignored in such calculations. The fluctuations in the proportions of total credit issues in particular maturity classes may be seen from World Bank data summarised in Table 9.6. Credits with a maturity of three years or less have been fairly rare in the period from 1974 to mid-1981 covered in the table. After the worsening of market conditions in 1975 in the wake of the Herstatt collapse, the gradual improvement of these conditions after 1976 was symbolised by a fall in the proportion of credits with a maturity of five years or less from 66.2% in 1975 (42.8% in the three-year period from 1974–6) to only 8.2% in 1978. Similarly while 56.8% of all credits had a maturity of over seven years in 1974, this fell to only 5.5% in 1975 before rising rapidly again to 74% in 1979. Since 1979, maturities have shortened very slightly although the predominant feature has been a levelling-off of the upward trend of average maturities apparent since 1976. (See also Figure 9.2.) Therefore in the first half of 1981 over 15.9% of total credits carried a maturity of five years or less, up two percentage points from 1979, with the share of total credits of over seven years being little changed at 72.4% in the first half of 1981. The credit of over ten years to maturity, which became virtually non-existent between 1975 and 1977, has reappeared with 17.3% of the total being of this maturity in 1979, although this share fell again to only 7.6% in the first six months of 1981.

These broad conclusions are confirmed in the top half of Fig. 9.2[14] in which the weighted average maturity is plotted on the left-hand scale. This chart shows the sharp fall in this average from over eight years in 1973–4 to just over five and a half years in mid-1976. The optimality of market conditions, as far as the borrower is concerned, in 1979 is seen with average maturity peaking at over nine years at that time, before levelling out at just over seven and a half years in 1980–1. In addition to such aggregate information, both the OECD and World Bank have in recent years published an increasing amount of individual country information on the maturity structure of new credit arrangements. The OECD publishes periodically details of 'minimum loan conditions' (maximum maturities and minimum spreads) for major borrowing countries, while the World Bank has

---

[14] The data on the average maturity and size of eurocurrency credits is annual to the beginning of 1976 and 1977 respectively. All remaining observations in Figs 9.2 and 9.3 (except the maturity differentials in the latter graph which are at half-yearly intervals) are on a quarterly basis. All credits of unknown maturity or spread are omitted from the relevant series.

MATURITY/SPREAD (PERIOD AVERAGES)

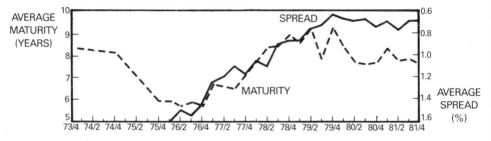

SIZE (AVERAGE)/INTEREST RATE

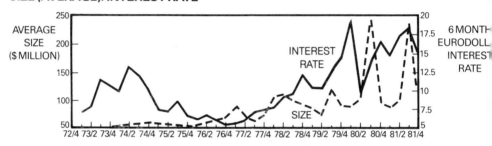

FIGURE 9.2
Eurocurrency credits: borrowing conditions

published country detail on weighted average maturities and spreads
in particular periods.

The spread or margin charged over the base interest rate is of great
importance in assessing borrowing conditions in the euro-credit
market. This margin is, in general, either a fixed percentage for the
whole life of the loan or a split spread involving an increase in the
spread to another fixed level after a number of years. For example,
the $600 million loan to Electricité de France in August 1980 carried a
spread of 0.35% for the first five years of the loan and one of 0.45%
for the remaining five years. This spread is essentially the premium or
profit margin (over the cost of its funds) of the lending bank. Table 9.7
sets out a margin breakdown of eurocurrency credits from 1975 to
mid-1981. The tightness of borrowing conditions in 1975–6 is confirmed by the low figure of 1.4% of total credits carrying a spread of
1% or less, a proportion that rose to 85% in 1979–80 and stood at
62.9% for the period as a whole. Even more notable, in 1980–81
around 35% of all new eurocurrency credits had a margin of 0.5% or
less representing a dramatic change from the 1975–7 period when no

TABLE 9.7
Eurocurrency Credits by Spread
(IBRD Data; Shares in Total[1])

	1975–1976	1977	1978	1979	1980	1981[2]	Total (1975–81[2])
Up to 0.50%	—	—	11.5	22.7	33.3	37.7	18.4
0.501–0.750%	—	4.1	33.5	41.7	38.4	29.9	27.9
0.751–1.000%	1.4	30.8	22.8	20.5	13.3	10.3	16.6
1.001–1.250%	16.5	20.3	14.1	9.5	7.4	7.5	12.0
1.251–1.500%	35.2	12.4	10.3	3.6	4.6	2.8	10.8
1.501–1.750%	26.1	20.0	3.8	1.3	0.9	1.9	7.4
1.751–2.000%	17.2	8.9	2.9	0.5	0.9	5.9	5.0
Over 2.000%	3.7	3.5	1.1	0.2	1.2	4.0	1.9
Memo Fixed rate credits (% of total)	10.5	7.3	9.0	12.1	7.1	3.3	8.7

[1] Excluding credits of unknown spread and fixed-rate credits.
[2] First half only.

credits carrying such a low spread were completed. At the other end of the scale, 47% of all credits in 1975–6 had a spread of over 1.5% compared to only 3% in 1980 (although this share rose to over 10% in the first half of 1981) and 14.3% in the period as a whole.

The extent to which movements in the average maturity and spread on eurocurrency credits have moved together since 1976 is clear from Fig. 9.2. (The spread is measured on the right-hand scale and from the top downwards to allow upward movements in both series to symbolise finer borrowing conditions and for downward movements the reverse.) Therefore the weighted average spread fell from 1.6% in the first quarter of 1976 to 0.64% at the end of 1979 representing a remarkable and rapid change in market conditions. However, while in 1980–81 some slight falls in average maturities from their peak values were recorded, no equivalent, significant, hardening of spreads occurred. In the second half of 1981, the weighted average spread was still as low as 0.69%. Likewise, no significant rise in spreads in 1980–81 is perceptible from the classified data in Table 9.7.

One problem with aggregate data of the type in Tables 9.6 and 9.7 and the top half of Fig. 9.2 is the lack of information on any differences in conditions, between prime and non-prime borrowers. This is a particular omission in the case of spreads where the differential between prime and non-prime margins — the tiering of

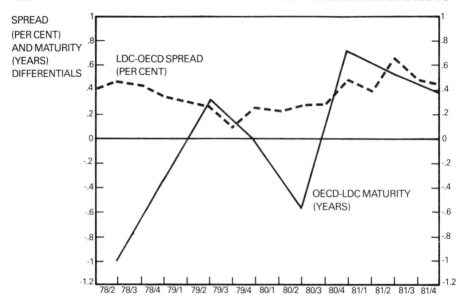

FIGURE 9.3
Eurocurrency credits-spread and maturity differentials

spreads — is frequently considerable and a source of much discussion in the markets. Figure 9.3 seeks to fill this gap by including the differential between conditions on credits to developing countries and those to OECD countries in terms both of average spread and maturity.[15] The data are defined in such a way that upward move-- ments in both graphs indicate increased positive differentials between developing country and OECD borrowing conditions (i.e. developing country credits have higher spreads and lower maturi- ties).

It is now generally accepted that, as far as spreads are concerned, the usual pattern is that when the average spread is tending to rise, the increase in non-prime margins is much more significant, leading to a widening of the differential between prime and non-prime spreads. In contrast, when spreads are generally falling the differential nar- rows, perhaps due to the banks' switching to non-prime lending opportunities (due to the low margins on prime credits) so competing

[15] This is not a particularly sophisticated measure as it does not allow for a developing country being a 'prime' borrower (e.g. Malaysia) and an OECD borrower being a non-prime borrower (certain Spanish borrowers). However it is a good general guide to the tiering of spreads and to maturity differentials.

non-prime spreads downwards also (Llewellyn 1981). This pattern is confirmed from the short span of data in Fig. 9.3. Therefore in 1979 when borrowing conditions were at their most favourable the spread differential virtually disappeared (OECD, 1982c). However it rose again to around 0.5 percentage points in late-1980 and 1981 (similar to the figure for mid-1978) as the market tightened somewhat.

In the case of maturities, differentials are much less noticeable or uniform. In fact, for the early part of the observation period in Fig. 9.3, the average maturity of developing country credits actually exceeded that on credits to OECD countries. Also in early 1979, when borrowing conditions eased and the spread differential fell amost to zero, the average maturity on developing country credits actually fell relative to that on credits to OECD countries. Only in 1980–81 did the expected pattern emerge with a slight increase in the tiering of spreads being matched by the development of a significant positive maturity differential on credits to OECD countries.

To a borrower, while the margin[16] charged over the base interest-rate is an important feature of a eurocurrency credit so is the base interest-rate itself. Most credits are priced over LIBOR — the London Inter-Bank Offered Rate — with the most widely used rate being the six-month eurodollar rate. This is defined for each credit as the average of the rates *offered* by banks and is fixed at the beginning of each six-month period. The bottom half of Fig. 9.2 (right-hand scale) plots the end-quarter observations of the six-month eurodollar rate (average of 'bid' and 'offer' rates) from 1973 to 1981. Clearly fluctuations such as the dramatic rise in the six-month LIBOR from 5.4% at the end of 1976 to 19.1% in the first quarter of 1980 with the subsequent fall to only 10% three months later, followed by a new increase to 18.3% in mid-1981 are of overwhelming importance to the borrower and in principle, reflect demand and supply conditions in the short-term eurocurrency markets (OECD, 1982c). Generally, the base interest rate has been emphasised less than the spread in discussions of borrowing conditions presumably as it, in itself, does not affect the profit margins of lending banks. Since 1979 however the sharp fluctuations of dollar interest rates and the additional debt-servicing costs of developing countries arising from the high dollar rates in 1981–82 have led to a much-needed increase in the awareness of this element of the cost of borrowing.

Finally, the average size of eurocurrency credits is by far the least-

[16] The fees charged on such credits are also important costs to the borrower. These fees and the lack of published statistics on them are discussed briefly in the following section.

discussed indicator of borrowing conditions, partly as it is easily distorted by the completion of 'jumbo' loans such as those over $1 billion. Figure 9.2 (left-hand scale) indicates that the average size of credits did not rise much after 1976 when conditions in terms of maturities and spreads improved so dramatically. When the average size did increase in 1980–81, the movements were very erratic, although an overall upward trend — an improvement in market conditions — may be said to have occurred.

Many types of tabular summaries of these borrowing conditions may be devised. One published by the OECD in *Financial Market Trends* contains (in addition to the total of new loans) details of the average size, maturity and spread on credits plus both the longest maturity and lowest spread. The one discussed here is set out in Table 9.8[17] and includes a group breakdown of eurocurrency credits by various categories of maturity, size and spread for 1978 and 1979. Many interesting conclusions emerge from this table. Firstly, there is evidence that on average, loans to developing countries carried longer maturities than those to industrialised countries (a result apparent from Fig. 9.3). Therefore, in 1979, 57.3% of the loans to industrialised countries had a maturity of ten years[18] or over, the equivalent figure for developing countries being 70.5%. Secondly, in the case of spreads, finer terms were obtained by industrialised countries with 96% of total credits for that group in 1979 carrying a spread of less than 1% compared to 71.9% for developing countries. Thirdly, a slightly greater proportion of the number of credits to developing countries were less than $50 million in size in comparison to the proportion of such loans to industrialised countries. Fourthly, a close study of Table 9.8 confirms the improvement in borrowing conditions in 1979 compared to those existing one year earlier.

Two points may be made to summarise this survey of data on borrowing conditions. Firstly, there is considerable correspondence between the maturity, spread and size of credit as indicators of market conditions. Therefore, all three characteristics indicated the existence of a lenders' market in 1975/6 with the gradual switch to a borrowers' market in 1979 being confirmed by all three series also. One potentially important divergence does however occur in 1980–81 when the average maturity fell slightly (and the average size

---

[17] Reproduced from Banker Research Unit *'Trends in International Banking and Capital Markets'*, October 1980, p 78. This is the most recent data available from this source, which is no longer being published.

[18] This is not inconsistent with the figures in Table 9.7 which included a maturity category of *over* ten years.

TABLE 9.8
Eurocurrency Credits — Borrowing Conditions (IBRD Data; 1979 (1978))

	Maturity (% of total Value of Credits of known Maturity)			Size (% of total No.)					Spread (% of Total Values of Credits of known Spread)			
	less than 6 years	6-less than 10 years	10 years and over	less than $50m	$50-99m	$100-499m	$500-999m	$100m and over	less than 1%	1%-less than 1½%	1½%-less than 2%	2% and over
Industrialised countries	10.8 (8.8)	32.0 (56.5)	57.3 (34.6)	47.8 (50.8)	26.9 (17.6)	21.4 (23.3)	2.2 (5.7)	1.6 (2.6)	96.0 (92.9)	2.8 (6.3)	1.0 (0.8)	0.2 (—)
Developing: Oil exporting	7.2 (24.4)	92.8 (59.2)	— (16.4)	76.5 (69.0)	— (17.2)	23.5 (13.8)	— (—)	— (—)	22.5 (48.1)	70.6 (24.6)	6.1 (9.5)	0.8 (17.8)
High and Upper Middle Income	7.8 (6.4)	12.9 (36.1)	79.3 (57.5)	50.2 (53.3)	25.1 (25.8)	23.5 (20.4)	0.8 (—)	0.4 (0.4)	79.4 (35.7)	19.1 (39.8)	1.5 (18.9)	— (5.6)
Intermediate and Lower Middle Income	10.9 (8.5)	22.9 (52.8)	66.2 (38.7)	52.6 (47.0)	21.1 (24.0)	22.4 (24.6)	3.9 (3.3)	— (1.1)	67.7 (26.1)	27.6 (61.2)	3.9 (11.4)	0.8 (1.2)
Low Income	7.2 (6.4)	30.8 (74.8)	62.0 (18.8)	72.8 (74.1)	12.1 (7.4)	15.2 (14.8)	— (3.7)	— (—)	64.1 (21.0)	18.6 (49.9)	9.0 (25.9)	8.4 (3.3)
Developing Countries total	9.4 (8.0)	20.2 (46.9)	70.5 (45.1)	53.5 (53.0)	21.7 (23.5)	22.4 (21.3)	2.1 (1.5)	0.2 (0.6)	71.9 (30.7)	24.4 (50.2)	3.1 (15.3)	0.7 (3.8)
Centrally Planned Economies	54.0 (3.0)	27.9 (73.7)	18.1 (23.4)	13.5 (27.8)	21.6 (11.1)	56.8 (61.1)	5.4 (5.4)	2.7 (—)	88.2 (79.5)	11.8 (20.5)	— (—)	— (—)
Total	14.6 (8.2)	24.0 (51.8)	61.4 (40.0)	50.1 (52.2)	23.1 (21.1)	23.9 (22.9)	2.3 (2.6)	0.7 (1.2)	79.2 (56.9)	18.1 (31.9)	2.2 (9.0)	0.5 (2.2)

became more erratic) while the average spread levelled off. This very *ad hoc* conclusion is supported by more rigorous empirical work completed at the Bank of England[19] which suggests that spreads and maturities are inversely correlated. This has the very important implication that the use of only one of these two pieces of information as an indicator of market conditions as a whole may be valid. Secondly, it appears that the differences in the quality of prime and non-prime borrowers is reflected mainly in a tiering of spreads with only limited evidence that variations in the size of credits are crucial. The position is less clear on maturities where there are considerable cross-country variations. However, any evidence that average maturities on credits to prime borrowers are higher is not clear cut, as seen from the data in Fig. 9.3 and Table 9.8.

STATISTICAL PROBLEMS

The problems of the statistical series discussed in this chapter will be briefly considered in this section in two senses. Firstly, a discussion is made of certain crucial omissions from the spectrum of statistics on eurocurrency credits. Secondly, the fact that capital market data refer to commitments of funds while banking data refer to actual drawings or disbursements will be noted as a flavour of the general issue of the consistency and comparability of capital market and banking data to be discussed at greater length in Chapter 15.

The most notable information gaps in published data on eurocurrency credits are on the fee structure[20] and the length of the grace and drawdown periods. A variety of fees are charged on eurocurrency credits in addition to the published cost of a credit in terms of the base interest-rate plus the margin or spread. These fees [21] (including commitment, management and participation fees) effectively increase the cost to the borrower of a eurocurrency credit often by as much as one or two percentage points. Lack of knowledge of such fees is a considerable drawback to an observer of this market as lower spreads (which tend to be publicised more fully) may at times be 'traded' for higher fees by a borrower in liaison with the lending banks to create the impression that 'prime' conditions are attached to

---

[19] Reported in Fleming and Howson (1980).

[20] Despite this, the World Bank formerly published a small amount of summary information on the fee structure for many loans.

[21] For a fuller description of these fees see *IMF Survey* 22 June 1981, and Davis (1978).

a loan. In practice, therefore, the overall cost of the credit may be unchanged by such manipulations. Notwithstanding this, the general trend in recent years has been for fees to move in a similar way to spreads (Fleming and Howson, 1980) making the lack of data on the fee structure less serious in practice.

Many loan arrangements include a 'drawdown' period during which the borrower must draw that part of the loan that is needed and after the end of which any undrawn balances are cancelled. In addition, a period of time may then elapse termed the 'grace period' before the repayments of loan must begin. These institutional features effectively increase the maturity of any given credit. The lack of published information on these drawdown and grace periods is therefore another significant omission in the state of knowledge of the eurocurrency credit market.

Despite such remarks and an acceptance by data sources that these gaps exist, it is difficult to provide information on fees and drawdown and grace periods for two reasons. Firstly, information on these characteristics of euro-credits are scanty even to public-sector organisations like the OECD and World Bank. Secondly, it is felt that the publication of such information would violate the confidentiality between the lenders and the borrowers to an excessive extent. The details of individual loans previously published by the World Bank, for example, are essentially non-confidential information; further publicity would, it is felt, exceed the accepted limits of privacy on such loans.

A perceived and frequently-discussed problem of statistics in this area is the difficulty in reconciling data on new eurocurrency credit arrangements with the banking statistics discussed in Section 2. The major point to note should such a comparison be made is that the figures in this chapter refer to gross new eurocurrency credit *commitments* while the banking data reflect actual *drawings* and also, by definition, the repayment of past loans and the redepositing of any borrowed or other funds in the banking system. This factor is perhaps the most important and most commonly-aired source of variation between capital market and banking statistics but many others exist. A full discussion of all these discrepancies is left until Chapter 15 in which many of the statistical systems surveyed in this book are put into comparative perspective. It is important, however, to note at this stage that organisations such as the OECD which publish capital market data are well aware of the divergence between commitments and drawings — particularly as some loans may not be drawn at all. However they argue that data on drawings of previously-reported individual credit arrangements are virtually impossible to obtain at any acceptable level of accuracy, so that 'commitments' data is the best available indicator of capital market activity of this type.

SUMMARY

This chapter has demonstrated that with the rapid growth of the eurocurrency credit market during the 1970s and early 1980s has come an increasing amount of statistical information on this market from a variety of sources. Despite the differences in certain definitional issues, there is a considerable degree of consistency between the statistical outputs of the three sources under survey. Therefore, although individual country totals do differ between sources, the estimates of total new eurocurrency credits for a particular time-period are usually fairly close. Clearly, a sound and reliable picture of the overall growth of this very important source of finance is feasible therefore from any of these sources.

Chapter 10

External Bonds

DEFINITIONS

The definitional problems in the external bond markets are generally less severe than those encountered in the markets for eurocurrency credits. The general concept of a 'bond' refers to a credit instrument which includes a promise to pay a specified amount of money at a fixed date and to pay interest periodically at stated intervals. Bonds are therefore marketable securities and are usually issued in standard denominations. An external bond is one issued by a borrower in a capital market (or markets) outside the country in which the borrower is domiciled. Conventionally, external bonds include both *foreign* (traditional) issues and *euro* (or *international*) bonds. A foreign bond is defined by the OECD as

> 'one which is placed (on behalf of a non-resident) by a domestic syndicate, on the market of a single country and is denominated in that country's currency'.[1]

To be a non-resident, a borrower must come from one of the following categories:

(a) . . . governments, government agencies or political sub-divisions which are not located in the country in which the issue is made.

(b) . . . international organisations.

(c) . . . officially-sponsored international enterprises except when their registered office is in the country concerned.[2]

[1] OECD, *Financial Statistics.*
[2] OECD, *Financial Statistics.* In addition, operating subsidiaries and financial subsidiaries are classified as foreign or domestic borrowers according to rules laid out with respect to eurocurrency credits in Chapter 9.

Similar definitions are adopted by the World Bank and Morgan Guaranty.

Alternatively, the OECD defines an international (euro) bond issue as one that

'is placed simultaneously on the market of at least two countries and is denominated in a currency which need not necessarily be that of either, usually through international syndicates of financial institutions of several countries.'[3]

Again, the definition utilised by the World Bank was conceptually equivalent. (Such similarity would be anticipated given the close link between the OECD and the World Bank in the publication of data on all external bond issues.) However, Morgan Guaranty adds to the basic definition the condition — which is persumably implicit in the OECD definition — tha the bond is sold outside the country of the currency in which the issue is denominated.[4] This latter condition is, in fact, a more commonly-used definition of a euro-bond. In practice, the definitions adopted by all three sources to be surveyed in this chapter are effectively equivalent.

One minor complication does exist in relation to the label attached to the second type of bond defined above. While the OECD and World Bank use the 'international' bond label (where *both* are not utilised), Morgan Guaranty refers to this class of external issue as 'euro'-bonds. In this chapter, the euro-bond label is used and it should be remembered therefore that this is equivalent to the OECD and World Bank concepts of international bonds.

The breakdown of total external bond into foreign and euro-issues is set out in Table 10.1. Over the observation period as a whole (1973-81) the share of the two types in the total have been very similar ($140.8 billion of foreign bonds or 50.6% of the total and $133.5 billion (48%) in the case of euro-bonds). However, in individual years the shares have at times differed much more noticeably. In general, euro-bond issues are less prominent in periods of considerable exchange rate uncertainty such as 1974 (36.9%) and 1978-9 (43.3%). In addition, Table 10.1 separately identifies 'special placements' made since 1979. There are private bond placements issued by international organisations (such as the World Bank itself) and international development institutions (such as the European Investment Bank and the Inter-American Development Bank) and placed directly with central banks, monetary authorities and governments. They are

[3] OECD, *Financial Statistics.*
[4] See, for example, *World Financial Markets,* September 1981, p.22.

TABLE 10.1
External Bond Issues
(OECD Data; $ Billion)

	1973	1974	1975	1976	1977	1978	1979	1980	1981	Total (1973–81)
Euro-Bonds	4.7	4.5	10.5	15.4	19.5	15.1	17.3	20.0	26.5	133.5
Foreign Bonds	5.3	7.7	12.3	18.9	16.6	20.7	20.0	18.0	21.3	140.8
Special Placements	—	—	—	—	—	—	1.6	1.4	1.0	4.0
Total	10.0	12.2	22.8	34.3	36.1	35.9	38.9	39.4	48.8	278.3
Shares in Total										
Euro-Bonds	47.0	36.9	46.1	44.9	54.0	42.2	44.5	50.8	54.3	48.0
Foreign Bonds	53.0	63.1	53.9	55.1	46.0	57.8	51.4	45.7	43.6	50.6
Special Placements	—	—	—	—	—	—	4.1	3.5	2.1	1.4

separately identified by the OECD as they do not 'come to the market' in the conventional way, even in comparison with private placements (see below). Between 1979 and 1981, $4.0 billion of special placements were issued (3.1%), although since 1974 as much as $12.9 billion of such issues have been made. (For the earlier period, these placements were not distinguished from foreign and euro-issues by the OECD).

A second level of disaggregation of total external bonds is a division into publicly-issued bonds and private placements. Publicly-issued bonds are those that are either offered for sale to investors at large (including those subscribed by an issuing house) or, according to the bond prospectus, are to be quoted on a stock exchange. In contrast, private placements do not come to the market this way being taken up entirely by institutional investors or are not quoted on a stock exchange. This distinction is not made, however, by Morgan Guaranty in their data series.

Despite these clear definitions of certain categories of bonds, one problem in their application should be noted. This is the possibility that it may be difficult to allocate a particular issue to the foreign or euro-bond classification. This is particularly common with private placements where it may be difficult to ascertain exactly where the bonds are sold. An explicit procedure is adopted by Morgan Guaranty to allocate such issues where there is a lack of full information, based on the nationality of the bank arranging the placement (Morgan Guaranty, 1977). This problem arises most frequently in the case of privately-placed Deutschemark bonds. Applying the Morgan Guaranty procedure to this type of bond would classify such bonds as foreign issues if all the banks arranging the issue were located in Germany and as euro-bonds otherwise. A related problem is that, at times, insufficient information may be available to identify whether a particular issue is a public offering or a private placement. Such 'semi-private' placements are allocated by the OECD and World Bank once all the information on that issue is obtained and verified with the use of the bond prospectus, in particular, for this process. Clearly the successful operation of this general cross-checking procedure by these organisations should also enable them to solve many of the difficulties noted earlier in this paragraph over whether a particular issue is of the foreign or euro-bond type. In practice, with information and procedures of this degree of refinement, the correct category in which to place a particular bond issue is eventually quite clear in most cases. However, as capital markets become increasingly internationalised over time this ability to distinguish between foreign and euro issues may be reduced.

From Table 10.2, it is clear that the proportion of public offerings is much higher in the euro-bond sector than is the case in the foreign bond market. From the unusually low figure of 33.3% in 1974, the share of public offerings in the euro-bond total rose gradually during the data period to over 80% in 1979–80% and as high as 92.1% in 1981; over the period as a whole the share of such public issues in this market was 77.4%. In contrast, public and private issues in the foreign bond market were very similar in volume between 1973 and

TABLE 10.2
Public/Private Bond Offerings
(IBRD/OECD Data; Shares in Total)

	1973–6	1977	1978	1979	1980	1981[1]	Total (1973–81)
Euro-Bonds:							
Public Offerings	58.6	79.0	73.0	81.5	85.8	92.1	77.4
Private Placements	41.4	21.0	27.0	18.5	14.2	7.9	22.6
Foreign Bonds:							
Public Offerings	51.0	53.6	57.7	51.5	56.8	67.0	54.0
Private Placements	49.0	46.4	42.3	48.5	43.2	33.0	46.0
Total External Bonds:							
Public Offerings	54.2	67.3	64.3	65.6	73.9	80.6	65.4
Private Placements	45.8	32.7	35.7	34.4	26.1	19.4	34.6

[1] First half only.

1981 (54% being public offerings) with, as in the euro-bond market, a peak level (67.5%) of private placements being attained in 1974. For external bonds as a whole, private placements accounted for only 34.6% of the total between 1973 and 1981, with 1974 being the only year when such issues outstripped the volume of public offerings.

A final breakdown of external bonds published by the World Bank allocates bond issues into certain groups by type. A 'straight' bond is one that carries a fixed rate of interest and therefore guarantees a given sum to be repaid at a future date with interest payable at specified dates. From Table 10.3,[5] it is clear that such bonds dominate with 84.6% of total issues between 1974 and 1981 being of the 'straight' variety, although after 1979, a significant decline in this share occurred. In contrast to such straight bonds, the interest rate on floating rate notes (FRNs) is tied to a base interest rate (usually LIBOR) to which a margin is then added. To prevent interest income from falling too low these FRNs usually have a minimum interest rate clause attached. FRNs first appeared in 1969 and came to prominence in 1974–5 when conditions in both the foreign exchange and bond markets were volatile with interest rates expected to rise. Since 1973, over $20 billion of FRNs have been issued representing 8.8% of total issues. Their chief advantages are in giving some protection to both borrowers and lenders at times of volatile interest rates and, by being something of a hybrid between 'straight' bonds and euro-credits, perhaps allowing a borrower to enter the bond markets when it would have been unable to float a straight bond. Despite a low share in the complete data period in Table 10.3, FRNs increased significantly in 1979–81, mirroring the slight decline in 'straight' issues, and reached 13.4% of the total over that period.

TABLE 10.3
External Bonds by Type
(OECD Data; Shares in Total)

	1973–6	1977	1978	1979	1980	1981	Total (1973–81)
Straight Bonds	94.5	90.0	86.0	79.6	77.1	74.5	84.6
Floating Rate Notes	2.5	6.3	8.1	11.3	12.6	15.7	8.8
Convertible Bonds	3.0	3.7	5.9	9.1	10.3	9.2	6.5
Deep Discount Bonds	—	—	—	—	—	0.6	0.1

[5] From Table 10.3 onwards (apart from the tables on euro-bonds by currency and foreign bonds by market country) the statistics are presented for all external bonds together (i.e. combining euro and foreign issues).

Convertible bonds allow holders to convert their holdings into the common stock of the borrower or, in some cases, the guarantor, of the issue. This conversion may occur at a fixed time in the life of the bond and at a price set by prior agreement. The high yields available on such equity-linked finance have been attractive to potential investors (in addition to the possible capital gain), so that the share of convertibles in total bond issues has risen steadily over the data period to reach 10.3% in 1980 and stood at 6.5% over the whole period since 1973.[6]

Deep discount bonds made an appearance on external bond markets in 1981 with $300 million of issues being made. These securities are issued at a discount and with a low coupon so that much of the investor's return is in the form of a capital gain. Such an issue will be attractive to a lender if the tax treatment of capital gains is more favourable than is that of interest income. It is expected that these issues will become of considerable importance in the near future. A procedural point applying particularly to deep discount bonds is that the OECD measures all securities at their nominal values except where a discount of over 5% to par applies in which case the issue price is used.

Finally in this section, it is important to note that in the conversion of non-dollar bond issues into dollar values no differences in procedure exist between the sources being surveyed here. This is both helpful in itself and an improvement over the situation in the eurocurrency credit market. The OECD (and, therefore, the World Bank too, given the close relationship between the organisations on bond statistics) converts non-dollar bonds into dollar values using the average market exchange rates for the month in which the bond is listed. A similar procedure is used for bonds denominated in composite currencies.[7]

[6] See also 'Convertible Issues on External Bond Markets' *Financial Market Trends,* November 1981.
[7] Nevertheless, valuation effects (due to the differences in procedure concerning the allocation of bonds to particular months by different sources — see the next section) may arise due to exchange rate changes from one month to another.

DISCREPANCIES BETWEEN STATISTICAL SERIES[8]

Three areas of potential discrepancy between different sources in the treatment of external bonds are discussed in this section. Firstly, and mirroring a major problem in the eurocurrency credit statistics, differences exist in the procedures adopted by the various sources for allocating bonds to particular time periods. The OECD and World Bank use, in general, the offering date as the guide to the allocation of a bond issue to a particular month. Two exceptions to this rule should however be noted. Firstly, in the case of foreign bonds issued in Switzerland, where the practice is to have an offering week rather than a particular day, the key date is the first day of subscription. Secondly, if, due to a lack of sufficient information, neither of these procedures is, in fact, operational the date of notification to the press is used by these organisations.

In contrast, Morgan Guaranty captures bond issues in its series slightly earlier in that

'The date of issuance for bonds is considered to be the date on which the final terms are set and announced, even though the receipt of some or all of the proceeds by the borrower may be spread over a period of months or even years in the case of issues providing for deferred delivery.'[9]

However, if this date when the final terms are set is unknown, the date of press notification is used by Morgan Guaranty in a way consistent with that adopted by OECD and the World Bank. In practice, although these two differences in procedure will lead to certain data entries being out of phase, the discrepancies will be less severe than was the case in the eurocurrency credit market. Specifically the time variation as a result of the adoption of these different procedures is likely to be one or two weeks only for most issues, given that once the final terms of a bond are set offering usually begins soon afterwards.

Secondly, differences exist between sources in the treatment of short-term bonds. The OECD and World Bank include all bonds with

---

[8] In addition to the discussion in this section it should be remembered that the points raised in Chapter 9 on eurocurrency credits concerning the identification of the borrowing country in the cases of certain classes of subsidiaries and multinational companies are equally relevant for the statistics on external bonds.

[9] Morgan Guaranty (1977), p.7.

an original maturity (defined as the period between the expected settlement date and the date of final maturity)[10] of over one year. This procedure is therefore consistent with the OECD and CMS treatments of eurocurrency credits and is indicative of the assumption that bonds of over one year's original maturity are 'long-term' in nature. On the other hand, the 'cut-off' point adopted by Morgan Guaranty is at three years so that its series omits all bonds of three years or less to maturity. It is believed by Morgan Guaranty that the three-year maturity limit results in a more meaningful definition of a long-term financing instrument while, in addition, this is a long-standing historical convention in the Morgan Guaranty statistics on external bond issues.

The extent of the discrepancy between the two series on this count may be seen in Table 10.10. Between 1974 and the middle of 1981, $8.7 billion of bond issues (3.6% of the total) included by the World Bank carried a maturity of over one but less than three years. There is an offset to this discrepancy in Morgan Guaranty data, however. In its series, Morgan Guaranty includes (while the OECD and CMS exclude) Certificates of Deposits (CDs) issued by banks with a maturity of over three years on the grounds that, being discountable, such CDs represent a form of long-term finance similar in nature to bond issues. It is argued by Morgan Guaranty that its inclusion of such CDs will roughly match the inclusion of bonds of over one but less than three years to maturity by the World Bank. If this is true (which is impossible to gauge from published information) the slight variations in the components of each series will be concealed by the broad consistency of the overall totals themselves.

Thirdly, the 'special' placements of bonds defined earlier in this section are automatically excluded from Morgan Guaranty data. This procedure is justified by Morgan Guaranty given that it is seeking to measure the volume of funds raised in the private financial markets and as such 'special' placements do not come to market in the normal way they should be excluded from the data series on methodological grounds. As noted earlier, both the OECD and CMS include them, given that the World Bank itself is the major issuer of bonds of this type. Therefore as part of the Bank's sources of finance, they are not ignored in the construction of the OECD and CMS data series. As reported above, $12.9 billion of such special placements were issued between 1974 and 1981 representing 4.8% of total issues. Clearly this factor is a major source of statistical disparity between on the one

[10] For bonds which are redeemable prior to maturity at the bondholder's
    discretion, the maturity is still calculated on the basis of the final maturity date.

hand the World Bank and the OECD and, on the other hand, Morgan Guaranty. On the evidence of 1979–81, when the share of such special placements rose to 3.1%, this discrepancy is likely to increase in the future, particularly if the World Bank's demand for external finance continues to rise.

THE DATA

The annual fluctuations in the volume of funds raised in the external bond markets in the 1970s were much less significant than those in the eurocurrency credit markets (Table 8.1). Apart from the decline in new issues from $11.3 billion in 1972 to $10 billion in 1973 and the very small fall in 1978, each year saw an increase in new issues over the previous year. Dramatic increases in bond financing occurred in 1975 when the issue volume was $22.8 billion, an increase of 86.9% from 1974, and again in the following year when a rise of 50.4% took the new issue volume to $34.3 billion. After that, bond financing reaching something of a plateau, with the 1980 volume of $39.4 billion being only 14.9% higher than the 1976 level (in a period when new eurocurrency credit financing more than doubled) before rising sharply again to $48.8 billion in 1981.

Although many of the demand factors that affect the volume of eurocurrency financing and also the supply factors (to the extent that banks themselves may use surplus funds to invest in external bonds) are relevant in the external bond markets, other factors specific to these markets have affected new issue volumes. In particular, the volumes of new bond issues are rather more dependent on world economic condition than is the case in the eurocurrency credit market (Fleming, 1981). The volume of bond financing has been held back in certain years by the tendency at times for a reverse yield gap to develop — that is when short-term interest-rates are higher than long-term rates such as external bond yields. In such circumstances, non-bank investors are more likely to place investable funds in the banking system rather than buy fixed rate bonds so that the volume of bond issues falls off. At the same time, banks themselves will not want to use their relatively expensive deposit liabilities to purchase low yield bonds. Conversely, at times of a significant positive yield gap (when long-term bond yields exceed short-term interest rates), bond issuance is likely to increase. Therefore, comparing the timepath of LIBOR (Fig. 9.2) with estimates of the eurodollar bond yield (Fig. 10.3), it is clear that the considerable increase in issue volume in

TABLE 10.4
External Bonds by Borrowing Country
(OECD Data; $ Million)

	1973–6	1977	1978	1979	1980	1981	Total (1973–81)
OECD Countries	(51034)	(24344)	(23248)	(26627)	(28430)	(36740)	(190423)
Australia	1893	1024	1421	605	437	695	6075
Austria	2340	1433	1431	1221	1829	1408	9662
Belgium	292	239	38	303	234	523	1629
Canada	17272	5374	4758	4131	3181	10959	45675
Denmark	1367	799	954	687	1202	826	5835
Finland	1141	397	1047	697	321	587	4190
France	4167	1906	1304	2050	2433	2885	14745
Ireland	367	87	83	180	267	516	1500
Italy	221	300	225	351	1081	985	3163
Japan	3956	1929	2794	4186	3789	4919	21573
Luxembourg	233	581	415	105	83	61	1478
Netherlands	1821	513	426	976	1126	745	5607
New Zealand	990	545	738	553	291	600	3717
Norway	2960	2562	2625	2075	808	356	11386
Spain	474	531	324	481	463	332	2605
Sweden	2447	1563	742	1571	2792	1660	10775
UK	3531	1637	1448	1237	1582	1353	10788
USA	2406	1522	1697	4081	5764	6553	22023
Oil Exporters	(438)	(752)	(1865)	(434)	(178)	(312)	(3979)
Algeria	314	215	729	183	—	—	1441
Venezuela	60	438	689	174	132	241	1734

Other Developing Countries	(4450)	(3390)	(3396)	(2639)	(1553)	(3024)	(18452)
Brazil	155	856	935	735	317	61	3059
Israel	1625	340	426	200	180	117	2888
Mexico	925	1348	688	363	382	2179	5885
Eastern Socialist Countries	(313)	(255)	(30)	(73)	(50)	(—)	(721)
International Organisations[1]/ Development Institutions	(21947)	(7161)	(6781)	(8851)	(8868)	(8529)	(62137)
ECSC	2882	655	825	688	731	192	5973
EEC	1096	600	30	251	191	275	2443
EIB	3254	1089	2198	2302	2345	1567	12755
IBRD[2]	12472	4269	2995	4342	4640	4934	33652
IDB	1117	301	92	371	326	635	2842
Unattributable and Other Countries[3]	(1239)	(193)	(544)	(310)	(365)	(188)	(2839)
Total	79419	36094	35862	38933	39444	48793	278545

[1] ECSC = European Coal and Steel Community.

EEC = European Economic Community.

EIB = European Investment Bank.

IBRD = International Bank for Reconstruction and Development (The World Bank).

IDB = Inter-American Development Bank.

[2] Including special placements.

[3] Liechtenstein and South Africa. In the earlier part of the data period, South Africa was classified as a non-OECD developed country and included in a separate category.

1975–6 was related to the substantial positive yield gap and the general downward trend of long-term interest rates in those years. In addition, the rise in LIBOR above the eurodollar bond yield in mid-1978 (where it remained until the end of 1981 despite some dramatic fluctuations in the yield gap in 1980–81 as LIBOR became very volatile) played a major rôle in the lack of significant growth in bond financing (except perhaps in 1981) and therefore the declining share of this form of finance in total external financing in this period. Therefore while 51.6% of total funds raised on international capital markets in 1977 were from bond issues this proportion fell to 35.2% one year later and stood at only 25.1% in 1981.

A second specific factor that influences the volume of bond financing is the attitude of central monetary authorities. For example, the development of a balance of payments deficit may encourage the monetary authorities in the country concerned to liberalise overseas access to its bond markets. The desire to maintain orderly market conditions will encourage national authorities to monitor closely issuing activity in bond markets denominated in that country's currency. To this end, issue calendars are common features of certain traditional foreign bond markets, notably in Germany. The consequent desire to protect traditional foreign bond markets is a key factor behind the limited size of external markets relative to both the purely domestic markets and the volume of eurocurrency credits. The extent to which the volume of foreign bond issues in particular countries is influenced by these factors will become clear later in this section when data on the breakdown of foreign bonds by market country are presented.

Finally, the volume of bond financing has been maintained in the 1970s in part, by innovations in the technique of raising funds. Such innovations have included new types of debt instrument, in particular FRNs and, more recently, deep discount bonds, and also modifications in existing instruments to revive market demand. Currency diversification has increased, both in terms of new currencies being used for issues and also greater use of bonds denominated in currency baskets.

Table 10.4 indicates the extent to which the external bond markets are dominated by OECD borrowers. It is this group of countries that has benefited, in particular, from the new types of bond financing noted in the previous paragraph. Amongst OECD countries by far the most important borrower between 1973 and 1981 has been Canada which took up $45.7 billion from these markets (16.4% of the overall total) including a particularly high figure of $11 billion in 1981 (22.5% of the total in that year). Other major borrowers in this period were the USA ($22 billion), Japan ($21.6 billion), France ($14.7 billion), Norway ($11.4 billion), Sweden and the UK (both $10.8 billion). In general, despite the Canadian figure, the concentration of borrowing among industrialised countries is slightly lower in this market than in the eurocurrency credit market (Table 10.5). Therefore, between 1973 and 1981, 46.9% of all funds raised by OECD countries in external bond markets was borrowed by three countries and 83.3% by ten countries compared with 49.1% and 84.4% respectively in the eurocredit market.

The main conclusion concerning borrowing by developing countries in these markets between 1973 and 1981 was the limited number of such countries that had access to external bond markets and therefore the low level of overall fund-raising by this group. For much of this period, it is likely that developing country borrowers were effectively crowded out from these markets by the better-risk industrialised country borrowers. In 1977–8, only, did funds raised by this group (including oil-exporting countries) through the issue of external bonds exceed $4 billion and even in these years this comprised only 19.8% of the borrowing by OECD countries. Major

TABLE 10.5
Concentration of External Bonds Amongst Country Borrowers (OECD Data; %)

	1973–6	1977	1978	1979	1980	1981	Total (1973–81)
Proportion of Total Bonds Absorbed by:							
3 Countries	42.7	33.8	29.4	32.5	36.0	46.0	36.4
5 Countries	52.1	44.4	42.9	48.9	51.1	62.0	49.4
7 Countries	60.0	53.3	51.6	59.5	63.2	69.9	58.1
10 Countries	69.7	65.2	63.2	69.9	74.9	78.7	69.3
Proportion of Bonds to OECD Countries absorbed by:							
3 Countries	49.8	40.5	43.8	46.7	44.8	61.1	46.9
5 Countries	62.5	55.1	57.3	62.1	63.2	73.4	60.6
7 Countries	72.0	67.7	69.6	72.6	75.2	80.9	71.9
10 Countries	83.9	81.1	83.8	83.5	87.2	87.9	83.3
Proportion of Bonds to Developing Countries absorbed by:							
3 Countries	60.0	56.5	44.7	49.3	49.9	77.5	52.7
5 Countries	70.9	69.9	65.9	61.7	65.0	85.6	66.9
7 Countries	77.6	77.6	75.1	73.2	76.0	91.2	76.3

borrowers in the 1973–81 period included Mexico ($5.9 billion), Brazil ($3.1 billion) and Israel ($2.9 billion). It is remarkable that as many as NINE individual countries in the OECD area borrowed more than the heaviest developing country borrower over this period. In addition, the re-appearance of the dominant borrowers in the eurocredit market (Mexico, Brazil) in these figures is also notable. In general, therefore, given the limited number of developing countries with access to these markets, the concentration of borrowing among these countries was considerably greater than in the eurocredit market. In particular, between 1973 and 1981, 52.7% of total funds were raised by three countries and 76.3% by seven countries compared with figures of 40.8% and 58.5% respectively in the eurocredit market.

Borrowing by centrally-planned economies in the external bond markets between 1973 and 1981 at $0.7 billion was very small indeed accounting for only 0.25% of total funds raised in the data period. The second heaviest single borrower in these markets between 1973 and 1981 was the World Bank itself which raised $33.7 billion (12.1% of the total) while other major borrowers amongst the international organisations were the European Investment Bank ($12.8 billion) and the European Coal and Steel Community ($6 billion). Overall, the international organisations raised $62.1 billion (22.3% of the total) between 1973 and 1981.

Considering all borrowers together, the overall conclusion is that a greater concentration of bond issuance among individual borrowers existed in the data period as a whole compared with the eurocredit market. Therefore 28.5% of total funds raised in the bond markets between 1973 and 1981 was borrowed by Canada and the World Bank, with 69.3% of the total going to the top ten borrowers compared with only 57% in the eurocredit market. The smaller number of countries having access to the external bond markets is clearly reaffirmed by such figures.

Table 10.6 demonstrates that, as in the eurocurrency credit market, public sector borrowers dominate the external bond markets. However, with only 55.9% of total funds going to such borrowers between 1973 and 1981 compared with 60.6% in the eurocredit market, this position of dominance is less marked in the external bond markets. Major borrowers in this sector included central governments (19% of the total) although this share fluctuated considerably, peaking at 37.8% in 1978 when $10.8 billion was raised; public non-financial enterprises (17.6% of the total) and public financial enterprises (12%). The extent to which private sector borrowers have had, in general, relatively greater access to external

TABLE 10.6
External Bonds[1] by Type of Borrower
(OECD Data; Shares in Total)

	1973–1976	1977	1978	1979	1980	1981	Total (1973–81)
Central Government	13.0	21.3	37.8	21.9	18.2	10.8	19.0
State and Local Government	12.1	9.0	5.2	5.2	2.0	6.2	7.2
Public Financial Enterprises	7.9	12.6	11.4	15.5	15.9	12.3	12.0
Public Non-Financial Enterprises	24.8	16.6	11.6	12.0	15.2	18.6	17.6
Private financial enterprises	11.1	13.2	11.4	14.0	17.0	15.1	13.4
Private Non-Financial Enterprises	31.0	27.3	22.5	31.3	31.7	37.1	30.7
Memo							
Public Sector	57.8	59.5	66.1	54.7	51.3	47.8	55.9
Private Sector	42.1	40.5	33.9	45.3	48.7	52.2	44.1

[1] Excluding those issued by Eastern Socialist countries and international organisations.

bond markets than to eurocurrency credit funding is clear from the fact that the single major sectoral borrower was the private non-financial enterprise sector which raised $65.3 billion between 1973 and 1981 amounting to 30.7% of the total. Private financial enterprises borrowed $28.5 billion (13.4% of the total). Overall, the share of the private sector borrowing in the total fluctuated around 40% for much of the period in Table 10.6, before rising above 50% in 1981. This sharp increase in private sector borrowing in bond markets mirrored — although less dramatically — the rise in private sector take-up of eurocredits (Table 9.3). Once again, the increased share of the non-financial enterprises in private borrowing more than accounted for the increase in the sector's overall share in 1981.

Table 10.7 illustrates that, when classified by borrowing sector, the largest share of bond issues bewteen 1974 and mid-1981 was for 'general purpose' (27.7%) with a further 25.8% going to banking and finance. The share going to industry at 21.4% was higher than the comparable share (for manufacturing) recorded in the eurocredit market, reflecting in part the greater share of private sector borrowing through external bond markets recorded in Table 10.6. Public utilities accounted for 12.6% of the total volume of funds raised while the reliance of energy and transport sectors on bond financing at 5.6% and 4.9% respectively over the data period is significantly lower than their dependence on eurocurrency bank lending.

TABLE 10.7
External Bonds by Borrowing Sector[1]
(IBRD Data; Shares in Total)

	1974–1976	1977	1978	1979	1980	1981[2]	Total (1974–81)
Banking and Finance	21.7	25.3	23.7	25.8	32.7	30.1	25.8
Transport	5.6	4.2	4.5	5.2	4.1	6.0	4.9
Public Utilities	20.1	9.7	7.2	7.6	10.9	15.7	12.6
Petroleum and Natural Gas	4.6	10.7	4.1	4.1	5.1	6.0	5.6
Natural Resources	1.8	1.4	0.3	0.3	0.3	—	0.9
Industry	21.7	18.0	16.8	25.8	25.2	22.3	21.4
Public and Community Purposes	0.6	0.7	0.3	1.0	1.0	3.0	1.0
General Purpose	24.0	30.1	42.6	29.6	20.7	16.9	27.7

[1] Excluding international organisations.
[2] First half only.

The currency distributions of the two segments of the external bond markets are set out in Tables 10.8 and 10.9 with the major components graphed in Figs 10.1 and 10.2.[11] In the euro-bond sector, dollar issues amounted to $85.2 billion between 1973 and 1981 accounting for 63.8% of the total; although this is a position of considerable dominance, the role of the non-dollar currencies in this sector and even more so in the foreign bond sector is considerably higher than in figures for eurocurrency credit commitments. The dollar's share in total euro-bond issues has fluctuated greatly over the data period and gradually fell from 82.8% in 1964–8[12] to 63.6% in 1969–73 and as low as 48.3% in 1978. The weakness of the dollar, particularly in 1971–3 and again in 1976–8 was the primary cause of this declining share with dollar bonds difficult to sell in these conditions. Combined with the general rise in short-term interest-rates this factor counteracted in part the initial advantages of the dollar in this market, namely the lack of restrictions on dollar euro-bond issues and the overwhelming importance of the currency as the international monetary system's key reserve asset and pivot of the pre-1970s fixed exchange rate system. However, since the end of 1979 the dollar's decline has been arrested and the share of dollar

[11] See 'The Use of Currencies for External Bond Issues' *Financial Market Trends*, November 1980 for a more detailed discussion of the currency breakdown of bond markets and a general overview of the issues that arise from the use of currencies for external bond offerings.

[12] All data for the pre-1974 period in this section are taken from 'The Use of Currencies for External Bond Issues' op.cit.

TABLE 10.8
Eurobonds by Currency of Denomination
(OECD Data; Shares in Total)

	1973–1976	1977	1978	1979	1980	1981	Total (1973–81)
US Dollar	59.5	63.3	48.3	58.9	66.3	80.2	63.8
Deutschemark	21.8	26.8	41.0	27.5	17.2	5.2	21.6
Canadian Dollar	5.9	3.4	—	2.7	1.3	2.6	3.1
Netherlands Guilder	4.8	1.9	2.4	1.8	2.7	1.6	2.7
French Franc	1.5	—	0.6	2.2	4.4	2.0	1.8
Sterling	0.2	1.1	1.8	1.7	4.9	2.0	1.8
Kuwaiti Dinar	1.5	0.7	3.0	2.2	0.1	1.5	1.4
EUA (European Unit of Account)	2.2	—	1.3	1.8	0.4	0.5	1.1
Japanese Yen	—	0.6	0.5	0.7	1.5	1.5	0.8
SDR	0.5	—	—	0.6	0.1	1.5	0.5
ECU	0.1	—	0.2	—	—	0.9	0.2

issues in total euro-bonds reached 80.2% in 1981, reflecting renewed strength of the currency over this period.

The only other significant currency of denomination in the euro-bond markets is the Deutschemark. Issues in this currency totalled $28.8 billion between 1973 and 1981 a share of 21.6%. However this proportion has also fluctuated dramatically within the data period from 41% in 1978 to the exceptionally low share of 5.2% in 1981. These individual figures illustate the general point that the share of DM euro-bonds has moved inversely with the dollar's share. Also, the

TABLE 10.9
Foreign Bonds by Market Country
(OECD Data; Shares in Total)

	1973–1976	1977	1978	1979	1980	1981	Total (1973–81)
USA	50.8	46.2	29.7	21.8	15.2	35.6	36.2
Switzerland	25.9	29.9	34.9	47.4	41.6	38.2	34.6
Germany	6.3	9.1	7.8	13.1	27.6	5.6	10.4
Japan	3.6	8.4	21.9	13.3	8.6	12.8	10.3
Saudi Arabia	3.6	3.9	1.2	0.2	0.7	—	1.9
Netherlands	2.1	1.1	1.6	0.8	1.8	2.3	1.7
UK	0.1	—	—	—	1.0	4.3	0.8
Belgium	1.1	0.2	0.7	0.7	0.4	0.3	0.7
France	0.4	0.8	1.0	1.0	1.5	0.4	0.7
Luxembourg	0.3	0.5	1.0	1.0	1.1	0.6	0.7
Venezuela	1.3	—	—	—	—	—	0.4

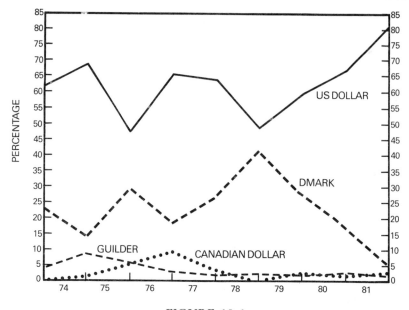

FIGURE 10.1

Shares of euro-bond market by currency

DM share of this market was, until 1980–1, increasing gradually, having stood at only 13.4% in 1964–8; this reflected the desire of investors to diversify their asset portfolios as response to both an increase in the level of wealth and the general weakness of the dollar over that period. A number of other currencies had minor shares of the euro-bond market between 1973 and 1981, namely the Canadian dollar (3.1%), Dutch guilder (2.7%), French franc and Sterling (both 1.8%) and the Kuwait dinar (1.4%). Finally, euro-bonds denominated in composite currencies or currency 'baskets' totalled only $2.4 billion between 1973 and 1981 (1.8% of the total) of which $1.5 billion were denominated in European Units of Account. This represents little change from the share of such bonds in the late-1960s, despite the expectation that this proportion would rise over time.

The dominance of the dollar in the foreign bond sector between 1973 and 1981 (Table 10.9) was much less marked than in the euro-bond sector. However despite a lower concentration of such foreign offerings by currency than in the euro-bond sector the market was still dominated by only four currencies — the US dollar, the Swiss Franc, the Japanese Yen and the Deutschemark.

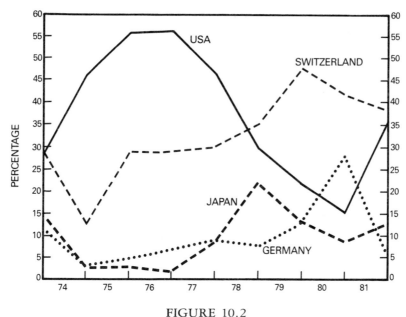

FIGURE 10.2
Shares of foreign bond market by market country

It is clear from Fig. 10.2 that considerable annual fluctuations have occured in the shares of individual sectors in the foreign bond markets. These are primarily related to the regulatory stance of the monetary authorities in the various market countries, in addition to the conventional exchange rate and interest rate considerations that also impinge on the euro-bond sectors. For example, the Swiss Franc share rose from only 6.4% in 1964–8 to 28.7% in 1975–6 and attained its high average share of 34.6% for the 1973–81 period due primarily to the large issue volume of $17 billion in 1979–80 (nearly 45% of the total). This recent surge in Swiss Franc bond issue was closely related to the removal of restrictions on the investment of overseas funds in such foreign bond issues and the temporary shift in policy away from targetting the money supply to targetting on the exchange-rate leading to a control of the upward movement of the currency in foreign exchange markets. Similarly the doubling of DM foreign bond issues to $5.0 billion in 1980 (27.6% of the total) reflected official concern with the substantial oil-induced external payments deficit in Germany in 1980 and, in particular, the reduction of the minimum maturity of DM foreign issues sold to overseas investors from 4 to 2 years.

The share of the dollar in the foreign bond market fell from 67.9% in 1964–8 to 56.1% in 1976 and only 16.7% in 1980 before rising again to 35.6% in 1981. This long-term decline in the dollar's share reflects in large measure the general liberalisation of conditions on the investment of overseas funds in all non-dollar foreign bond markets, not simply those markets in Switzerland and Germany alone. The share of issues in Japanese Yen reached 21.9% in 1978 compared to only 2.5% in 1974 and averaged 10.3% over the whole 1973–81 period. Finally, the shares of foreign bonds denominated in Saudi-Arabian riyals and Dutch guilders were each sufficiently high to exceed 1% of the total in the data period as a whole.

BORROWING CONDITIONS

Borrowing conditions in the external bond market are conventionally represented by data on:

  i) The maturity of a bond offering.
 ii) The initial offering yield on a bond issue.

Table 10.10 sets out a maturity breakdown of external bond issues as reported by the World Bank where the original maturity is defined as the period between the expected settlement date and the date of final maturity. An immediate observation from Table 10.10 is the pattern of considerably longer maturities in the external bond markets in comparison to the market for eurocurrency credits (Table 9.7). therefore over the period from 1974 to 1981, 11.5% of total

TABLE 10.10
External Bonds by Maturity
(IBRD Data; Shares in Total[1])

	1974–1976	1977	1978	1979	1980	1981[2]	Total (1974–81)
Over 1–3 years	3.3	3.0	2.9	2.6	4.4	7.3	3.6
Over 3–5 years	21.2	19.4	21.3	20.6	19.1	27.7	21.1
Over 5–7 years	20.2	22.7	14.7	18.8	22.7	15.5	19.5
Over 7–10 years	20.8	20.5	23.2	26.2	33.2	26.2	24.4
Over 10–15 years	13.4	20.5	25.3	20.1	14.6	14.5	17.7
Over 15–20 years	8.7	5.8	6.4	5.3	2.6	1.5	5.8
Over 20 years	9.4	6.4	3.2	5.0	1.8	4.9	5.7
Weighted Average Original Maturity (years)	10.03	9.30	9.09	9.05	8.64	8.82	9.29

[1] Excluding bonds of unknown maturity.
[2] First half only.

external bonds had an original maturity of over fifteen years with as many as 5.7% being over 20 years.

In general, bond maturities have fluctuated rather less during the observation period in Table 10.10 than was the case with eurocurrency credits. Therefore, although the weighted average maturity dropped sharply from 10.88 years in 1974 to 8.89 years in 1975, it subsequently levelled out at around the nine-year level; in 1980 it fell slightly again to 8.64 years before rising to 8.82 years in the first half of 1981. Similarly, the share of total external bonds having a maturity of seven years or less jumped from 27.9% in 1974 to 52.2% one year later but soon settled down at around 40% before a further rise in the first half of 1981 to 50.5%. Over a period as a whole this proportion stood at 44.2%. The pattern was therefore for a more rapid improvement in borrowing conditions after 1975 than the gradual amelioration felt in the eurocredit market with considerable stability of bond maturities being recorded in the latter half of the 1970s. The slight decline in average maturities in 1980–1 in the external bond markets also mirrors a similar development in the eurocredit market (as demonstrated in Fig. 9.2).

The major problem in commenting on the time paths of secondary market yields on external bonds is the difficulty of obtaining reliable data on particular bond types and of ensuring consistency between the sources of this information. The construction of such a reliable picture of some major bonds yields is, however, attempted in Fig. 10.3. The yield fom holding a particular bond depends on the rate of interest and maturity of the issue and on whether the bond is held to maturity. Therefore, the yields in Fig. 10.3 are initial offering yields to maturity and so are calculated on the basis that the bonds are held to maturity. In addition, the yields are discounted semi-annually to facilitate cross-bond yielded comparisons. A reconsideration of Tables 10.8 and 10.9 indicates that the yields represented in Fig. 10.3 refer to those on the major bond types in the foreign (US and Swiss) and euro (dollar and Deutschemark) bond markets.[13]

[13] The US foreign bond yields are as published in various issues of 'Borrowing in International Capital Markets' and are weighted average yields for publicly-offered bonds by industrial companies. The other three series are taken from various issues of Morgan Guaranty's 'World Financial Markets'. The dollar euro-bond yields are calculated as an (unweighted) average of ten issues made by US companies, the DM euro-bond yields from ten issues made by European companies and the Swiss Franc foreign bond yields from four issues made by US companies.

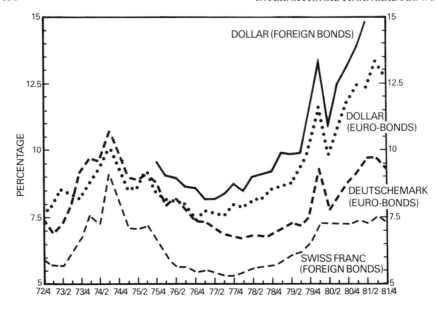

FIGURE 10.3
External bond yields

Despite the use of different sources, markets and borrowers[14] it is clear from Fig. 10.3 that the pattern of yields is fairly consistent across the bond samples chosen. Therefore, peak yields were recorded in the third quarter of 1974 when DM euro-bond yields reached an average of 10.8% before a general decline in the next four years. Continuing this example, the average DM euro-bond yield fell to 6.7% in the first quarter of 1978 while that on Swiss Franc foreign bonds fell equally dramatically from 9.2% in late 1974 to 5.3% at the end 1977. However, since 1978, an upward rebound of external bond yields has occured with, in particular, the yields on foreign bonds floated on the US market rising very steeply to 14.8% in mid-1981. Despite these movements, the short-term variations in external bond yields are considerably lower than those noted in Fig. 9.2 for LIBOR and also than other eurocurrency deposit rates.[15] This is exemplified by the development of a significant reverse yield gap as

[14] However as all the companies noted in Footnote 13 are 'prime' borrowers, this variation in borrower type is likely to be of limited importance in Fig. 10.3.

[15] The standard deviation of the six-month LIBOR used in Fig. 9.2 was 3.86 and that of the average dollar euro-bond yield was 1.63 between 1973 and 1981.

eurodollar rates soared in late 1979/early 1980 and again in mid-1981.

A major information gap in the data on external bonds, as was the case for eurocurrency credits, is the relative paucity of information on the fee structure of individual issues. Again, the delicate issue of confidentiality limits the amount of published detail in this respect although for a 'true' picture of the cost to a boroower of floating a new external bond, a considseration of the fee structure in addition to the interest rate on the bond is essential.

SUMMARY

It is clear that the basic format of published information on new external bond issues is similar in style to that available for eurocurrency credits. Indeed, as the OECD, World Bank and Morgan Guaranty all have done, the two should be considered together with the overall survey corresponding to borrowing in the international capital markets as a whole. The conclusion made a the end of Chapter 9 is equally valid here namely that despite important inter-source differences in certain aspects of the data on external bond issues, there is a considerable amount of consistency between sources on the overall totals involved.

Section 4
External Debt Statistics

Chapter 11

The World Bank's Debtor Reporting System

INTRODUCTION AND ORIGINS

In addition to its statistics on new borrowing in international capital markets (the CMS) discussed in Section 3, the World Bank has for many years published information on the outstanding external debt of major developing countries. This is compiled in the Bank's Debtor Reporting System and is discussed in detail in this chapter; it is at present the major source of external debt statistics.[1] Essentially external debt data refer to the STOCK of outstanding debt at one point in time in contrast to FLOW data on new capital market borrowing (although some data on flow changes in external debt are also published by the DRS). In this limited sense, the figures are conceptually closer to the banking data of Section 2 than the capital markets data of Section 3.

The DRS originated in 1951, when the World Bank began to require member countries to furnish it with details of outstanding external public and publicly-guaranteed private debt statistics.[2] In effect, therefore, any country that had at any time borrowed from the

[1] The concentration in this chapter on World Bank data should not be taken to mean, however, that external debt data are not published by other organisations. In particular, the OECD publishes data on the external debt of developing countries alongside the broader operation of the collection of data on the transfers of funds from Development Assistance Committee (DAC) members. These two types of data published by the OECD, which are the subject of Chapter 12, interlink considerably with DRS data. (See OECD 1974, 1982a.) In addition, Morgan Guaranty Trust Company have at times attempted to estimate outstanding external debt (e.g. Morgan Guaranty 1976, 1983). See also Abbott 1981, Solomon 1981, *The Economist* 1978, 1982.
[2] For a very detailed survey of the history of the DRS, see Saxe (1979).

International Bank for Reconstruction and Development (IBRD) and International Development Association (IDA) parts of the World Bank group was required to provide this information. Initially the information was published, in increasing detail, in successive World Bank *Annual Reports* and in a series of general studies of the debt problems of developing countries (e.g. Avramovic, 1958, 1965). Publication was made more formal from 1966 with the incorporation of these data into a new Bank document which eventually (in 1973) became known as '*World Debt Tables*'[3] and has been published since then on an annual basis. EC-167 has been gradually improved during the 1970s and in recent years has carried a series of supplements to the main document including new debt information as it becomes available, to overcome, in part, the problem of long lags in the reporting of this information by certain countries.

In 1970, countries were asked for the first time to provide information on outstanding private non-guaranteed debt. At first, such figures as were available were included in supplements to '*World Debt Tables*' primarily due to the small number of countries that report such data and the non-standard form in which this information is made available to the DRS. However the issue of '*World Debt Tables*' containing data to the end of 1980, published in December 1981, included data on such private non-guaranteed debt for the first time.[4]

The initial objective of the DRS was to furnish the Bank itself with full details of a potential borrower's current external debt position. Essentially then the information available in the DRS is for internal use in the assessment of a project in a particular country. In addition, however, a more general appraisal of a country's financial position is facilitated by such data while the publicity that the Bank has gained through the quality of these figures should not be overlooked as a major advantage of the DRS.

The data included in the DRS come from three major sources. Firstly, and of overwhelming importance, are the reports submitted by developing countries:

'on the annual status, transactions and terms of the external debt of public agencies and that of private ones guaranteed by a public agency in the debtor country.[5]

These are requested by the DRS at the end of each calendar year and

[3] This document carried the codes of EC-149 and EC-156 before the current code of EC-167 was established.
[4] EC-167/81.
[5] *World Debt Tables* (1982/3), p.xvii.

are augmented by quarterly reports of new debt commitments. For public and publicly-guaranteed private debt, new debts are reported on a loan-by-loan basis while for private non-guaranteed debt a consolidated report is accepted by the DRS. In general there is no requirement for countries to report information on debt owed to the World Bank itself, the IMF or regional development banks as these institutions, in principle, report transactions with debtor countries direct to the DRS.[6]

Secondly, the above information is both verified and at times supplemented from a variety of sources including:

'statements and reports of several regional development banks and government lending agencies, as well as the reports received by the World Bank under the Creditor Reporting System (CRS) from the members of the Development Assistance Committee (DAC) of the OECD.[7]

When such procedures are used to supplement the basic reporting of debt transactions by debtor countries this is more likely to be due to inefficient and inadequate reporting than deliberate concealment of the information. For many developing countries, particularly where debt information is computerized, the verification and supplementation procedures are not required.

Thirdly, information gained from the previous two sources is usually augmented when a World Bank mission is sent to a particular developing country. By gathering data and providing technical assistance, a greater and more efficient flow of debt information may be derived (Holsen, 1978).

The most recently published DRS information on outstanding external public and publicly-guaranteed debt covers one hundred and one developing countries. Although generally including data to the end of 1981, no information beyond the end of 1978 was available for three of these countries — Afghanistan, Iran and Iraq. At the time of publication of the annual document however, data for only fifty-three countries were actual figures, with those for twenty-one countries being preliminary. For the remaining twenty-four countries DRS estimates were included.[8]

Despite this coverage, the number of countries included in the DRS is significantly lower than the figure of over 160 included in DAC data. This is for two main reasons.[9] Firstly, the DAC makes use of

[6] Unfortunately the reporting of debt transactions by certain regional development banks is itself inefficient, leading to problems in this respect.
[7] *World Debt Tables* (1982/3), p.xvii.
[8] *World Debt Tables* (1982/3), p.xviii.
[9] *World Debt Tables* EC-167/77, p.49.

creditor reports in addition to the debtor reports of the World Bank and so is able to augment information in this way, given that countries who have not borrowed from the World Bank group do not have to report to the DRS. Secondly, DAC data specify a broader country coverage including many 'quasi-territories' such as Gibraltar, Macao and certain small Caribbean states, for example St. Lucia, that may have been linked at times in past history to larger countries. Many of these types of country are not separately identified in the DRS. Therefore in principle the DRS includes nearly all the major developing country debtors although there are examples of countries that have borrowed in recent years on international capital markets (and therefore are included in the CMS) but are excluded from the DRS. These include Kuwait, Qatar, Saudi Arabia, United Arab Emirates, Antigua, Bermuda, Netherlands Antilles, Nauru and Mozambique.

Data on private non-guaranteed debt were available for 1981 for forty-three countries only. Actual figures were published for eighteen countries while, for a further twenty-five countries whose debt of this type was considered significant at the global level, estimates were made by the DRS which were included in regional totals, although not set out in individual country pages. This figure is considerably lower than the number of countries reporting public and publicly-guaranteed private debt data due to the enormous variation in debt types in this sector and the lack of reliable procedures in many countries for the collection of this information. In the case of both debt types the principle is adopted that available data or estimates must be sufficiently reliable before they are included in EC-167.

Countries are requested to report debt data on a sectoral basis by both debtor and creditor. Table 11.1 sets out the degree of detail requested by the World Bank and compares the sectorisation adopted in the reported and published figures. On the debtor side, it is noticeable that although a fairly detailed sectoral breakdown is requested by the World Bank from reporting countries, the information is published in EC-167 in aggregate form. Therefore by adopting this procedure, presumably for justifiable reasons of confidentiality, considerable detail available to the World Bank is not published.[10]

Finally certain procedures for the conversion of non-dollar data into dollar values are adopted by the DRS given that debt information is typically reported to the World Bank in currencies in which the debts are repayable or in which the transactions occurred. For *stock* data on outstanding external debt, the exchange rate ruling at the end of the period in question is used, while for *flow* data an average rate

[10] The creditor classification by sector is discussed later in the chapter.

TABLE 11.1
Debtor/Creditor Classification in DRS

Reported Information	Published Information

Debtor Classification
  Public and Publicly-Guaranteed
  Private Debt
  — Central Government
  — Central Bank
  — Public Corporations
  — Mixed Enterprises
  — Official Development Banks
  — Local government
  — All other if publicly-guaranteed
	In aggregate

Private Non-Guaranteed Debt
  — Commercial Banks
  — Direct Investment Enterprises
    (excluding commercial banks)
  — All other enterprises
	In aggregate

Creditor Classification
  Public and Publicly-Guaranteed
  Private Debt
  Official
  — Bilateral
  — Multilateral[1]
 	
  Private
  — Suppliers (Exporters)
  — Commercial Banks and other
    financial institutions
  — Bonds
  — Other (excluding direct invest-
    ments).
	As for reporting except that commercial banks, other financial institutions and bonds are combined as 'financial markets'[2]

Private Non-Guaranteed Debt
  NON-STANDARD but full break-
    down is:
 	
  Official
  — Bilateral and multilateral
 	
  Private
  — Commercial Banks and other
    financial institutions (Financial
    Institutions)
  — Foreign parents and affiliates
  — Suppliers and all other private
    creditors
	As for reporting.

[1] Debt owed to the IBRD and IDA are separately identified in the total of multilateral debt.

[2] Prior to EC-167/81, debt held in the form of external bonds was separately listed in *World Debt Tables*.

for the relevant period is used. For data on projected debt service payments, the end-period rate for the period in which these projections are made is used. The only exceptions to these rules are for debt repayable in multiple currencies, goods or services or debt with a constant value repayment clause all of which are measured at book value.

DEFINITIONS

External public debt is defined by the DRS as:

'debt owed to non-residents repayable in foreign currency, goods, or services, which has an original or extended maturity of over one year and which is an obligation of either a public debtor or a private debtor, publicly guaranteed for repayment'.[11]

The category of a public debtor includes national governments, political sub-divisions (e.g. provinces or states) or agencies of either and autonomous public bodies.

Specific problems may arise over the interpretation of the terms 'external' and 'public'. A non-resident is defined in the DRS in accordance with the procedures adopted in the IMF Balance of Payments Manual, namely any person, agency or organisation physically located outside the country of origin. Therefore residency not nationality is crucial in DRS statistics. In cases where despite the above definitions it is not clear whether a particular debt is held, or guaranteed, by the public sector one of the following criteria should be satisfied for its inclusion in the public debt category. Either the budget of the organisation that incurs the debt must be subject to central government approval, the government must own over half of the voting stock of the organisation, over half the members of the board of directors must be governemnt representatives or finally in case of default the state must be liable to cover that organisation's debt.[12]

Any private debt that does not satisfy any of these conditions is included in the DRS's definition of external private (non-guaranteed) debt. Specifically, external private debt has all the characteristics of the public debt definition noted above except that a public guarantee is absent. The only exception to this rule is that private debts

[11] *World Debt Tables* EC-167/8: p.iii.
[12] This latter criterion is effectively equivalent to the public guarantee of a private debt.

guaranteed for exchange transfer *only* are included in the category of non-guaranteed debt.

Clearly the categories of debt covered by these definitions are both broad and numerous. The concept includes 'loans, lines of credit, bonds whether publicly-issued or privately-placed and revolving credits' (Saxe, 1979). Data are also collected by the DRS on commitments as yet undisbursed to give an indication of possible future trends in external debt.

However the concepts of external debt are not completely comprehensive. Omissions from the statistics should be considered in two groupings. Firstly, certain types of 'debt' are omitted due to the definition of external debt utilised by the DRS, while secondly inadequate and incomplete reporting of certain transactions may reduce the coverage of DRS data.

The most notable deliberate omission from the DRS is data on short-term debt. The maturity of a debt is calculated as the time-period that elapses from the initial signature of a credit arrangement to the final maturity date (ignoring 'rollover' dates in the case of floating rate loans). Any debt with a maturity defined in this way of one year or less is omitted from the DRS, a procedure that is consistent with the World Bank's CMS. Three further reasons may be advanced for this neglect of short-term debt. Firstly and very simply, the reporting of such debt may not be justifiable given that it may be repaid and the transaction completed before the data on such debt are processed by the DRS and published. Secondly, as in the field of syndicated eurocurrency credits, the whole concept of short-term debt is something of a 'grey' area with many debt transactions of different types that may at times be indistinguishable from each other. Finally, when the DRS began its work such short-term debt was negligible. This is no longer a valid argument, however. Katz (1979) estimated that such short-term debt totalled $50–60 billion at the end of 1977 (around 20% of the total of external debt). It is likely to have risen considerably since then, primarily due to the increase in short-term borrowing consequent upon the high interest cost of long-term finance, in particular since the end of 1978, and the tendency for most short-term debt to be liable to interest charges at market rates (in contrast to some long-term concessional finance) (Nowzad 1982). It has been estimated that debt of less than one year to maturity stood at around $130 billion at the end of 1981 (Gasser and Roberts, 1982) and may now constitute as much as 23% of total developing country debt. To ignore short-term debt is therefore a significant omission which will bias downwards the DRS data and, more seriously, its estimates of countries' debt-servicing capacity. Indeed it may be more appropriate, in an ideal world, to use a type of cash flow approach to estimating a country's debt servicing burden that specifically takes account of the rapid turnover of short-term funding (Amex Bank, 1982).

Secondly, the DRS excludes reserve-related transactions with the IMF (except Trust Fund loans) on the grounds that detailed statistics on outstanding borrowing by all countries in this way are published by the IMF itself. These figures are described in Chapters 13 and 14. At the end of 1981, outstanding Fund credit against developing countries totalled SDR 12.8 billion, equivalent to $14.9 billion.

Thirdly, the DRS omits all debts repayable in the domestic currency of the debtor country. Fourthly, no data on direct investment are included in the DRS except to the extent that contractual obligations of direct investment enterprises to foreign parent companies are now included in external private non-guaranteed debt data. However, at this early stage, such data are of relatively low quality as many countires do not separately report such transactions to the DRS. Finally, all grants are omitted from EC-167 as, by definition, they are not repayable, while data on these are separately drawn by the World Bank from the OECD and recorded in an individual table in the Bank's *Annual Report*. Despite the concept of a grant as a transfer of funds that is fully concessional, the DRS does still include 'grant-like loans' which are defined as debt with a grant element of 25% or above.[13]

The main type of debt that is included, in principle, in EC-167 but where, it is believed, information reported to the DRS is seriously incomplete is military debt. There is no requirement for military debts to be separately identified by reporting countires and due to their political sensitivity it is likely that many countries receiving credit in this form (particularly where the debt transactions are not computerised by the country concerned) do not report this information in full or conceivably at all. Clearly this is, by definition, an area where the quality of data is uncertain and where it would be very difficult to persuade many borrowers to provide such information fully.

Despite the situation on military debt, the DRS data, within the confines of the concept of debt utilised by the World Bank, are likely to be virtually complete for many countries in the case of external public debt. This is due both to the increasingly common practice of computerisation by individual countries of their debt and to the

---

[13] Such loans are labelled 'concessional' by the DRS when this 25% limit is exceeded despite the fact that up to 75% of the flow of funds has to be repaid in the future.

sophisticated cross-checking techniques of the DRS itself. Where there is no computerisation of this information, incomplete reporting is more likely to exist. However, the coverage of the data on private non-guaranteed debt is much less complete. Apart from the fact that fewer countries report such debt anyway, the quality of the information that is reported to the DRS varies enormously from country to country and probably from year to year for any one country. In part, this is due to the absence of any requirement for countries to report such debt on a loan-by-loan basis. The resultant consolidated reporting of private non-guaranteed debt — due to the perceived privacy of much private debt and the weight of work that would fall on the DRS if a loan-by-loan listings were tendered — is likely *per se* to lead to a lower capture rate compared to public debt. Therefore, the World Bank is aware of the need to improve both the quality and country coverage of the private non-guaranteed debt data in particular.

THE DATA

Total External Debt

In this section, external debt data compiled by the DRS are set out in a number of forms. Table 11.2 quantifies the main aggregates of outstanding external debt (both public and private) for 1973 and on an annual basis from 1976 to 1981. Disbursed external debt rose by nearly three times from $117.7 billion in 1973 to $461.9 billion at the end of 1981, with the average annual increase amounting to 18.6%. Although this is a rapid rate of growth, the figures in Table 11.2 do not show that external debt actually rose at an average rate of over 20% per annum in the four years to 1973; in real terms too the rate of growth of external debt was higher in the earlier period. In fact, the real external debt of developing countries rose by only 56% between 1972 and 1979 (Kincaid, 1981). The most notable development within the total of external debt has been the fall in the share of public debt (excluding publicly-guaranteed private debt) from 45.9% in 1973 to 36.5% in 1981 with the share of private debt rising accordingly to 63.5%. Within the total of private debt the share of non-guaranteed debt fell from 48.9% in 1973 to 32% in 1979. It is clear therefore that the debt type that experienced the most rapid rate of growth was private debt guaranteed by the public sector which rose more than fivefold between 1973 and 1981 from 27.8% of the overall total to 43.2%. In consequence, the share of public debt and

TABLE 11.2
Outstanding External Debt of Developing Countries
(IBRD Data; $ Billion; End-Year).

		Disbursed Debt				Total including undisbursed Debt[1]
		Private Debt				
	Public Debt	Guaranteed	Non-Guaranteed	Total	Total Debt	
1973	54.0	32.7	31.0	63.7	117.7	150.6
1976	83.4	71.2	40.8	112.0	195.4	263.5
1977	99.6	93.4	47.0	140.4	240.0	321.7
1978	119.0	125.7	54.1	179.8	298.7	398.5
1979	134.3	154.6	63.3	217.9	352.3	467.7
1980	154.6	176.5	73.3	249.8	404.5	529.2
1981	168.5	199.6	93.8	293.4	461.9	592.4
Shares in Total (%)						
1973	45.9	27.8	26.3			
1976	42.7	36.4	20.9			
1977	41.5	38.9	19.6			
1978	39.8	42.1	18.1			
1979	38.1	43.9	18.0			
1980	38.2	43.6	18.1			
1981	36.5	43.2	20.3			

[1] Undisbursed public and publicly-guaranteed debt only.

publicly-guaranteed private debt in the total rose from 73.7% in 1973 to 79.7% in 1981.

Some of the *flow* data published by the DRS are set out in Table 11.3 in aggregate form for 1979–81. In each of the three parts of this table Line F corresponds to the stock of outstanding debt at the end of the year in question. The flow data in Lines A-E determine the change in that stock position over a particular twelve-month period. For example, the outstanding external debt at the end of 1978 of $298.7 billion (Line 3F) was increased by the *flow* transactions during 1979 (Lines 3A–3E) to yield a new total of outstanding debt of $352.3 billion at the end of 1979.[14]

[14] The data in Table 11.3 are such that, in general, Equation 11.3 is not satisfied exactly. This is for two reasons. Firstly, cancellations of debt may occur. Secondly, given the different procedures for converting stock and flow debt data into dollar values (noted earlier in the chapter), valuation effects are present.

TABLE 11.3
Flow Data on External Debt During Calendar Years
(IBRD Data; $ Billion)

	1978	1979	1980	1981
1 Public and Publicity-Guaranteed Private Debt				
A Net flow (addition to debt) equal		45.9	44.2	49.1
B Disbursements minus		74.9	72.1	79.6
C Amortisation		29.0	27.9	30.5
D Debt service equals		46.0	51.3	59.2
C Amortisation plus		29.0	27.9	30.5
E Interest		17.0	23.4	28.7
F Outstanding Debt	244.6	288.9	331.2	368.1
2 Private Non-Guaranteed Debt				
A Net Flows equal		8.6	10.7	17.4
B Disbursements minus		19.3	22.6	30.4
C Amortisation		10.8	11.8	13.0
D Debt Service equals		16.3	19.1	23.9
C Amortisation plus		10.8	11.8	13.0
E Interest		5.5	7.2	10.9
F Outstanding Debt	54.1	63.3	73.3	93.3
3 Total External Debt				
A Net flows equal		54.5	55.0	66.5
B Disbursements minus		94.3	94.7	110.0
C Amortisation		39.8	39.7	43.5
D Debt Service equals		62.3	70.4	83.1
C Amortisation plus		39.8	39.7	43.5
E Interest		22.5	30.7	39.6
F Outstanding Debt	298.7	352.3	404.5	461.9

The relationships in Table 11.3 may be defined in the following way

$$NF_t = D_t - A_t \qquad (11.1)$$
$$DS_t = A_t + I_t \qquad (11.2)$$
$$ED_t = ED_{t-1} + NF_t \qquad (11.3)$$
and

where NF, D, A, DS, I and ED refer to Net Flows, Disbursements, Amortisation, Debt Service, Interest Payments and Outstanding External Debt respectively while t is a time subscript. Strict definitions of the terms newly introduced in Equations 11.1–11.3 are given by the DRS.[15] Disbursements (D) refer to those loan commitments (the total of loans for which contracts are signed in the year specified) actually drawn during the year in question. With amortisation (A) representing repayments of principal, net flows or net lending (NF)

[15] e.g. *World Debt Tables* EC-167/8, pp. v, vi.

are defined in Equation 1.1 as disbursements minus amortisation. Debt service payments (DS) include both amortisation and interest payments (I) and are defined in this way in Equation 11.2. At times, the division of particular debt service payments into repayments of principal and payments of interests is not clear; in such cases, that part of the payments over which uncertainty exists is included in the amortisation data. Finally, Equation 11.3 states that the change in the stock of outstanding debt (ED) from one year to the next is determined by the size of net flows (notwithstanding the information in Footnote 14). This confirms that external debt data in stock form exclude undisbursed debt and future interest obligations and are presented net of repayments.

In 1981, total disbursements of $110 billion were offset in part by amortisation of $43.5 billion giving a residual of net flows totalling $66.5 billion. This figure was larger than that in 1980 despite the lower amortisation of that year, as disbursements rose sharply in 1981. Amortisation payments as a proportion of gross new borrowing (disbursements) have varied around the 40% level since 1973 (Katz, 1979). Debt service payments have risen rapidly during the 1970s from $18.3 billion in 1973 (Katz, 1979) to $83.1 billion in 1981. Within this total, while amortisation payments rose more than threefold from $12.8 billion to $43.5 billion over this period, interest payments increased even more rapidly from $5.4 billion to $39.6 billion between 1973 and 1981. Therefore while 29.7% of debt service was accounted for by interest payments in 1973, this share had risen to 47.7% by 1981. This increase is not in itself particularly significant and a much more dramatic picture of the recent increased burden of debt service is given by the evidence that, in 1981, 75.5% of the value of new disbursements of debt was 'accounted for' by debt service payments compared to 58.7% in 1973, while, in 1981, interest payments amounted to 59.5% of the value of 'net flows' compared to only 34.4% in 1973; both these figures illustrate the extent to which funds newly acquired by developing countries have been increasingly allocated to the servicing of previously-accumulated debt.

Public Debt
(including publicly-guaranteed private debt)

The majority of the tables published by the DRS refer to external public and publicly-guaranteed debt only. Table 11.4 allocates the aggregate figures from Table 11.2 (disbursed debt only) to the cate-

TABLE 11.4
External Public Debt by Creditor
(IBRD Data: $ Billion; End-Year)

	Official Creditors			Private Creditors[1]				Total Debt	Memo Share of Variable Rate Debt in Total
	Govern-ments	International organisations	Total	Suppliers	Financial Markets	Other	Total		
1973	41.0	12.9	54.0	10.5	21.1	1.2	32.7	86.7	15.7[2]
1976	60.8	22.6	83.4	14.3	54.9	2.0	71.2	154.6	22.6
1977	71.0	28.6	99.6	17.2	74.7	1.5	93.4	193.0	24.5
1978	83.6	35.4	119.0	21.0	103.3	1.4	125.7	244.6	27.0
1979	91.7	42.6	134.3	21.2	132.2	1.2	154.6	288.9	31.7
1980	103.2	51.4	154.6	21.4	154.4	0.7	176.5	331.2	33.4
1981	109.0	59.5	168.5	19.4	179.6	0.6	199.6	368.1	37.4
Shares in Total (%)									
1973	47.3	14.9		13.3	24.3	1.4			
1976	39.3	14.6		9.2	35.5	1.3			
1977	36.8	14.8		8.9	38.7	0.8			
1978	34.2	14.5		8.6	42.2	0.6			
1979	31.7	14.7		7.3	45.8	0.4			
1980	31.2	15.5		6.5	46.6	0.2			
1981	29.6	16.2		5.3	48.8	0.2			

[1] Guaranteed by the official sector in the debtor country.
[2] 1974.

gories of creditor identified earlier in this chapter (Table 11.1). Debt owed to official creditors is subdivided into that payable to governments (including central banks and autonomous public bodies) known as *bilateral* loans and to international organisations known as *multilateral* loans. The only exception to this rule is that any loan administered by an international organisation on behalf of one donor government only is included as a bilateral debt. Loans from governments to developing countries — mainly in the form of bilateral export credits — grew relatively slowly over the data period rising from $41 billion in 1973 to $109 billion in 1981. The share of such bilateral debt in all debt owed to official creditors therefore fell from 75.9% to 64.7% and in total debt from 47.3% to 29.6% over this period. External debt incurred against international organisations rose more than threefold to $59.5 billion between 1973 and 1981 with its share in debt owed to official creditors rising from 22.9% to 35.4% over this period. Its share in the overall total remained remarkably steady at around 15% between 1973 and 1979 before a significant increase to 16.2%, in 1981.

Much of the debt made available by official creditors to developing countries is on 'concessional' terms. Concessional debt is defined as that having a grant element of 25% or more, calculated as the 'grant equivalent' (the face value of the debt commitment minus the discounted[16] present value of the future flow of repayments of principal and payments of interest) as a percentage of the face value of the commitment. Detailed data on the share of concessional debt in total external debt and some of its components were published by the DRS to the end of 1979, with summary data only since then. Some of this information is set out in Table 11.5.[17]

Although more than doubling in size from $44.6 billion in 1974 to $103.8 billion, concessional debt has grown relatively slowly compared to total public debt with its share falling accordingly from 43% to 28.2% over this period. It is likely that the primary cause of this fall was the restriction on the rate of increase of such credit from developed countries, although no data on this specific point are published by the DRS. The share of concessional debt granted by governments in total (official) concessional debt fell from 87.8% in

---

[16] The discount rate used is 10%, consistent with that used by the DAC of the OECD.

[17] Given the share of *total* debt that was on concessional terms at the end of 1980 and 1981, and assuming a continuing decline of just under two percentage points per annum of the share of total concessional debt that is owed to governments, the estimates for 1980–1 in the remainder of Table 11.5 were made. Their accuracy is therefore critically dependent on the validity of the above assumption.

TABLE 11.5

External Public Debt: Proportion of Concessional Debt
(IBRD Data; %; End-Year)

	1974	1976	1977	1978	1979	1980	1981
Proportion of concessional Debt in:							
Bilateral Official Debt	83.6	81.6	81.2	78.7	77.3	74.9[e]	72.8[e]
Multilaterial Official Debt	35.7	36.6	39.3	41.1	41.2	41.6[e]	41.0[e]
Total Official Debt	71.9	69.9	69.2	67.5	65.9	63.8[e]	61.6[e]
Total Debt	43.0	37.9	35.9	33.0	30.3	29.8	28.2
Proportion of Official concessional Debts owed to:							
Governments	87.8	85.7	83.7	81.9	80.1	78.3[e]	76.5[e]
International Organisations	12.2	14.3	16.3	18.1	19.9	21.7[e]	23.5[e]

[e] = estimates

1974 to an estimated figure of 76.5% in 1981, mirroring in part the decline in the share of total debt owed to governments noted in Table 11.4. Overall in 1981, only 72.8% of all debt owed to governments was on concessional terms compared to 83.6% in 1974.

A reverse pattern is apparent from the figures on debt owed to international organisations. The share of such debt on concessional terms has been historically lower than is the case of debt to governments but has risen between 1974 and 1981 from 35.7% of total multilateral debt to an estimate of 41% in 1981. However, all of this increase came in the first part of the period in Table 11.5 and there was no further increase in this share after 1978. Given these trends it was inevitable that the share of multilateral concessional debt in total concessional debt should have increased. In fact, it has virtually doubled from 12.2 %per cent. in 1974 to an estimate of 23.5 per cent. at the end of 1981.

Private debt that carries a public guarantee is subdivided by the DRS into;

  (i) Suppliers' credits
 (ii) Financial credits and
(iii) Other debt.

Suppliers' creditors are mainly short-term 'loans' which arise when a manufacturer or exporter automatically extends credit to the country in question by allowing it time to pay for a shipment of goods. Financial credits include loans from commercial banks and other financial institutions and also the floating of publicly-issued or privately-placed bonds. Finally 'other' debt includes 'debt on account of nationalised properties and unclassified debts.[18]

The growth in the share of total debt owed to private creditors is fully explained by the enormous increase in publicly-guaranteed liabilities to the financial markets from $21.1 billion in 1973 to $179.6 billion in 1981, an average annual growth rate in this period of over 30%. The figures reflect in the main the growth of the eurocurrency market in general and specifically of syndicated eurocurrency credit over this period (Chapter 9). The share of this form of debt in the private debt total rose from 64.5% in 1973 to 90% in 1981 and as a proportion of total public and publicly-guaranteed debt from 24.3 to 48.8% over the same period. With external bond financing still essentially limited to a small group of developing nations, outstanding debt of this type accounted for just over 10% of total debt to the financial markets in 1980, down from over 20% in 1973. The share of bonds in total external debt stood at around 5% at the end of 1980.

[18] *World Debt Tables* EC-167/8, p.v.

(No separate figures on the size and proportion of debt held in the form of external bonds were published by the DRS for 1981.) This rise in the share of external debt owed to the financial markets as a whole has been matched very closely by the rising share of floating interests rate debt in the total from 15.7% in 1974 to 37.4% at the end of 1981. This development has had the effect of generating greater uncertainty over future debt-service commitments which was most clearly felt in 1980–1 when nominal interest rates rose sufficiently rapidly to raise markedly the volume of service payments in those years. (See also Neuhaus, 1982.)

In contrast, suppliers' credits grew much more slowly than bank credits as to a large extent the latter began to replace suppliers' credits as the most convenient source of private sector finance in the 1970s. The share of suppliers' credits in guaranteed debt owed to private creditors fell from 32.1% in 1973 to only 9.7% in 1981 with their share in total public debt falling from 13.3% to 5.3% over the same period.

Turning to available information on outstanding external public debt from the side of the debtors themselves, the DRS groups countries in terms of both region and income and provides, in addition, individual country data. The regional and income groupings are set out in Tables 11.6–11.8 while major country debtors whose debt exceeded $5 billion at the end of 1981 are listed in Table 11.9.

By far the largest regional debt total is that of Latin America and the Caribbean. From a figure of £27.4 billion at the end of 1973, the external debt of this group of countries rose at at an aveage annual rate of 23.2% to stand at $145.1 billion at the end of 1981. The share of this group's debt in the total rose from 31.6% in 1973 to 39.4% in 1981. However this figure was heavily concentrated with Brazil ($44 billion) and Mexico ($42.6 billion) accounting for 59.7% of the debt of Latin American and Caribbean countries at the end of 1981. In fact, these two countries — the two individual largest country debtors in each year since 1976 — accounted for 23.5% of total external public debt in 1981 (up from 15.1% at the end of 1973).

The shares of the debt of other geographical regions in total external public debt are fairly similar. Between 1973 and 1981, the most rapid growth amongst these other regions was recorded by the debt of countries in North Africa and the Middle East which rose from $7.9 billion (9.1% of the total) to $45.6 billion (12.4%) over the period. Major country debtors in this total for 1981 included Algeria ($14.4 billion) and Egypt ($13.9 billion). In contrast the external debt of countries in South Asia rose by only 108.5% between 1973 and

TABLE 11.6
External Public Debt by Region
(IBRD Data; $ Billion; End-Year)

	Africa, South of Sahara	East Asia and Pacific	Latin America and the Caribbean	North America and the Middle East	South Asia	More developed Mediterranean	Total	Memo: Major Debtors[1]
1973	9.2	12.5	27.4	7.9	16.4	13.2	86.7	53.7
1976	16.5	22.5	58.4	17.4	22.3	17.5	154.6	99.8
1977	20.6	27.9	73.4	25.6	25.0	20.5	193.0	122.7
1978	27.0	34.8	94.6	34.3	27.7	26.2	244.6	155.3
1979	33.5	40.2	112.1	40.3	28.9	33.9	288.9	182.1
1980	38.9	47.3	126.9	43.7	32.7	41.6	331.2	205.6
1981	42.3	55.2	145.1	45.6	34.2	45.7	368.1	227.5
Shares in Total (%)								
1973	10.6	14.4	31.6	9.1	18.9	15.2		61.9
1976	10.7	14.6	37.8	11.3	14.4	11.3		64.6
1977	10.7	14.5	38.0	13.3	13.0	10.6		63.6
1978	11.0	14.2	38.7	14.0	11.3	10.7		63.5
1979	11.6	13.9	38.8	13.9	10.0	11.7		63.0
1980	11.7	14.3	38.3	13.2	9.9	12.6		62.1
1981	11.5	15.0	39.4	12.4	9.3	12.4		61.8

[1] Algeria, Argentina, Brazil, China, Egypt, India, Indonesia, Israel, Korea, Mexico, Turkey, Venezuela and Yugoslavia.

TABLE 11.7
External Public Debt by Income Group
(IBRD Data; %; End-Year)

	Low-income Africa	Low-income Asia	Oil Exporters	Middle-income Importers
1974	6.1	17.4	28.4	48.1
1976	5.9	14.4	33.3	46.4
1977	5.8	12.9	35.2	46.1
1978	5.5	11.3	35.7	47.4
1979	5.6	10.0	35.0	49.4
1980	5.6	9.9	33.8	50.8
1981	5.5	9.3	34.0	51.2

1981 with their share falling from 18.9% to 9.3% over this period. India ($17.9 billion) accounted for just over 50% of this total in 1981. The shares of total external debt accounted for by countries in Africa (South of the Sahara) and East Asia and the Pacific remained fairly steady at just over 10% and under 15% respectively, while that of the more advanced Mediterranean countries fell from 15.2% in 1973 to 10.6% in 1977 before rising again to 12.4% by the end of 1981. Major individual country debtors in these three groups included Korea ($20 billion), Indonesia ($16.5 billion), Israel ($13.9 billion) and Turkey ($13.8 billion).

The income groupings included in the 1982/3 issue of *World Debt Tables* are given in Table 11.7. This is only a classification by income in partial terms as a geographical distinction is made between low income Africa and Asia, while a group of oil exporters[19] is also defined. Several major individual country debtors, such as Mexico (outstanding debt of $42.6 billion at the end of 1981), Indonesia ($16.5 billion), Algeria ($14.4 billion), Egypt ($13.9 billion) and Venezuela ($11.4 billion) are included in the latter group. As a result, this figure is heavily concentrated with these five countries accounting for 78.9% of the debt owed by oil-exporting countries at the end of 1981. The translation of the data in Table 11.7 for 1974 and 1981 to a Lorenz curve relating the cumulative proportion of external debt by income group to the cumulative proportion of total countries

[19] Algeria, Congo, Ecuador, Egypt, Gabon, Indonesia, Iran, Iraq, Malaysia, Mexico, Nigeria, Oman, Peru, Syrian Arab Republic, Trinidad and Tobago, Tunisia and Venezuela. Data from many OPEC members, including Saudi Arabia, the United Arab Emirates, Qatar and Kuwait, are not included in the DRS. Therefore the group of oil-exporting countries used by the DRS is different in its components from the conventional listing of such nations.

TABLE 11.8
Distribution of External Public Debt by Credit and Income Group
(IBRD Data; %; End-1981)

	Official Creditors			Private Creditors			
	Governments	International Organisations	Total	Suppliers	Financial Markets	Other	Total
Low Income Africa	49.0	26.4	75.4	6.6	18.1	—	24.6
Low Income Asia	58.2	36.1	94.3	1.4	4.3	—	5.7
Middle Income Oil Importers	26.6	15.3	41.9	5.2	52.8	0.2	58.1
Oil Exporters	23.1	10.5	33.6	6.2	60.0	0.2	66.4
Total	29.6	16.2	45.8	5.3	48.8	0.2	54.2
Memo Major Borrowers	25.5	12.8	38.3	5.7	55.8	0.2	61.7
Low Income Africa and Asia	54.8	32.4	87.2	3.4	9.4	—	12.8

TABLE 11.9
External Public Debt by Country
(IBRD Data; $ Billion; End-Year)

	1973	1976	1977	1978	1979	1980	1981
Brazil	7.5	17.6	22.1	30.3	35.6	39.2	44.0
Mexico	5.6	15.9	20.8	25.6	29.2	33.6	42.6
Korea	3.5	6.8	8.6	11.4	13.9	16.3	20.0
India	10.4	13.3	14.5	15.4	15.6	17.4	17.9
Indonesia	5.2	10.0	11.7	13.1	13.2	14.9	16.5
Algeria	2.9	5.8	8.3	12.7	14.9	15.1	14.4
Egypt	2.2	5.8	8.1	9.9	11.4	12.8	13.9
Israel	4.5	7.2	8.1	9.2	10.3	12.6	13.9
Turkey	2.9	3.6	4.3	6.4	11.0	13.5	13.8
Venezuela	1.5	3.0	4.4	6.9	9.8	10.9	11.4
Argentina	2.8	4.4	5.0	6.7'	8.6	10.2	10.5
Pakistan	4.2	6.0	6.8	7.6	8.0	8.8	8.8
Morocco	1.0	2.3	4.1	5.1	6.2	7.1	7.9
Philippines	0.9	2.1	2.9	4.2	5.1	6.4	7.4
Portugal	0.7	1.3	2.2	3.7	5.0	5.6	6.3
Peru	1.4	3.7	4.7	5.4	5.9	6.2	6.0
Greece	1.5	2.5	2.7	3.2	3.6	4.8	5.8
Yugoslavia	1.9	2.8	3.1	3.4	3.7	4.6	5.3
Thailand	0.4	0.8	1.1	1.8	2.8	4.1	5.2
Colombia	1.9	2.4	2.7	2.8	3.3	4.0	5.1

included in the DRS is therefore rather tentative, due to this limited classification by income.[20]

The uneven distribution of total debt is indicated by the fact that the twenty-two low income African countries (21.8% of the total number of countries) owed only 5.5% of external public debt in 1981. The main offset to this uneven distribution was in the group of seventeen oil exporting countries (16.8% of the total) which accounted for 34% of the debt at the end of 1981. In contrast, both the eight low income Asia countries (7.9% of the total) and the fifty-four middle income oil importers (53.5%) held shares of debt (9.3% and 51.2% respectively) broadly comparable to the number of countries in their groups. One other clear result from Fig. 11.1 is the increased maldistribution of external debt between 1974 and 1981 as the oil exporting countries and, to a lesser extent, the middle income oil importers have increased their share of external public debt at the expense primarily of the low income Asian countries.

With the aid of Table 11.8 some factors behind the small propor-

---

[20] It is assumed that the ranking of the groupings from highest per capita income downwards is oil exporters, middle income oil importers, low income Asia and finally low income Africa.

tion of total external debt owed by low income countries may be mooted. Firstly, the limited access of low income countries to the international capital markets has restricted the borrowing potential of such countries and therefore the growth of their debt. At the end of 1981, only 9.4% of the debt of low income countries (Africa and Asia combined) was owed to financial markets compared to 55.8% for all developing countries. Secondly, with the low income countries being particularly dependent on official flows of capital, the increased unevenness of the distribution of outstanding external public debt between 1974 and 1981 (Fig. 11.1) is likely to reflect in part the relatively slow growth (and therefore declining share) of debt granted by official creditors over this period noted earlier in this chapter (Table 11.4). Therefore there has been a slight decline in the proportion of the debt of low income countries owed to the official sector from 88.2% in 1974 to 87.2% in 1981. In general however the slower rate of growth of such debt granted by the official sector appears to have been accompanied by a concentration of such debt on the low income group. The decline in the proportion of total debt

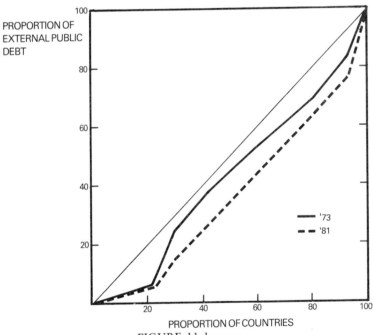

FIGURE 11.1
Distribution of External Public Debt by Income Group
(IBRD Data; End-1974, 1981)

owed to official creditors is much more dramatic in the case of the other income groups.[21] What is clear is that the increased maldistribution of external public debt between 1974 and 1981 indicated in Fig. 11.1 was *not* due to a lack of need of low income countries for new flows of funds.

Despite the large number of countries included in the DRS, it is apparent from Table 11.9 that outstanding external public debt is heavily concentrated amongst a small group of countries. At the end of 1981, 29% of total external debt was owed by three countries, 38.3% by five countries and as much as 56.6% by the ten major debtors. In fact, in the most recent issue of *World Debt Tables*, a group of major borrowers[22] is defined with data on these countries separately listed in an additional table. The memorandum item in Table 11.6 indicates that these thirteen major debtors have accounted for just over 60% of total public debt in recent years. This degree of concentration of developing country debt amongst a small number of countries has — as would be expected with stock data in comparison to the flow figures of new eurocurrency credits and external bonds — been very stable over the observation period in Table 11.9. However, if anything, there has been a slight reduction in the degree of country concentration of external public debt during the 1970s.

A certain amount of information on the conditions attached to new loan commitments is published by the DRS on both an aggregate basis and for individual countries. The aggregate data is reproduced in Table 11.10. The overwhelming impression from this table is not just the variation in conditions over time but between the different categories of debt at one point in time. Therefore in general the terms on new commitments from the official sector were notably softer than those on private sector debt. For example, in 1973 while the average interest rate and maturity on funds committed by the official sector was 4.1% and 26.7 years respectively the equivalent figures for credits from the private sector were 9% and 11 years. Similarly the grant element in official commitments was 44% in 1973 but was as low as 4.5% for private sector commitments

Another notable feature is the almost completely uniform deterioration in borrowing conditions on new debt commitments between

[21] Excluding low income countries, the share of total debt that was owed to official creditors fell from 50.2% in 1974 to 38.6% in 1981.

[22] The thirteen countries so defined (those having outstanding total debt, including non-guaranteed private debt of over $12 billion at the end of 1981) were Algeria, Argentina, Brazil, Chile, Egypt, India, Indonesia, Israel, Korea, Mexico, Turkey, Venezuela and Yugoslavia. (See Footnote 1 to Table 11.6.)

TABLE 11.10
Average Borrowing Terms on New Commitments of Public
Debt
(IBRD Data; Annual Averages)

	1973	1976	1977	1978	1979	1980	1981
Interest Rate (%)							
All Creditors		6.8	6.8	7.9	9.4	9.1	11.7
Official Creditors	4.1	5.4	5.2	4.8	5.1	5.3	6.7
Private Creditors	9.0	7.9	8.1	9.7	11.6	12.8	14.7
Maturity (years)							
All Creditors		15.0	14.5	14.8	13.9	16.2	14.0
Official Creditors	26.7	23.0	22.8	24.4	23.0	23.7	22.1
Private Creditors	11.0	8.7	8.0	9.0	9.2	8.9	8.9
Grant Element (%)							
All Creditors		18.8	18.6	14.5	6.9	10.2	- 3.6
Official Creditors	44.0	32.4	33.8	37.6	34.9	34.0	23.8
Private Creditors	4.5	8.2	6.9	0.6	- 7.7	- 12.5	- 20.4
Grace Period (years)							
All Creditors		4.5	4.5	4.7	4.6	4.7	4.3
Official Creditors		6.5	6.3	6.4	6.1	6.1	5.6
Private Creditors		2.9	3.2	3.7	3.8	3.4	3.4

1973 and 1981. (The only exception to this pattern was an increase in the grace period on private credits.) The most dramatic hardening of terms over this period came in the average interest rate on commitments by the private sector (mainly financial institutions) from 9% to 14.7% and the sharp fall in the grant element proportion of all commitments. From Table 11.10, the gradual decline in spreads on eurocurrency credits after the mid-1970s was not clearly evident mainly due to the rise in absolute interest rates in the latter years of the decade. In addition, the sharp increase in average interest rates on both official and private credits in 1980–81 is apparent, with the deterioration in other borrowing conditions being much more modest in that period.

Public Debt: Debt Service Payments

In addition to the aggregate historical data on debt service payments for all debt described in Table 11.3, the DRS also publishes estimates of future debt service payments. Those computed for 1982 to 1989 on the basis of external public debt data for the end of 1981 are set out in Table 11.11.[23] This information is computed on the basis of outstanding debt at the time that the figures were calculated and, for variable interest-rate debt, at current rates of interest. Therefore only a partial picture is afforded by such data, given that no provision is possible for flows of funds negotiated by developing countries after the calculations are complete.

TABLE 11.11
Projected Service Payments on Public Debt
(IBRD Data; $ Billion)

	1982	1983	1984	1985	1986	1987	1988	1989
Principal Payments	37.9	40.9	42.3	44.3	45.7	45.0	37.6	30.3
Interest Payments	34.0	33.2	30.6	27.3	23.3	18.9	14.3	10.7
Total Debt Service	71.9	74.1	72.9	71.6	68.9	63.9	51.9	41.1
Shares in Total (%):								
Principal Payments	53.4	55.2	58.1	61.9	66.3	70.4	72.4	73.8
Interest Payments	47.3	44.8	41.9	38.1	33.7	29.6	27.6	26.2
Payments to Official Creditors	26.2	28.4	30.7	32.6	35.3	36.4	41.7	49.6
Payments to Private Creditors	73.8	71.6	69.3	67.4	64.7	63.6	58.3	50.4

Certain tentative conclusions may however be drawn from Table 11.11. Firstly, the generally softer terms on debt repayable to the official sector noted in the previous table is confirmed by the fact that while 45.8% of total outstanding public debt at the end of 1981 was against this sector, only 26.2% of service payments in 1981 were to be paid to official creditors. Secondly, and related to the previous point, the growth of fund-raising from the private sector at market-related interest-rates and the absolute increase in these rates is indicated by the projection that 47.3% of total service payments for 1982 were to be interest payments. This contrasts with the actual proportion of interest payments in total debt service in 1973 of 29.7%, a figure which had risen to 47.7% in 1981. Thirdly, the longer-term nature of much debt owed to the official sector is indicated by the declining shares of service payments to the private sector and of interest payments in general in total debt service during the 1980s.

[23] Much more debt-service detail is published in EC-167 than given in Table 11.11. This table is merely indicative, therefore, of the type of information available.

Only a small part of the work of the DRS has involved the calculation of indicators of debt service in contrast to the aggregate debt service data of Table 11.11, although some aggregate and individual country indicators of a conventional type (such as the proportion of debt service or interest service in exports or Gross National Product) are published on a consistent cross-country basis. However the whole task of seeking to summarise a country's debt position in terms of such indicators is exceedingly complex and is worthy of a separate study of its own.[24] The DRS, itself, has only limited resources to use for the calculation of such indicators. In fact, the limitations of these indicators are stressed by the World Bank and should be borne in mind. These limitations may be summarised in the following way:

'None of the substantial efforts that have gone into the search for specific indicators or ratios which, alone or in combination, could be used to predict debt service capacity have been successful. There is no substitute for a thorough analysis of national economic management, with particular attention to the management of debt, in the assessment of creditworthiness. Such assessments must continue to rely heavily on judgement. The debt service ratio, because of the contractual charge of debt service on exports remains the relevant starting point in the analysis of creditworthiness, but it cannot substitute for an in-depth knowledge of a country's situation and prospects based on regular contact and analysis.' (Hughes, 1977, pp. 24–5)

A similar note of caution is valid for all aggregate data on external debt. Such information is of considerable interest and is indicative of general trends in the financial situation of the developing countries as a group. However, what is likely to be crucial for most observers is the debt situation and prospects of an *individual* country. This does not imply that the information presented so far in this section is of minimal value. Its usefulness in the context of this book (apart from the value of the debt data in an aggregate sense noted above) is that the material presented in aggregate form so far is, virtually without exception, also available for each individual country included in the survey. This section concludes by condensing much of the information contained in Tables 11.2–11.11 into one table for a sample country. This is done in Table 11.12 for Malaysia with data for 1973, 1977 and 1981.

[24] There are many useful descriptions and analyses of debt indicators and their problems. They include Abbott (1979), *The Economist* (1982), Gutmann (1980), Hughes (1977), Nagy (1979), Roberts (1981) and Saini and Bates (1978).

Although not clearly evident from Table 11.12, the indebtedness picture for an individual country may vary quite considerably from year to year due to sharp fluctuations in key flows of funds. Therefore, while in 1973, all new disbursements of debt were exactly 'accounted for' by the requirements of servicing previously accumulated debt and a fall in this ratio of service payments to disbursement to 71.2% had occurred by 1977 this ratio then fluctuated dramatically after that. It rose to 91.1% in 1980 before falling to only 21.4% one year later due, primarily, to a threefold increase in disbursements in 1981. The proportion of interest payments in total debt service fell from 49% in 1973 to only 28.7% in 1977 before rising steeply to

TABLE 11.12
Sample of Country Debt (Public) Statistics
(IBRD Data — Malaysia; $ Million; End-Year)

	1973	1977	1981
Total — All Lenders[1]			
1 Outstanding Debt (incl. undisbursed)	1210.2	3471.6	6280.1
2 Outstanding Debt (disbursed only)	720.3	1998.5	4627.3
3 Commitments	240.9	554.2	1876.9
4 Net Flows	42.2	304.6	1735.9
5 Disbursements	86.2	618.9	1873.6
6 Debt Service	86.2	440.7	401.7
7 Principal Repayments (amortisation)	44.0	314.3	137.7
8 Interest Payments	42.2	126.4	264.0
Average Terms on Commitments[2]			
9 Interest Rate (%)	6.6	7.4	14.9
10 Maturity (years)	17.3	12.8	12.3
11 Grace Period (years)	4.3	3.9	4.8
12 Grant Element (%)	18.1	12.8	− 25.9
Principal Ratios[3]			
13 Debt Outstanding/Exports (%)	22.0	29.2	36.1
14 Debt Outstanding/GNP (%)	9.7	15.8	19.6
15 Debt Service/Exports (%)	2.6	6.4	3.1
16 Debt Service/GNP (%)	1.2	3.5	1.7
17 Reserves/Debt Outstanding (%)	202.9	153.7	108.6
18 Reservers/Imports (months)	5.7	5.8	3.9
19 Debt Service[2]	829.5	915.3	868.9
20 Amortisation[2]	332.0	447.2	625.4
21 Interest Payments[2]	497.5	468.1	243.5

[1] Lines 1–8 are quantified for the creditor categories of Multilateral Official (including IBRD, IDA), Bilateral Official, Private (Suppliers) and Private (Financial Markets).
[2] Lines 9–12 and 19–21 are quantified for Official and Private creditors.
[3] Lines 13–18 are available in aggregate form only.

65.7% in 1981. The ratio of debt service to GNP of Malaysia (although remaining comparatively low) rose to 3.5% in 1977 before falling to 1.7% in 1981. However, the sharp increase in outstanding debt in 1981 (as net flows increased more than five times compared to the previous year) led to a rise in the proportion of debt to GNP to 19.6% in that year after this ratio had been as low as 9.7% in 1973. Future debt service payments are expected to rise only slowly to just over $1 billion in 1986 before falling to $868.9 billion (only 4.7% higher than in 1982) by 1988.

It is clear that many conclusions may be drawn from data of this type. Given the enormous differences in country experiences on external debt in the 1970s it is essential that a data collection such as that in Table 11.12 is utilised for the assessment of the financial situation of any individual developing nation illustrating therefore the value of such micro-level data.

Private non-guaranteed debt

Table 11.13 reproduces data on the external private non-guaranteed debt of forty-three countries. Eighteen countries for which actual data are available are separately listed with estimates for twenty-five other countries being included in the regional totals. One notable conclusion from this table is the extent to which the figures of actual (in contrast to estimated) debt are dominated by the private non-guaranteed debt of Brazil. Standing at $19.8 billion at the end of 1981, it is estimated that 33.6% of the published total of private debt of the eighteen countries that submitted actual data was against that country (compared to 54.9% in 1976). In fact it is believed that the data on private non-guaranteed debt submitted by Brazil are virtually complete and therefore of extremely high quality. Comparing Tables 11.9 and 11.13, the share of private non-guaranteed debt in the total external debt of Brazil stood at 31% at the end of 1981, illustrating the importance of this type of debt to the Brazilian economy. The only other countries with significant private non-guaranteed debt in absolute terms at the end of 1981 were Argentina ($12.2 billion), Yugoslavia ($10.9 billion), Chile ($8.1 billion), the Philippines ($2.8 billion) and Thailand ($2.1 billion). Of the countries submitting reliable data on private non-guaranteed debt, the share of such debt in total external debt is high for Yugoslavia (67.4% of total debt at the end of 1981 being owed by the private sector without any guarantee) and Chile (64.8per cent). Other significant shares of private non-

TABLE 11.13
External Private Non-Guaranteed Debt of Developing Countries
(IBRD Data; $ Billion; End-Year)

	1974	1976	1977	1978	1979	1980	1981
Mauritius	0.01	0.01	0.01	0.01	0.02	0.02	0.02
Senegal	0.02	0.02	0.01	0.01	0.01	0.01	0.01
Other Africa, South of the Sahara[1]	0.91	1.25	1.35	1.78	2.35	2.84	3.20
Total — Africa South of the Sahara[2]	0.94	1.28	1.37	1.80	2.38	2.87	3.23
Korea	0.37	0.44	0.43	0.39	0.37	0.43	0.69
Philippines	1.21	1.81	2.16	2.09	2.07	2.01	2.76
Thailand	0.65	0.79	0.88	0.93	1.24	1.70	2.10
Other East Asia and Pacific[1]	3.02	4.27	4.81	5.29	5.85	6.59	7.37
Total — East Asia and Pacific[2]	5.25	7.31	8.28	8.70	9.53	10.73	12.92
Argentina	n/a	n/a	n/a	3.10	5.43	6.59	12.17
Brazil	8.18	11.13	13.01	16.15	15.86	16.61	19.79
Chile	0.53	0.77	0.98	1.57	2.74	4.69	8.14
Colombia	0.32	0.40	0.40	0.36	0.46	0.53	0.90
Dominican Republic	n/a	n/a	0.30	0.30	0.30	0.25	0.23
Honduras	n/a	0.11	0.14	0.17	0.16	0.19	0.17
Paraguay	0.02	0.04	0.06	0.09	0.14	0.15	0.13
Uruguay	0.12	0.06	0.08	0.07	0.18	0.21	0.33
Other Latin American and The Caribbean[1]	11.29	11.87	12.24	8.60	9.18	12.34	16.21
Total — Latin America and The Caribbean[2]	20.46	24.38	27.21	30.41	34.45	41.56	58.07
Total — North Africa and the Middle East[1]	0.04	0.18	0.28	0.32	0.27	0.33	0.40
India	0.12	0.10	0.11	0.13	0.11	0.11	0.15
Pakistan	n/a	0.01	0.02	0.02	0.02	0.02	0.02
Sri Lanka	n/a	0.00	0.00	0.00	0.00	0.00	0.00
Other South Asia[1]	0.01	0.02	0.00	0.00	0.00	0.00	0.01
Total — South Asia[2]	0.13	0.12	0.13	0.15	0.13	0.13	0.18
Turkey	0.15	0.25	0.48	0.56	0.63	0.54	0.44
Yugoslavia	2.83	4.38	5.87	7.71	10.06	10.89	10.88
Other More developed Mediterranean[1]	2.26	2.93	3.37	4.41	5.27	6.26	7.71
Total — More developed Mediterranean[2]	5.24	7.56	9.72	12.68	16.56	17.69	19.03
Total — Actual Data	14.53	20.32	24.94	33.66	39.80	44.85	58.93
Total — Estimated Data[1]	17.53	20.52	22.05	20.40	23.52	28.36	34.90
Grand Total[2]	32.07	40.83	46.98	54.06	63.33	73.31	93.83

[1] Estimated data.
[2] Including estimated data.

guaranteed debt in total debt at the end of 1981 were recorded for Argentina (53.7%), Thailand (28.9%) and the Philippines (27.2%) while the shares dropped to less than 1% for India, Pakistan, Senegal and Sri Lanka. These latter results illustrate the importance of public and publicity-guaranteed debt to certain developing countries and, in all likelihood, the lower quality and coverage of data on non-guaranteed debt.

An attempt is made in Table 11.14 to allocate the country totals of private non-guaranteed debt at the end of 1981 to creditor categories. Despite the introduction of a standardised presentation of this information in EC-167/81, it is obvious from the table that few general conclusions on the distribution of private non-guaranteed debt by creditor are possible. Notwithstanding this, the importance of flows of funds from financial institutions to the private sectors of many of the countries listed in this table is clear, especially Chile (a share of this sort of debt in the total of 94.3%), Colombia (87.3%), Brazil (85.9%), Thailand (72.9%) and Honduras (71.8%).

A very limited attempt to derive debt service data for private non-

TABLE 11.14

External Private Non-Guaranteed Debt of 18 Developing Countries
(IBRD Data; $ Million; End-Year)

		Private Creditors			
	Official Creditors	Foreign Parent Companies	Financial Institutions	Suppliers	Total Debt
Argentina					12166.0
Brazil	516.4	1203.1	17008.3	1063.8	19791.6
Chile	—	—	7675.0	463.0	8138.0
Colombia	—	52.7	787.7	61.7	902.1
Dominican Republic	8.6	87.9	102.6	33.6	232.7
Honduras	30.6	—	123.2	17.9	171.7
India	—	150.4			150.4
Korea					687.6
Mauritius	—	7.2	2.9	8.9	19.0
Pakistan	—	24.6			24.6
Paraguay	4.1	5.3	1.3	122.1	132.7
Philippines					2760.7
Senegal					8.2
Sri Lanka	—		4.0		4.0
Thailand	—	272.7	1528.9	297.0	2098.6
Turkey	135 0	305.0			440.0
Uruguay					326.2
Yugoslavia					10876.1

guaranteed debt from DRS publicity is undertaken in Table 11.15. The table estimates debt service payments for 1982 to 1988 on the basis of outstanding debt and other information at the end of 1981. Once again, therefore, at best only tentative conclusions may be drawn, one of which is that interest payments are projected to account for 37.8% of total debt service in 1982 in comparison to 47.3% for public debt (Table 11.11).

TABLE 11.15
*Debt Service Payments on Private Non-Guaranteed Debt
(IBRD Data; $ Billion*

	1982	1983	1984	1985	1986	1987	988	1989
Principal Payments	17.6	18.2	12.6	12.2	10.6	8.7	6.4	3.6
Interest Payments	10.8	8.5	6.4	5.0	3.6	2.4	1.4	0.7
Total Debt Service	28.3	26.6	19.0	17.1	14.2	11.1	7.9	4.4
Share in total%								
Principal	62.2	68.4	66.3	71.3	74.6	78.4	81.0	81.8
Interest	37.8	31.6	33.7	28.7	25.4	21.6	19.0	18.2

DATA PROBLEMS AND SUMMARY

In an appraisal of external debt statistics published by the DRS it is apparent that the information provided is of a very high standard given the great complexity of the data-gathering process and the large number of countries in which the DRS maintains an interest. Within the limits of its operations, therefore, the DRS is clearly very comprehensive. However some problems of coverage and compilation of the figures, which make the task of the DRS more difficult, do exist. In this final section, five of these will be noted.

Firstly, as argued extensively in this chapter, the data are not complete due to the existence of less than comprehensive coverage of debtor countries, in particular in the case of information on external private non-guaranteed debt. Quite naturally, despite its inability to enforce reporting from many countries, the DRS is constantly seeking to increase the country coverage in order to provide an increasingly complete guide to developing countries' debt.

This issue of country coverage is linked to the second drawback relating to the received statistics themselves. This has a number of facets. Both within any one reporting country over time and between different reporting countries, considerable variations exist in the quality and coverage of the statistics. Once again, as in the issue of the number of countries covered, the DRS is constantly aiming to raise the 'capture' rate of external debt transactions.

Next, a major drawback is the sizeable time-lag before debt data relating to the end of a particular year are published. In the case of external public debt, countries are asked to report end-year data by the following March/April but many countries do not submit their 'returns' until much later in the year, in August or September, for example. Therefore it has been customary for the annual issue of *World Debt Tables* to be published late in the year following the end of the period to which the data refer or even later. For example, the 1982/3 edition of *World Debt Tables* with data to the end of 1981 was published in February 1983 with public debt data for only fifty-three countries being actual figures and the remainder being either preliminary or estimated data. Therefore, even in the annual document, actual data for the most recent year may not be available for all countries. However the recent publication of a series of supplements to the annual documents enables improvements to be made on this issue in two ways. Firstly, data for certain countries published in preliminary or estimated form in the annual document may be speedily converted into actual data when the latter are available, while secondly data for a certain year may, if available early enough, be published *before* the annual document itself. In general, the time-lags in the publication of data on private non-guaranteed debt are even longer than those in the case of public debt. Finally, a problem of considerable complexity is that countries very often report external debt data on a fiscal or financial year basis which is likely to differ from the calendar year basis adopted by the DRS in its data series.[25] The DRS therefore has to break down the data submitted by individual countries to seek to convert them into an unbiased calendar year form. This may not be easy in many cases. The alternative solutions appear to be to switch the whole DRS operation to the more common fiscal year reporting principle or alternatively established to standardised procedures — as the DRS actually aims to have — to convert fiscal year data into calendar year form. The problem may not in fact be particularly serious in the case of data from an individual country,

---

[25] Fortunately, this problem is eased somewhat by the fact that most developing countries have similar fiscal years — running from the beginning of April to the end of March. The considerable complexities that would surround the existence of different fiscal years are therefore generally avoided.

but in the compilation of regional totals for example, the mixing of calendar and fiscal year statistics is potentially very misleading.

Thirdly, a problem may arise in the allocation of particular debt transactions to the guaranteed or non-guaranteed debt category in that it may be difficult, at times, to identify whether a guarantor exists or not. In general the existence of a guarantor in the debtor country itself will be well-known to the reporting country but the existence of the increasingly common *creditor* guarantee may, in fact, never come to the notice of the debtor country. For example, a company granting a suppliers' credit to a developing country may have that financial arrangement guaranteed by a bank in its own country. If the existence of such guarantees does escape the notice of the debtor the proportion of total debt reported to be of public or publicly-guaranteed type may be underestimated. To seek to overcome this inaccuracy the DRS geneally adopts the procedure that if a private debt is *separately* reported by the debtor to the DRS it is assumed to bear a guarantee. This assumption may in its turn overestimate the extent of publicly-guaranteed debt and so may partly cancel out the downward bias imparted to the share of the total that is calculated to be public or publicly guaranteed debt.

Fourthly, a major problem in the compilation of statistics on external debt and one that is likely to become more serious as time goes on is the increasing number of debt types in existence. In particular, the increasingly sophisticated forms of bank and other credit flows make the task of achieving anything like a comprehensive coverage of external debt very difficult. This is particularly true given the final drawback discussed in this summary namely the political sensitivity of much of this information (most notably to do with military credits, as noted earlier in this chapter) and the confidentiality with which the DRS treats the country reports. However, the DRS argues that

> 'The amount of detail in this report *(World Debt Tables)* is believed to be sufficient to meet most analytical needs.[26]

Clearly, therefore, the DRS in its ability to gather full information on external debt transactions and its freedom to publish such information is faced with considerable constraints. However, the World Bank believes, nevertheless, that these do not prevent the information included in *World Debt Tables* being closely representative of the external debt situation of developing countries.

---

[26] *World Debt Tables* EC-167/77, p.3.

Chapter 12

The OECD's Development Assistance Committee (DAC) Statistics[1]

INTRODUCTION AND ORIGINS

The Development Assistance Committee (DAC) of the OECD consists of seventeen member countries[2] of the OECD itself, and the European Communities Commission.[3] The DAC makes available international financial data of two distinct types. Firstly, statistics on long-term transfers of financial resources from DAC countries (and more recently from OPEC) to both developing countries and international organisations are published. These *flow* figures are therefore distinct from the *stock* data on the long-term external debt and corresponding debt service of developing countries that constitutes the second set of data made available by the DAC. Given these two systems, it is logical to discuss DAC data in the section on the external debt of developing countries although, given the overlap with the material on the DRS in Chapter 11, the major focus of this chapter is on the first type of data just described. In addition, definite general emphasis is made in DAC figures on these 'resource flow' figures and this has been the particular expertise gradually developed by the DAC publicity in the overall collection of international financial statistics.

[1] A major source of information on the origin, coverage and quality of DAC data is Stein (1980).
[2] Australia, Austria, Belgium, Canada, Denmark, Finland, France, Germany, Italy, Japan, Netherlands, New Zealand, Norway, Sweden, Switzerland, UK and USA.
[3] In addition, observer status at DAC meetings is granted to the World Bank and the IMF.

The Development Association Group of the OEEC (as it was then known) was established in 1959 before being transformed into the Development Assistance Committee (DAC) when the OECD was founded in 1961. From this date, information began to be compiled and despatched to the OECD by individual DAC countries on the transfer by them of long-term resources to developing countries. In 1966, alongside this procedure a second reporting system was established. This was known as the Expanded Reporting System (ERS) — later known as the Creditor Reporting System (CRS)[4] — which was jointly sponsored 'by the OECD and the World Bank (Stein, 1980). The ERS, which sought to monitor every transaction between DAC members and developing countries and so facilitate the calculation of stock figures on outstanding external debt, was fully operational by 1972. At the time of writing, flows of resources to 163 developing countries and territories (including the East African Community, the Indus Basin and the Mekong Delta Project) are separately recorded in DAC statistics. This is a considerably greater number than the 101 countries that are included in the DRS, for reasons discussed in Chapter 11. The country coverage is therefore very comprehensive although this degree of detail introduces the problem of how to splice together the data for those countries included in both surveys with DAC data for those areas which are not part of the DRS. These procedures are discussed later in the chapter.

DAC data are published in two separate documents on a regular basis. Firstly, the *Annual Report* of the DAC (or the DAC Chairman's Review) entitled *'Development Co-operation: efforts and policies of the members of the Development Assistance Committee'* is typically published in the latter part — usually November — of the year following the end of the data period covered in the document. While certain country breakdowns are included in this *Annual Report*, essentially it is concerned with aggregate data on financial flows. In contrast, the second publication entitled *'Geographical Distribution of Financial Flows to Developing Countries'* includes a separate page for the major developing country recipients with information on certain financial flows, while the volume also includes breakdowns by country of aggregate data on official development assistance and total flows. This document appears less regularly than the *Annual Report* with the most recent version (at the time of writing — covering the period from 1978 to 1981) having been published at the end of 1982 (OECD, 1982b).

---

[4] This label indicates clearly the symmetry between this system and the Debtor Reporting System (DRS) of the World Bank.

Apart from the key advantage that has gradually evolved for DAC data over time, namely that of providing detailed information of a kind not available elsewhere in the international financial system, it is argued that the objectives served by the publication of DAC data are fourfold (Stein, 1980). Firstly, from the point of view of the donor countries, the initial function of these data was to provide an appraisal of the provision of aid by individual developed countries and therefore to permit a comparison between an individual country's performance in granting aid and successive internationally-agreed aid programmes. Secondly, and related to this point, the data therefore fulfilled the information needs of countries that granted development assistance. Thirdly, on a more general level, DAC data are a source of valuable information on development co-operation in the broadest sense. Fourthly, and perhaps of primary importance at present, the data allow a judgement to be made on the volume of flows of development assistance to an individual country relative to that country's resource requirements, and very importantly, to the economic, political and social conditions within that country.

Certain other introductory technical points should be made briefly. DAC data cover long-term financial transactions only, defined as those credit flows carrying an original or extended maturity of over one year. While this is a logical dividing-line between short- and long-term flows, it is also consistent with both the DRS and the (now defunct) CMS of the World Bank and accordingly facilitates the comparability of the three systems. Comparability between the data for separate countries within the DAC presentation is itself aided by the requirement that reported data should conform to balance of payments 'norms and definitions'. This is particularly relevant — as with DRS data — in the interpretation of residency principle. Finally, different currency conversion procedures are adopted dependent on the type of data in question. Stock data — for example, figures on external debt — are converted into dollar values using the *end-year* exchange rate. In contrast, flow data, such as figures of debt service payments or transfers of funds in a particular time-period, are converted into dollar values at the *average* exchange rate over the period in question. Any variations between these average and end-year exchange rates will, therefore, generate valuation effects which may be very significant at a time of volatile exchange rate movements.

TRANSFERS OF FINANCIAL RESOURCES TO DEVELOPING COUNTRIES

Figures published by the DAC on transfers of long-term financial resources to developing countries cover four main categories of flows:

(a) Official Development Assistance (ODA),
(b) Other Official Flows (OOF),
(c) Non-Concessional Private Flows,
(d) Grants from Private Voluntary Agencies.

The main components of total resource flows may therefore be summarised as concessional flows or 'aid' which correspond to categories (a) and (d) above and non-concessional resource flows, that is funding at market-related terms, corresponding to categories (b) and (c). A further subdivision of the overall data is that flows (a) and (b) of the above list originate from the public sector and flows (c) and (d) are from the private sector. In fact, flows are included in DAC data whenever they are channelled from the public or private sectors of a DAC country directly to a developing country or indirectly through an international organisation. Despite the greater number of developing countries included as recipients of funds in DAC statistics compared to both DRS and CMS data (the latter for the reason that many of the countries included in DAC data have never borrowed on the international capital markets), the only cross-system discrepancy in the concept of a developing country to note is that South Africa was included as a developing country in the CMS but is not part of either the DRS or DAC list.

To be included in DAC data the purpose to which each particular loan or grant is put by borrowing countries must be included in the following list. The flow must be used for:

(i)   development programmes (in particular to finance the import-ation of goods and services),
(ii)   developments projects,
(iii) grants and capital subscriptions of those international organi-sations that actively finance development or
(iv)   technical co-operation (in particular to augment the stock of human capital in a developing country by improvements in skills, technical knowledge and education and to increase the efficiency of capital utilisation).[5]

---

[5] See Stein (1980), p. 7.

Those *grants* which are included in DAC statistics may be provided in foreign, convertible currencies or in kind for which no future repayment is required or may be *grant-like flows* which are loans denominated in the currency of the donor country but repayable in the recipient's own currency.[6]

Official Development Assistance (ODA) comprises those flows to developing countries and international organisations with a maturity of over one year, repayable in foreign currencies or in kind from governments or official agencies, which aim to promote the economic development and welfare of the developing country in question and are either wholly concessional or have a grant element[7] of at least 25%. These figures may include any rescheduling (i.e. maturity extension) or refinancing of indebtedness previously incurred in the form of ODA.

Other Official Flows (OOF) include all flows from the official sector which do not meet the conditions to be classified as ODA specified in the last paragraph. In particular, OOF are those flows with a grant element of less than 25% or where the primary objective for borrowing the funds is other than for development purposes. Therefore the main types of flow included in OOF are official export credits — but not those which have been re-discounted by central banks in the portfolios of commercial banks (Stein 1980) — the purchase by the official sector of equity interests in developing countries and portfolio investment.

Non-Concessional Private Flows to developing countries are funds loaned by the private sector on market terms and are not intended to aid development, as such, directly (although they may do so indirectly). The principal flows involved are guaranteed export credits,[8] direct investment, bank lending and transactions in the securities of developing countries. Finally, grants from private voluntary agencies are the private sector equivalent of ODA and have the characteristics of being both concessional and intended to assist development; such grants are frequently termed 'private aids'.

[6] Loans which are both extended and repaid in the recipient's own currency are completely excluded from DAC data.

[7] As noted in Chapter 11, the interest rate used for the calculation of the grant element is 10%. In general, a loan will not include a grant element of over 25% unless it has a maturity of ten years or more. The grant element of ODA programmes has averaged 90% in recent years. See Stein (1980), OECD (1982b).

[8] In general, no data are available on non-guaranteed export credits and no estimates are made by the DAC of these. Where the official and private (with a guarantee) sectors combine on the provision of an export credit, such a 'mixed' credit is allocated separately by volume to the sectors concerned.

Given these definitions of flows included in DAC statistics, certain omissions from the possible flows of funds to developing countries should be noted. As stated in the introduction, all short-term flows (with a maturity of one year or less) are automatically excluded. Other important exclusions are military grants or credits and financial flows from the IMF (other than from its Trust Fund), the latter as they are closely monitored by the IMF itself (Chapters 13 and 14). In these three senses, DAC statistics follow the conventions of the DRS. In addition, while DAC statistics essentially focus on flows from DAC and OPEC countries to the exclusion of resource flows from other sources, certain tables are published which estimate the latter in order to provide a conceptually complete picture of the receipt of funds by the developing countries. In this section, those concerned are Tables 12.1, 12.2 and 12.4–12.7.

Information on these transfers of funds to developing countries is derived from a variety of sources, dependent on the type of lender or donor. In the case of flows from DAC countries, themselves, standard tables are compiled by each member country annually and submitted in an almost complete form by early summer of the year following the end of the last year included in the statistics. However, certain details — in particular on direct private investment — may only be made available to the DAC with a lag of over 12 months. For flows from multilateral agencies[9] (or international organisations) statistics are collected from the various documents published by the agencies themselves and augmented by information provided by the agencies directly to the DAC on request. Finally, data on flows from OPEC countries are collected from published sources and from information made available directly by such countries to the DAC, UNCTAD or the World Bank.

These detailed data accumulation procedures ensure that in the case of certain flows — in particular Official Development Assistance and Other Official Flows — the coverage is effectively complete. In addition, broad comparability has been achieved in the reporting of such flows by individual countries. However, in the case of private flows, certain problems of coverage do exist. These mainly arise from limitations on the reporting procedures of individual members or alternatively from the inability of a country to disclose information on confidential financial arrangements. Finally, cross-country comparability is often poor, also. These problems are particularly severe with data on direct investment which

[9] A full list of the multilateral agencies included in the survey is given in OECD (1982b), p. vii.

'are perhaps the weakest area of DAC statistics in terms of comparability, reliability and available detail' (Stein 1980, p. 17).

In addition, while the problems of calculating accurately the volume of banking flows to individual developing countries were considerable in the past, recent gradual improvements in BIS banking statistics have reduced these to a large extent. (However, even now, many adjustments of BIS figures must be made before they conform to DAC conventions on maturity and valuation effects in particular.)

Table 12.1[10] quantifies annual flows of resources to developing countries from *all* sources. The total receipts of developing countries rose over threefold in the observation period from $33.6 billion in 1973 to $106.0 billion in 1981. Although a breakdown of these flows by the donor/lender country group is available in Table 12.1 for ODA only, reference to Tables 12.2 and 12.3 indicates that 83% ($88.0 billion) of the estimated total of $106 billion of flows in 1981 had their origin in DAC countries, although the peak share of 86.1% was recorded in 1979.

Over the period from 1973 to 1981 there were few significant changes in the shares of individual types of flow (Table 12.2). While bilateral ODA fell from 31.2% of the total in 1973 to 25.9% in 1981, this fall was partly offset by the steady rise in the share of multilateral ODA from 5.8% of the total to 7.5% between 1973 and 1981. In turn, bilateral non-concessional flows jumped in size by over 70% in one year to stand at $31.7 billion in 1975 causing the share of such flows, having fallen from 55% in 1973 to 49.2% one year later, to rebound to 56.9% in that year. This share of bilateral non-concessional flows peaked at 62.4% in 1978 before falling again to 59.9% in 1981, illustrating clearly its considerable volatility. The share of non-concessional multilateral flows rose steadily from 3.8% in 1973 to 5% in 1980 before falling to 4.7% in 1981, while that of private sector grants tumbled from 4.1% to 2.2% between 1973 and 1976 before levelling out at 1.9% of the total in 1981. Therefore, bilateral flows dominated the total although the rise in the share of all multilateral flows from 9.6% of the total in 1973 to 12.2% in 1981 was a notable development.

There is little clear evidence from Tables 12.1 and 12.2 of a substantial decline in the share of concessional flows (both ODA and private sector grants) in the total receipts of developing countries, despite tentative evidence to this effect from DRS data in Chapter 11.

[10] While Tables 12.1–12.7 are drawn from the *DAC Annual Report,* Tables 12.4–12.7 are also available in the more detailed document (OECD, 1982b) and Table 12.8 is published in the latter exclusively.

TABLE 12.1
Total Net Resource Receipts of Developing Countries
(OECD Data; $ Billion)

	1973	1976	1977	1978	1979	1980	1981
Official development assistance (ODA)							
I Bilateral	9.4	15.7	15.6	21.2	24.4	28.7	27.5[e]
of which							
DAC countries	7.1	9.5	10.1	13.1	15.9	18.0	18.3
OPEC countries	2.0	5.2	4.3	6.9	6.6	8.3	6.9
CMEA countries[1]	1.4	1.0	1.1	1.2	1.8	2.1	2.1
Other countries[2]	—	0.1	0.1	0.1	0.1	0.2	0.2[e]
II Multilateral	2.0	3.9	4.8	6.0	6.2	7.7	8.0[e]
Total ODA	11.4	19.6	20.4	27.2	30.6	36.4	35.5[e]
Non-concessional flows (NCF)							
I Bilateral	18.5	35.9	40.5	53.0	50.8	54.5	63.5[e]
of which:							
Bank sector	9.7	15.0	15.5	22.9	19.7	19.0	25.0[e]
Private export credits	1.2	7.2	9.1	10.2	9.5	12.2	10.6[e]
II Multilateral	1.3	2.7	2.9	3.1	4.2	4.8	5.0[e]
Total NCF	19.8	38.6	43.4	56.1	54.9	59.3	68.5[e]
Private Sector Grants[3]	1.4	1.3	1.5	1.7	2.0	2.3	2.0
Total receipts	33.6	59.5	65.3	85.0	87.6	98.0	106.0[e]

[1] Council for Mutual Economic Assistance.
[2] Includes India, Ireland, Israel, Luxembourg, Spain, Yugoslavia.
[3] From DAC countries.
[e] = estimate.

TABLE 12.2
Relative Shares in Resource Flows to Developing Countries
(OECD Data; %)

	1973	1976	1979	1981
Share in bilateral ODA from:				
DAC	67.7	60.5	65.2	66.5
OPEC	19.4	33.1	27.0	25.1
CMEA	12.9	6.4	7.4	7.6
Other countries	—	0.6	0.4	0.7
Share in total receipts of:				
ODA — bilateral	31.2	26.4	27.9	25.9
— multilateral	5.8	6.6	7.1	7.5
NCF — bilateral	55.0	60.3	58.0	59.9
— multilateral	3.8	4.5	4.8	4.7
Private sector grants[1]	4.1	2.2	2.3	1.9
Share in total receipts from DAC countries	66.8	77.3	86.1	83.0
DAC countries ODA/GNP	0.29	0.33	0.35	0.35
DAC countries total flows to developing countries/GNP	0.72	1.10	1.17	1.21
OPEC ODA/GNP	2.70	2.14	1.88	1.46

[1] From DAC countries only.

However the fact that throughout the period from 1973 to 1981 around 60–65% of the new funds transferred to developing nations were at non-concessional (market) terms will have had the effect of exacerbating the future debt servicing commitments of such countries. The slower growth in bilateral ODA from DAC countries between 1973 and 1981 — reflected in the small decline in its share to 66.5% in 1981 — is potentially serious. This declining share (and that of ODA from CMEA countries from 12.9% to 7.6% between 1973 and 1981) was taken up by bilateral aid from OPEC. This stood at 25.1% in 1981 (up from 19.4% in 1973, although a figure of 33.1% had been obtained in 1976) and remains a minor part of total ODA. Indeed with the halving in the proportion of bilateral OPEC ODA to the national income of these countries from 2.7% in 1973 to 1.46% in 1981, the performance of this group of countries in transferring funds to the developing world is clearly not as good as the absolute figures and shares would indicate. The relatively slower growth of national income in DAC countries is reflected — despite its declining share of total bilateral ODA — by the gradual increase in the proportion of bilateral ODA granted by such countries relative to their aggregate national income from 0.29% in 1973 to 0.35% in 1981 (although a share of 0.36% was achieved as early as 1975). However this is still far below the objective of 0.7% of GNP recommended by the United Nations in 1970. This target was reached by the Netherlands (1.08%), Sweden (0.83%), Norway (0.82%), Denmark (0.73%) and France (0.73%) only in 1981 with the figure for Italy, as a case in point, being as low as 0.19%.

Table 12.3 disaggregates total flows from DAC countries (only) to developing countries and multilateral institutions by type of flow. Overall the annual flow of resources rose from an average of $17.8 billion in 1970–2 to $88 billion in 1981. Within this total the trends in the shares of each type of flow which developed during the 1970s have been arrested somewhat in 1980–1. The most notable development has been the increase in the share of private non-concessional flows from 41.7% in 1970–2 to 64.1% in 1979 before falling sharply

TABLE 12.3

Annual Flow of Financial Resources from DAC Countries to Developing Countries and Multilateral Agencies (OECD Data; $ Billion)

	1970–1972 (average)	1977	1978	1979	1980	1981
I *Official Development Assistance (ODA)*	7.9	15.7	20.0	22.4	27.3	25.6
A Bilateral	6.2	10.1	13.1	15.9	18.1	18.3
B Contributions to multilateral institutions	1.7	5.7	6.9	6.5	9.2	7.4
II *Other Official Flows (OOF)*	1.5	3.4	5.5	2.8	5.3	6.6
A Bilateral	1.2	3.3	5.3	3.0	5.4	6.5
B Contribution to multilateral institutions	0.3	0.1	0.2	– 0.2	– 0.1	0.1
I & II *Total Official Flows*	9.4	19.2	25.5	25.2	32.5	32.2
III *Grants by private voluntary Agencies*	0.9	1.5	1.7	2.0	2.4	2.0
IV *Private flows at market terms*	7.4	31.3	44.0	48.5	40.4	53.8
A Direct investment	3.7	9.5	10.8	12.9	9.8	14.6
B Bilateral portfolio investment and others	1.1	10.7	21.1	23.5	17.7	24.7
C Multilateral portfolio investment	0.6	2.6	2.2	2.1	1.5	3.8
D Private export credits	1.9	8.5	9.9	10.0	11.5	10.6
V *Total resource flow* (I + II + III + IV)	17.8	52.0	71.2	75.7	75.4	88.0
Shares in total						
I	44.4	30.3	28.1	29.6	36.2	29.1
II	8.7	6.6	7.7	3.7	7.0	7.5
III	5.3	2.9	4.4	2.6	3.2	2.3
IV	41.7	60.2	61.8	64.1	53.6	61.1

in 1980 and settling at 61.1% in 1981. This upward movement was linked to the rapid growth of the eurocurrency market, and in particular of syndicated eurocurrency credits, during the 1970s. All other flow types fell in share, with the decline in ODA (both multilateral and bilateral) from 44.4% of the total in 1970–2 to only 29.6% in 1979 being indicative of the considerable part played by aid from OPEC (excluded from Table 12.3) in bolstering the share of ODA in flows from all sources in Tables 12.1 and 12.2; subsequently, in 1980, the share rose to 36.2% before falling again to 29.1% in 1981. The share of OOF remained around 6–9%, apart from a sharp fall to 3.7% in 1979 when contributions to multilateral institutions were negative, while as in Table 12.2 the share of private grants fell significantly to stand at only 2.3% in 1981. Therefore, over the observation period the share of total flows that were concessional (ODA plus private grants) fell significantly from 49.7% in 1970–2 to 39.4% in 1980 and to as low as 31.4% in 1981. Relative to GNP however, the performance of DAC countries in transferring funds to the developing world has been good. Total flows as a proportion of GNP rose from 0.72% in 1973 to a peak of 1.24% in 1978, although this share fell again to 1.04% in 1980 and stood at 1.21% in 1981 (Table 12.2). Therefore as with ODA alone the proportion of resource flows from DAC countries relative to those countries' aggregate national income rose significantly in the observation period.

Breakdowns by the recipient country are published for both ODA and all financial flows from, firstly, DAC countries only and, secondly, from all countries and multilateral agencies. To avoid repetition, Tables 12.4–12.7 provide some of this detail for the case of all flows from all countries to developing nations. A breakdown by geographical area is given in Table 12.4. Clearly, financial flows are relatively well-spread across these areas and it is notable that an area such as the South of Sahara, which received relatively little finance in the form of bank credits in the 1970s, should have, over the same period, been a major recipient ($13.2 billion in 1981 — 13.9% of the total), when all flows are considered. Other significant shares in 1981 went to Far East Asia (16.7%), South America (16.6%) and North Central America (11.8%).

The same data are grouped essentially by income in Table 12.5.[11] The distribution by income group is fairly even (and certainly more so than that in the data on the stock of external debt — Figure 11.1) with,

---

[11] Only 159 countries are separately grouped in Table 12.5. The four other countries/entities that are included in DAC data (East African Community, Indus Basin, Mekong Delta Project and Timor) are included in the unallocated totals in this table.

TABLE 12.4
Net Disbursements from all Sources Geographical Area
(OECD Data; $ Billion)

	1977	1978	1979	1980	1981
Europe	4.21	5.05	7.34	7.45	6.71
North of Sahara	6.26	8.64	6.45	6.39	4.94
South of Sahara	7.58	8.76	10.19	13.33	13.20
North and Central America	4.25	6.27	7.90	10.16	11.25
South America	5.74	9.35	10.81	11.15	15.77
Middle East	5.61	7.72	8.29	3.45	4.02
South Asia	2.93	3.88	4.32	6.19	5.15
Far East Asia	4.42	5.98	7.65	8.32	15.82
Oceania	0.68	0.87	0.99	1.12	1.04
Unspecified	11.73	19.09	17.96	15.46	17.07
Total	53.42	75.62	81.90	83.06	94.96
Shares in total					
Europe	7.8	6.7	9.0	9.0	7.1
North of Sahara	11.7	11.4	7.9	7.7	5.2
South of Sahara	14.2	11.6	12.4	16.0	13.9
North and Central America	8.0	8.3	9.6	12.2	11.8
South America	10.7	12.4	13.2	13.4	16.6
Middle East	10.5	10.2	10.1	4.2	4.2
South Asia	5.5	5.1	5.3	7.5	5.4
Far East Asia	8.3	7.9	9.3	10.0	16.7
Oceania	1.3	1.2	1.2	1.3	1.1
Unspecified	22.0	25.2	21.9	18.6	18.0

in 1981, 67.6% of total flows going to the highest income groupings (including middle income and the newly industrialising countries and OPEC) which comprised 57.9% of all countries sampled. This represents a similar degree of concentration of total flows on the higher income countries to the share of 67% in 1977.[12]

Table 12.6 lists the major individual country recipients of resource flows from all sources with the concentration ratios for these flows being calculated in Table 12.7. It is clear that concentration amongst individual countries is relatively limited with in 1981 only 33.4% of the total going to the ten major recipients in comparison to figures for developing country borrowing in the international capital markets of 67.3% (credits) and 91.2% (bonds — seven countries).[13] This dramatic difference is primarily caused by the widely-dispersed nature of ODA over many countries including many in Africa and Oceania, in particular, that do not have access to capital market borrowing. It is also notable that while Mexico, Brazil, Indonesia,

[12] A Lorenz curve would be drawn from the data in Table 12.5 in the same way as it was done for external debt statistics in Fig. 11.1.

[13] See Tables 9.2 and 10.5.

TABLE 12.5
Net Disbursements from all Sources to Income Groups[1]
(OECD Data; $ Billion)

	1977	1978	1979	1980	1981
Least developed countries[2]	3.85	4.40	5.75	7.16	6.39
Other low income countries[3]	9.13	11.50	10.35	14.16	16.38
China	—	—	0.13	0.32	1.89
Middle income countries[4]	10.86	15.14	20.88	22.54	23.89
Newly industrialising countries[5]	9.57	14.17	18.21	18.19	25.44
OPEC[6]	5.96	10.44	4.96	5.24	2.13
Unallocated	14.05	19.97	21.62	15.45	18.85
Total	53.42	75.62	81.90	83.06	94.96
Shares in total (%)[7]					
Least developed countries	9.8	7.9	9.5	10.6	8.4
Other low income countries	23.2	20.7	17.2	20.9	21.5
China	—	—	0.2	0.5	2.5
Middle income countries	27.6	27.2	34.6	33.3	31.4
Newly industrialising countries	24.3	25.5	30.2	26.9	33.4
OPEC	15.1	18.8	8.2	7.8	2.8

[1] Income groups are based on 1980 GNP per capita in US dollars, see DAC *Annual Report* (1982) PP. 171–2, 254–6.
[2] As defined by the United Nations (36 countries at present).
[3] Less than $600 per capita (31 countries).
[4] Over $600 per capita, excluding newly industrialising countries and OPEC (70 countries).
[5] 11 countries — Argentina, Brazil, Greece, Hong Kong, Korea, Mexico, Portugal, Singapore, Spain, Taiwan, Yugoslavia.
[6] 11 countries — Algeria, Ecuador, Gabon, Iran, Iraq, Kuwait, Libya, Qatar, Saudi Arabia, United Arab Emirates, Venezuela.
[7] Excluding unallocated.

Argentina, Spain and Hong Kong appear in the list of the ten major recipients of funds in 1981 in both the aggregated capital market data and those on total resource flows,[14] certain countries which were major recipients of resource flows when considered in aggregate were minor capital market borrowers. This is particularly true of Egypt, India, Netherlands Antilles, Jordan and Bangladesh. The tentative conclusion from the data in Tables 12.6 and 12.7 is therefore that, when capital market borrowing is combined with all other types of resource flow, a much more even dispersion of financial flows was apparent in the later years of the 1970s.

In addition to the data surveyed above, country breakdowns are also published in the DAC *Annual Report* for:

[14] Some overlap should be anticipated as the data on resource flows in Table 12.6 include capital market borrowing surveyed in Chapters 8–10.

TABLE 12.6
Net Disbursement from all Sources to Major Countries
(OECD Data; $ Million)

	1977	1978	1979	1980	1981
Brazil	2426	5030	5086	4309	7377
Mexico	1868	2500	3379	4463	6822
Indonesia	908	1446	430	1780	4545
Argentina	427	1187	2002	2773	2690
Egypt	2745	2802	2075	2356	2404
India	1049	1314	1288	2517	2289
Turkey	888	1129	1851	1878	1979
Spain	1188	1151	1543	1347	1905
China	—	—	129	324	1887
Hong Kong	265	171	1053	910	1634
Thailand	284	643	946	1114	1561
Korea	1353	1500	1571	823	1533
Nigeria	416	648	686	1201	1501
Chile	− 123.2	129	289	409	1435
Panama	570	575	669	761	1320
Netherlands Antilles	605	851	111	215	1299
Singapore	215	364	527	752	1283
Colombia	239	333	506	833	1240
Philippines	716	1061	1153	972	1236
Algeria	2363	3866	1507	1559	1197
Jordan	375	422	1224	1342	1167
Bangladesh	1096	1394	1687	1342	1167
Israel	773	1000	1190	1259	1072
Venezuela	803	1394	575	1303	1036

TABLE 12.7
Concentration of Resource Flows Amongst Country Borrowers
(OECD Data; %)

	1977	1978	1979	1980	1981
Proportion of flows to:					
3 countries	14.1	15.5	12.9	13.9	19.7
5 countries	20.1	20.8	17.6	19.8	25.1
7 countries	24.4	24.5	21.6	24.2	29.0
10 countries	29.7	29.7	26.9	29.3	33.4

(a) ODA *commitments* from all countries (in contrast to disbursements),
(b) the grant/loan distribution of ODA commitments from DAC countries, and
(c) food aid from DAC countries.

The second of this list allows the calculation of the grant element of ODA commitments to developing countries which is a particularly useful 'micro'-statistic in the assessment of the status of financial flows to individual countries.

Finally in this section, table 12.8 presents an example of a country page (for the Ivory Coast) published by the DAC with, however, only a sample of the available information for each country.[15] Although not included in Table 12.8, the DAC published on each such country page a creditor or donor breakdown by country for all flows and, in addition, by multilateral agency for net and gross flows of ODA, commitments of ODA and for total net receipts. In addition, certain economic indicators and external debt data are included. All this information is provided in an annual time-series form usually for four years; it clearly represents an enormous stock of detail on an individual country's receipts of resource flows and other crucial macroeconomic variables and would be of considerable interest when an assessment of country risk is made.

OUTSTANDING EXTERNAL DEBT OF DEVELOPING COUNTRIES

Data compiled by the DAC on the long-term external debt (disbursed only) and debt service of developing countries are generally very comprehensive. They cover virtually all types of public and private debt whether concessional[16] or non-concessional and whether such debt is bilateral or multilateral in nature. The exclusions from these debt series are, in the main, consistent with those discussed in the previous section, in particular short-term debt (with an original or extended maturity of one year), military debt, debt owed to the IMF (except the Trust Fund), domestic currency debt and debt service arrears. Any debt incurred by a country that functions as an offshore banking centre or 'flag of convenience' shipping centre but which is not used in the domestic economy of that country is also excluded from these figures. Therefore, any funds channelled through an offshore centre to the domestic economy of the ultimate borrower is deemed to be the debt of that country and not the offshore centre.

As was the case with DRS data, external debt figures are presented

---

[15] Separate pages were published for one hundred and eleven countries in the most recent edition of the 'Geographical Distribution' document. Information on other countries has to be drawn from country breakdowns such as Table 12.6.

[16] Not including, of course, flows with a 100% grant element.

TABLE 12.8
Sample of Statistics on Disbursements from DAC Countries and Multilateral Institutions to an Individual Country
(OECD data — Ivory Coast; $ Million, 1981)

Net disbursements	Bilateral	Multilateral	Total	Gross disbursements	Bilateral	Multilateral	Total
ODA loans	26.0	2.8	28.8	ODA loans	41.5	4.1	45.5
+ ODA grants	65.2	29.7	94.9	+ ODA grants	65.2	29.7	94.9
⌈ of which: ⌊ Technical co-operation grants	58.0	4.8	62.8	⌈ of which: ⌊ Technical co-operation grants	58.0	4.8	62.8
= Total ODA	91.2	32.5	123.7	= Total ODA	106.6	33.8	140.4
+ Total OOF	31.6	33.5	65.1	+ Total OOF	42.5	58.2	100.7
= Total official flows	122.7	66.1	188.8	= Total official flows	149.1	92.0	241.1
+ Private flows	71.9	—	71.9	+ Private flows	255.0	—	255.0
⌈ of which:							
Direct investment	22.4	—	22.4				
Portfolio investment	63.0	—	63.0				
⌊ Export credits	− 13.5		− 13.5				
= Total receipts	194.6	66.1	260.6	= Total receipts	404.1	92.0	496.1
Memo: ODA commitments	156.5	52.6	209.1				

in net terms in the sense that any repayments or cancellations of debt are netted out. However, the exclusion of any assets of each developing country (such as foreign exchange reserves and other claims on overseas residents held by that country's private sector or government), as again was the case with DRS figures, has led the DAC to state that in this particular sense the debt figures are expressed in *gross* terms. Therefore any country that borrows $50 million exclusively to build up reserves has, according to DAC and DRS procedures, incurred an increase in external debt of that amount despite the existence of an equivalent rise in foreign assets.

The sources of information that are used for the compilation of these debt statistics vary according to the debt type involves and whether the country concerned does or does not report information on that debt type to the DRS. Table 12.9 should help to clarify the relevant procedures.

TABLE 12.9
Sources of Information for DAC External Debt Statistics

	CRS	*DRS*	*Other*[1]
Public debt to DAC countries			
Countries in DRS (101)	✔		
Countries outside DRS	✔		
Public debt to non-DAC countries			
Countries in DRS (101)		✔	
Countries outside DRS			✔
Private debt to all countries			
Countries in DRS (43)		✔	
Countries outside DRS[3]			✔

[1] See text.
[2] CRS data re used as they are generally more comprehensive than the corresponding data reported by debtors under the DRS.
[3] This will, of course, include those countries (58 in number) who are included in the DRS for public and publicly guaranteed debt but not for private debt.

Essentially, three main sources are used. Firstly, the Creditor Reporting System (jointly-sponsored by the OECD and World Bank) includes reports by DAC countries on the official or officially-guaranteed debt of 158 developing countries[17] in the forms of ODA, OOF (mainly official export credits) and Officially-Guaranteed Pri-

[17] This figure, which therefore is indicative of the number of countries whose debt data are collected by the DAC, is drawn from OECD (1982a).

vate Export Credits (OGPEC)[18] owing to those DAC countries. Secondly, the Debtor Reporting System is used, where appropriate, covering as it does public and publicly-guaranteed debt data for 101 countries and private non-guaranteed debt for 43[19] of the above total of countries. Finally, where necessary, a variety of other sources are used to augment the information derived from the two main reporting systems. These sources include the central banks of debtor countries, private banks, the annual reports of various Multilateral Development Finance Institutions, the IMF and the BIS. In addition, internal estimates may be made of any remaining gaps in the debt information.

Therefore, referring to Table 12.9, to quantity the public debt of all developing countries owed to DAC members, CRS information is used. (This is so even in the case of a country that is part of the DRS as CRS data are likely to be more comprehensive than those reported to the DRS by the debtor countries themselves). However once public debt owed to non-DAC countries and all private debt is to be evaluated, the relatively narrow base of the CRS is apparent as these two elements are not included. In the case of public debt to non-DAC countries, therefore, DRS figures are used for those 101 countries that report and for other countries reliance has to be placed on 'other sources'. A similar distinction occurs in the case of private non-guaranteed debt with the difference of degree that recourse to 'other sources' will be more common due to the much smaller number of countries (43) that at present report such information in reliable form to the DRS.

Clearly such a complex data-generation operation may lead to some double-counting of certain debt types and perhaps the omission of others. One particular form of potential double-counting that, in principle, is eliminated from DAC statistics, is that data for private debt do not, where this is feasible, include OGPEC from banks and other financial institutions.

In principle, all this information is accumulated by the DAC on an on-going basis, although it is processed for publication once a year only. Reporting countries are, however, asked to submit a 'status report' on their outstanding claims on developing countries every six months as part of this continuous information-gathering process, with loan-by-loan listings for official sector assets and debt service schedules for the succeeding eight years (Stein, 1980). The time-lags

[18] The operations of the CRS in collecting information on OGPEC is undertaken in co-operation with the Berne Union.

[19] As noted in Chapter 11, however, actual figures for only 18 countries are published with estimates being made for the remaining 25 countries.

before publication of these statistics are considerable however, with the first systematic presentation of definite figures being included in the *Annual Report* of the year following the year after the end-period to which the latest figures refer. However, attempts are made to reduce this lag by providing preliminary and estimated figures for the two intervening years. Therefore the 1982 *Annual Report* contains firm data for 1980, with preliminary figures for 1981 and estimates only for 1982.

As would be expected from such complex reporting conventions, the quality of the DAC external debt data varies enormously according to debt type, country and time-period. In principle the coverage varies from being virtually complete for public debt, owed to DAC members, of countries who report to the DRS, to being of more dubious quality for public debt owed to non-DAC members and for private debt of those countries that do not report to the DRS. However the data are 'best estimates' and it should be remembered that:

> 'their coverage, availability and the reporting methodology are such that they represent the fullest and most comparable information presently available on the total debt position of each country shown *vis-à-vis* all its creditors' (*OECD Survey of External Debt*, 1980, p. viii)

A sample of the available statistics on external indebtness published by the DAC is set out in Tables 12.10–12.13. Concentration is placed in these tables on the presentation of figures which differ from the information available in the DRS, both to avoid too much duplication and to illustrate the alternative information available in DAC data. Unlike the DRS, it is only in the most recent external debt report published by the OECD (OECD, 1982a) that the degree of breakdown of detail at the individual country level has matched that of the aggregate data.

Table 12.10 sets out a time-series from 1971 to 1982[20] of developing countries' external debt by type. The most notable conclusion from this (and the following tables) is the slightly higher figures of developing country indebtedness compared to those of the DRS. This is for two main reasons. Firstly, DAC data cover all debt types and, while Table 11.2 does aggregate external public and private debt figures of the DRS, it is more common for concentration to be focussed on DRS public debt data alone due to the higher quality of such figures. Secondly, the DAC estimates, as already noted in this

---

[20] Figures for 1981 and 1982 are preliminary and estimated respectively. This breakdown by type is not published by the DRS.

TABLE 12.10
Outstanding External Debt of Developing Countries
(OECD Data; $ Billion; End-Year)

	DAC countries, multilateral organisations and capital markets						Debt from other sources	Total disbursed debt	Annual increase (%)
	Bilateral and multilateral ODA	Other multilateral lending	Total export credits	Bank loans	Other capital market loans	Total			
1971	30	4	27	11	9	81	9	90	—
1975	44	12	42	49	12	159	21	180	18.9[1]
1976	49	14	51	64	16	194	26	220	22.2
1977	55	19	65	81	22	243	31	274	24.5
1978	67	22	85	105	29	308	37	345	25.9
1979	73	27	100	131	31	362	44	406	17.7
1980	81	32	114	155	35	417	48	465	14.5
1981[2]	85	37	128	180	42	472	58	530	14.0
1982[3]	95	44	148	210	55	552	74	626	18.1

Shares in total debt owed to DAC countries, multilateral organisations and capital markets

	Bilateral and multilateral ODA	Other multilateral lending	Total export credits	Bank loans	Other capital market loans
1971	37.0	4.9	33.3	13.6	11.1
1976	25.3	6.2	26.3	33.0	8.2
1980	19.4	7.7	27.3	37.2	8.4
1982[3]	17.2	8.0	26.8	38.0	10.0

[1] 1971–1975 at annual rate.
[2] Preliminary.
[3] Estimates.

TABLE 12.11
Outstanding External Debt of Developing Countries by Source
(OECD Data; $ Billion; End-Year)

	DAC countries and capital markets	Multilateral organisations	CMEA countries	OPEC	Other LDCs	Unspecified and adjustments	Total debt
1971	71	10	6	6	2	1	90
1975	137	22	9	8	4	3	180
1976	168	26	9	8	4	5	220
1977	210	33	11	11	5	4	274
1978	268	40	12	13	6	6	345
1979	315	47	14	15	7	7	406
1980	361	56	15	18	8	7	465
1981[1]	407	65	17	23	10	8	530
1982[2]	476	76	20	29	13	12	626

Shares in total debt

	DAC countries and capital markets	Multilateral organisations	CMEA countries	OPEC	Other LDCs
1971	78.9	11.1	6.7		2.2
1976	76.4	11.8	4.1	3.6	1.8
1980	77.6	12.0	3.2	3.9	1.7
1982[2]	76.0	12.1	3.2	4.6	2.1

[1] Preliminary.
[2] Estimates.

TABLE 12.12
Annual Debt Service Payments by Debt Type
(OECD Data; $ Billion)

			DAC countries, multilateral organisations and capital markets						Total debt service	of which:	
	Bilateral and multilateral ODA	Other multilateral lending	Total export credits	Bank loans	Other capital market loans	Total	CMEA countries	OPEC		interest	amortisation
1971	1.6	0.7	5.1	— 2.7 —		10.1	0.6		11.0	3.3	7.7
1975	2.4	1.1	10.7	8.1	1.4	23.7	0.8	0.2	25.8	9.3	16.5
1976	2.5	1.4	12.4	10.6	2.2	29.1	0.9	0.2	31.9	10.5	21.4
1977	2.7	1.9	16.5	14.4	3.4	38.9	1.1	0.6	42.1	12.9	29.2
1978	3.1	2.5	20.5	24.6	4.2	55.0	1.4	1.0	59.0	17.6	41.4
1979	3.3	3.1	25.6	33.1	5.2	70.3	1.7	1.3	75.6	26.0	49.6
1980	3.7	3.9	29.6	38.1	5.3	80.6	1.8	1.9	86.9	37.2	49.7
1981[1]	3.9	4.6	35.5	49.6	7.9	101.5	2.1	2.4	109.3	48.5	60.8
1982[2]	4.6	5.5	44.8	56.0	11.0	121.9	2.5	3.0	131.3	60.1	71.2

			Shares in debt service payments to DAC countries, multilateral organisations and capital markets							Shares in total debt service payments	
1971	15.8	6.9	50.5	— 26.7 —						30.0	70.0
1976	8.6	4.8	42.6	36.4	7.6					32.9	67.1
1980	4.6	4.8	36.7	47.3	6.6					42.8	57.2
1982	3.8	4.5	36.8	45.9	9.0					45.8	54.2

[1] Preliminary.
[2] Estimates.

TABLE 12.13
External Debt and Reserves by Country
(OECD Data; $ Billion; End-Year)

	External debt				Reserves				Reserves as % of debt	
	1978	1979	1980	1981[1]	1978	1979	1980	1981	1978	1981
Brazil	44.4	50.8	57.0	65.6	11.9	9.0	5.9	6.7	26.8	10.2
Mexico	30.5	37.6	43.5	54.4	1.9	2.2	2.9	4.2	6.2	7.7
Spain	13.1	16.3	20.7	25.1	10.8	13.9	12.5	11.4	82.4	45.4
Korea	12.5	15.5	17.6	20.8	2.8	3.0	2.9	2.7	22.4	13.0
Argentina	7.9	12.6	15.6	20.0	5.2	9.6	6.9	3.4	65.8	17.0
India	15.9	16.5	18.0	19.4	6.8	7.8	7.3	5.0	42.8	25.8
Indonesia	14.5	15.1	16.6	18.2	2.6	4.1	5.5	5.1	17.9	28.0
Algeria	14.9	17.0	17.2	17.0	2.2	2.9	4.0	3.9	14.8	21.8
Yugoslavia	11.4	13.5	15.1	16.8	2.5	1.3	1.5	1.7	21.9	10.1
Turkey	7.3	11.6	14.5	15.5	1.0[2]	0.9	1.4[2]	1.4	11.3	9.0
Venezuela	9.7	12.3	14.7	14.7	6.6	7.8	7.1	8.7	68.0	58.4
Egypt	10.4	12.2	13.8	14.0	0.6	0.6	1.2	0.8	54.8	5.7
Chile	5.1	7.1	9.0	12.3	1.2	2.0	3.2	3.3	23.5	26.8
Philippines	6.2	7.4	8.5	9.5	1.8	2.3	2.9	2.3	29.0	24.2
Pakistan	7.8	8.4	9.2	n/a	0.7[2]	0.9[2]	1.7[2]	1.5[2]	9.0	18.5[3]
Morocco	5.4	6.7	7.3	8.0	0.7	0.6	0.4	0.3	13.0	3.8
Israel	5.7	6.7	7.8	n/a	2.7[2]	3.1[2]	3.4[2]	3.5[2]	47.4	43.6[3]
Greece	4.7	5.6	6.9	7.6	1.2	1.5	1.3	1.2	25.5	15.8
Peru	6.1	6.5	7.1	7.3	0.4	1.6	2.0	1.3	6.6	17.8
Nigeria	2.6	4.2	5.5	6.0	1.9[2]	5.6	10.3[2]	3.9	73.1	65.0
Nigeria	2.6	4.2	5.5	6.0	1.9[2]	5.6	10.3[2]	3.9	73.1	65.0
20 country total	236.1	283.6	325.6	352.4[4]	65.5	80.7	84.3	72.3	27.7	19.1[4]
% of LDC total	68.4	69.9	70.0	66.5[4]	60.8	64.6	58.0	46.0		

[1] Preliminary.
[2] From IMF data.
[3] 1980.
[4] Calculated from 18 countries only.

chapter, are for a much larger number of countries than DRS figures.[21] In addition it is possible that, despite the sophisticated search and cross-checking procedures of both the DAC and DRS, significant variations in estimates of debt type included by both systems may exist.

The developing trends in the shares of each debt type in Table 12.10 are very definite. Therefore, there has been a secular decline in the share of bilateral and multilateral ODA in outstanding debt owed to DAC countries, multilateral organisations and capital markets from 37% in 1971 to an estimated figure of 17.2% in 1982. The volume of outstanding private lending rose from $20 billion (24.7% of the total) in 1971 to $265 billion (48%) in 1982. The bulk of this was accounted for by bank loans which rose from 13.6% of the debt at the end of 1971 to an estimated figure of 38% in 1982. The share of 'other multilateral lending' rose from 4.9% in 1971 to 8% in 1982 while that of export credits declined sharply from 33.3% in 1971 to 26.3% five years later before levelling out. These share movements are slightly different from those observed in DAC flow data in Table 12.2. However, it is likely that the absence of clear secular trends in the shares of combined ODA and bilateral non-concessional flows observed in that table is consistent with the trends in Table 12.10 due primarily to the high grant element (which may reach 100% for some flows which would not therefore, of course, appear in Table 12.10) in many of the ODA flows. A somewhat reassuring piece of evidence from Table 12.10 is the dramatic deceleration in the rate of growth of developing countries' indebtedness from over 20% in all years from 1975 to 1978 (and a peak of 25.9% in 1978) to under 15% in 1980 and 1981. This is somewhat surprising given the great concern expressed about the development of external indebtedness in recent years, particularly since the second oil crisis of 1979.

Table 12.11 presents a different breakdown of the same aggregates, this time by creditor country. No major shifts in country group shares occurred between 1971 and 1982, although the rise in debt owed to OPEC from $1.2 billion (in 1973) to $29 billion in 1982 was a substantial proportionate increase taking the share from 1% of total outstanding debt to 4.6%. However, given the enormous accumulated external surpluses of this group of countries, this remains a very low figure. The share of debt owed to DAC countries themselves declined slightly from 78.9% of the total in 1971 to 76% in 1982

[21] Using data for 1981 external public debt (including publicly-guaranteed private debt) for 101 countries was, according to DRS figures, $368.1 billion. When private debt data for forty-three countries were added, the figure rose to $461.9 billion (Table 11.2). The end-1981 DAC estimate for one hundred and forty-three countries covering public and private debt was $530 billion.

although still being completely dominant nevertheless. The share of debt owed to CMEA countries, as expected, declined more significantly from 6.7% to 3.2%, while a moderate increase in share occurred for debt owed to international organisations (from 11.1% in 1971 to 12.1% in 1982). Finally, the share of inter-developing country debt in the total remained steady at around 2% over the same period.

While no projections of future debt service payments are made by the DAC, information on historical service payments is available and is set out by debt type in Table 12.12. Aggregate service payments have increased significantly over the observation period and, within this total, the growing importance of interest payments (as was also observed in the flow specification of DRS data in Table 11.3) is apparent, with the share of such payments rising from 30% of the total in 1971 to 45.8% in 1982. In addition, service payments overall are generally rising faster than the debt itself by anything up to ten percentage points each year. An interesting conclusion from this table is the greater share of service payments on export credits and other private lending at market terms compared to the share of these debt types in the total outstanding debt itself. This reflects the non-concessionary terms on such financial flows — in particular, higher interest charges and shorter maturities — compared to the softer, concessionary terms on ODA, in particular, and other multilateral lending. In fact the share of payments to service ODA and other multilateral debt relative to total debt service payments had fallen as low as 8.3% in 1982 in comparison to the share of such debt in total outstanding indebtedness of 25.2% in that year.

Finally, Table 12.13 presents annual data on the outstanding external debt of the twenty largest country debtors (at the end of 1981) for the period from 1978 to 1981. The DAC also publishes figures of reserves held by individual developing countries which is additional information of immense value and is presented alongside the debt totals in Table 12.13 in a similar way to that used in the DAC *Annual Report*. All but three of the major country debtors listed in Table 12.13 also appear in the list of major debtors from DRS data on *public debt only* in Table 11.9 (one of these being Spain which is not classified as a developing country and so is excluded from the DRS), while the more comprehensive nature of DAC data is confirmed by higher country totals occurring in Table 12.13 in comparison with Table 11.9 for the remaining seventeen countries.[22]

In the final two columns of table 12.13, the proportion of reserves to outstanding debt is calculated in aggregate and for the individual

[22] This would be expected given that Table 12.13 includes all external debt while Table 11.9 covers public debt only.

countries. Although a comparison of reserves with debt service obligations in the immediate future would be a better indicator of the 'liquidity' of individual countries, these calculations are of considerable interest and permit the practice of countries' borrowing and therefore incurring new debt to build up reserves to be allowed for in the data. The share of outstanding debt that is 'covered' by reserves varies greatly across countries, and, over the twenty countries in aggregate, fell sharply from 27.5% in 1978 to a preliminary estimate of 19.1% in 1981 (eighteen countries only). Countries whose coverage of debt by reserves fell to very low levels during this period included Morocco (13% to 3.8%), Egypt (5.8% to 5.7%), Turkey (11.3% to 9%), Yugoslavia (21.9% to 10.1%) and Brazil (26.8% to 10.2%), while Mexico (6.2% to 7.7%), Peru (6.6% to 17.8%) and Pakistan (9% to 18.5%) all improved, in differing degrees, positions of serious relative shortage of reserves. Many other countries continue to have adequate reserve coverage of external debt including Nigeria (65% at the end of 1981), Venezuela (58.4%), Spain (45.4%) and Israel (43.6%).

SUMMARY

It is said that

'DAC statistics are a unique source of information on the flow of financial resources to developing countries and are recognised as providing a comprehensive, comparable, neutral and useful body of data' (Stein, 1980, p. 4).

The task that is tackled by these figures is enormous and the outflow of detailed information both in aggregate and at the individual country level is indicative of the importance and scope of this work. In the compilation of these figures, the DAC Secretariat encounters a number of problems many of which have been considered in some depth at various points in this chapter. These may be summarised as problems of concept, reporting and confidentiality. While the achievement of cross-country comparability particularly with respect to private sector flows is very difficult, the overriding constraint on these figures concerns the disclosure of confidential data. The uncertainty over whether full information on certain financial flows is reported is, at times, considerable but such doubts do not detract from the overall value and benefits of these figures on resources flows to developing countries and their external indebtedness.

Section 5
Statistics of IMF Borrowing and Lending

Chapter 13

Structure of IMF Credit Activities

INTRODUCTION

The subject of this section is the data on credit flows from the IMF. In Chapter 13, the structure and development of IMF borrowing and lending activities will be described and some aggregate data presented. In Chapter 14, the complex tabular presentation of the Fund's accounts sumarising these activities, which is published in *International Financial Statistics*, will be explained. Although this presentation includes all operations and transactions involving Special Drawing Rights (SDRs)[1] through the Special Drawing Rights Department, concentration in these chapters is almost exclusively placed on the activities of the Fund's General Department. The Fund's borrowing operations and the drawing of resources by member countries are completed through the General Resources Account of the General Department.

Under the articles of agreement that established the IMF at the Bretton Woods conference in 1944, six main objectives of the Fund were set out (Hooke, 1981). The organisation was (1) to promote international co-operation by providing the machinery required for members to consult and collaborate on international monetary issues; (2) to facilitate the balanced growth of international trade and, through this, contribute to high levels of employment and real

---

[1] SDRs are an international reserve asset created by the IMF. They are a combination or basket of currencies of fixed, nominal amounts; originally 16 currencies were included in the basket but this was reduced and simplified to only 5 currencies (the US dollar, Deutschemark, pound sterling, French franc and Japanese yen) in January 1981. All IMF accounts and therefore all tables in this chapter which include totals expressed in absolute terms are denominated in SDRs.

income and the development of productive capacity; (3) to promote exchange stability and orderly exchange arrangements and facilitate the avoidance of competitive currency depreciation; (4) to foster a multilateral system of payments and transfers for current transactions and seek the elimination of exchange restrictions that hinder the growth of world trade; (5) to make financial resources available to members, on a temporary basis and with adequate safeguards, to permit them to correct payments imbalances with resorting to measures destructive of national and international prosperity; and (6) to seek reduction of both the duration and magnitude of payments imbalances.

In the context of the survey of data on credit flows to individual countries undertaken in this book, emphasis is placed in this section on the fifth of the above objectives; in particular the objectives in relation to exchange rate arrangements, as enshrined in the Bretton Woods system, and the general promotion of international co-operation are played down.

To appreciate the environment in which these credit flows have occurred it is essential to be aware of the significant change of role of the IMF particularly during the last ten years.[2] At its establishment, the IMF comprised forty-five member countries (of which twenty-eight were developing nations) and its major functions were to monitor the newly-created fixed exchange rate system and to provide short-term funds to countries suffering temporary balance of payments disequilibria. There was no explicit reference to the goal of economic development and implicitly it was believed that industrialised countries, in particular, would be the major recipients of IMF credit flows.[3]

However with the final collapse of the Bretton Woods exchange rate system in 1973, the rapid development of the eurocurrency market in the 1970s and the rise in its membership, the IMF's role was compelled to change. Despite certain abortive attempts to re-establish fixed exchange rates on a global basis or alternatively to create rules of intervention that would apply in a world of essentially

[2] For short discussions of this changing role see de Larosière (1979), Forrest, (1981) Gorman (1981) and for a much more detailed survey see Williamson (1982).

[3] The charge against the IMF that it has under-emphasised economic development may be answered by stating that the World Bank — established at the same time as the IMF — was planned to be more directly concerned with encouraging the development of the poorer nations, while it may also be argued that economic development would be indirectly promoted by the pursuit of a major IMF objective, namely that of facilitating the expansion of international trade (see, for example, Nowzad, 1981).

flexible parities, the role of the IMF in monitoring the exchange rate system since 1973 has, by definition, declined. With the growth of the eurocurrency markets — in particular, the market for syndicated bank credits — the industrialised countries now have less need to have recourse to the IMF when short of funds. The only heavy borrowers from the IMF amongst the advanced countries in the 1970s have been the UK, USA and Italy, with the last major drawing by one of these countries being made by the USA in 1978 (Table 13.2). In contrast the ability of many of the poorer developing countries to raise credit in large amounts and at fine terms in the eurocurrency markets is generally limited. In addition, with the two major periods of oil price increase pushing the developing countries as a group into substantial long-term balance of payments disequilibrium, it is apparent that these countries in particular now have a much greater need to borrow funds from the IMF (Bird, 1981a). Finally the expansion of the membership of the IMF to 143 countries by the end of December 1981,[4] of which only 21 were not designated as developing countries, has increased the importance, at least in this sense, of the poorer nations in the organisation.

Given that much of the IMF's activity at the present time is the provision of credit to the poorer nations, it may be argued that as a result, the Fund is becoming more akin to a development institution, and is moving away from its initial role of providing short-term balance of payments support. Three points need to be made concerning such a development. Firstly, developing countries often approach the IMF for funds as a last resort once their ability to raise private credit has been virtually exhausted. Developing countries, in general, dislike the often rigid conditionality attached to IMF credits. Therefore with the IMF acting as a 'lender of last resort', when the economic conditions in a particular country have deteriorated markedly, it may be necessary for the Fund to attach rigid adjustment conditions to seek to improve a country's difficult economic circumstances.[5] A type of vicious circle is created with the IMF, due to the perceived harsh conditionality that it often imposes, seen to be the villain and to be generally unsympathetic to the problems and requirements of developing countries. Secondly, a basic conflict may now exist between the original role that the IMF was perceived to be

[4] This rose further to 146 countries, with the admission of Hungary, in May 1982.
[5] See Reichmann and Stillson (1978), Donovan (1982a, 1982b) and Kelly (1982, 1983) for broad studies of the effects of IMF adjustment programmes on member countries' economic performance.

going to play of generating temporary balance of payments financing and its more recently-developed function of providing long-term structural support for the developing countries. Finally, with this change of role, it may be argued that there is now a blurring of functions between the IMF and the World Bank. A case could therefore be made for either amalgamating the two organisations or reversing the gradual evolution in the IMF's role back towards the contribution it was initially designed to make. It is clear, however, that there is great pressure from the developed countries for the IMF to retain its traditional role (Howe, 1982), although many developing nations would prefer the transformation of the Fund into a source of longer-term transfers of resources.

These general features of the evolution of the IMF are illustrated in Table 13.1. While 64.8% of the funds lent by the IMF between 1947 and 1974 were drawn by industrialised countries, this share fell to 32.2% in 1975–81. The most recent observations point to a continuation of this trend with there being little drawing from the Fund by industrial countries in 1979 and none in 1980 or 1981. Nevertheless a consideration of Table 13.2 of major drawing countries suggests some tempering of this conclusion. There is evidence that the major industrial country borrowers (the UK, USA and Italy, although not France) continued to use Fund resources fairly heavily in the 1970s. The largest developing country borrower between 1975 and 1981 was India (SDR 2.43 billion), but this total was little more than half of total UK drawings over this period. It seems therefore that the 1970s has seen more recourse by developing countries to the IMF at the expense of the less heavy users of IMF resources amongst the industrial countries; at times, certain other industrial countries continued to draw heavily from the Fund.

SOURCES OF IMF FUNDS

The main source of IMF resources is the subscriptions of members. These have been augmented during the IMF's existence through the General Arrangements to Borrow (GAB) and, more recently, by direct borrowing from certain member countries to finance specific drawing facilities.

Each member of the IMF is required to pay a subscription to the Fund equal to its assigned quota. Under the original articles of the Fund, 25% of the quota (equivalent to the gold tranche to be defined later) was to be paid in gold and the remaining 75% in the member's own domestic currency. However with the declining role of gold

TABLE 13.1
Gross Drawings from the IMF by Geographical Area
(SDR m)

	1947–1974	1975	1976	1977	1978	1979	1980	1981	1947–1981
Industrial countries	19127.5	2043.7	3174.9	2389.4	2473.8	72.8	—	—	29282.1
Oil-exporting countries	597.8	80.0	—	—	—	—	—	—	677.8
Non-oil developing countries	9666.9	2474.5	3835.0	1035.2	1210.7	1769.9	3752.7	7081.7	30826.6
of which:									
Africa	1212.9	465.3	914.2	320.2	309.1	539.7	874.1	1875.9	6511.4
Asia	3143.2	722.9	776.4	295.7	334.9	355.7	1586.6	3299.4	10514.8
Europe	1068.3	486.1	731.0	148.2	241.4	389.4	966.0	1299.7	5330.1
Middle East	669.6	190.1	220.9	117.5	147.4	—	31.6	45.9	1423.0
Western Hemisphere	3572.6	610.2	1192.6	153.7	177.9	485.1	294.4	560.8	7047.3
Unallocated	138.1	60.0	—	—	60.0	—	—	—	258.1
Total	29530.3	4658.1	7009.9	3424.6	3744.3	1842.8	3752.7	7081.7	61044.6
Shares in total									
Industrial countries	64.8	43.9	45.3	69.8	66.1	4.0	—	—	48.0
Non-oil developing countries	32.7	53.1	54.7	30.2	32.3	96.0	100.0	100.0	50.5

TABLE 13.2
Gross Drawings from the IMF by Country
(SDR m)

	1947–1974	1975	1976	1977	1978	1979	1980	1981	1947–1981
UK	7868	—	2400	2250	—	—	—	—	12518
USA	3552	—	—	—	2275	—	—	—	5827
Italy	2001	1080	—	90	—	—	—	—	3171
France	2388	—	78	—	—	—	—	—	2466
India	1664	201	—	—	—	—	266	300	2431
Yugoslavia	567	16	186	—	—	268	339	554	1929
Turkey	320	245	129	—	202	70	492	400	1859
Philippines	317	126	223	109	93	136	303	200	1506
Korea	150	107	104	—	—	—	499	576	1437
Pakistan	425	161	107	67	40	21	105	483	1409
Argentina	715	311	270	—	—	—	—	—	1295
Spain	216	614	76	—	99	—	—	—	1004
South Africa	337	91	390	162	—	—	—	—	980
Romania	95	40	150	73	39	41	121	346	905
Chile	587	177	124	—	—	—	—	—	888
Zambia	76	57	38	19	149	100	50	359	848
China, People's Republic of	—	—	—	—	—	—	218	600	818
Peru	208	—	190	10	86	177	111	—	781
Germany	684	30	—	49	—	—	—	—	763
Thailand	2	—	67	—	101	45	—	531	747
Sri Lanka	265	42	28	55	38	80	30	194	732
Egypt	413	—	126	105	75	—	—	—	719

over time and the increasing share of total international liquidity held as foreign exchange, particularly the dollar, the gold tranche was renamed the reserve tranche under the second amendment of the Fund's articles in April 1978; it has now become more common for the first 25% of quota to be paid in foreign exchange in part or in full. A further change occurred with the implementation of the Sixth General Review of Quotas also in April 1978. This stated that less than 25% could now be subscribed in gold and foreign exchange by a member with the remainder being subscribed in domestic currency. The exact proportion to be deposited in *domestic currency* was determined by the 'norm'.[6] Clearly, the effect of the definition of the 'norm' is that over time the share of a member's quota subscribed in reserve assets (including gold) will fall. However notwithstanding this, the Seventh General Review of Quotas, effective in November 1980, stated that the previous formula of 25% of the quota to be paid in reserve assets was to be applied to the quota *increase* sanctioned in that Review.

Since the establishment of the IMF, the quotas themselves have been calculated using a variety of formulae (*IMF Survey*, 1978). Essentially, however, a country's quota is based on certain key macroeconomic variables such as national income, reserves, the variability of exports and the export/income ratio. According to the Articles of the Fund, a general review of quotas has to be undertaken at least once every five years while at any other time selective adjustments to quotas (normally involving changes in the shares of individual countries' quota within a fixed total) may be made. In recent years, such adjustments have typically been made to reflect the increased importance of oil exporting countries and the greater need of non-oil developing countries to have access to adequate liquidity. For example, in September 1981 a quota increase for Saudi Arabia from SDR1.04 million to SDR2.10 million was made effective, although in this case no compensating quota reductions of other members were made; total quotas therefore rose. In addition to determining its subscription to the Fund, a country's quota also determines its drawing and voting rights and its share of an SDR

[6] The norm is not a uniform amount; it is determined according to the date of entry of each country to the Fund. For a member country which joined before the Second Amendment of the Fund's articles became effective on April 1, 1978 the 'norm' is equal to 75% of its quota prior to the Second Amendment plus the whole of subsequent quota increases. For countries joining since April 1, 1978, the 'norm' is the weighted average of the 'norms' applicable to all members on the date at which that country joined the Fund. At the end of 1981, the average 'norm' was 87.9%.

allocation. As a result, the size and distribution of quotas are of great significance in the whole operation of the Fund.

Table 13.3 sets out the SDR value of individual country quotas and their size relative to total quotas at the end of 1981. For most members, the Seventh General Review raised quotas by 50%, with, however, greater increases for eleven countries. Total quotas stood at SDR 60.674 billion at the end of 1981 and SDR 61.060 billion at the end of May 1982 when the membership of the Fund had expanded to 146 countries. The Eighth General Review, which under Fund rules had to be completed by the end of December 1983, was advanced in time such that at a meeting of the Interim Committee of the IMF in February 1983, an increase of 47.5% to approximately SDR 90 billion was agreed in principle. Forty per cent of this total was to be spread over all members according to their current quotas, with the remainder of the increase being in the form of selected adjustments to individual members' quota sizes. This increase of just under half was viewed as a satisfactory compromise between the developing countries who sought a doubling of quotas, most of the industrialised nations who wanted an increase of around 50–75% and the USA which initially wanted no increase at all and apparently accepted the agreed increase as an absolute maximum. At the time of writing, the Eighth General Review of Quotas still had to be ratified by individual member governments. As a result the information in the second half of Table 13.3 on the proposed increases in quotas under this latest review is tentative, in particular with respect to the country shares in the total which may be significantly affected if a number of countries fail to ratify the proposed increases. Despite recent moves to reallocate members' quotas in favour of OPEC and the non-oil developing nations, as much as 48.6% of the total at the end of 1981 was accounted for by seven major industrial nations (the USA, UK, Germany, France, Japan, Canada and Italy); only 11% of total quotas was allocated to the group of oil exporting countries (as designated by the IMF) and 27.4% to the non-oil developing countries.

The IMF first borrowed to raise resources in October 1962, when, under the *General Arrangements to Borrow* (GAB), ten industrialised countries (and later Switzerland) agreed to lend $6 billion to the IMF. These arrangements were to be activated when requests for drawings on the reserve or credit tranches were made by one or more of the ten countries concerned. In other words, the GAB sought to finance drawings by any of the ten countries themselves without using the Fund's normal resources which could therefore be lent to other countries. Despite being renewed frequently the dollar value of the GAB was not altered in size until the beginning of 1983. At that time it

TABLE 13.3
Quotas of Largest Fund Members (SDR m; End-1981)

	Actual quotas (end-1981)		Proposed quotas (Feb-1983)	
	SDR m	% of total	SDR m	% of total[1]
Industrial countries total	37410.0	61.66	56089.0	62.32
Australia	1185.0	1.95	1619.2	1.80
Austria	495.0	0.82	775.6	0.86
Belgium	1335.0	2.20	2080.4	2.31
Canada	2035.5	3.35	2941.0	3.27
Denmark	465.0	0.77	711.0	0.79
Finland	393.0	0.65	574.9	0.64
France	2878.5	4.74	4482.8	4.94
Germany	3234.0	5.33	5403.7	6.00
Italy	1860.0	3.07	2909.1	3.23
Japan	2488.5	4.10	4223.3	4.69
Netherlands	1422.0	2.34	2264.8	2.52
Norway	442.5	0.73	699.0	0.78
Spain	835.5	1.38	1286.0	1.43
Sweden	675.0	1.11	1064.3	1.18
UK	4387.5	7.23	6194.0	6.88
USA	12607.5	20.78	17918.3	19.91
Developing countries total	23264.0	38.34	33911.0[1]	37.68
Oil exporting countries total	6662.1	10.98	10392.5	11.55
Algeria	427.5	0.70	623.1	0.69
Indonesia	720.0	1.19	1009.7	1.12
Iran	660.0	1.09	1117.4	1.24
Iraq	234.1	0.39	504.0	0.56
Kuwait	393.3	0.65	635.3	0.71
Libya	298.4	0.49	515.7	0.57
Nigeria	540.0	0.89	849.5	0.94
Saudi Arabia	2100.0	3.46	3202.4	3.56
Venezuela	990.0	1.63	1371.5	1.52
Non-oil developing countries total	16601.9	27.36	23518.5[1]	26.13
Argentina	892.5	1.32	1113.0	1.24
Brazil	997.5	1.64	1461.3	1.62
China	1800.0	2.97	2390.9	2.66
Hungary	—	—	530.7	0.59
India	1717.5	2.83	2207.7	2.45
Malaysia	379.5	0.63	550.6	0.61
Mexico	802.5	1.32	1165.5	1.30
Pakistan	427.5	0.70	546.3	0.61
Romania	367.5	0.61	523.4	0.58
South Africa	636.0	1.05	915.7	1.17
Yugoslavia	415.5	0.68	613.0	1.68
Total	60674.0		90000[1]	

[1]Approximate figures.

was proposed that the GAB should be increased nearly threefold as one contribution to the provision of extra liquidity during the international financial crisis at that time. The proposed distribution of the augmented GAB is set out in Table 13.3. Three features of the newly-expanded arrangements (in addition to the redistribution of members' shares to reflect relative changes in the size and role of each member in the international economy) should be noted. Firstly, it is planned that Switzerland will become a full member of the GAB. Accordingly, that country gave a commitment to provide SDR 1020 million to the GAB. Secondly, the funds are planned to be available to non-members (of the GAB) for drawing in contrast to the previous restriction to members only. However such drawings will only be available on conditional terms and when the Fund is faced with an inadequacy of other resources such that there is a danger to the stability of the international financial system. Finally, it is envisaged that, in the future, other countries may either become members of the GAB or be associated with it. At the time of writing, discussions had already occurred with Saudi Arabia on this basis.

In recent years, borrowing has also been completed by the IMF to provide direct finance for some of the newly-established drawing facilities. The two oil facilities in 1974 and 1975 were financed by SDR6.91 billion of loans from 16 member countries and the Supplementary Financing Facility by loans totalling SDR7.78 billion from thirteen member countries, including six oil-exporting countries and from Switzerland. Finally, much of the Fund's Policy on Enlarged Access to Resources, effective from May 1981, was expected to be financed by a two-year SDR8 billion loan from the Saudi-Arabian Monetary Agency (SAMA) with a further SDR1.3 billion being made available by a group of thirteen industrial countries, part of the latter being through the BIS. Details of this direct borrowing are also set out in Table 13.4.

The possibility that the IMF may have to enter the private markets to supplement its resources has also been raised in recent times. However, member countries see this option very much as a last resort or at least only 'a temporary expedient' (Howe, 1982), given that it may alter the character of the Fund as a mutual association of governments and an international monetary authority. It may also require an increase in the rates of interest charged on members' drawings and a tightening of conditionality if the IMF itself has to pay a market rate of interest on any private borrowing (Frowen, 1981), while there is a fear that banks might then lend funds to the IMF rather than directly to borrowing countries. In this light a compromise solution such as sales of SDR-denominated bonds to member coun-

TABLE 13.4
Direct Borrowing Agreements of the IMF Under GAB and Various Special Facilities
(SDR m)

Official Agencies or Central Banks of:	General arrangements to borrow:		Oil facility:		Supplementary financing facility: 1979	Enlarged access policy: 1981
	at end-1981¹	1983 proposed increase	1974	1975		
Austria				100	50	
Belgium	167.5	595		200	150	
Canada	157.7	892.5	246.9		200	
Denmark						
France	403.6	1700				
Germany	1524.1	2380		600	1050	
Italy	249.9	1105				1305
Japan	1333.2	2125			900	
Netherlands	252.6	850	150	200	100	
Norway				100		
Sweden	81.1	382.5		50		
Switzerland		1020		250	650	
UK	578.6	1700				
USA	1718.3	4250			1450	
Abu Dhabi			100		150	
Guatemala					30	
Iran			580	410		
Kuwait			400	285	400	
Nigeria			100	200	220	
Oman			20	0.5		
Saudi Arabia			1000	1250	1934	8000
Trinidad and Tobago				10		
Venezuela			450	200	500	
	6466.7	17000	3046.9	3855.5	7784	9305

¹Equivalent to the $6 billion GAB agreement at the end-1981 exchange rate for the SDR (see Chapter 14).

tries is a much more likely course of action in any future Fund liquidity shortfall (*The Banker*, 1982).

CONDITIONALITY

Much of the credit made available to member countries by the IMF is subject to 'conditionality' to a greater or lesser extent. The whole issue of Fund conditonality is a controversial and important one that should be treated separately before the various tranche policies and credit facilities are described individually in the next section. Only a brief survey of the subject is given here with the aim of providing just sufficient background detail to place the information of the next section in proper perspective.[7]

Conditionality refers to the imposition of certain economic adjustment policies on member countries seeking access to the resources of the Fund. Its main objective is:

'to help members to attain, over the medium-term, a viable payments position, if feasible in the context of reasonable price and exchange rate stability, as well as a sustainable level and rate of growth of economic activity' (Guitian, 1980, p. 24)

In the pursuit of this objective, certain performances criteria may be established by the IMF to monitor the implementation of the agreed programme. These criteria concentrate on the traditional macroeconomic variables such as quantified ceilings on bank credit, the money supply and public sector deficits, key elements of the price system such as the exchange rate and rates of interest and other crucial variables such as the levels of external debt and international reserves (Crockett, 1982). In general, therefore, adjustment programmes typically include reference to fiscal and monetary measures, frequently a change in the country's exchange rate and, at times, the introduction of an incomes policy. In observing such conditionality clauses, lending by the IMF is aimed to facilitate the international adjustment process, through the sensible combination of short-term financing and medium-term adjustment of exteral payments disequilibria. Although often perceived so, conditionality should not be treated by a country as a 'penalty' for past excesses.

The principles which underly the imposition of conditionality are

[7] Recent comprehensive studies of conditionality include Gold (1979a), Guitian (1980, 1981a, 1981b, 1981c), Bird (1981a) and Dell (1981). See also Hooke (1981).

long-established and, in theory, non-controversial. Most importantly, conditionality assumes that any external payments imbalance (unless of a transotory nature in which case a short-term financing programme would suffice) must be corrected in time. In the imposition of conditions on a member country in pursuit of this principle, the IMF seeks to achieve uniformity of treatment for all its members while, nevertheless, taking account of institutional variations across the countries.

As early as 1952, a decision was made to incorporate a certain degree of conditionality — in particular with respect to the length of the repayment period — into Fund lending. A major review of conditionality in 1968, which essentially confirmed all the evolving elements of policy in this field, was effectively overtaken by the economic disruption of the early 1970s in particular the collapse of fixed exchange rates in 973 and the substantial increases in the prices of oil and other commodities in 1973/74. In these circumstances, the immediate requirement of many countries was for access to large volumes of funds to assist in balance of payments financing. To this end, the IMF established the 1974 and 1975 Oil Facilities, the Trust Fund in 1976 to provide credit at low conditionality and the Extended and Supplementary Financing Facilities in 1974 and 1979 respectively — in addition to the increase in quotas — to deal with the need for medium-term financial support of significant volume.

The more flexible approach evidenced by the new facilities called for a new set of guidelines on conditionality, eventually made effective in 1979. The new elements of these guidelines recognised the need for a longer-term adjustment for many (particularly structural payments deficits and the consideration of a borrowing country's social and political objectives, while embracing the crucial importance of the introdcution of effective adjustment measures at an early stage of balance of payments difficulties. Therefore, there is no doubt that the IMF has responded flexibly — both in the provision of the facilities themselves and the conditionality attached to them — to the global economic problems of the last decade. This flexibility has been enhanced by the more explicit reference to measures to expand supply potential in recent lending agreements with member countries. While such supply measures have never been ignored completely (at least implicitly) throughout the history of the Fund, the recent emphasis on measures to stimulate investment, promote exports, increase the productive efficiency of public sector spending and raise employment and production incentives reflects the macroeconomic environment of the early 1980s.

Moves towards increased flexibility of borrowing conditions have not, however, prevented heavy criticism of conditionality, notably on the part of developing countries.[8] The central complaint is a general insensitivity of IMF conditonality to development needs. In particular, it is argued that a distinction should be drawn not simply between transient and permanent external deficits but also between those which have external rather than internal origins. For example, if a deficit is caused by adverse movements in the terms of trade associated with global recession or a rise in the price of oil, the imposition of strict monetary and fiscal policies on a non-oil developing country may be inappropriate; such policies treat the symptoms of the payments deficit and may acutally *discourage* the structural adjustment which may be needed to deal with the fundamental cause of disequilibrium. Conditionality is said to be too reliant on the operation of markets in ways most identifiable with advanced industrial nations and also to compromise the long-term growth objectives of developing nations. The almost mandatory depreciation of a country's exchange rate may also not be sensible for all developing countries particularly given the short-term J-curve effects of a devaluation in worsening the rate of inflation and the balance of payments.

More generally, despite recent greater flexibility in this respect, it is argued that too rapid adjustment speeds are frequently imposed on many developing countries. Although the IMF believes such immediate adjustment may be necessary given that it is often approached for assistance only as a last resort, the dangers of a political and social backlash in the face of harsh conditionality may be considerable. In itself, the perceived insensitivity of IMF conditionality to the political stability in a borrowing country represents an additional general criticism of conditionality. Finally, conditionality frequently has to be severe due to the limited pool of IMF resources and has had to become tougher precisely because of the worsening situation in individual economies and the world economy as a whole in recent years. The solution to the first of these problems may be a continuation of the recent process of increasing resources rather than rationing, on unrealistically harsh terms, those resources which are already available.

Clearly conditionality should not be abandoned, particularly as the IMF is the only truly global financial institution that is able to impose conditionality on a formal basis. Despite the recent switch in emphasis towards more lending to the developing countries, the IMF must

---

[8] Some of the counter-arguments to the following criticisms of IMF conditionality have been put by Nowzad (1981).

retain its character as an institution providing balance of payments support and it should not become a foreign aid agency. Therefore the real challenge for the future is to mould and develop the process of conditionality according to the international economic situation and, most importantly, to the needs and long-term viability of the Fund's member countries.

BORROWING FROM THE IMF[9]

Member countries may borrow funds from the IMF for balance of payments purposes. These borrowings are completed through the sale of domestic currency of the country concerned to the Fund in return for other countries' currencies or SDRs. Therefore while such 'purchases' or 'drawings' effectively raise the foreign exchange reserves of the drawing country, they do not alter the total volume of funds available to the IMF, but simply alter its composition. Over time, a country must repay its drawing (or make 'repurchases' of its own currency from the Fund) according to the repayment conditions for the particular borrowing arrangement in question; a country is, however, expected to complete repurchases earlier than scheduled if its balance of payments situation improves sufficiently.

Before the various drawings from the Fund are described a further statistical concept has to be introduced at this stage. This is the *Use of Fund Credit* which is defined by the IMF as the net use by a member of its conditional drawing rights in the Fund or alternatively it is the outstanding *stock* of credit owed by a member country to the Fund at any particular point in time. In effect, it is the cumultive total of all *net* purchases made over the history of the Fund. Therefore if net purchases from the Fund in a given year are positive, the Use of Fund Credit at the end of that year is greater than that at the end of the previous year.

The Use of Fund Credit is quantified in aggregate form in Table 13.5 and also sub-divided into the use of credit under the various tranche policies and facilities to be defined below.[10] From Table 13.5, it is clear that sharp increases in the Use of Fund Credit were recorded in 1974–1976 due to heavy use of the Oil Facilities and also, in 1976,

[9] See Williamson (1982) and the conference papers quoted therein, for a very detailed, up-to-date analysis of all aspects of fund lending policies.

[10] Given that the Use of Fund Credit covers drawings of conditional credit only, Table 13.5 excludes any drawings on the reserve tranche. Such drawings simply return to the member its own reserves rather than using the credit of the IMF. Therefore data on all drawings are not exactly compatible with the information on the Use of Fund Credit in Table 13.5.

due to substantial drawings on the ordinary credit tranches and on the Compensatory Financing Facility. In contrast by the end of 1979, the Use of Fund Credit had fallen back to SDR8 billion under the influence of repurchases under the Oil Facilities and ordinary credit tranches. The increase in the Use of Fund Credit in 1981 was also considerable and was mainly due to Ordinary and Supplementary drawings on both credit tranches and the Extended Fund Facility. In gross terms, in fact, purchases in 1981 were a record.

Time-series data for the Use of Fund Credit by country are set out in Table 13.6. The industrial countries and non-oil developing countries substantially increased their borrowing from the IMF in 1974–76. While much of this credit was repaid by the industrialised countries in the remainder of the decade, the Use of Fund Credit by developing nations continued to rise albeit erratically and generally slowly until a sharp increase occurred in 1981. For example, outstanding credit owed by Italy of SDR2.46 billion in 1975–6 had been repaid by the end of 1979, while by the end of 1981 the UK accounted for 57.3% of outstanding credit owed by industrialised countries to the IMF. Borrowing by the developing countries was much more widely spread across member countries, with significant outstanding Fund debts held by Turkey (SDR1.14 billion), Yugoslavia (SDR1.08 billion), Korea (SDR1.07 billion), the Philippines (SDR0.82 billion), Pakistan (SDR0.65 billion), Zambia (SDR0.63 billion) and Thailand (SDR0.61 billion) at the end of 1981.

Tranche Policies

Details of the cumulative possible tranche drawings with their effects on the Fund's holding of a member country's domestic currency and reserves and the related conditionality are given in Table 13.7. The drawing of the first 25% of a country's quota (the reserve tranche) effectively reduces the reserves of the drawing country in the Fund from 25% to zero, while increasing the Fund's holdings of that country's domestic currency from 75% to 100%.[11] Given that this tranche effectively furnishes a member country with some of its own reserves (previously deposited at the Fund), it is available unconditionally[12] and is part of any calculation of that member country's

[11] This calculation of the proportion of a members' quota held in domestic currency at the IMF in Table 13.7 is independent of any holdings of members' currencies that arise from transactions under the Fund's other policies and special facilities. All reserve tranche drawings may be made independent of a country's position *vis-à-vis* these other facilities.
[12] Except for the requirement of balance of payments need.

TABLE 13.5
Use of Fund Credit
(SDR m; End-Year)

	Total	Credit tranche drawings			Compensatory Financing Facility drawings	Buffer Stock Financing Facility drawings	Extended Fund Facility drawings			Oil Facility drawings
		Ordinary	SFF[1]	EAR[2]			Ordinary	SFF[1]	EAR	
1973	1.0	0.5	—	—	0.5	—	—	—	—	—
1974	3.7	1.4	—	—	0.5	—	—	—	—	1.7
1975	7.4	1.8	—	—	0.7	—	—	—	—	4.8
1976	12.6	3.1	—	—	2.7	—	0.1	—	—	6.7
1977	13.1	3.9	—	—	2.8	—	0.3	—	—	6.4
1978	10.3	1.9	—	—	2.9	—	0.3	—	—	5.0
1979	8.0	1.4	0.2	—	2.8	0.1	0.5	0.1	—	2.8
1980	8.5	1.5	1.1	—	2.8	—	0.8	0.4	—	1.9
1981	13.4	3.1	2.6	0.3	3.3³	—	1.7	0.9	0.5	0.9

[1] Supplementary Financing Facility.
[2] Policy on Enlarged Access to Resources.
³ From 1981, this is divided into Compensatory Financing Facility Drawings for Export Shortfalls (SDR 3260 million in 1981) and Compensatory Financing Facility Drawings for Cereal Import-Excesses (SDR 12 million in 1981).

TABLE 13.6
Use of Fund Credit by Country
(SDR m; End-Year)

	1975	1976	1977	1978	1979	1980	1981
Industrial countries	3298	5695	6456	4107	1660	1044	546
Australia	—	333	333	247	271	62	—
Italy	2457	2457	1581	880	—	—	—
New Zealand	242	390	388	361	270	132	34
Spain	496	572	572	615	205	205	142
UK	—	1700	3340	1805	813	563	313
Oil exporting countries	—	—	—	—	—	—	—
Non-oil developing countries	4137	6913	6622	6170	6317	7442	12822
Argentina	250	456	345	—	—	—	—
Chile	331	402	301	267	136	96	42
China, People's Rep. of	—	—	—	—	—	—	450
India	698	406	125	—	—	266	566
Ivory Coast	11	23	13	—	—	—	319
Jamaica	13	69	88	139	267	243	404
Korea	217	302	280	202	104	535	1071
Mexico	—	319	419	229	103	—	—
Morocco	—	116	116	173	151	248	387
Pakistan	374	440	438	395	337	300	650
Peru	—	159	169	256	373	372	333
Philippines	165	348	418	441	507	669	823
Romania	88	238	270	256	247	257	507
South Africa	—	315	392	314	77	—	—
Sri Lanka	125	134	170	186	234	211	347
Sudan	113	119	100	121	171	268	414
Thailand	—	67	67	136	182	143	606
Turkey	208	337	337	478	480	827	1136
Yugoslavia	155	319	213	183	346	596	1076
Zambia	76	95	95	245	320	308	628
Total	7435	12608	13078	10277	7976	8486	13367

Reserve Position in the Fund, defined in the next chapter. There are no charges for reserve tranche drawings and no obligation to repurchase.

Four other tranches of equal size are also available to a member for drawing. These are known as 'credit tranches' and if drawn in full take the Fund's holdings of that member's currency from 100% to 200% of quota. They are subject to increasingly severe conditionality. Since the major review of conditionality in 1968, no performance criteria have been applied in the case of a drawing in the first credit tranche, although an economic adjustment programme has to be discussed by the IMF and the country concerned. This programme is likely to be the same as that considered when drawings in the upper credit tranches are requested; however in the case of these upper

TABLE 13.7
Possible Tranche Drawings and Related Conditionality

Transaction	IMF Holdings of Member's:[1]		Reserve position in the fund (RPF) (% of quota)	Conditionality
	Domestic currency (% of quota)	Reserves (% of quota)		
Deposit of quota	75	25	25	—
Drawings				
Reserve tranche[2]	100	—	—	None[3]
Credit tranche 1	125	—	—	⎫ Increasingly severe,
Credit tranche 2	150	—	—	⎬ involving programme
Credit tranche 3	175	—	—	⎨ agreed by IMF and
Credit tranche 4	200	—	—	⎭ member to overcome balance of payments disequilibrium[4]

[1] Assuming no drawing on special facilities of the Fund and no borrowing of relevant members' currency by other members.
[2] Formerly the gold tranche.
[3] Except balance of payments need.
[4] Performance criteria attached in credit tranches 2–4 only.

credit tranche drawings, performance criteria are monitored, while the funds themselves are drawn in phases. While reserve tranche drawings are always by direct purchase, most drawings under the first credit tranche and all drawings in the upper credit tranches are made under stand-by arrangements. These usually permit drawing over a period of up to one year although since 1979 a maximum of three years has been allowed.[13] All credit tranche drawings are subject to repurchase within a fixed time period, usually in equal instalments between three and five years after drawing although, once again, early repayment is required if a member's external payments position improves.[14]

[13] As with stand-by credits in private markets, such arrangements may have an 'announcement' effect which, by restoring market confidence in that country's credit rating, could ensure, paradoxically, that the country will not ultimately have to draw much, if any, of the stand-by facility, as access to private funds is unlocked.
[14] If sufficient improvement occurs and the Fund is able to lend that member's currency to other members as a result, this has the same effect as repurchases by the original member itself.

Special Facilities

In this section, the special facilities created by the IMF over time are described briefly. Table 13.8 tabulates some information including the maximum possible drawing and conditionality on each of these facilities. The reader is also referred back to Table 13.5 for aggregate data on the use of these facilities in 1973–81 and forward to Table 13.10 for data on the outstanding drawings on these facilities by country at the end of 1981.

The *Compensatory Financing Facility* (CFF) was established in 1963, to provide financial assistance to members experiencing balance payments difficulties due to falling export values.[15] To qualify for assistance, a country should be suffering from an export shortfall[16] which is of a short-term nature only and due to circumstances — such as a recession in those countries where the country in payments difficulties has its major markets — beyond that member's control. Given these drawing conditions it is apparent that the facility is aimed primarily at the primary-producing developing countries whose export earnings may be severely reduced by a collapse in the market for their major export commodity. The CFF may not be drawn upon when the shortfall is due to factors (such as an inappropriate economic policies or excess demand) within the member's control.

Initially, under the CFF, up to 25% of a country's quota could be drawn in addition to normal tranche drawings. This was extended to 50% in 1966, 75% in 1975 and 100% in 1979. Three other major liberalisations of the CFF have also been introduced. Under the original design of the CFF, any country which produced its trade statistics with a lag of over 6 months was unable to draw from the CFF, given that a rule existed forcing requests for assistance to be made within six months of the end of the shortfall year. An early drawing procedure was introduced in 1975 incorporating *estimates* for up to half of the shortfall year. In 1979, the CFF was extended to a shortfall on the invisibles account of a country's balance of payments. Finally in 1981, the CFF was extended to allow countries to draw from the facility when faced with temporary increases in the costs of cereal imports due to exogeneous circumstances such as poor harvests or sharp rises in import prices. The integrated facility (encompassing both export shortfall and excessive cereal import costs) now

[15] See Goreux (1980) for a full history and discussion of the CFF.
[16] A shortfall is defined as the discrepancy between export earnings in the shortfall year and the medium-term trend of exports defined as a five-year moving average of export earnings centred on the shortfall year.

TABLE 13.8

Cumulative Purchases under Regular Tranche Policies and Special Facilities[1]
(% of Quota)

	Regular Tranche Policy	Extended Fund Facility	Conditionality	Ordinary Resources
Reserve Tranche	25.0	25.0	} See Table 14.3	EFF
Credit Tranches	100.0	25.0[2]		
Extended Facility	—	140.0	Medium-Term Programme to overcome structural balance of payment disequilibrium including the monitoring of performance criteria.	
Sub Total	125.0	190.0		
Supplementary Financing Facility Credit Tranche 1	12.5		As for upper credit tranches and extended facility; for use for long-term balance of payments adjustment through a stand-by arrangement reaching into the upper credit tranches or under the Extended Facility; subject to performance criteria and phasing of purchases.	SFF
2	30.0			
3	30.0			
4	30.0			
	102.5			
Under Extended Facility		140.0		
Sub Total	227.5	330.0		
With Enlarged Access	600.0	600.0	As for the Supplementary Financing Facility.	ER
Sub Total[3]	600.0	600.0		
Compensatory Financing Facility[4]	125.0	125.0	Existence of export shortfall and/or import cost increase, beyond member's control; co-operation with Fund on payments adjustment, but no performance criteria.	CFF
Buffer Stock Financing Facility	50.0	50.0	Existence of international bufferstock accepted by Fund; co-operation with Fund on payments adjustment but no performance criteria.	BSFF
Total	775.0	775.0		

[1] Excluding any outstanding drawings on the oil facilities.

[2] In effect, only one credit tranche may be drawn.

[3] Assistance under the Enlarged Access Policy (EAR) is limited to 150 per cent of quota annually or 450 per cent of quota over a three year period with a limit on cumulative purchases of 600% of quota. These limits do not include drawings on the CFF

allows total drawings of up to 125% of quota although drawings may still be made up to the original 100% limit for either the export shortfall or the excessive cereal import costs. Conditionality on the CFF is limited. For any drawing up to 50% of quota, a member must agree to co-operate with the IMF on finding a solution to its payments problem and for any higher level drawing the IMF itself must be satisfied with this level of co-operation (although no formal programme is required). Repurchases of CFF drawings must be made in instalments between three and five years after drawing.

The CFF was relatively underused until the mid-1970s. Between 1963 and 1975 gross purchases under the CFF amounted to only SDR1.2 billion (Goreux, 1980) although the effect of the liberalisation of 1975 was apparent with gross purchases totalling SDR2.3 billion and net purchases of SDR2.0 billion in 1976 alone. Since then activity has slowed again and at the end of 1981, SDR3.3 billion of drawings under the CFF were outstanding, of which only SDR12 million were under the newly-created compensation for the excess cost of cereal imports. This relatively limited usage may, in part, be due to the short-term nature of the facility and the fact that it may not deal adequately with the long-term structural problem of a particular country's balance of payments (Bird, 1981b). Nevertheless, the sharp falls in commodity prices in 1981–2 make greater immediate future use of the CFF very likely.

The *Buffer Stock Financing Facility* (BSFF) set up in June 1969 has been the least used of the IMF special facilities. It seeks to provide financial assistance (up to 50% of quota for five years) to members wishing to meet contributions to buffer stock arrangements which themselves aim to limit the export price variability that causes the CFF to be drawn upon. However in effect, the conditionality agreement on an acceptable buffer stock and on co-operation to deal with external payments problems have made it unlikely that many countries would use the scheme, while successful international buffer stocks are difficult to organise. To date, drawings have only been made with respect to agreements on tin and sugar and between 1973 and 1981, total purchases totalled only SDR79 million.

The next special facilities in chronological sequence set up by the IMF were the temporary *Oil Facilities* of 1974 and 1975. These were designed to assist members in coping with and ultimately solving the payments problems caused by the sharp increases in oil prices in late 1973. They are unique in the list of IMF special facilities due to their very short-term nature. The 1974 facility was established in June of that year and the later one in April 1975. Drawings from the facilities were completed by the end of May 1976. Both facilities were financed by direct borrowing from oil exporting countries and certain other countries whose external payments positions did not deteriorate seriously following the oil price increases (notably Germany, Switzerland, Belgium and the Netherlands — see Table 13.4).

In other respects, however, each of the two Oil Facilities had a number of separate features. Under the 1974 facility, drawings could be made up to 75% of a members quota[17] or to an amount equal to balance of payments need during 1974 as defined by a formula including the estimated cost of members' net imports of oil and oil-based products and its level of reserves. A judgement was made that adjustment of external positions to the oil price rises would be difficult in the short-term; therefore *financing* of the deficits was considered to be the main objective with, accordingly, conditionality requirements being limited. A member wishing to draw from the 1974 facility had to demonstrate to the IMF that it was not pursuing policies (such as competitive devaluations) designed to aggravate the payments positions of other members, to be willing to discuss energy conservation and development and long-term balance of payments adjustment with the Fund and to agree not to impose restrictions on current international transactions while in receipt of an oil facility drawing. Repurchases had to be made in equal instalments between four and seven years after the initial drawing.

In contrast, the 1975 oil facility was different in design and by concentrating more on adjustment rather than financing (due to the assumed non-reversibility of the price rises) incorporated tighter conditionality requirements. Under this facility, the relative importance of the quota was raised with drawings now allowed up to 125% of quota or 85% of the formula noted above. Conditionality involved members furnishing the IMF with details of balance of payments adjustment and energy policies for approval (rather than simply consulting the Fund as with the 1974 facility), although no performance criteria were established. The repurchase requirements were identical to those under the 1974 facility although the charges levied on drawings were higher than under the earlier facility.

A further difference with the 1975 Oil Facility was the establishment by the IMF (in August 1975) of an *Oil Facility Subsidy Account*. This was the first of the special facilities designed exclusively for developing country use. Under this arrangement, the Fund subsidised the interest payments (under the 1975 Oil Facility) of up to twenty-five developing countries who had drawn from this facility and were

[17] Once the reserve tranche (at that time the gold tranche) had been drawn in full. Oil Facility drawings were over and above any drawings on the credit tranches.

most seriously affected by the oil price increase. In the financial year 1981, for example, the rate of subsidy on outstanding Oil Facility drawings was 5%. This subsidy account was financed by donations from twenty four Fund members and Switzerland.

The two Oil Facilities were very well used. Combined drawings under the facilities of SDR6.9 billion were made in 1974–6 of which SDR0.93 billion remained outstanding at the end of 1981. The one country with a large outstanding drawing at that time was the UK (SDR0.31 billion). Table 13.9 sets out information on country drawings from the Fund-Administered Accounts. The table lists all those countries which had at the end of 1981 received SDR5 million or more from the Oil Facility Subsidy Account. By that time a total of SDR163.2 million of subsidy payments had been made to the planned number of twenty five countries.

A second facility established in 1974 was the *Extended Fund Facility* (EFF), set up in September of that year. This was designed to assist members through the provision of resources of larger amounts, relative to quota, than available under regular tranche policies and for longer periods. Specifically, assistance under the EFF is available to members suffering from either of two types of balance of payments difficulty. First, a member may draw from the EFF when it is suffering from a long-term structural maladjustment of not only its international trade but also production and prices. Secondly, the EFF provides assistance to any member which is unable — due to the weakness of balance of its payments — to pursue an 'active development policy'. Therefore the EFF accepts the principle that, under certain circumstances, external payments adjustment may only be possible over a long period; such adjustment may, as a result, be inconsistent with the shorter-term nature of the Fund's normal tranche policies.

Drawings under the EFF are phased over a period of three years and may not exceed 140% of quota or together with credit tranches 165% of quota.[18] This implies that the Fund's holdings of that member's domestic currency (which stands at 75% of quota before any tranche drawings) must not exceed 265% of quota under the EFF.

The conditionality attached to the EFF requires a member to draw

[18] Both the above figures exclude drawings under the reserve tranche. As demonstrated in Table 13.8, which *includes* reserve tranche drawings, a member may either draw up to 125% of quota in five equal tranches (without the EFF) or to 190% of quota which includes the full EFF and the value of one credit tranche and the reserve tranche. In other words the EFF should only be used after the reserve and first credit tranches have been drawn, and any EFF assistance is deemed to be making effective use of the upper credit tranches.

TABLE 13.9
Drawings by Country from Fund-Administered Accounts (SDR m; End-1981)

	Trust fund				Of subsidy payments	SFF subsidy payments
	Loan Disbursements			Distribution of profits from gold sales		
	Period 1 [1]	Period 2 [2]	Total			
Argentina	—	—	—	54.4	—	—
Bangladesh	51.8	70.4	122.2	15.5	9.5	1.3
Brazil	—	—	—	54.4	—	—
Burma	24.9	33.8	58.6	7.4	—	—
China, People's Republic of	—	309.5	309.5	—	—	—
Egypt	77.9	105.8	183.7	23.3	7.3	—
India	—	529.0	529.0	116.3	27.0	—
Indonesia	—	—	—	32.2	—	—
Iran	—	—	—	23.7	—	—
Ivory Coast	21.6	29.3	50.8	6.4	1.4	0.1
Kenya			46.9	5.9	6.7	0.8
Malaysia	—	—	—	23.0	—	—
Mexico	—	—	—	45.8	—	—
Morocco	46.8	63.6	110.4	14.0	4.1	0.9
Pakistan	97.4	132.3	229.7	29.1	26.5	1.4
Peru	—	—	—	15.2	—	4.5
Philippines	64.2	87.2	151.5	19.2	35.9	3.8
Romania	—	—	—	23.5	—	—
Sri Lanka	40.6	55.2	95.8	12.1	8.0	—
Sudan	29.8	40.5	70.4	8.9	4.4	2.5
Tanzania			41.0	5.2	5.0	0.4
Thailand	55.5	75.4	131.0	16.6	—	—
Venezuela	—	—	—	40.8	—	—
Vietnam	25.7	34.9	60.6	7.7	—	—
Yugoslavia	—	—	—	25.6	—	—
Zaire	46.8	63.6	110.4	14.0	7.4	—
Zambia			42.8	9.4	3.4	3.4
Total	841.0	2150.4	2991.3	1003.5	163.2	22.9
No of countries in receipt of funds	43	53	55	104	25	20

[1] July 1, 1976–June 30, 1978.
[2] July 1, 1978–February 28, 1981.

up a three-year programme to deal with structural payments problem with performance criteria monitored on a successive twelve-month basis. Despite the short length of the adjustment programme, repurchases under the EFF begin four and a half years after the first drawing and finish ten years after this,[19] giving such assistance a relatively long-term character.

The EFF was relatively under-used until the end of 1979. Since then however with the introduction of the Supplementary Financing Facility and Enlarged Access Policy elements of the EFF, total outstanding credit under the facility rose from SDR0.6 billion in 1979 to stand at SDR3.1 billion at the end of 1981. This latter figure was however spread over only nineteen countries. Greater use of the EFF in the immediate future may be expected given that agreed, but as yet undrawn, EFF arrangements totalled SDR9.3 billion in December 1981.

The *Supplementary Financing Facility* (SFF) which became effective in February 1979, is designed to help member countries whose balance of payments deficits are large in relation to quota. More strictly, three criteria have to be satisfied before a member is eligible for assistance under the SFF. Firstly, the expected period of payments adjustment has to be longer than one year and secondly the resources required by the member in question must be greater than those available under normal tranche policies or the EFF. Finally, access to the SFF is only permitted with the use of ordinary resources, specifically a stand-by arrangement reaching into the upper credit tranches, or an EFF arrangement.

The SFF is wholly financed by direct borrowing from member countries in balance of payments surplus (Table 13.4). Following the announcement of the facility in August 1977, arrangements were gradually completed with thirteen member countries (including six oil exporting nations) and Switzerland to provide SDR7.78 billion to the facility. Upon completion of these borrowing arrangements, the SFF became effective in early 1979. The period of commitment by the Fund of resources to member countries was scheduled to end by February 1982 but, by March 1981, in fact, the available resources under the facility were fully committed to twenty-five member countries, with the major agreements being with Yugoslavia (SDR1.48 billion), Turkey (SDR1.37 billion), Pakistan (SDR0.87 billion), Morocco (SDR0.64 billion) and Korea (SDR0.62 billion). By the end of 1981, however, only SDR3.57 billion of the total SFF commitments had been borrowed by the IMF and drawn by members from the Fund. None of that sum had been repaid by that time.

Under the SFF, strict rules are applied to the apportionment of funds between ordinary resources and borrowed (SFF) resources, dependent also on whether the drawings are made on a stand-by

[19] Extended from a repurchase period of 4–8 years in December 1979, see *IMF Survey*, 10 December 1979.

arrangement in the regular tranches or by an extended arrangement.[20] For an SFF drawing on regular tranche policies, ordinary and borrowed (SFF) resources are used in the proportion 2:1 on the first credit tranche and 1:1.2 on the upper credit tranches. To put this another way, a supplementary drawing of 12.5% of quota may be made alongside the first credit tranche (25% of quota) and three drawings of 30% of quota alongside the remaining credit tranches which are also 25% of quota.[21] Under an extended arrangement, the proportion of ordinary to borrowed resources is 1:1 with a maximum of 140% of quota being available on ordinary resources and supplementary financing. In sum and including reserve tranche drawings, the maximum drawing under regular tranche policies, including SFF, is 227.5% of quota, while under the Extended Facility it is 330% of quota. However the facility is in a sense open-ended as additional resources may be made available to a member under the conditions of the SFF if all resources as set out in Table 13.8 are exhausted and further borrowing needs remain.

Given the close link between the drawing arrangements for the SFF and those for the upper credit tranches and the EFF, the conditionality requirements are the same as those imposed under the latter agreements. As the SFF is financed by direct borrowing, charges are levied on drawings under the facility to compensate those countries which lend resources. Repurchases under the SFF must begin $3\frac{1}{2}$ years after the initial drawing and be completed after seven years.

In like manner to the 1975 Oil Facility, the Fund established, in December 1980, the *Supplementary Financing Facility Subsidy Account* to reduce the cost of interest payments on SFF drawings made by certain developing countries. Given the method of financing the SFF, the costs of drawing on this facility are higher than those on drawings from the facilities financed out of the Fund's own resources. The subsidy paid may be up to, but not above, 3% of the interest charges per annum for seventy developing countries whose per capita income qualifies them for assistance from the International Development Association (IDA) arm of the World Bank and half this level for a further fifteen countries who, although not qualifying for IDA assistance, are eligible to borrow from the Trust Fund.

The SFF subsidy account is itself to be financed by repayments of interest on Trust Fund loans amounting to SDR750 million and donations from member countries and elsewhere of a further SDR250

---

[20] This paragraph should be made much clearer by reference to Table 13.8.

[21] Therefore, ignoring the reserve tranche, borrowing under regular tranche policies is possible up to 102.5% of quota under the SFF, in conjunction with 100% of quota using ordinary resources.

million. In December 1981, resources available under the Subsidy Account had reached SDR43.3 million[22] with, by the same time, the IMF having made the first payments under the Subsidy Account of SDR 22.9 million to 20 developing countries. (Table 13.9).

The most recent form of special financial assistance introduced by the IMF is the policy on *Enlarged Access to Resources* (EAR) announced in March 1981 and operational from May of that year. Given that the EAR only became effective when all resources under the SFF had been committed and financing arrangements for the policy had been concluded, it is clear that the EAR is designed to be a continuation of the SFF. Assistance is available under the EAR on the same terms as previously enforced under the SFF. In particular, conditionality and repurchase arrangements are similar and the proportions of ordinary and borrowed resources drawn by members, according to whether regular tranche policies or an Extended Facility are utilised, are retained. However the EAR includes a guideline — independent of any drawings on the CFF and BSFF and any outstanding balances on the Oil Facilities — that up to 150% only of quota may be borrowed under any one-year arrangement and up to 450% of quota under a three-year arrangement. Cumulative net purchases should not exceed 600% of quota from any combination of ordinary resources, the SFF and EAR, whether regular tranche policies or the EFF are used. Exceptions to these all-embracing rules are possible, however. For any country with a low quota relative to the size of its economy or which is implementing an 'exceptionally strong' adjustment programme, the normal limits set out above may be waived. In addition, the specified drawing limits are subject to regular review.

As with the SFF, the EAR is financed by direct borrowing. In May 1981, the Saudi-Arabian Monetary Agency (SAMA) agreed to provide up to SDR8 billion over the following two years to finance the EAR with the possibility that a further SDR4 billion may be provided in the future.[23] In addition, an agreement was made with thirteen industrial countries to lend SDR1.1 billion to the Fund (part of which was to be made available through the BIS and which was soon increased to SDR1.3 billion) to contribute to the financing of the EAR over a two-year period (Table 13.4). By the end of 1981, SDR0.79 billion had been drawn by eight countries under the EAR.

---

[22] This was particularly small at that time as repayments of Trust Fund loans were not scheduled to begin until July 1982. These resources were therefore in large part derived from eight member countries and Switzerland.

[23] This agreement was concluded in conjunction with the doubling of Saudi Arabia's quota to SDR2.1 billion.

The Trust Fund

The activities of the Trust Fund are reported separately by the IMF as its assets are not part of the general resources of the Fund (Gold, 1979b). The Trust Fund was set up in May 1976 as a further segment of the programme for providing special balance of payments assistance to developing countries. Like the Oil Facility Subsidy Account, the Trust Fund was a temporary facility and it was terminated, when all the resources in the Fund had been disbursed to members, in April 1981.

The resources of the Trust Fund were, in the main, derived from profits accummated from IMF gold sales. Following the considerable reduction of the monetary role of gold embodied in the Second Amendment of the IMF's Articles of Agreement, the Fund decided to sell one-third of its gold holdings or 50 million ounces. While 25 million ounces were sold directly to member countries at the official price (SDR35 per ounce), the remaining 25 million ounces were sold by public auction over a four year period. Between June 1976 and May 1980, these sales raised $4.64 billion of profit for the Fund.[24] Of this profit $1.3 billion was allocated directly to the developing country members of the Fund, according to quota, while the remainder was placed in the Trust Fund for lending to eligible developing countries. The direct distribution of gold was completed in 1980, except for the share allocated to Kampuchea. Table 13.9 includes those countries which received a distribution of SDR20 million or more. The value of the total distribution to one hundred and four developing countries was almost exactly SDR1 billion at the end of 1981. Trust Fund resources were augmented by the transfer by the oil-exporting countries of their quota share of the gold profits, partial transfer of its share by Yugoslavia, the loan of part of its share by Romania and by other investment income.

Trust Fund loans were made in two phases.[25] To be eligible for assistance from the Trust Fund under the first phase, developing countries had to have an income per capita of SDR300 or less in 1973, and one of SDR520 or less in 1975 for second phase assistance. In addition, a country had to demonstrate to the IMF that it had a balance of payments need and was willing to make a reasonable effort to strengthen its external position. Trust Fund loans carried similar conditionality to that applicable in the first credit tranche, while

[24] Profit in this sense is defined as the difference between the market price at which the gold was sold and the official price per ounce of gold sold.

[25] The first period ran from July 1, 1978 to June 30, 1978 and the second period from July 1, 1978 to February 28, 1981 (see Table 13.9).

given that they are direct loans denominated in SDRs and disbursed in dollars, they do not require the purchase of IMF resources with the member country's own currency. Trust Fund loans carry an interest charge of only 0.5% and have a final maturity of ten years.

Over the two periods of Trust Fund operations, SDR2.99 billion was disbursed to eligible members (Table 13.9) with 55 members in total receiving assistance in this way. Given that no part of any of these loans had been repaid by the end of 1981, no outstanding stock data need be reported alongside the flow data of Trust Fund disbursement in Table 13.9. As noted earlier, the first SDR750 million of repayments of and interest on Trust Fund loans will be allocated to the SFF Subsidy Account while the subsequent repayments will be transferred to the Fund's Special Disbursement Account.

SUMMARY

To summarise the material in this chapter, Tables 13.10 and 13.11 pull together data on the various aspects of IMF borrowing and lending operations. Table 13.10 disaggregates data on the Use of Fund Credit outstanding at the end of 1981 by country and also by the type of drawing. This table is, in fact, a disaggregated version of the 1981 entry for the Use of Fund Credit in Table 13.5. The extent to which the outstanding drawings of developing drawings of developing countries dominates the total use of fund credit is clear from this table. Only five developed countries still owed funds to the IMF at the end of 1981, all on the CFF or the two Oil Facilities. The total is dominated by an outstanding Oil Facility drawing by the UK of SDR312.5 million. In contrast, outstanding credit owed by developing countries is more evenly spread both across countries and across the facilities concerned. The largest volume of outstanding credit was on the CFF (SDR3.22 billion) although combined credit tranche drawings totalled SDR6.01 billion, while the only facility on which no credit was outstanding in 1981 was the little-used BSFF. In addition, there is evidence in this table of considerable scope for further drawing with undrawn stand-by credits of SDR3.77 billion and arrangements under the EFF of SDR9.33 billion.

Finally, Table 13.11 re-establishes the flow data form by presenting a summary of the Fund's operations in the General Resources Account on an annual basis from 1975 to 1981. This table therefore includes aggregate data on all purchases from the Funds by facility (including reserve tranche drawings), total repurchases, borrowing by the Fund and repayments by it of previous loans. It is in fact a full,

TABLE 13.10
Use of Fund Credit — Major Countries
(SDR m: End-1981)

	Credit tranche drawings				Extended fund facility			Oil facility	Use of fund credit	Undrawn extended fund	
	ordinary	SFF	EAR	CFF	ordinary	SFF	EAR			Standbys	facility
UK	—	—	—	—	—	—	—	312.5	312.5	—	—
Industrial countries	—	—	—	49.4	—	—	—	496.4	545.8	—	—
Oil exporting countries	—	—	—	—	—	—	—			—	—
Bangladesh	44.1	—	—	—	110.0	110.0	—	12.7	276.8	—	580.0
China, People's Republic of	450.0	—	—	—	—	—	—	—	450.0	—	—
India	—	—	—	266.0	150.0	—	150.0	—	566.0	—	4700.0
Ivory Coast	28.5	—	—	114.0	88.4	88.4	—	9.1	319.2	—	307.8
Jamaica	22.9	—	—	80.6	145.5	145.5	—	38.6	403.5	—	332.9
Korea	255.9	616.1	—	160.0	—	—	—	38.6	1070.6	—	—
Morocco	56.3	—	—	49.0	137.4	137.5	—	6.8	386.9	—	680.6
Pakistan	106.9	—	—	—	257.1	257.1	—	29.0	650.0	—	749.0
Peru	67.5	195.1	—	53.8	—	—	—	16.5	332.9	—	—
Philippines	168.3	333.0	—	137.5	145.4	—	—	38.9	823.0	—	—
Romania	97.9	—	53.2	355.5	—	—	—	—	506.7	962.5	—
Sri Lanka	51.4	—	—	25.3	260.3	—	—	9.9	346.9	—	—
Sudan	33.0	—	—	124.8	123.2	127.8	—	5.6	414.8	—	176.0
Thailand	189.2	—	179.5	237.6	—	—	—	—	606.2	469.5	—
Turkey	176.1	780.0	—	127.5	—	—	—	52.0	1135.6	590.0	—
Yugoslavia	392.2	398.0	—	277.0	—	—	—	8.3	1075.5	1108.0	—
Zaire	97.1	—	—	7.0	67.4	—	107.6	17.8	297.0	—	737.0
Zambia	223.1	—	—	95.9	77.0	—	223.0	8.8	627.8	—	500.0
Non-Oil developing countries	3089.9	2617.4	305.5	3222.1¹	1720.1	947.5	480.6	438.5	12821.6	3772.1	9331.7
Total	3089.9	2617.4	305.5	3271.5¹	1720.1	947.5	480.6	934.9	13367.4	3772.1	9331.7

¹ Of which SDR12.0 m was on the Compensatory Financing Facility for Cereal Import-Excesses.

TABLE 13.11
Summary of IMF Operations in the General Resources Account
(SDR m)

	1975	1976	1977	1978	1979	1980	1981
1 Purchases	4658.1	7009.9	3424.6	3744.3	1842.8	3752.7	7081.7
Reserve tranche	722.6	990.8	80.1	2535.5	147.1	359.1	310.4
Credit tranche	640.9	1477.6	2895.3	421.0	853.1	1798.6	3436.6
of which:							
SFF	(—)	(—)	(—)	(—)	(205.4)	(943.1)	(1468.9)
EAR	(—)	(—)	(—)	(—)	(—)	(—)	(305.5)
CFF	239.0	2308.1	240.5	577.7	572.0	980.4	1230.5
EFF	7.7	90.0	208.8	174.0	233.0	614.5	2092.2
of which:							
SFF	(—)	(—)	(—)	(—)	(101.5)	(275.2)	(570.8)
EAR	(—)	(—)	(—)	(—)	(—)	(—)	(480.6)
BSFF	4.7	—	—	—	37.7	—	—
Oil Facilities	3043.2	2143.4	—	36.1	—	—	—
2 Repurchases	492.1	1272.0	2936.6	4845.3	4215.3	3344.8	2109.9
3 Net purchases (1–2)	4166.0	5737.9	488.0	-1101.0	-2372.5	407.9	4971.8
4 Trust Fund loans	—	—	152.9	688.1	526.6	1256.1	367.8
5 Fund borrowing	3042.9	2143.4	1730.0	777.3	306.9	1218.3	3098.2
of which:							
GAB	3042.9	2143.4	1730.0	777.3	—	—	—
Oil Facilities	—	—	—	—	—	—	—
SFF	—	—	—	—	306.9	1218.3	2039.6
EAR	—	—	—	—	—	—	1058.6
6 Fund repayments	—	200.0	261.8	2564.7	2806.2	900.5	1023.1
of which:							
GAB	—	—	—	1142.1	587.9	—	—
Oil Facilities	—	200.0	261.8	1422.6	2218.3	900.5	1023.1
SFF	—	—	—	—	—	—	—
EAR	—	—	—	—	—	—	—
7 Net borrowing (5–6)	3042.9	1943.4	1468.2	-1787.4	-2499.3	317.8	2075.1

although aggregated, picture of all Fund activity in the relevant years. As would be expected the patterns established in the earlier tables in this chapter are clear from this presentation; these include the heavy drawing in 1975–76 mainly on the Oil Facilities, the substantial repurchases in the subsequent four years giving total net repurchases of as much as SDR2.58 billion between 1977 and 1980, the significant borrowing on the CFF in 1976 and 1980 and the heavy use of the SFF (particularly under credit tranche policies) in 1980. In addition, Table 13.11 shows the jump in gross purchases in 1981. This increase was spread fairly evenly across the various drawing arrangements and represents an early signal of the much more substantial increase in purchases that occurred during much of 1982. The information on the borrowing activities of the Fund shows that in 1974/6 all borrowing was undertaken to finance the Oil Facilities with the same pattern applying to borrowing under the GAB in 1977–8 and for the SFF in 1979–80. In 1981, in addition to further borrowing for the SFF, the first portion of funds was raised for the Enlarged Access Policy. Repayments under the Oil Facilities have been made on a regular basis in recent years, while the whole of the GAB borrowing of SDR1.73 billion in 1977 was repaid in 1978–9. As a result, having been a net borrower of SDR8.17 billion in 1974–7, the Fund repaid amounts totalling SDR4.29 billion in the following two years, before becoming a net borrower again in 1980–1.

Chapter 14

The IMF's Accounts

INTRODUCTION

The main objective of this chapter is to explain the tabular presentation of the IMF's accounts which is published every month in *IFS*. Most of the items of data included in the table of the Fund's Accounts correspond to a certain part of the borrowing or lending activities of the Fund as described in detail in Chapter 13. Therefore, the present chapter should be seen as providing a guide to the methods adopted by the Fund in *IFS* to summarise their borrowing and lending activities and as such is a crucial addition to the material presented in the previous chapter.

To facilitate the explanation of these accounts, statistics for the transactions of three countries[1] (the Netherlands, Kuwait and Pakistan) with the Fund will be presented at various points in the chapter. These data all refer to the Fund's accounts as they stood at the end of 1981. Given that data on the IMF's accounts are published two months in arrears, the stock data for the end of 1981 are drawn from the *IFS* edition for February 1982. However, the form in which these accounts are presented was altered in the August 1982 issue of *IFS*. To enable an up-to-date description of these accounts therefore, the data for the end of 1981 are ordered in this chapter in a way consistent with the more recent presentation.[2] The data on the Fund's accounts are arranged in forty-two columns in *IFS*. All member countries are

[1] A diverse sample of countries was used (an industrial country, an oil exporter and a non-oil developing country) to illustrate all aspects of the accounts.

[2] See also the recently published *IFS* Supplement on Fund Accounts (IMF, 1982). Even more information is contained in this document with data on the current position (end-December 1981) in as many as fifty-six columns. It should be repeated therefore that while the statistical detail in this supplement is consistent with the data in this chapter, the ordering of the columns of data is different.

listed in the main body of the table with data on their borrowing and lending transactions with the Fund.

GENERAL DEPARTMENT

The first thirty-eight columns of the newly-reconstituted Fund Accounts table refer to the transactions completed in the General Resources Account of the Fund's General Department.

Quotas (Column (1))

The quotas assigned to each member are set out in Column (1). The practice of identifying in separate columns those parts of each country's quota subscribed in reserve assets and domestic currency respectively, was dropped from the table in the first half of 1981 to accommodate data on the EAR and other changes. The quotas of the three sample countries are set out in Table 14.1.

TABLE 14.1
Quotas
(SDR m; End-1981)

	Quotas (1)
Netherlands	1422.0
Kuwait	393.3
Pakistan	427.5
Total — all countries	60674.0

Fund Borrowings (Columns (2)–(10))

Details of borrowing by the IMF, to augment resources made available by members from quota subscriptions, are given in Columns (2)–(10); the information includes, in addition to actual borrowing, details of borrowing arrangements that have been made but not drawn upon at the time these accounts were drawn up (See Table 14.2). The current situation concerning the General Arrangements to Borrow is summarised in Columns (3) and (4). Actual borrowing undertaken by the Fund is presented in Column (3) and given the current GAB agreement, the remaining amount available to be drawn in the future is given in Column (4). At the end of 1981, despite a GAB

TABLE 14.2
Fund Borrowings
(SDR m; End-1981)

| | Outstanding borrowings (net) | | | | EAR | | Available funds | | | |
	Total	GAB	OF	SFF	Medium-term	Short-term	GAB	SFF	EAR[1]	Total
	(2)	(3)	(5)	(6)	(8)	(9)	(4)	(7)	(10)	
Netherlands	77.0[2]	—	33.9	43.1	—		252.6	56.9		309.5[2]
Kuwait	287.4[2]	—	95.6	191.8	—		—	208.2		208.2[2]
Pakistan	—		—	—			—	—		—
Total — all countries	6366.5	777.3[3]	875.8	3564.8	1048.0[4]	100.6	5737.2	4219.1	8156.1	18112.4

[1] Due to the confidential nature of the policy on EAR, no country breakdowns of the short-term borrowings by the Fund or the funds available are published in IFS.

[2] Not including any short-term borrowing or availability of funds under the EAR.

[3] Two countries — Germany (SDR 582.9 m), Japan (194.3)

[4] One country — Saudi Arabia.

agreement with a value of SDR 6467 million,[3] the Fund had outstanding borrowings at that time against Germany (SDR582.8 million) and Japan (SDR194.3 million) only.

However, in the case of these two countries and any other future lenders to the Fund through the GAB, the size of the GAB agreement with these countries does not exactly equal the sum of the amount already lent by them and the remaining funds available to be borrowed. The discrepancy is due to valuation effects. Specifically, while the GAB agreement and the remaining funds available to be drawn (Column (4)) are converted into SDRs at current end-month exchange rates, the figures for actual outstanding borrowing (Column (3)) are converted at the end-month exchange rate applicable at the time of borrowing. Therefore while the total GAB agreement had a value of SDR6467 million at the end of 1981, net borrowing was SDR777.3 million and the funds still available were SDR5737.2 million, slightly higher than the difference between the two former figures.

Column (5) gives outstanding Fund borrowing to finance the Oil Facilities, while Columns (6) and (7) provide a similar presentation for the Supplementary Financing Facility (SFF) as that for the GAB. Therefore, Column (6) sets out actual borrowing at a particular point in time under the SFF and Column (7) evaluates those funds still available to be borrowed by the IMF under this facility. In this case, however, adjustments are made for valuation effects.

Finally, Columns (8)–(10) refer to the Policy on Enlarged Access to Resources (EAR). The presentation of these data is different from that of the data on the GAB and SFF. Specifically, while the total of funds still available to be borrowed under the EAR is set out in Column (10), actual borrowings are divided into net medium-term borrowing by the Fund (Column (8)) and net short-term borrowing (Column (9)). However due to the confidential nature of this facility, no country breakdowns are published for the EAR agreement or for short-term borrowings. At the end of 1981, an EAR agreement of SDR9.3 billion had been completed but actual borrowings totalled only SDR1148.6 million, of which SDR1048 million was medium-term borrowing from Saudi Arabia.

Aggregate Fund borrowing (Column (2)) may therefore be defined as:

$$IMF_B(2) = GAB_B(3) + OF_B(5) + SFF_B(6) + EARMT_B(8) + EARST_B(9) \tag{14.1}$$

[3] This information is taken from the February 1982 edition of *IFS*, where it is included in the old format of the Fund's accounts. See also Table 13.4.

where MT and ST, in the context of the EAR, refer to short-term and medium-term borrowing respectively and the subscript B refers to borrowing. The remaining funds available to be borrowed by the Fund may be defined as:

$$IMF_A = GAB_A(4) + SFF_A(7) + EAR_A(10) \qquad (14.2)$$

where the subscript A refers to completed but undrawn borrowing agreements. At the end of 1981, total outstanding net borrowing by the Fund under the GAB, EAR and the specified facilities was SDR6366.5 million to which the Netherlands and Kuwait made small contributions under the OF and SFF. A further SDR 18112.4 million had been agreed but not yet drawn upon by the IMF (Table 14.2).

Lending Commitments (Columns (11)–(14))[4]

Before presentation of data on the gross purchases by member countries over the history of Fund, Columns (11) to (14) give figures on drawn and undrawn (but agreed) stand-by and EFF arrangements (Table 14.3). Along with the figures on the Use of Fund Credit (Columns (28)–(38) below), such information is a much more accurate representation of the current lending position of the Fund than are the gross purchases data which cover a total period of nearly four decades.

Columns (11) and (13) give data on drawings under stand-by and EFF arrangements *in effect* at the time the accounts are drawn up. At the end of 1981, all outstanding drawings and commitments under stand-by and EFF arrangements were in respect of non-oil developing country borrowers. Total outstanding drawings (Columns (11) + (13)) were SDR4786 million at that time. Given total stand-by and EFF arrangements of SDR17889.8 million, the undrawn balances totalled SDR1310.8 million (Columns (12) + (14)) at the end of 1981. Under both these types of arrangement, resources are frequently allocated to a particular borrowing country and then not used in full, and sometimes not at all. To provide revenue in such circumstances, the Fund levies a commitment charge on all such undrawn balances. This may be offset against the service charges levied by the Fund on all drawings of foreign currencies and SDRs, apart from reserve tranche drawings, and on all outstanding balances of a member's domestic currency held in the General Resources Account of the Fund arising

[4] The IMF also publishes a time-series flow data on *new* commitments on a regular basis in the *IMF Survey* and other Fund publications.

TABLE 14.3
Lending Commitments
(SDR m; End-1981)

	Stand-bys		EFF		Total	
	Drawn	Undrawn balance	Drawn	Undrawn balance	Drawn	Undrawn balance
	(11)	(12)	(13)	(14)		
Netherlands	—	—	—	—	—	—
Kuwait	—	—	—	—	—	—
Pakistan	—	—	170.0	749.0	170.0	749.0
Total[1]	2777.5	3772.1	2008.5	9331.7	4786.0	13103.8

[1] There were no entries in columns (11)–(14) for industrial or oil-exporting countries at the end of 1981.

from drawings under the credit tranches, the CFF, BSFF, OFS, SFF, and the EAR.

Cumulative Gross Purchases/ Drawings from the Fund (Columns (15)–(24))

Considerable detail is given in Columns (15)–(24) on the gross drawings from the Fund — that is without adjustment for repayments — since its inception. These data are set out in total and for the three sample countries in Table 14.4. Cumulative gross drawings (CUM_D) may be defined as:[5]

$$CUM_D = RT_D + CFFES_D(15) + CFFIE_D(16) + BSFF_D(17)$$
$$+ OF_D(18) + CTORD_D(19) + CTSFF_D(20)$$
$$+ CTEAR_D(21) + EFFORD_D(22)$$
$$+ EFFSFF_D(23) + EFFEAR_D(24) \qquad (14.3)$$

where RT and CT are the reserve tranche and credit tranches, respectively, CFFES and CFFIE refer to the export shortfall and the cereal import excess elements of the CFF, ORD are ordinary drawings and the subscript D refers to drawings in general. It is apparent from Table 14.4 that, taking the history of the Fund as a whole, the heaviest drawings have been on the credit tranches (ordinary) representing 38.2% of the total and the reserve tranche (28.2%), with the special

[5] Data for cumulative total drawings and reserve tranche drawings are not presented in the current version of the Fund's Account set out in *IFS*. Data on reserve tranche drawings are taken from IMF (1982).

TABLE 14.4
Cumulative Gross Purchases from the Fund
(SDR m; End-1981)

	Total	Reserve tranche	CFF Export short-falls	CFF Cereal import excesses	CFF BSFF	CFF OF	Credit tranche Ordinary resources	Credit tranche SFF	Credit tranche EAR	EFF Ordinary resources	EFF SFF	EFF EAR
			(15)	(16)	(17)	(18)	(19)	(20)	(21)	(22)	(23)	(24)
Netherlands	524.5	517.9	—	—	—	—	6.6	—	—	—	—	—
Kuwait	—	—	—	—	—	—	—	—	—	—	257.1	—
Pakistan	1409.1	28.5	117.5	—	—	236.0	508.1	—	—	261.9	—	—
Total–all countries	61044.6	17209.9	7130.4	12.0[1]	103.7	6902.5	23343.1	2617.4	305.5[2]	1992.1	947.5	480.6[3]
Shares in total		28.2	11.7	0.02	0.2	11.3	38.2	4.3	0.5	3.3	1.6	0.8

[1] Drawn by one country — Malawi.
[2] Drawn by five countries — Ethiopia (SDR19.7 m), Romania (53.2), Somalia (13.2), Thailand (179.5), Uganda (39.9).
[3] Drawn by three countries — India (150.0 m), Zaire (107.6), Zambia (223.0).

facilities, due to their more recent introduction, appearing to be quantitatively less important. In particular, up to the end of December 1981, the BSFF had accounted for only 0.17% of total drawings while, as yet, the EAR had led to drawings from the Fund, under both the credit tranches and the EFF, to a small extent only. The special facilities to have been most heavily used have been the CFF (11.7% of total drawings) and the Oil Facilities (11.3%).

Fund Holdings of Currency (Columns (25)–(26))

As explained in Chapter 13, drawings by a member country from the IMF are completed through the transfer of that member's domestic currency to the Fund in return for foreign currency or SDRs. Therefore Fund holdings of the domestic currency of any member are indicative of the extent to which that member holds outstanding loans from the Fund. To provide evidence of this sort, Column (25) quantifies these holdings of domestic currency by the Fund in absolute terms, while they are expressed as a percentage of quota in Column (26) (see Table 14.5).

Given that the Fund's holdings of member currencies alter when drawings are made on any of the five ordinary tranches and from the special facilities, it is difficult to make a judgement from the information in Column (25) on the extent to which any particular member country has drawn separately on either the tranches or the facilities.[6] However any figure of above 75% in Column (26) is indicative of a positive aggregate outstanding drawing from the IMF by the member country in question. Therefore, in Table 14.5, IMF holdings of the domestic currency of Pakistan stood at SDR 1077.5 million at the end of 1981, or 252% of quota, indicating that Pakistan had outstanding credit from the Fund of 177% of quota[7] at that time.

In contrast, any figure below 75% in column (26) indicates that the currency of the country in question has been used to sell to other (drawing) countries, to repay the Fund's own borrowings or for other purposes. These activities reduce the Fund's holdings of a member's currency from the basic 75% figure, so that the country concerned is a net *lender* to the Fund. In Table 14.5, both the Netherlands and Kuwait are net lenders to the Fund showing that their currencies have been used for one or more of the three purposes outlined above. The

[6] Formerly, the Fund published a series of its holdings of members' currencies exclusive of changes due to drawings on the special facilities. This enabled a calculation to be made of the extent to which drawings had been made by members on the reserve and credit tranches.

[7] 252%–75% (i.e. domestic currency held by the Fund minus the initial deposit by Pakistan of its quota in domestic currency).

TABLE 14.5
Fund Holdings of Currency
(SDR m; End-1981)

	Fund holdings of currency	
	Absolute amounts	As % of quota
	(25)	(26)
Netherlands	1001.3	70.4
Kuwait	271.0	68.9
Pakistan	1077.5	252.0
Total — all countries	58976.1	97.2

75% figure is therefore the dividing line between the net drawer or lender status of each country *vis-à-vis* the IMF. It is very rare for a country to be a net lender to the Fund and a net drawer from it simultaneously. However, at the end of 1981, Guatemala was in this position having lent SDR 8.4 million to the Fund under the SFF facility, while having outstanding net drawings of SDR 95.6 million under the Credit Tranches (Ordinary Resources — SDR 19.1 million) and the CFF (SDR 76.5 million).

Use of Fund Credit (Columns (28)–(38))[8]

The Use of Fund Credit (UFC) was discussed briefly in Chapter 13 and the reader is asked to look again at that passage. In principle the UFC is the sum of the outstanding *stock* of credit owed to the IMF by each member country at the time the Fund's Accounts are drawn up. Credit, in this case, includes outstanding conditional drawings only and as such omits reserve tranche drawings which, as argued earlier, allow the member country to use its own funds and not those of the IMF. The basic definition of the UFC is therefore:[9]

---

[8] Column (27) on members' Reserve Positions in the Fund is discussed after the Use of Fund Credit.

[9] When a member makes payments in its own currency for Fund charges or for gold distributed by the Fund, total UFC (28) will exceed its components in Columns (29)–(38). This arises as such payments raise UFC, through increasing the volume of its own currency that a country eventually must repurchase from the Fund, without altering any of the components of UFC.

$$UFC(28) = NETCFFES_D(29) + NETCFFIE_D(30) + NETBSFF_D(31)$$
$$+ NETOF_D(32) + NETCTORD_D(33) + NETCTSFF_D(34)$$
$$+ NETCTEAR_D(35) + NETEFFORD_D(36)$$
$$+ NETEFFSFF_D(37) + NETEFFEAR_D(38) \qquad (14.4)$$

where NET refers to net outstanding drawings of a country from the IMF or credit owed to the IMF and the remaining symbols are defined as in Equation (14.3).

Total UFC and that of the sample countries at the end of 1981 are given in Table 14.6. Neither the Netherlands nor Kuwait had any outstanding liabilities to the IMF at that time, while the UFC by Pakistan stood at SDR650 million of which the majority (79.1%) was on the Extended Fund Facility (EFF). The main components in total UFC at the end of 1981 were the SFF (credit tranche drawings and Extended Facility combined — 26.7% of the total) and the CFF (24.5%). Ordinary credit tranche drawings in net terms were 23.1% of the total, with the use of ordinary resources under the Extended Facility amounting to 12.9% of the total. EAR credit, at only 5.9% of UFC, was still small and there were no outstanding drawings on the BSFF at the end of 1981.

Given that reserve tranche drawings do not constitute part of the Use of Fund Credit, any such drawings which take the domestic currency holdings of the Fund for a particular member from 75% of quota up to the size of the quota itself (i.e. 100%) leave UFC at zero. However, any drawings beyond that raise the domestic currency held by the Fund above the member's quota and cause UFC to become positive. Accordingly, UFC may be defined in a second way — for those member countries who have drawn the reserve tranche in full as well as drawing other credit — as the excess of the Fund's holdings of a member's currency over that member's quota:

$$UFC(28) = DOMC_{IMF}(25) - QUOTA(1) \qquad (14.5)$$

where $DOMC_{IMF}$ is the domestic currency of a member held by the IMF.

An example may help to clarify this second method of calculating the UFC and when it may be used. Consider two countries (A and B) each with a quota of SDR100 million. Assume each has drawn SDR100 million from the IMF on the Compensatory Financing Facility and a further SDR100 million as an ordinary credit tranche drawing. In addition, Country A has drawn its reserve tranche in full while Country B has not drawn any of its reserve tranche. The UFC is

TABLE 14.6
Use of Fund Credit
(SDR m; End-1981)

| | | CFF | | | | Use of fund credit[1] | | | | | | Fund holdings of currency (25) | Quota (1) |
| | Total[1] (28) | Export shortfalls (29) | Cereal imports excesses (30) | BSFF (31) | OF (32) | Credit tranche | | | Extended facility | | | | |
						Ordinary resources (33)	SFF (34)	EAR (35)	Ordinary resources (36)	SFF (37)	EAR (38)		
Netherlands	—	—	—	—	—	—	—	—	—	—	—	1001.3	1422.0
Kuwait	650.0	—	—	—	—	—	—	—	—	—	—	271.0	393.3
Pakistan		—	12.0	—	29.0	106.9	—	—	257.1	257.1	—	1077.5	427.5
Total–all countries	13367.4[2]	3259.5	12.0	—	934.9	3089.9	2617.4	305.5	1720.2	947.5	480.6	58976.1	60674.0
Shares in total		24.4	0.1	—	7.0	23.1	19.6	2.3	12.9	7.1	3.6		

[1] UFC (28) = (29 + 30 + 31 + 32 + 33 + 34 + 35 + 36 + 37 + 38) or for net borrowers (i.e. UFC > 0) = (25) − (1)

[2] Total UFC differs from the sum of its components. See footnote 9 in text.

TABLE 14.7
Calculation of Use of Fund Credits
(SDR m)
Quota of Country A, B = SDR100 million

	IMF holding of A's:		IMF holdings of B's:	
	Domestic currency	Foreign exchange reserves	Domestic currency	Foreign exchange reserves
Deposit of quota	75	25	75	25
Cumulative effect of Drawings:				
Reserve tranche	100	—	175	—
FF	200	—	175	—
CTORD	300	—	275	—
UFC calculation				
1: CFF + CTORD	200		200	
2: Domestic currency minus quota	200		175 ×	

calculated for these countries in Table 14.7.

Under the standard calculation (designated here as the first calculation), as defined in Equation (14.4), UFC equals SDR200 million for both countries. However the secondary calculation achieved by subtracting a country's quota from the IMF holdings of that country's currency (Equation 14.5) provides the correct answer for Country A only. For Country B, given that it has not drawn any of its reserve tranche, the CFF and CTORD drawings raise the Fund's holdings of its currency to SDR275 million only, leading to an underestimate of UFC. Therefore for the calculation of a country's UFC, the aggregation of columns (29)–(38) will always provide the correct answer while the secondary method is only appropriate if the reserve tranche has been drawn in full.

In Table 14.6 the methods of calculating UFC provide the same answer of SDR650 million for Pakistan, indicating that the country has drawn its reserve tranche in full. However the effects of some countries using IMF credit without drawing their full reserve tranche and of many being net lenders to the Fund are shown in the aggregate UFC. While the total UFC at the end of 1981 was SDR 13367.4 million, this could not be derived by subtracting the quota (1) from total Fund holdings of domestic currency (25). Finally, if for an individual country (e.g. Netherlands and Kuwait) Equation (14.5) gives a negative figure (i.e. the reserve tranche has been drawn in part only or not at all and that country has made no other drawings from the Fund), UFC is given a value of zero. There is no such thing as a negative UFC. In this case, Equation (14.4) would also give a zero value for the UFC.

Reserve Position in the Fund (RPF — Column (27))

To give credit to the member which transfers part of its quota to the IMF in foreign currency and which may not then draw any or all of its reserve tranche, a concept is defined by the Fund to represent the volume of foreign exchange reserves held by a member in the accounts of the IMF. This is known as the Reserve Postion in the Fund. The RPF is defined as the outstanding amount that a member may draw unconditionally from the Fund (i.e. that part of the reserve tranche, if any, as yet undrawn) plus the equivalent of that member's lendings to the Fund. This concept — which is effectively treated as a reserve asset of the member country — is therefore increased by any new borrowings by the Fund of that member's currency and reduced by reserve tranche drawings by the member itself, to reflect the return of a country's own reserves to its national accounts. The RPF is unaffected by all other drawings (on the special facilities and four credit tranches) and cannot fall below zero.[10] In principle therefore:

$$RPF(27) = 0.25(QUOTA\ (1)) + IMF_B(2) - RT_D \qquad (14.6)$$

where IMF_B and RT_D will generally not both be non-zero for any country (i.e. a country is rarely both a lender to the Fund and a drawer from the Fund simultaneously).

The actual calculation of the RPF completed by the Fund, although equivalent to Equation (14.6), is set out in a more complex way. Therefore:

$$
\begin{aligned}
RPF(27) =\ & QUOTA(1) - DOMC_{IMF}(25)^{[11]} + GAB_B(3) + OF_B(5) \\
& + SFF_B(6) + EARMT_B(8) + EARST_B(9)^{[12]} \\
& + NETCFFES_D(29) + NETCFFIE_D(30) \\
& + NETBSFF_D(31) + NETOF_D(32) + NETCTORD_D(33) \\
& + NETCTSFF_D(34) + NETCTEAR_D(35) \\
& + NETEFFORD_D(36) + NETEFFSFF_D(37) \\
& + NETEFFEAR_D(38) \qquad\qquad\qquad\qquad\qquad (14.7)
\end{aligned}
$$

[10] The RPF will fall to zero when a country draws its reserve tranche in full.
[11] Any subscription received by the IMF from a member and not included in (25) should, if possible, be subtracted also.
[12] Although $EARST_B$ (9) should in principle be included in the definition of the RPF, in practice, due to the confidential nature of the short-term borrowings by the Fund under the EAR, it is omitted.

which, using Equations (14.1) and (14.4), may be simplified to:

$$RPF(27) = QUOTA(1) - DOMC_{IMF}(25) + IMF_B(2) \\ + UFC(28) \qquad (14.8)$$

In virtually all cases, the RPF calculation will be simplified as either the UFC or IMF_B will be zero (the one exception at the end of 1981 was, as noted earlier, Guatemala.)

To explain the logic behind the RPF concept and to demonstrate its use, six country examples are drawn from the Fund's accounts and set out in Table 14.8. Case 1 is of a net lender to the IMF (the Netherlands) where, as a result, its UFC is zero. In this example the Fund's holdings of the Dutch domestic currency (SDR1001.3 million) are less than 75% of the quota indicating that some of this currency has been used to lend to other member countries, to repay a Fund borrowing or for other purposes. The use of its domestic currency in this way is credited to the Netherlands by the subtraction of $DOMC_{IMF}$ from its quota as the first element in the RPF calculation. To put this another way, if no additional use had been made of the Dutch currency, Fund holdings of it would have been 75% of quota or SDR1066.5 million (with the remainder of the Dutch quota being made up of foreign currency reserves deposited at the IMF). To this difference between the quota and $DOMC_{IMF}$ (Column 3) must be added Fund borrowing from the Netherlands (SDR77 million) giving a RPF figure of SDR497.8 million.

Case 2 is of a country which has not lent any funds to the IMF except in the sense that its reserve tranche has not been drawn in full. Fund holdings of the domestic currency of Australia are 78.7% of quota indicating that a small part of the reserve tranche has been drawn but SDR252.5 million remains to be drawn[13] leaving a RPF figure of that amount.

Case 3 is the most unusual one of a country (Guatemala) that, at the end of 1981, was both a lender to the Fund and had outstanding drawings from it. Given a quota of SDR76.5 million and Fund holdings of the Guatemalan currency of SDR172.1 million, this indicates a Use of Fund Credit of SDR95.6 million, with the reserve tranche drawn in full. In addition, however, the SDR 8.4 million borrowing by the IMF under the SFF appears in Column (4) of Table 14.8, corresponding to a Reserve Position in the Fund for Guatemala of the same amount at the end of 1981.

Case 4 is something of a special case in which the reserve tranche is

[13] This figure will also include, as did the total for the Netherlands, any use of the Australian currency by the Fund to, for example, lend to other countries.

TABLE 14.8
Reserve Position in the Fund — Calculation for Sample Countries
(SDR m; End-1981)

	Quota (1)	Fund holdings of domestic currency (25)	Sub-total	Borrowing by IMF	Use of Fund Credit (28)	Reserve position in the Fund (27)	Memo: $DOMC_{IMF}$ (25) as % of quota (1)
	(1)	(2)	(3) = (1) − (2)	(4)	(5)	(6) = (1) − (2) + (4) + (5)	(7)
Case 1: net lender to Fund: Netherlands	1442.0	1001.3	420.7	77.0	—	497.8	70.4
Case 2: net lender to Fund/full reserve tranche not drawn Australia	1185.0	932.5	252.5	—	—	252.5	78.7
Case 3: lender to Fund and borrower from fund simultaneously Guatemala	76.5	172.1	−95.6	8.4	95.6	8.4	225.0
Case 4: Reserve tranche only drawn Yemen Arab Republic	19.5	19.5	—	—	—	—	100.0
Case 5: Net borrower from Fund/full reserve tranche drawn Pakistan	427.5	1007.5	−650.0	—	650.0	—	252.0
Case 6: Net borrower from Fund/full reserve tranche not drawn Finland	393.0	367.6	25.4	—	52.1	77.4	93.5

drawn in full, but no other drawings are made by the country concerned. As a result, the quota of the Yemen Arab Republic is exactly equal to the domestic currency of that country held by the IMF such that the RPF is zero. The RPF is also zero in Case 5 (Pakistan) but under very different circumstances. In this case, Fund holdings of domestic currency exceed the quota considerably, due to the extensive Use of Fund Credit by Pakistan (SDR 650 million). Given that the RPF cannot be negative for any country, a zero figure is obtained by an accounting procedure of *adding* the UFC to the sub-total in Column 3. This should not be taken to mean however, that a rise in UFC will, except in this accounting sense, raise a country's RPF.

Finally, Case 6 is of a net drawer from the Fund, in this case Finland, which has not drawn its reserve tranche in full. This may be seen from the figures presented in Table 14.8. If Finland's UFC had been zero, it would not have had to sell an amount of its domestic currency, equivalent to its UFC, to the IMF in return for foreign currency drawings. A zero UFC would therefore have yielded a figure for Fund holdings of the Finnish currency of only SDR315.5 million.[14] Such a 'notional' total of $DOMC_{IMF}$ gives a RPF figure for Finland of SDR77.4 million as the difference between the quota and this 'notional' $DOMC_{IMF}$, i.e. this is the undrawn part of Finland's subscription of reserve assets. The positive UFC has, in fact, raised Fund holdings of the Finnish currency to SDR367.6 million; therefore to calculate the correct RPF, the figure of the UFC (SDR52.1 million) must be added to the sub-total given in Column 3. The occurrence of this situation of a country drawing IMF credit without using its reserve tranche in full is identified in the table of Fund accounts by there being a non-zero figure for both the UFC and RPF. This applied to thirty countries at the end of 1981.

These procedures for calculating the RPF of member countries have an important implication for the aggregate RPF. The example in Table 14.9 will demonstrate this. Let both member countries (A and B) have quotas of SDR100 million. In the initial position countries A and B have RPFs of SDR25 million due to their reserve assets subscription and there are no drawings. In line 2, Country A is assumed to draw its reserve tranche in full, increasing the Fund's holdings of A's domestic currency to SDR100 million and accordingly reducing A's RPF to zero. It is assumed that this drawing is made possible by some existing IMF holdings of the currency of Country B being lent to Country A so reducing the Fund's holdings of

---

[14] This figure is 80.3% of quota indicating that part of the reserve tranche has been drawn, i.e. 315.5−0.75 (393) = SDR20.7 million.

TABLE 14.9
Example of Calculation of Aggregate RPF (SDR m)

| | Country A | | | | | Country B | | | | | |
	Quota	$DOMC_{IMF}$	Fund borrowing	UFC	RPF^1	Quota	$DOMC_{IMF}$	Fund borrowing	UFC	RPF^1	Total RPF^2
	(1)	(2)	(3)	(4)	(5)	(6)	(7)	(8)	(9)	(10)	(11)
1 Initial position	100	75	—	—	25	100	75	—	—	25	50
2 Drawing of reserve tranche (A)³	100	100	—	—	—	100	50(75)	—(25)	—	50	50
3 Positive UFC (A)³	100	125	—	25	—	100	25(75)	—(50)	—	75	75

¹ RFP = (1) – (2) + (3) + (4) = (6) – (7) + (8) + (9).
² Aggregate RPF = (5) + (10).
³ The secondary case in parentheses assumes the Fund borrows from country B to finance country A's drawings.

B's currency to SDR50 million. Alternatively, the Fund could have borrowed a further SDR25 million from Country B leaving its holdings of B's currency unchanged on a net basis. In both cases, B's rises to SDR50 million and the aggregate RPF remains at SDR50 million also. Now consider, as in line 3, a further borrowing by Country A on, for example, a special facility of SDR25 million. Country A's UFC rises to SDR25million, but given that its RPF cannot be negative, this remains at zero. However whether this is financed by a further run-down of existing Fund holdings of Country B's currency to SDR25 million or by a new Fund borrowing from Country B (leaving total borrowing by the Fund from B at SDR50 million and the domestic currency of B held by the Fund at SDR75 million), B's RPF rises to SDR75 million. Aggregate RPF therefore increases to SDR75 million. This asymmetrical effect implies that the aggregate RPF rises whenever a country increases its UFC such that the country's RPF goes to a notionally negative figure although remaining at zero in the Fund's Accounts. Conversely when a country repays some of its UFC, part of the asymmetrical effect on aggregate RPF is unwound. In this case, if Country A repurchases its own currency by selling back Country B's currency to the Fund, Country A's RPF remains at zero until the domestic currency of A held by the Fund falls below A's quota, while as its currency is repaid by the other country, country B's RPF falls back again.

Time-series data for the Reserve Position in the Fund of certain member countries are set out in Table 14.10. The domination of aggregate RPF by the industrial and oil-exporting countries is notable. In addition the rise in the aggregate RPF in 1975–6 and 1980–1, which were years of heavy borrowing from the Fund, demonstrate the effects of the asymmetry just described.

SDR DEPARTMENT (COLUMNS (39)–(41))

The activities of the SDR Department are briefly summarised in Columns (39)–(41). At the end of 1981, all members of the IMF were participants in the SDR Department and so received an allocation of SDRs, determined according to quota.[15] These are set out in Column (39) in IFS. Total SDR allocations stood at SDR21.43 billion at that time (see Table 14.11); six SDR allocations have been made, including the first one in January 1970 and the most recent one in January 1981. Participants in the SDR department may use SDRs for transactions

[15] As does Switzerland, which is not a member of the IMF. See footnote 16.

TABLE 14.10
Reserve Position in the Fund by Country
(SDR m; End-Year)

	1973	1974	1975	1976	1977	1978	1979	1980	1981
Industrial countries	4899	6196	7713	11847	12246	9579	7731	10708	13548
Australia	167	176	167	167	166	161	156	255	253
Austria	126	131	177	344	325	254	232	228	224
Belgium	492	511	591	814	779	606	524	489	390
Canada	280	433	554	813	702	427	297	454	345
France	377	429	623	843	736	461	479	837	884
Germany	1207	1290	1581	2133	2185	3302	2372	1796	2117
Italy	297	—	—	—	—	243	237	646	631
Japan	529	603	686	1144	1329	1642	1121	1044	1339
Netherlands	309	442	747	900	954	632	458	510	498
Norway	63	69	112	247	235	206	188	201	214
Spain	104	121	—	—	—	136	133	206	206
Sweden	88	89	95	232	225	191	181	194	166
Switzerland	—	—	81	250	391	309	207	252	397
UK	117	206	304	—	—	—	—	1045	1236
USA	458	1513	1890	3817	4072	804	951	2237	4342
Oil-exporting countries	322	1892	4338	5428	5360	4398	2991	4051	5771
Iran	48	422	959	998	986	725	325	235	141
Kuwait	20	256	574	743	722	588	390	411	410
Nigeria	33	34	212	334	340	366	295	371	446
Saudi Arabia	34	595	1570	2206	2215	1896	1290	1896	3428
Venezuela	112	401	805	926	833	588	408	490	549
Non-oil developing countries	947	726	574	461	483	862	1038	2077	2005
Argentina	—	11	—	—	—	131	154	263	239
Brazil	116	116	116	162	160	139	183	270	227
India	76	—	—	—	—	69	162	330	330
Total	6168	884	12624	17736	18089	14838	11760	16835	21323

TABLE 14.11
SDR Department
(SDR m; End-1981)

	SDRs		
	Net cumulative allocations	Country holdings	Holdings as % of allocations
	(39)	(40)	(41)
Netherlands	530.0	648.0	122.2
Kuwait	26.7	42.3	158.3
Pakistan	170.0	40.7	23.9
Total — all countries	21433.4	16868.7	78.7

with other country participants, with 'other holders'[16] of SDRs and with the General Resources Account of the Fund. Column (40) sets out the actual SDR holdings of member countries at the time the Accounts were drawn up and so reflects the extent of each member's transactions as listed in the previous sentence. Column (41) calculates each member's holdings of SDRs as a percentage of its allocation:

$$\text{Column (41)} = \frac{\text{SDR HOLDINGS (40)}}{\text{SDR ALLOCATION (39)}} \times 100 \qquad (14.9)$$

Therefore if Column (41) includes a figure of less than 100% that country has been a net user of part or all of its SDR allocation (e.g. Pakistan — Table 14.11); a figure exceeding 100% indicates that the country in question has made net acquisitions of SDRs (e.g. Netherlands, Kuwait).

Trust Fund Loans Outstanding (Column (42))

Finally, as one of the administered accounts of the Fund, the Trust Fund is listed separately in the IMF's accounts in *IFS*. In Column (42) the outstanding loans made by the Trust Fund are set out by country. The reader is referred to Table 13.9 for information on the major borrowers from the Trust Fund (including Pakistan — SDR229.7 million at the end of 1981) and the other administered accounts of the Fund.

[16] These officially prescribed 'other holders' numbered ten at the end of 1981 — the Bank for International Settlements, the World Bank, the International Development Association, the Andean Reserve Fund, the Arab Monetary Fund, the Central Bank for West African States, the East Caribbean Currency Authority, the International Fund for Agricultural Development, the Nordic Investment Bank, and the Swiss National Bank.

OTHER TABLES AND SUMMARY

To conclude this chapter, it should be noted that eight of the most important concepts included in separate columns in the Fund's accounts are also published in time-series form in a set of world tables, immediately following the accounts themselves in *IFS*.

Four of these tables are in *flow* form. They record cumulative Total Drawings, Repayments by Repurchase, Currencies Drawn and Repurchases by Currency of Repurchase during a particular time period. The main time-series information on Total Drawings has already been set out in Tables 13.1 and 13.2 and in aggregate form in Table 13.11. The aggregate figures for Repayments by Repurchase and Repurchases by Currency of Repurchase are similar but not identical as the latter includes repurchases resulting from firstly, currency subscriptions, secondly, charges paid in a member's own currency and finally, payments for gold subscriptions, all of which are excluded from the Repayments by Repurchase table. The main information on the currencies of drawing is set out in Table 14.12. Over the history of the IMF, the main currency drawn by members has been the US dollar which accounted for 28.9% of the total from 1947 to 1981 although this was slightly lower than the figure of 30.1% which applied on cumulative drawings to the end of 1972. In recent years the shares of the currencies of the other industrial countries (except the Japanese yen which represented 6.1% of total drawings up to 1981) have declined in the face of the growing role of SDRs and the currencies of the oil-exporting countries. Since the end of 1972, 20.1% of all drawings have been in SDRs, a figure that is rising sharply given that, in 1979–81, 32.4% of the total (68.7% in 1979 alone) were SDR-denominated drawings. Of the currencies of oil exporting countries, the share of the Saudi Arabian riyal in total drawings rose most steeply from zero before the end of 1973 to 14.3% in 1974–6; it now stands at 5.9% over the whole history of the Fund and at 9.9% since 1972.

The final four world tables are in *stock* form. These give figures for the outstanding Use of Fund Credit, Reserve Positions in the Fund, Net Credit Tranche Drawings under Ordinary Policies and SDRs at the end of the period to which the data refer. Detailed breakdowns of the UFC and RPF have already been included in Tables 13.6 and 14.10, respectively, while less detailed, aggregate information has also been recorded on the other two stock concepts at various points in the last two chapters.

In summary it should be reiterated that the lay-out of the Fund's Accounts as presented in *IFS* is complicated, liable to change and relies unavoidably on a thorough knowledge of the procedural

TABLE 14.12
Currencies of Drawing
(SDR m)

	1947–1972	1973	1974	1975	1976	1977	1978	1979	1980	1981	Total 1947–1981
Industrial countries	23901.4	687.6	2525.1	2287.4	5229.4	2821.7	2602.7	177.7	1279.4	3741.5	45253.9
Belgian francs	1580.0	28.3	132.1	111.4	291.4	64.6	5.0	6.6	5.7	—	2225.1
Canadian dollars	1642.7	33.6	60.5	43.0	308.5	75.0	4.0	—	—	—	2167.3
French francs	1695.4	82.2	137.3	224.9	400.6	69.5	—	17.7	80.9	30.0	2738.5
Deutschemark	4360.0	323.8	474.5	280.0	324.2	670.0	1654.1	—	—	186.0	8272.6
Italian lira	1974.9	18.8	—	—	—	—	—	—	243.4	—	2237.1
Japanese yen	987.2	61.5	132.7	148.7	600.3	427.2	766.0	42.1	144.5	423.2	3733.4
Netherlands guilders	1734.1	29.7	154.2	91.8	186.0	153.1	5.0	—	—	33.4	2386.6
Pound sterling	1312.8	—	89.0	97.7	—	—	101.8	—	—	190.6	1791.9
US dollars	7449.8	—	1199.5	1182.2	2720.0	1277.5	59.9	108.0	800.8	2826.2	17624.2
Other countries											
Iranian rials	—	—	374.0	536.8	99.2	1.5	7.0	—	—	—	1081.5
Kuwaiti dinars	—	—	236.0	320.9	171.1	3.0	—	22.8	90.6	114.9	964.2
Saudi Arabian riyals	—	—	561.8	953.4	734.8	35.0	30.0	180.5	345.7	745.3	3586.5
Venezuelan bolivars	37.3	—	291.0	405.6	167.2	10.0	4.0	20.0	75.7	153.5	1164.3
SDRs	—	45.0	31.9	101.0	501.9	455.8	1024.9	1266.0	1555.9	1298.3	7300.8
Total	24744.8	732.6	4053.1	4658.1	7009.9	3424.6	3744.3	1842.8	3752.7	7081.7	61044.7

operations of the IMF in both raising resources and lending. Therefore, Chapters 13 and 14 complement each other and should be read together, although in terms of the content of this book the main objective of this section has been a survey of the statistical presentation of the Fund's Accounts as described in Chapter 14.

Section 6
Empirical Evidence

Chapter 15

Empirical Evidence on the Comparability of Statistical Sources

INTRODUCTION

To conclude this survey of the available sources of data on international financial stocks and flows, this chapter draws together these disparate sources in two ways. Firstly, the coverage in particular statistical series of certain flows of funds (broadly grouped as banking flows and flows from non-banks) is considered in an abstract way. This enables a general picture to be derived of the extent to which different statistical series will be consistent in their treatment of such flows. Secondly, empirical evidence is presented for ten countries and a group of oil exporters from certain of the statistical sources surveyed in this volume to shed light on the degree of association, if any, between the amounts of new borrowing completed by the countries as estimated by the alternative statistical systems.

Data for the sample of countries is compared from four different sources. These are:

   (i) BIS data on banking flows (Chapters 3, 5 and 6)[1]
  (ii) OECD data on borrowing in international capital markets (Chapters 8–10)
 (iii) The World Bank's CMS (Chapters 8–10).
 (iv) The World Bank's DRS (Chapter 11).

The restriction of the scope of this empirical study to these

---

[1] There is no consideration in this chapter of data from the six-monthly BIS *Press Release* on the maturity distribution of international bank lending or of other (national) sources of maturity figures. Sole use is made of the data from the quarterly BIS *Press Release* on aggregate international banking flows.

statistical systems necessarily involves the omission of certain sources which have been surveyed earlier in the book. In particular, no evidence on the flows of funds to the countries concerned is presented from IMF banking data published in *International Financial Statistics* or from data published by the Development Assistance Committee (DAC) of the OECD. *IFS* banking data are omitted as they do not include a borrower country breakdown of the sort needed for this study, while DAC data are left out due to the conceptual similarity between them and DRS data. In contrast, the maxim of excluding one of two similar data series was not invoked in the case of the two series — from the OECD and the World Bank — on international capital market borrowing. An investigation of the degree of overlap between these two, theoretically very similar, series was considered to be of major interest. Finally, data on flows from the IMF (Chapters 13 and 14) to the countries included in the study were omitted as such flows are automatically excluded from all other series.

Apart from the expectation that CMS and OECD capital market data should correspond closely, the fact that the data sources and the forms in which the statistics are presented differ between the various sources does generate the expectation that general, cross-source consistency would be difficult to achieve. In particular, the BIS publish data on bank *stock* positions while the OECD/CMS produce data on new commitments *(flows)* of funds from banks and on new bond issues, while most DRS data is on the outstanding *stock* of external debt. Therefore, anticipating the results of the empirical tests somewhat, limited correspondence between the data series for any one country is found. It may be argued that this is primarily due to conceptual differences between the sources, although it may also be traceable to inefficient reporting.

Despite such unconvincing evidence and the general conclusion that it is difficult to achieve a clear and comprehensive picture of total financial flows to a particular country — which is itself a serious problem — each individual data series has its own merits and value. For example, the announcements or commitments data of the OECD and CMS are important if a summary of market conditions is needed, while the BIS data on actual bank flows (and therefore completions) are equally crucial in that they indicate the actual volume of funds drawn. Therefore, while total consistency may be desirable from a particular viewpoint, it is difficult to achieve and the lack of it does not affect the value of individual series.

In the survey to follow, the reporting of bank flows and commitments by the various systems will be considered first. This is based on the fact that all systems cover some concept of bank flows while the number and importance of conceptual differences between the sources is greatest in the case of these statistics. Following that, a briefer comparative survey will be made of statistics on firstly, external bond issues sold in part or wholly to non-banks and, finally, other non-bank flows.

BANKING FLOWS

The logical starting point for a survey of available statistics on flows of funds from banks is the data issued by the BIS. Whereas all other reporting systems to be examined in this chapter aim to include certain specified non-bank flows, the BIS alone considers banking flows exclusively. Table 15.1 sets out the differences in reporting coverage for a variety of banking flows and is designed in the following way. On the left-hand side of the table, a set of conditions is listed that must be satisfied for a completed loan, that is drawn in full, to be included in all statistical systems (All Systems Coverage). On the right-hand side, should one or more conditions not apply, but in all other respects the original conditions are satisfied, then that flow is included in the reporting system that is ticked. Due to the lack of uniformity across systems for these variants of the basic financing instrument, this part of the table is termed a 'Partial System Coverage'. An example may clarify this. A loan that satisfies all conditions on the left-hand side of the table except that it is short-term (i.e. with a maturity of one year or less) is included in the BIS reporting system only, as such short-term flows are excluded, by definition, from the other statistical systems.

Drawings of Banks Funds

As shown in Table 15.1 there is a certain type of flow from banks to ultimate borrowers that is included by all reporting systems. Specifically, any published, medium- or long-term credit to an overseas, non-bank borrower without the guarantee of an official institution, funded in the eurocurrency market and drawn in full should in principle be included in the data issued by all four systems.

However the BIS include in their banking data certain other flows which are excluded from all or some of the other reporting systems. Firstly, certain bank flows are not well publicised and therefore elude the search processes of the OECD and CMS in the compilation of data on eurocurrency credits. It is estimated that around 20% of the

TABLE 15.1
Systems Coverage of Statistics on Bank Drawings and Commitments

A Bank drawings: all systems coverage	Bank drawings of: partial systems coverage	BIS	OECD	CMS	DRS
if — publicised	if — unpublicised or	✓			✓
— financed in external (eurocurrency) markets	— financed in domestic markets[1] or	✓			✓[2]
— granted to overseas borrowers	— granted to domestic borrowers or	✓[3]	✓	✓	
— granted to non-bank borrowers	— granted to bank borrowers (inter-bank deal) or	✓			
— granted to borrower who does not have a guarantee from official institutions[4]	— granted to borrower with guarantee from official institutions or	✓			✓
— medium and long-term debt[5]	— short-term debt[6]	✓			
B Bank commitments					
if conditions under A (All Systems Coverage) satisfied			✓	✓	

Memorandum

	BIS	OECD	CMS	DRS
Gross or Net reporting of drawings of fund	Gross/Net	Gross	Gross	Gross/Net[7]

Credits advanced by foreign banks would be included by the OECD and CMS even if the loan was partly funded in the domestic markets.

[1] Excluding loans denominated in the debtor's domestic currency.
[2] With the exception of domestic currency loans to residents by foreign banks in the country concerned.
[3] For example, Export Credit Agencies, EEC Agencies but not Central Government or other parts of government.
[4] Original maturities of over one year.
[5] Original maturities of one year or less.
[6] Original maturities of one year or less.
[7] Most DRS data are in net form but some gross series are published, in particular, new disbursements of funds (flow data).

number of bank credits is not captured by the CMS and OECD but, as many of these unpublicised flows are very small[2] (less than $10 million for example), the proportion of the total *volume* of funds that is missed by these systems is significantly lower than this. Such unpublicised flows are however included in BIS data as, in general, they will be reported by the lending banks, while they will also appear in the DRS as they are part of the outstanding debt of the borrower.

Secondly, the procedures of the reporting systems differ on the question of foreign and domestic currency loans. The OECD and CMS use compatible definitions of eurocurrency credits, which emphasise the financing of the new credit in the eurocurrency markets. In contrast, the BIS includes flows to overseas borrowers where the funds are raised in domestic money markets. Therefore while the BIS, CMS and OECD would all include in their data a dollar credit to Brazil that is funded outside the country in which the lending banks are located,[3] the BIS would also include the same credit flow even if it were funded in domestic money markets. The only exception to this general rule is that a credit funded in domestic markets would be included in OECD data when that credit is advanced by foreign banks in the country concerned. This latter condition encompasses the likelihood that such foreign banks would rely on both domestic and foreign sources for funding such a loan (see Chapter 9). The complexity of this issue is heightened by the procedure of the DRS to include all of the flows specified in this paragraph (consistent therefore with the BIS) except any liabilities to international banks denominated in the domestic currency of the *debtor* country. Continuing the example, all flows are included in the DRS unless a liability is created to international banks in Brazilian cruzeiro.

Thirdly, a set of data differences arises from the identification of the borrower. All systems report bank credits to overseas (external), non-bank borrowers who do not have a guarantee from an official institution (as defined in Footnote (4) to Table 15.1). Any foreign

---

[2] See BIS (1979), although this may be a less valid conclusion more recently as in 1980/81 it is believed that certain large loans were arranged but not publicised (see Chapter 8).

[3] The CMS and OECD figures therefore include what may be termed 'domestic currency' loans. For example, in the case noted above should the dollar credit be granted by US banks it is included as long as it is funded outside the US. Therefore it should not be assumed that the part of the BIS banking figures that specifies domestic currency loans is automatically excluded from the CMS and OECD series on eurocurrency credit flows. The crucial criterion is the location of the market in which the credit is funded.

currency loan to a domestic non-bank resident is included in the eurocurrency credits data of the OECD and CMS (assuming it is funded externally). For example a dollar loan by a group of UK banks to a UK firm would be included in this category. Such flows are also included in some of the tables published by the BIS,[4] although emphasis is placed by this source on external positions. In addition, the OECD and CMS include domestic currency loans to residents from foreign banks in the country concerned. This covers, for example, dollar loans to US residents by non-US banks based in the United States. This case is a rare example of a banking flow being included in capital markets' data but excluded by the BIS to which the residency of the lending banks and not their country of ownership is the crucial factor in determining the allocation of loans to particular series. The debt of any sector in a country to any other domestic sector is, however, automatically excluded from the DRS whatever the currency of the debt. In addition, the BIS gross data includes all reported cross-border interbank flows. To the extent that such on-lending may occur before funds reach the ultimate borrower, double-counting of the 'true' volume of new bank credit will occur. Figure 15.1 repeats the example (from Fig. 6.3) of a flow from a non-bank

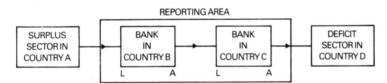

FIGURE 15.1
Flow of funds involving an inter-bank transaction

surplus sector (in country A) to a deficit sector (in country D) through two international banks (in countries B and C). Assuming both banks involved in such a flow are reporting banks, double counting would occur as this flow would be included in BIS data twice. The liability of the bank in country B to country A and of the bank in country C to the bank in country B would be included with a similar situation existing on the claims side of the composite balance-sheet of the reporting banks.[5] On the other hand, the OECD and CMS series would ignore

[4] However, these positions against domestic residents were reported by the group of European reporting banks only until 1979 and by banks in Canada and Japan also since then.

[5] This double-counting only applies to BIS data series on gross flows and is eliminated from the net figures published by the BIS.

the claim of C's bank on the ultimate borrower in country C and include the claim of C's bank on the ultimate borrower in country D only. Similarly, the debt of country D to the international banking system would alone be included in the DRS. However, a further difference may exist in this system also. Should country D be borrowing funds ahead of need, part or all of the funds may be redeposited in the international banking system. In this case, the net change in country D's external debt is zero, for a flow which was counted twice in BIS data and once in OECD and CMS figures. One other inter-system difference exists concerning the borrower category. In contrast to the OECD and CMS practice, any funds lent to a borrower but guaranteed by an official institution are included in the data of the BIS and DRS.

Fourthly, OECD and CMS figures on eurocurrency credits and DRS data on outstanding external debt are limited to medium- and long-term flows. These are defined as flows having an original maturity of greater than one year. In contrast, the BIS does not make this distinction including all flows whatever their maturity. (Given this procedure of the BIS and the exclusion of the maturity data of the BIS from the empirical work in this chapter, the potentially difficult problem of the distinction between 'original' and 'residual' maturity may be ignored.) The size of the discrepancy between the BIS series on the one hand and the DRS and the capital markets data on the other is both uncertain and likely to be fairly volatile. However, in stock terms, it may be around $130 million (23% of total external debt) at the end of 1981 (Gasser and Roberts, 1982) although the BIS estimate of bank claims of up to and including one year to maturity of $230.1 billion at the end of 1981 is not comparable, being based on residual maturities.

Gross and Net Drawings

Having identified the differences in the types of banking flow included in the various systems, it is now important to make a distinction between the reporting of such data in *gross* or *net* terms.[6] Banking data are said to be in gross terms when new flows of funds are evaluated without considering repayments. Alternatively and repeating some of the material in Chapter 6, a net flow of bank credit occurs when the figure for new drawings minus payments is positive. Two examples will illustrate this difference. Firstly, in a given year if a borrower in country A negotiates a loan of $500 million while the same or a separate borrower in that country repays a loan of $100

[6] See memorandum item (Table 15.1).

million in the same period, the gross flow of new eurocurrency credit is $500 million and the net flow $400 million. Secondly, if a lender refinances a loan of $500 million for a borrower in country A in a given year so that the repayment of that amount coincides with a new credit being granted, then the gross rise in bank lending is $500 million but in net terms, no new bank lending has occurred.

Both the OECD and CMS report new eurocurrency credits in gross terms. In contrast, in considering the outstanding external debt of individual countries, the DRS evaluates new bank credit net of repayments so that the change in outstanding debt is calculated in this way. Finally, BIS figures of both assets and liabilities of reporting banks enable either a gross or net flow of credit to be calculated for a particular borrowing country. Given the rapid expansion of eurocurrency credits since the beginning of 1970s and the typical maturity of such credits of 7–10 years plus the benefits at certain times to borrowers of renegotiating part of their outstanding debt or repaying debt, the differences between gross and net figures for new bank have at times become significant. Clearly the divergence between gross and net new bank credit will be highly volatile and dependent on many factors including the willingness of lenders and borrowers to conclude refinancing agreements and the current conditions available on refinancing loans.

Commitments of Bank Funds and Valuation effects

A further complication in the comparison between banking and capital– market data is that the OECD and CMS report completed eurocurrency credits (commitments) while BIS data cover actual drawings of bank credit. The problems caused by this difference are of two forms. Firstly, certain completed eurocurrency credits may not be drawn in full or even, in certain cases, drawn upon at all. The latter situation is most common in the case of 'stand-by' credits. Such agreements have the effect of guaranteeing to the borrower a certain volume of bank credit should that borrower wish or need to draw upon these funds in the future. They are usually signed with a particular possible future contingency in mind, such as the mobilization of resources to defend the countrie's currency against speculative attack. Very often the mere signature of a stand-by credit — which demonstrates to the market the existence of a significant volume of funds that are available to defend the currency — is sufficient to stem the attack and paradoxically render the stand-by credit unecessary. To this extent, OECD and CMS data over estimate the volume of funds actually drawn, with BIS data presenting a very different, but more accurate, guide to funds actually used.

Secondly, should a certain period of time elapse between signature of the credit and drawing of the funds, data for a particular credit flow will, even if drawn in full, appear in OECD and CMS series in a different time period compared to BIS data. Conventionally, eurocurrency credits specify a 'drawdown' period to run from signature for a stipulated time after which any undrawn part of the credit is automatically cancelled. This drawdown period may run for up to five years. Therefore for a credit that is drawn either in full, but not immediately after signature, or in separate amounts right through this period, the ability to achieve close correspondence between OECD and CMS capital markets data and BIS banking data is limited.

This situation generates two further technical problems. Firstly, it is possible that the details of a eurocurrency credit may alter after signature. Any such changes may affect bank positions but would mean that the original capital market data of signed eurocurrency credits were inaccurate and would need to be revised. Secondly, it is possible, particularly when a substantial time-period elapses between signature and drawdown, that a credit will be drawn in a currency different from the one in which the credit is denominated.[7] Many agreements stipulate an option for the borrower to switch the currency of the loan from that in which it was originally denominated. The borrower is usually allowed to do this at the end of any interest-payment period enabling it to take a view on expected interest rate and exchange rate developments. In the cases of a non-dollar credit or a dollar credit drawn in non-dollar currencies, with BIS data recording the dollar value of these drawings, the possibility of a type of valuation effect exists. Such effects occur when, due to movements in exchange rate between two currencies, the dollar value of the non-dollar drawings (which may occur sometime after the signature of the credit itself) is different from the dollar value of the original credit, leading to a further disparity between capital markets data and the BIS banking figures.

Further discrepancies may arise between the different series as a result of the possible combination of general valuation effects and the different procedures adopted by the statistical systems concerning the conversion of non-dollar flows into dollar values. Those procedures to be described in this paragraph will occur even if signature

[7] In 1981, 93% of all publicised eurocurrency credits were denominated in dollars (Table 9.5), but it is likely that a much smaller proportion of total funds actually drawn was denominated in this currency.

and drawdown occur in the same time-period used for reporting by the different series. Given their use of flow data, the OECD and CMS convert non-dollar credits into dollar values using the average market exchange rate over the month in which the loan is signed. In contrast, the BIS series converts non-dollar bank positions into dollar values using the market rate ruling at the end of the quarter or half-year to which the data refer. Therefore, for example, a movement in the dollar rate of a particular currency between the January signature date of a credit denominated in that currency to the end of March when the credit — assuming it has been drawn — appears in the BIS figures will lead to valuation effects and a further discrepancy between the data series. More seriously, but to be expected for annual stock data, the DRS converts any outstanding non-dollar debt into dollar values at the exchange rate ruling at the end of the year in question. Continuing the example it is likely that, in the recent era of floating exchange rates, a movement in the dollar value of the currency in which the credit is denominated will occur between its inclusion in the capital markets data in January and in the DRS data at the end of the year, leading to a significant discrepancy in the published statistics of the different systems.

Reporting Group

Yet another source of variation between BIS banking and other statistical sources arises from the limitation on the BIS Reporting Group. At present, as discussed in Chapters 3 and 5, this is restricted to a group of twelve European countries, the USA, Canada and Japan and, using the broadest available coverage of such centres, branches of all banks in eight offshore banking centres. To the extent that the countries included in this survey borrow funds from banks outside the BIS Reporting Group, or from financial institutions within the BIS group but which do not form part of BIS statistics (Table 5.4), a new discrepancy is created between the BIS series and the other sources included in this study, given that, in principle, these other series include all banking flows from whatever territorial or institutional source. However, as argued in Chapter 5, the discrepancy is not large. The BIS estimate of outstanding external bank lending at the end of 1981 of $1778 billion was 89.4% of the IMF figure for the equivalent Reporting Group and 84.7% of the IMF 'world' total of external bank lending.

A further point to note in this comparision of statistical sources is the absence of a full country breakdown for all BIS reporting countries. (See Chapter 3.) Although this does not affect the global totals of international banking activity, the allocation of many of the foreign assets of banks in Switzerland and the USA to a residual hampers the analysis of an individual country's outstanding debtor/creditor relationship with reporting banks and, by definition, reduces the consistency between the statistical sources being studied. However, it is important to note that, at present, no country breakdown of banking flows at all is published by the IMF which as argued above, was the main practical reason for the exclusion of IMF banking data from this study.

Borrower Groupings

The objectives of the statistical systems under study in this book frequently differ and this leads to an additional problem when comparing them, namely that of the classification of the borrowers or debtors. In essence, the DRS is a system designed to collect information on the outstanding debt of developing countries while BIS, OECD, and CMS data aim to include all countries and international organisations as borrowers. In addition, the DRS is hampered at times by the lack of willingness of developing countries to report their debt statistics. It is a requirement that when a country borrows from the World Bank Group it must furnish the DRS with the appropriate information on its outstanding debt on an annual basis.

Despite this, for 1981 the DRS has information on the outstanding external public debt of 98 countries only (that is excluding Afghanistan, Iran and Iraq, data for which does not extend beyond 1978). DAC statistics, on the other hand, which have the advantage by being the output of a creditor reporting system of securing information more easily, include data for over 160 developing countries. Therefore, although as argued in Chapter 11, the DRS covers most of the major debtors in the developing world, the coverage is not complete.

The adoption of different grouping procedures also hampers a comparative survey of these systems. Table 15.2 sets out the regional and/or income groupings adopted by the alternative reporting systems, noting that, in the case of the BIS series, two separate geographical classifications, which overlap partially, are specified. Given the wide variety of conventions it is clear that any cross-system data comparison on a regional or income basis is cumbersome. As a result, such comparative studies as are feasible are, strictly, those completed at the global level (or at the level of the developing country aggre-

Cross-System Country Groupings

BIS (By Region) [1]	BIS (By region) [1],[2]	OCCD (By Region)	CMS (By region/income)	DRS (By region)	DRS (By region)
Reporting countries[2] (Intra-Group)	Reporting countries[2] (intra-Group)	OECD countries	Industrial countries		
Offshore centres	Other Western Europe				
Other Developed	Other Developed				
Eastern Europe	Eastern Europe	Eastern Socialist countries	Non-market countries/organisation		
		Developing	*Developing*	*Developing*	*Developing*
OPEC countries	Caribbean Area	Oil-exporters	Oil-exporters	Africa, South of the Sahara	Oil Exports
Latin America	Latin America	Other	Middle Income	East Asia and the Pacific	Middle Income Oil-Importers
Middle East	Middle East		Low Income	Latin America and the Caribbean	Low Income Asia
Other Africa	Other Africa		Other	North Africa and the Middle East	Low Income Africa
Other Asia	Other Asia			South Asia	
International Institutions	International Institutions	Interntional Organisations based in Europe/ International Development Institutions	International Organisation	More Developed Mediterranean countries	
Memorandum Oil Exporters	*Memorandum* Oil Exporters			*Memorandum* Major Borrowers	

[1] This classification is also used by the BIS in its maturity data (Chapter 7).

[2] Excluding offshore centres.

gate)[8] or for an individual country. This may, in itself, not be a significant handicap but the danger of regional and income group comparisons should not be underestimated.

NON-BANKING FLOWS

Turning to flows from non-banks to borrowing countries, Table 15.3 illustrates the extent to which these flows are covered by the various statistical systems being surveyed.

To provide a link with the previous section, the first item in this table is the credit advanced to borrowing countries through the purchase by non-banks of external bond issues. Such issues are reported on a quarterly basis by the OECD and CMS and are also included in the outstanding external debt statistics of the DRS. The link between this item and banking flows is provided in two ways. Firstly, although not set out explicitly in that section, any bond holdings of reporting banks will, by definition, be reflected in banks' external asset positions as described in the previous section. Therefore despite the absence of any separate categorisation of advances through bond purchases above, such flows are part of those statistics. Secondly, the OECD and CMS reporting systems do not identify the sectoral split on the creditor side with respect to bond issues. Therefore the dividing-line between the figures for bank and non-bank purchases of external bonds in the capital market data of the OECD and CMS is not apparent, generating an overlap between flows from banks and from non-banks in these statistical systems. However, should the distinction between bank and non-bank bond purchases be feasible, and given that the OECD and CMS include both creditor categories in their external bond data, this is the only flow from the non-bank sector that is included by more than one statistical system in Table 15.3.[9]

[8] Even this should be done with care because in the BIS series no overall developing country category is separately identified, while certain countries included as developing nations by the DRS (viz. Cyprus, Greece, Malta, Portugal, Turkey and Yugoslavia) are included in the BIS categories that imply a non-developing country status (viz. other countries in Western Europe and other developed), while the OECD also includes Yugoslavia as an Eastern Socialist country in contrast to BIS procedure.

[9] In addition, the DRS, in its data on public and publicly-guaranteed private debt, reports bond issues in the creditor category of financial markets, while in the private non-guaranteed debt category, bond issues are included as the assets of 'financial institutions'. However, this aggregation of bond holdings into a single sector is purely for convenience due to the frequent difficulty of identifying accurately all bond-holders. Although this should not be taken to mean that non-bank holdings of bonds are zero, it does perpetuate the statistical ground-rule that no distinction is made between bank and non-bank holders.

Table 15.3
Systems Coverage of Statistics on Non-Bank flows

	BIS	OECD	CMS	DRS
External Bonds held by non-banks		×	×	×

Loans from official institutions[1]
—Multilateral (e.g. IBRD, regional
    development banks)
—Bilateral (e.g. central banks,
    public corporations)
				×
				
				×

Private Flows
from — suppliers
    — non-bank financial
        institutions
    — foreign parent companies
				×
				×
				
				×

[1]Excluding the IMF (except for Trust Fund loans which are included in the DRS).

All other categories of non-bank flows to borrowing countries are reported by the DRS alone.[10] In Table 15.3 these have been subdivided into official and private flows. Official flows themselves are reported by the DRS as either multilateral credits[11] from international organisations such as the World Bank Group, regional development banks such as the Inter-American Development Bank and export credit agencies such as Exim Bank, or bilateral credits from central banks or public corporations in an individual country. In turn, private capital flows are subdivided into suppliers' credits and loans from non-bank financial institutions and foreign parent companies. The category of non-bank financial institutions is intended to capture any funds loaned by a financial institution that does not report to the BIS system and whose external loans are not included in the OECD and the CMS eurocurrency credits data. Such institutions would include, for example, finance companies, although it is clear that only a small proportion of external finance raised by borrowing countries would come from such sources. Finally, credit may be extended by a parent company to a subsidiary or affiliate located in a foreign country and such funds are also included only in the DRS.

[10] All of these flows are also included, in principle, in the DAC statistics on the flows of funds to developing countries (see Stein, 1980), which are not part of this empirical study (see Chapter 12).

[11] As the OECD and CMS eurocurrency credits data exclude any credits granted by official institutions, the external claims of such multilateral organizations, despite being one interpretation of the concept of a 'banking' flow, are included in Table 15.4 and not in the previous section. Loans from the IMF (except Trust Fund loans) are excluded from the DRS too.

EMPIRICAL EVIDENCE

This section looks at data for eleven countries from the four statistical systems surveyed above. It seeks to identify any association between these series through graphical inspection and the reporting of some simple regression results. In the choice of countries, a broad mix of country type was used in the study (see Table 15.4) with data for 3 industrialised countries, 1 centrally-planned economy, 2 Latin American countries, a group of low-absorbing oil-exporters (as defined by the World Bank), 1 African country and 3 Asian countries being compared. This type of cross-section was selected for two reasons. Firstly, there may exist a greater or lesser degree of correspondence between published statistics for one or other of these geographical groupings; any pattern of this sort may be identifiable in such a sample. Secondly, for pure interest, it was felt desirable to cover as broad a range of country-types as possible wih some of the major individual country borrowers being chosen for empirical study.

Table 15.4 presents annual figures (in millions of dollars) used for this comparative survey for the period from 1974 to 1981. All data are in flow form and therefore should be interpreted as $ × billion of new borrowing by country Y in any particular twelve-month period. The columns are defined as follows. Columns (1) and (2) are the flows of new, publicised eurocurrency credits completed by a particular country in any one year as published by the CMS of the World Bank and by the OECD respectively. Column (3) is the change in the value of reporting banks' outstanding claims on a country (in gross terms) over a particular calender year. Column (4) is on the same basis as Column (3) except that these figures are given net of the change in reporting banks' liabilities to the borrower over the calendar year. Both these columns may be derived from published BIS stock figures. Finally, Column (5) is the change in the stock of outstanding external public and publicly-guaranteed private debt of a country over a particular calendar year.

Certain statistical coverage restrictions are apparent from Table 15.4. A country breakdown of reporting banks' external assets and liabilities was first published by the BIS for end-December 1975.[12] This allows the derivation of a flow series beginning only in 1976. Data on new eurocurrency credits for 1981 drawn from the CMS are available for five of the countries included in Table 15.4 only while, finally, external debt data are not published for industrial countries, Eastern European countries and the low-absorbing oil-exporters.

[12] *Bank for International Settlements.* 46th Annual Report (1975), June 1976.

The variables in each of the columns were chosen and arranged in the form of Table 15.4 for a number of reasons. Firstly, it is clear that the closest correspondence between the series should exist between the eurocurrency credits data of the CMS and OECD. Secondly, these data for new credit commitments – which do not include any repayments or new bank deposits made by borrowers — should be most closely related to the gross concept of BIS data. Thirdly, the net concept of BIS data should correspond as closely as any series to the change in outstanding external debt which similarly is a net figure.

Apart from the close correspondence between the CMS and OECD series, it is difficult to identify any consistently close association between the series as they are set out in Table 15.4. To facilitate comparison therefore, these data are graphed for each country (Fig 15.2). In addition, a number of simple regressions were carried out and the results of these are reported in Table 15.5.[13] In addition to the regressions completed on a contemporaneous basis, BIS (gross) data were related to OECD and CMS data with one- and two-year lags to try to capture the expected result that countries may not draw on new bank credits immediately after their arrangement. On the same grounds, DRS data were correlated with OECD and CMS figures with similar lag lengths. Despite the simplicity of the regressions and the small number of observations, the results do give a general indication of the basic strength of the relationships between the various statistical series for individual countries.

(a) CMS/OECD (Table 15.5 (a))

As might be expected the regression results in the table indicate an extremely close association between these two data series on eurocurrency credits. For all countries the CMS data series is significantly related to the OECD series at the 1%. level with the exception of

---

[13] The basic regression equation fitted was (for example, for the relationship between CMS and OECD data):

$$CMS_{it} = \alpha_i + \beta_i OECD_{it} + U_t \quad \text{for i countries.}$$

The β-values are reported in the various parts of Table 15.5 with t-statistics, which measure the degree of significance, being in brackets. A + sign means the co-efficient is significant at the 5% level and a * sign at the 10% level. In certain equations in parts b), c) and d) of Table 15.5, time-lags of up to two years were specified on the independent variable. The adjusted co-efficient of determination ($\bar{R}^2$) is reported as is the Durbin-Watson (DW) statistic which indicates whether auto-correlation is present. Given the sample sizes for these tests, a DW statistic of between 1.54 and 2.46 indicates a lack of auto-correlation, with one of between 0.95 and 1.54 or between 2.46 and 3.05 being in the inconclusive range.

TABLE 15.4
Data Series for Selected Countries ($million)

		CMS[1]	OECD	BIS (gross)[2]	BIS (net)[2]	DRS[3]
France	1974	3331	3331			n/a
	1975	506	506			
	1976	734	769	400	− 1004	
	1977	1865	1762	7515	− 877	
	1978	2475	2365	16298	426	
	1979	2735	2787	12120	− 2110	
	1980	1960	1922	9026	− 1082	
	1981		3847	11030	19456	
Italy	1974	2390	2390			n/a
	1975	120	120			
	1976	20	20	200	2534	
	1977	779	676	3915	767	
	1978	2808	2811	7213	− 1617	
	1979	3415	3361	5146	− 1546	
	1980	6177	6483	9655	8326	
	1981		6984	10194	4924	
USA	1974	1354	1354			n/a
	1975	572	514			
	1976	407	288	2641	− 11663	
	1977	848	843	5817	− 11852	
	1978	2465	2637	13325	− 14504	
	1979	3845	3722	28829	− 6910	
	1980	7489	6387	7128	− 28973	
	1981		58192	44682	− 23595	
Poland	1974	508	509			n/a
	1975	475	475			
	1976	499	469	1572	1437	
	1977	19	19	1349	1608	
	1978	374	406	2647	2238	
	1979	819	861	3226	3037	
	1980	338	736	88	565	
	1981		—	− 465	− 565	
Mexico	1974	1478	1478			2728
	1975	2151	2166			3227
	1976	2140	1974	4385	3370	4391
	1977	2895	2657	1446	57	4828
	1978	6554	5664	3337	2150	4857
	1979	7655	10438	7426	5645	3627
	1980	5017	5980	10369	9155	4345
	1981	6594	10571	14244	11540	9056
Venezuela	1974	50	50			− 48
	1975	200	200			− 231
	1976	1129	1099	2362	2354	1699
	1977	1650	1648	2440	1496	1465
	1978	2051	1720	4877	3626	2466
	1979	3238	3035	5710	1740	2912
	1980	2898	2937	2758	425	1068
	1981	689	1333	922	− 1831	479

Country	Year					
Oil-exporters[4]	1974	151	151			n/a
	1975	6	6			
	1976	244	175	861	-4742	
	1977	1560	1634	1808	-539	
	1978	1347	1104	2429	1149	
	1979	661	786	1527	-9114	
	1980	452	478	482	-11765	
	1981		761	371	-15646	
Morocco	1974	—	—			220
	1975	200	200			535
	1976	409	389	467	276	577
	1977	702	757	328	124	1739
	1978	620	667	902	899	1054
	1979	450	590	645	567	1059
	1980	450	450	166	463	916
	1981		543	270	347	782
Indonesia	1974	368	368			1109
	1975	1608	1608			1637
	1976	510	464	961	-10	2008
	1977	88	88	243	-664	1657
	1978	1623	1592	430	97	1449
	1979	670	695	-295	-1896	127
	1980	1080	967	63	-2348	1648
	1981	1093	1101	294	865	647
Korea	1974	300	300			961
	1975	326	326			1057
	1976	980	1061	593	-375	1276
	1977	796	682	1355	475	1778
	1978	1699	1582	862	1396	2767
	1979	2590	2694	3425	2831	2570
	1980	1903	2037	3714	3542	2343
	1981	2352	3174	2935	3047	3691
Philippines	1974	853	883			221
	1975	223	253			279
	1976	873	827	601	467	745
	1977	705	637	150	158	816
	1978	1872	1463	941	548	1269
	1979	1673	1774	1364	856	926
	1980	1121	1277	1608	845	1272
	1981	947	1141	243	798	982

Note
All data are in *flow* terms:
OECD, CMS figures are the volume of new eurocurrency credits completed for each country in a particular year.
BIS figures are the change in the outstanding bank external claims (gross and net of liabilities) each country in a particular year.
DRS figures are the change in the outstanding external public and publicly-guaranteed private debt (disbursed only) of each country in a particular year.
[1] Although full data publication under the CMS ended in June 1981, certain fragmentary data collected under the CMS were published for the whole of 1981 in *IMF Survey*, 25th January 1982. All entries for 1981 in this column are drawn from that source.
[2] For 1976–7, the previous series was used, i.e. excluding data on banks in Austria, Denmark and Ireland. For 1978–81 the new series was used. A country breakdown is not available for data before December 1975.
[3] These data are only available for non-oil developing countries.
[4] Low absorbers, — Kuwait, Qatar, Saudi Arabia, the United Arab Emirates.

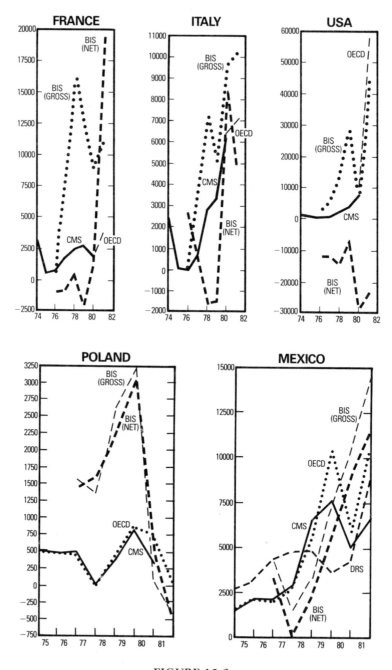

FIGURE 15.2

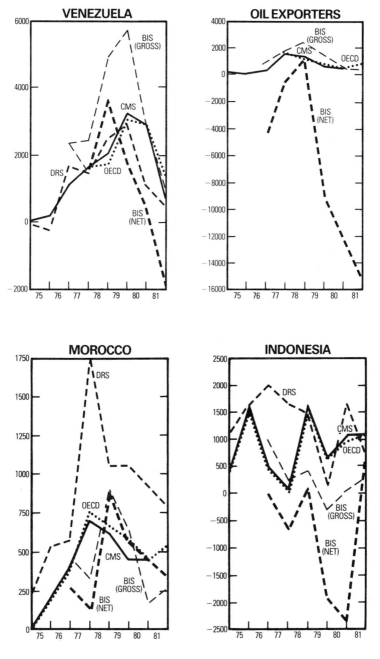

FIGURE 15.2

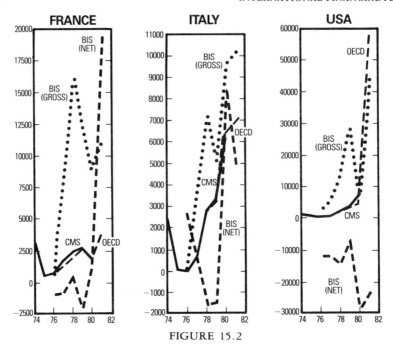

FIGURE 15.2

Poland where a 5%. level of significance is achieved. In fact for the majority of the sample countries, the data are identical for the first two years (1974–5) and only begin to diverge significantly later in the observation period and then only for certain countries. The lower significance for Poland is largely accounted for by the sharp fall in the CMS eurocredits series from $819 million in 1979 to $338 million in 1980, while a much smaller fall to $736 million was recorded by the OECD.

In drawing conclusions from these figures of total eurocurrency credits, however, two points should be borne in mind. Firstly, these absolute volumes of new credits reported by the series may diverge considerably due to the reporting by one source and the omission by another of one or two large loans. For example, in 1977, of the 128 credits reported by the OECD for this sample of borrowers at least 112 were captured by the CMS. Therefore the degree of divergence between credit volumes may be very different from the extent to which the series may overlap in terms of the *number* of separate credit agreements captured. In fact, it may be more likely that the discrepancies between the two series are of greater importance than the absolute figures would suggest if a large number of small loans —

TABLE 15.5(a)
Results from CMS/OECD and BIS (Gross)/BIS (Net) Regressions (Annual Data)

Dependent variable		CMS	BIS (gross)
Independent variable		OECD	BIS (net)
France:	β	1.004⁺	0.116
		(36.27)	(0.36)
	$\bar{R}^2$/DW	0.99/2.28	− 0.21/1.10
Italy:	β	0.956⁺	0.441
		(58.57)	(1.02)
	$R\bar{2}$/DW	0.99/1.99	0.01/0.85
USA:	β	1.148⁺	− 0.256
		(21.39)	(− 0.26)
	$\bar{R}^2$/DW	0.99/1.54	− 0.23/1.98
Poland:	β	0.746⁺	1.101⁺
		(3.34)	(9.35)
	$\bar{R}^2$/DW	0.63/1.76	0.95/2.88
Mexico:	β	0.609⁺	1.095⁺
		(6.35)	(20.46)
	$\bar{R}^2$/DW	0.85/1.55	0.99/2.86
Venezuela:	β	1.050⁺	0.663
		(10.14)	(1.93)
	$\bar{R}^2$/DW	0.94/0.88	0.35/1.26
Oil-exporters:	β	0.998⁺	0.110⁺
		(11.13)	(3.44)
	$\bar{R}^2$/DW	0.95/3.19	0.68/1.35
Morocco:	β	0.881⁺	0.766*
		(11.71)	(2.33)
	$\bar{R}^2$/DW	0.96/2.39	0.47/1.26
Indonesia:	β	1.009⁺	0.215
		(31.69)	(1.67)
	$\bar{R}^2$/DW	0.99/3.09	0.26/1.65
Korea:	β	0.800⁺	0.811⁺
		(10.12)	(4.98)
	$\bar{R}^2$/DW	0.94/0.94	0.83/2.85
Philippines	β	1.021⁺	1.415
		(6.43)	(1.74)
	$\bar{R}^2$/DW	0.85/1.54	0.29/1.81

many of which tend to be less publicised than large credits — are not captured by one or other of the sources. Secondly, part of the discrepancies in the series for a particular two-year period may simply be a problem of timing — that is the allocation of a credit to two separate years by the different sources. This is quite likely to occur when the exact signature date of a credit is unknown and it occurs around the turn of a year.

(b) BIS (Gross)/BIS (Net) (Table 15.5 (a))

It would not be expected that the series for gross and net new banking flows would be necessarily very closely related. However, a perfect correlation would occur when the series coincided due to unchanged liabilities of reporting banks to a particular country. However, a positive coefficient with a high degree of significance would also be obtained when the series move together but do not coincide. The best example of this in the country sample is Mexico where the difference between the gross and net positions remains fairly steady due to a fairly constant annual increase in bank liabilities to Mexico.[14] The results in Table 15.5 (a) are rather mixed with significant results for 5 of the 11 countries in the sample, although only in the case of the sample of industrial countries is there a complete lack of association, due to the highly volatile nature of reporting banks liabilities to these countries.

(c) BIS (Gross)/CMS and OECD (Table 15.5 (b) and (c))

These are perhaps the most interesting in theory of the results due to

[14] The change in a banks' gross claims (G) on a country may defined as:

$$G_t = A_t - A_{t-1} \tag{15.1}$$

and the change in their net position (N) as:

$$N_t = (A_t - L_t) - (A_{t-1} - L_{t-1}) \tag{15.2}$$

where A and L are assets and liabilities respectively and t indicates time.

For perfect correlation:

$$G_t = N_t \tag{15.3}$$

from (15.1), (15.2):

$$A_t - A_{t-1} = (A_t - L_t) - (A_{t-1} - L_{t-1}) \tag{15.4}$$

simplifying:

$$L_t = L_{t-1} \tag{15.5}$$

i.e. constant liabilities

For a constant difference between G and N (also perfect correlation)

$$G_t - N_t = C_t \tag{15.6}$$

where C is a constant:

$$(A_t - A_{t-1}) - [(A_t - L_t) - (A_{t-1} - L_{t-1})] = C \tag{15.7}$$

simplifying:

$$L_t - L_{t-1} = C \tag{15.8}$$

i.e. A constant absolute growth of banks liabilities.

the frequently expressed hope of discovering whether any relationship exists between capital market and banking data. Unfortunately the regression results from these relationships are rather poor. For both the CMS and OECD as alternative independent variables only ten of the thirty-three co-efficients are significantly greater than zero (including one- and two-year lagged observations), while a further three co-efficients are significantly negative.

A cursory glance at Fig. 15.2 confirms that despite there being, for many countries, certain years when the series moved together this pattern was generally not maintained throughout the observation period. When entered without a lag, CMS data are significantly related to gross BIS data for France, Italy, Venezuela, the oil exporters and Korea while for OECD data significance was achieved for Italy, the United States, Mexico, Korea and the Philippines. Perhaps the most impressive association is in the case of Italy, apart from 1979 when both the CMS and OECD recorded a rise in new eurocurrency credit commitments at a time when there was a decline in the gross amount of new bank lending to that country. When one and two year lags are included, significant co-efficients were recorded for Italy, the United States, Mexico and Korea. When included contemporaneously, the lack of significance of CMS data for the United States, while the OECD series is highly significant, is explained by the capture by both OECD and BIS series of the enormous increase in lending to US companies in 1981. (No CMS observation for the full year was available for the United States.)

Three explanations may by advanced for these mixed results. Firstly, it may simply be the case that, due to all the theoretical factors noted earlier in the chapter, any greater degree of correspondence between the series should not be anticipated. Secondly, the use of annual data may be inappropriate. It is possible that an analysis using quarterly data would permit a more successful identification of correspondence between the series. In particular many of the short-run related fluctuations in the series may be lost in the annual figures. A final explanation may be that such poor results are due to a shortage of observations and therefore degrees of freedom.

The latter argument may simply have to await the availability of more annual observations; however, it does link up with the previous point to suggest a quarterly analysis of these series. Therefore Table 15.5 (c) presents a set of regression results from quarterly BIS (Gross) and OECD data from the first quarter of 1977 to the fourth quarter of 1981. Lags of up to four quarters were tried individually and in combination. For each country, the best equation in terms of the

TABLE 15.5(b)
Results from Regressions of BIS (Gross) Against CMS and Against OECD (Annual Data)

Dependent variable		BIS (gross)					
Independent variable		CMS_t	CMS_{t-1}	CMS_{t-2}	$OECD_t$	$OECD_{t-1}$	$OECD_{t-2}$
France	β	7.092+ (4.29)	3.843 (1.73)	-2.707 (-1.40)	3.567 (1.93)	3.703 (1.57)	-2.728 (-1.40)
	$\bar{R}^2$/DW	0.81/3.21	0.28/1.75	0.16/1.04	0.35/1.53	0.23/1.75	0.16/1.10
Italy:	β	1.344+ (3.95)	1.234* (2.53)	0.868 (0.72)	1.225+ (5.34)	1.158* (2.42)	0.858 (0.71)
	$\bar{R}^2$/DW	0.79/2.03	0.52/2.32	-0.11/0.93	0.85/1.94	0.49/2.29	-0.11/0.91
USA:	β	0.900 (0.44)	4.846+ (2.74)	7.212 (1.45)	0.606+ (3.07)	5.553+ (2.69)	6.597 (1.29)
	$\bar{R}^2$/DW	-0.25/2.14	0.57/2.78	0.18/2.46	0.63/2.12	0.56/2.84	0.12/2.46
Poland:	β	2.487 (1.27)	-2.807 (-1.20)	-3.908 (-2.02)	1.870 (1.06)	-3.947 (-2.78)	-4.055 (-2.38)
	$\bar{R}^2$/DW	0.13/1.34	0.08/1.30	0.38/1.64	0.02/1.25	0.57/2.20	0.48/1.78
Mexico:	β	1.075 (1.14)	1.437* (2.01)	1.703+ (4.98)	0.965* (2.21)	1.092* (2.23)	1.269+ (4.55)
	$\bar{R}^2$/DW	0.06/0.75	0.38/1.25	0.83/2.69	0.44/1.29	0.44/1.77	0.80/1.88
Venezuela:	β	1.376* (2.40)	-0.142 (-0.18)	-0.314 (-0.43)	1.251 (1.43)	-0.292 (-0.36)	-0.281 (-0.36)
	$\bar{R}^2$/DW	0.49/1.89	-0.24/1.18	-0.19/1.23	0.17/1.39	-0.21/1.16	-0.21/1.24
Oil Exporters:	β	1.144* (2.55)	0.792 (1.46)	-0.450 (-0.76)	1.064 (1.70)	0.746 (1.30)	-0.457 (-0.76)
	$\bar{R}^2$/DW	0.58/2.35	0.18/0.71	-0.09/1.00	0.28/1.51	0.12/0.76	-0.09/1.05
Morocco:	β	0.396 (0.31)	0.951 (1.55)	0.027 (0.05)	0.660 (0.70)	0.678 (1.18)	-0.071 (-0.15)
	$\bar{R}^2$/DW	-0.29/2.22	0.22/1.50	-0.25/1.77	-0.11/2.25	0.07/1.59	-0.24/1.79
Indonesia:	β	-0.021 (-0.05)	0.006 (0.02)	-0.065 (-0.21)	-0.040 (-0.10)	0.013 (0.04)	-0.066 (-0.21)
	$\bar{R}^2$/DW	-0.25/1.53	-0.25/1.46	-0.24/1.43	-0.25/1.59	-0.25/1.47	-0.24/1.42
Korea:	β	1.468* (2.42)	1.571+ (6.19)	0.952 (1.56)	1.078* (2.27)	1.443+ (5.01)	0.808 (1.28)
	$\bar{R}^2$/DW	0.49/2.54	0.88/3.09	0.22/2.10	0.45/2.53	0.83/2.67	0.11/1.94
Philippines:	β	0.752 (1.48)	0.609 (1.63)	0.349 (0.79)	1.040* (2.12)	0.586 (1.35)	0.146 (0.28)
	$\bar{R}^2$/DW	0.19/2.10	0.25/2.64	-0.08/1.51	0.41/2.60	0.14/2.14	-0.23/1.64

TABLE 15.5 (c)
Results from OECD/BIS (Gross) Regressions — Quarterly Data

Dependent variable — BIS (gross)	Constant	OECD					$\bar{R}^2$	DW
		t	$t-1$	$t-2$	$t-3$	$t-4$		
France	8475.83 (4.96)			1.87 (1.48)			0.759	2.69
Italy	7492.51 (5.25)	1.49* (1.96)					0.832	1.96
USA	−821.40 (−0.32)	0.14 (1.14)	0.45+ (3.71)				0.477	1.67
Poland	428.93 (0.34)	0.25 (0.25)					−0.062	1.87
Mexico	99.39 (0.11)	0.53* (2.05)	0.49* (1.90)				0.354	0.82
Venezuela	1154.97 (3.84)	0.49* (1.89)					0.345	1.50
Oil Exporters	−0.65 (−0.01)			1.64+ (2.26)	0.38 (0.52)		0.397	1.83
Morocco	4.38 (0.05)			0.90+ (2.95)	0.31 (1.10)	0.70+ (2.49)	0.455	2.79
Indonesia	104.02 (1.27)	0.09 (0.52)					0.063	1.67
Korea	132.73 (0.95)			1.02+ (6.35)	0.24 (1.33)		0.779	1.99
Philippines	147.16 (1.06)				0.49* (1.88)		0.180	2.02

significance of the OECD variable and the overall fit of the equation was chosen and the results are set out in this table.[15]

These results represent a marked improvement on the regression equations using annual data. Only for France, Poland and Indonesia was it possible to achieve a significantly positive coefficient on any of the OECD variables (defined contemporaneously and with a lag of up to four quarters). For the latter two countries, this result is not surprising given the poor quality of the annual results. For the other countries a variety of lag patterns is apparent although the relative weight placed on current and one-quarter lagged values of the independent variable is perhaps unexpected given the belief that OECD commitemnts data are not likely to be reflected in BIS data particularly rapidly.

The equation for Korea is very well-determined with the coefficient on OECD data lagged by six months being highly significant. The lag pattern for Morocco suggests a similar six month lag before fluctuations in eurocurrency credit commitments are reflected in gross bank claims but in this case it is augmented by a coefficient of almost equal significance on the OECD variable when lagged by four quarters. The impressive result for Italy using annual data is not really matched when quarterly observations are used (although a 10% level of significance is achieved on the contemporaneous OECD variable), while there is strong evidence for a one-quarter lag in the case of the United States.

Clearly, the quarterly regressions have established certain links between the BIS and OECD data series where evidence was rather limited in the annual tests. However, the lack of overall pattern in the results and particularly in the time-lags for the different countries suggests that a considerable amount of work remains to be done to relate these series in a stable and predictable way at the micro-level. Certainly, the quarterly results are a great improvement for many of the countries in the sample, particularly given the small number of observations and the relatively crude modelling of the lag structure. However, it is still true that the problems involved in deriving a stable relationship between BIS banking figures and capital market figures for an individual country are, as expected, quite considerable.

---

[15] In each case, dummy variables were included in the regressions to allow for the heavy seasonal influences — mainly due to window-dressing and other operations by lending banks — in the BIS data series. These dummy variables were all highly significant for France and Italy only, with one or other of them being significant in the other 'best' equations except those for Poland, Mexico, Korea and the Philippines.

(d) DRS/CMS and OECD (Table 15.5 (d))

The correlation coefficients reported in Table 15.5 (d) suggests a stable positive relationship between contemporaneous DRS and both CMS and OECD data for Venezuela, Morocco, Korea and the Philippines. From Fig. 15.2, it is clear that the relationship is particularly close for Morocco, with the gradual acceleration in the rate of growth of external public dept to its peak in 1977 being reflected by an increase in eurocurrency credit agreements over this period. Similarly, the subsequent fall in the rate of increase of external debt in 1978, before levelling off at around $1 billion per annum to the end of 1981, is mirrored in OECD data and (to the end of 1980) CMS figures also.

However, the general absence of any evidence of significant association between the series when capital markets data is lagged places some uncertainty on the contemporaneous results. Given that CMS data are for commitments only while the DRS covers actual debt transactions, a lagged relationship may, *a priori,* be more expected. The only exceptions are for Korea, where a two-year lagged relationship is highly significant and for Mexico (using OECD data only) where again a two-year lag provides satisfactory results. Therefore, without dismissing the apparent stability of the unlagged relationship, some uncertainty must still remain over the links between CMS and DRs data and further evidence to confirm the positive conclusions noted above would be useful. More generally, the good results for Korea and Mexico are consistent with the overall picture from Table 15.5, that the association between the different statistical series is generally better for Korea and Mexico than for any other developing country.

(e) BIS (Net)/DRS (Table 15.5 (d))

This is the only set of correlations undertaken in this study between flow changes of published stock series and so the results should be of particular interest. Unfortunately, only for Venezuela and Korea is a significant relationship derived between these two series with the results for the other four developing countries in the sample being very poor. The good result for Venezuela is based on a fall in the absolute increase of net bank claims on that country and of its external debt in 1977 followed by a sharp increase in both series one year later. Although the series diverged in 1979 with net claims decelerating again while the increase in debt continued to rise, there was again close correspondence between the two series in 1980–1

TABLE 15.5(d)
Results from Regressions of DRS Against CMS, OECD and BIS (net) (Annual Data)

Dependent variable		DRS						
Independent variable		CMS_t	CMS_{t-1}	CMS_{t-2}	$OECD_t$	$OECD_{t-1}$	$OECD_{t-2}$	BIS (net)
Mexico:	β	0.380	0.121	0.498	0.309	0.125	0.484+	0.261
		(1.32)	(0.35)	(1.79)	(1.80)	(0.48)	(3.35)	(1.44)
	$\bar{R}^2$/DW	0.10/1.27	−0.17/1.37	0.31/2.01	0.24/1.46	−0.15/1.49	0.67/1.76	0.34/1.86
Venezuela	β	0.769+	0.117	−0.316	0.749+	0.072	−0.303	0.384+
		(3.34)	(0.30)	(−0.94)	(2.59)	(0.18)	(−0.81)	(2.65)
	$\bar{R}^2$/DW	0.59/2.03	−0.18/1.29	−0.02/1.55	0.45/1.60	−0.19/1.27	−0.07/1.57	0.55/2.26
Morocco	β	1.855+	0.850	0.031	1.641+	0.660	−0.061	−0.315
		(4.75)	(1.30)	(0.04)	(5.08)	(1.08)	(−0.09)	(−0.44)
	$\bar{R}^2$/DW	0.73/3.48	0.10/2.55	−0.25/2.36	0.78/2.84	0.03/2.45	−0.25/2.40	−0.19/2.01
Indonesia	β	0.038	−0.448	0.541	−0.013	−0.413	0.530	0.057
		(0.09)	(−0.99)	(1.13)	(−0.03)	(−0.88)	(1.09)	(0.20)
	$\bar{R}^2$/DW	−0.17/2.02	−0.01/1.78	0.05/1.60	−0.17/2.09	−0.04/1.80	0.04/1.64	−0.24/2.13
Korea	β	0.953+	0.702*	0.809+	0.807+	0.649	0.794+	0.391*
		(4.72)	(1.97)	(3.35)	(5.49)	(1.87)	(3.54)	(2.16)
	$\bar{R}^2$/DW	0.75/2.03	0.32/2.13	0.67/1.92	0.81/2.20	0.30/2.10	0.70/1.79	0.42/2.26
Philippines	β	0.528*	0.204	0.203	0.568*	0.242	0.168	0.383
		(2.42)	(0.81)	(1.36)	(2.35)	(0.89)	(0.92)	(1.07)
	$\bar{R}^2$/DW	0.41/1.30	−0.06/1.80	0.15/1.82	0.39/1.63	−0.04/1.71	−0.03/2.00	0.03/2.75

with sharp falls in the increase in net bank claims (with a negative figure of $1831 million in 1981) and in external debt.

Given the shortage of observations and the expectations that two series for bank debt and total debt should be most highly correlated, if at all, on a contemporaneous basis, no lagged relationships were investigated. The limited evidence on the linkages between the contemporaneous series is therefore rather disappointing.

CONCLUSION

The efforts made in this chapter to establish close correspondance between various statistical series on international financial flows have had limited success. Certain stable and positive relationships have been discovered and it is reassuring, in particular, that the CMS and OECD series on new eurocurrency credit agreements are very closely linked.

The rather uncertain conclusion from this chapter should not be unexpected however given the different definitions, constituents and coverage of these series and the different objectives of the various organisations in publishing them. The overall conclusion to the book itself should be that an enormous and often bewildering amount of statistical information is now available for monitoring the rapid growth of financial flows between countries. A close understanding of some of these series is essential for anyone seeking to achieve a firm grasp of the problems of international indebtedness, the growth of eurocurrency lending and many other financial topics of equal importance at the beginning of the 1980s. While it maybe hoped that,in time, an attempt will be made to establish a centralised, internally, consistent data, system covering all financial flows, it is important to be aware of the wealth of material that is already available on such flows. If the reader's understanding of this complex subject has been increased a little by studying this book, it may be said to have achieved its main purpose.

References

G. C. Abbott, (1979) *International Indebtedness and the Developing Countries* London and New York: Croom Helm and Sharpe.

G. C. Abbott (1981) 'International Indebtedness of Less Developed Countries: Structure, Growth and Indicators', *Aussenwirtschaft, Heft 4, pp. 340–351.*

Amex Bank (1982) 'LDC debt service burdens: A cash-flow analysis', *Amex Bank Review,* April, pp.1–3.

D. F. V. Ashby (1974) 'The $300 billion super-dollar market', *The Banker,* May, pp.449–454.

D. F. V. Ashby (1978) 'Challenge from the new Euro-centres' *The Banker,* January, pp.53–61.

D. F. V. Ashby (1979a) 'Changing patterns in the $800 billion super-dollar market', *The Banker,* March, pp.21–23.

D. F. V. Ashby (1979b) 'New Eurocurrency centres: attracting an increasing share of new business', *Investors Chronicle Euromarkets Survey,* 21–27 September, pp.34–39.

D. F. V. Ashby (1981) 'Will the Eurodollar market go back home?', *The Banker,* February, pp.93–98.

D. F. V. Ashby (1982) 'Eurocurrency mismatching does matter up to a point', *The Banker,* January, pp.79–81.

D. Avramovic (1958), *Debt servicing capacity and post-war growth in international indebtedness,* Johns Hopkins University Press, Baltimore.

D. Avramovic *et al.* (1965) *Economic growth and external debt,* Johns Hopkins University Press, Baltimore.

D. E. Baer (1981) 'Sources of information for country risk analysis' *Federal Reserve Bank of Atlanta Economic Review,* June, pp.37–39.

Bank for International Settlements (1979) *Manual on statistics compiled by international organisations on countries' external indebtedness,* Basle, March.

Bank of England (1981) 'Purposes of banking statistics' *Bank of England Quarterly Bulletin,* September, pp.374–381.

Bank of England (1982) 'The international banking markets in 1980–1', *Bank of England Quarterly Bulletin,* March, pp.42–55.

The Banker (1982) 'SDR Issues: New IMF Borrowing?', March, p.82.

G. Bird (1981a) 'The IMF and the Developing Countries: Evolving Relations, Use of Resources and the Debate over Conditionality' *Overseas Development Institute Working Paper*, No.2, March.

G. Bird (1981b) 'Financial Flows to Developing Countries: the role of the International Monetary Fund', *Review of International Studies*, pp.91–105.

M. Campbell (1978) 'Keeping track of developments in international borrowing', *Financial Times*, 1st August.

A. D. Crockett (1982) 'Issues in the use of Fund Resources', *Finance and Development*, June, pp.10–15.

S. Davis (1978) 'Techniques in International Banking' in S. Frowen (ed.) *A Framework of International Banking*, Guildford Educational Press, Guildford.

S. Dell (1981) 'On being grandmotherly: the evolution of IMF Conditionality', *Princeton Essays in International Finance*, No.144, October.

G. E. J. Dennis (1983) 'The Growth of International Bank Lending, 1972–82', *Aussenwirtschaft,*, *Heft 3*, pp.263–283.

D. J. Donovan (1982a) 'Macroeconomic Performance and Adjustment under Fund-Supported Programs: The Experience of the Seventies' *IMF Staff Papers*, June, pp.171–203.

D. J. Donovan (1982b) 'Economic Performance of Developing Countries under Stand-By Arrangements Traced by Study' *IMF Survey*, 25th October pp.337, 345–8.

G. Duffy and I. H. Giddy (1978) *The International Money Market*, Prentice-Hall, Englewood Cliffs, New Jersey.

P. R. Duncan (1981) 'When mismatching in international lending may matter' *The Banker*, December pp.57–9.

The Economist (1978) 'Must lend, will travel. International banking, a survey — Figuring on ldc debts' 4th March, p.9.

The Economist (1982) 'A nightmare of debt: a survey of international banking' 20th March.

J. G. Ellis (1981) 'Eurobanks and the inter-bank market' *Bank of England Quarterly Bulletin*, September, pp.351–364.

Euromoney (1979) 'How the British taxpayer gives London banks a hand-out', August, pp.121–122.

A. E. Fleming (1981) 'Private Capital Flows to Developing Countries and their Determination: Historical Perspective, Recent Experience and Future Prospects, *World Bank Staff Working Paper*, No. 484, August.

A. E. Fleming and S. K. Howson (1980) 'Conditions in the syndicated medium-term euro-credit market' *Bank of England Quarterly Bulletin*, September, pp.311–318.

G. Forrest (1981) 'IMF — Do its Functions Conflict?', *Barclays Review*, May, pp.25–6.

S. F. Frowen (1981) 'Why the IMF Is Increasing Its Role in Recycling', *Euromoney*, January, pp.123–32.

E. J. Frydl (1982) 'The Euro-dollar Conundrum', *Federal Reserve Bank of*

New York Quarterly Review, Spring, pp.11–19.

W. J. Gasser and D. L. Roberts (1982) 'Bank Lending to Developing Countries: Problems and Prospects', *Federal Reserve Bank of New York Quarterly Review*, Autumn, pp.18–29.

J. Gold (1979a) 'Conditionality', *IMF Pamphlet Series*, No. 31, Washington DC.

J. Gold (1979b) 'Financial Assistance by the International Monetary Fund. Law and Practice', *IMF Pamphlet Series*, No. 27, Washington DC.

L. S. Goodman (1980) 'The Pricing of Eurocurrency Credits', *Federal Reserve Bank of New York Quarterly Review*, Summer, pp.39–49.

L. M. Goreux (1980) 'Compensating Financing Facility', *IMF Pamphlet Series* No. 34, Washington DC.

D. Gorman (1981) 'A New Role for the IMF?', *Barclays Review*, May, pp.31–5.

S. Griffiths-Jones (1980) 'The Growth of Multinational Banking, the Eurocurrency Market and their Effects On Developing Countries', *Journal of Development Studies*, January, pp.204–23.

Group of Thirty (1982) 'Risks in international bank lending', New York.

M. Guitian (1980) 'Fund Conditionality and the International Adjustment Process: The Early Period, 1950–70', *Finance and Development*, December, pp.23–27.

M. Guitian (1981a) 'Fund Conditionality and the International Adjustment Process: The Changing Environment of the 1970's', *Finance and Development*, March, pp.8–11.

M. Guitian (1981b) 'Fund Conditionality and the International Adjustment Process: A Look into the 1980's', *Finance and Development*, June, pp14–17.

M. Guitian (1981c) 'Fund Conditionality: Evolution of Principles and Practices', *IMF Pamphlet Series*, No. 38, Washington DC.

P. Gutmann (1980) 'Assessing Country Risk', *National Westminister Bank Review*, May, pp.58–68.

C. Hardy (1981) 'Rescheduling developing country debts', *The Banker*, July, pp.33–8.

J. A. Holsen (1978) 'Sources of data on LDC external debt' in M. S. Wionczek (ed.). *LDC external debt and the world economy*, Collegio de Mexico.

A. W. Hooke (1981) 'The International Monetary Fund. Its Evolution, Organisation and Activities', *IMF Pamphlet Series*, No. 37, Washington DC.

G. Howe (1982) 'The International Monetary Fund and The World Bank: The British Approach', *International Affairs*, Spring, pp.199–209.

H. Hughes (1977) 'The external debt of developing countries', *Finance and Development*, December, pp.22–5.

K. Inoue (1980) 'Determinants of Market Conditions in the Eurocurrency Market — Why a borrower's market?', *BIS Working Paper*, No. 1, April.

IMF (1981) 'International Capital Markets: Recent Developments and Short-Term Prospects', *IMF Occasional Paper*, No.7, Washington DC.

IMF (1982) 'Supplement on Fund Accounts', *IFS Supplement Series*, No. 3.

IMF Survey (1976) 'Progress made in reporting capital flows to the developing world', 6th September, pp.263–266.

IMF Survey (1978) 'Multiformula Methods Add Flexibility in the Calculation of Members' Quotas', 5th June, pp.166–8.

R. B. Johnston (1979) 'Some Aspects of the Determination of Eurocurrency Interest Rates', *Bank of England Quarterly Bulletin*, March, pp.35–46.

R. B. Johnston (1983) *The Economics of the Euromarket: History, Theory and Policy*, Macmillan, London.

J. A. Katz (1979) 'Capital Flows and Developing Country Debt', *World Bank Staff Working Paper*, No. 352, August.

M. R. Kelly (1982) 'Fiscal Adjustment and Fund-supported Programs, 1971–80' *IMF Staff Papers*, December, pp.561–602.

M. R. Kelly (1983) 'Analysis of Stand-By Program during 1971-80 Confirms Importance Attached to Fiscal Targets' *IMF Survey*, 7th February, pp.35–8.

S. J. Key (1982) 'Activities of International Banking Facilities — the early experience', *Federal Reserve Bank of Chicago Economic Perspectives*, Fall, pp.37–45.

G. R. Kincaid (1981) 'Inflation and the external debt of developing countries', *Finance and Development*, December, pp.45–8.

P. Koenig (1982) 'Whatever happened to New York's IBF's?', *Institutional Investor*, April, pp.121–5.

J. de Larosière (1979) 'Towards a solution of international economic problems', *Finance and Development*, September, pp.12–14.

J. S. Little (1979) 'Liquidity Creation by Euro-banks: 1973–1978', *New England Economic Review*, January–February, pp.62–72.

D. T. Llewellyn (1978) 'International Banking in the 1970's' in S. Frowen (ed.) *A Framework of International Banking*, Guildford Education Press, Guildford.

D. T. Llewellyn (1980) *International Financial Intergration: The Limits to Sovereignty*, Macmillan, London.

D. T. Llewellyn (1981) 'The analytical framework of international banking', *Tape Manuscript*, Philip Thorn Associates, Guildford.

D. T. Llewellyn and G. E. J. Dennis (1979) 'Identified Flows of Funds through International Banking', Technical Note No. 3 *Trends in International Banking and Capital Markets*, Banker Research Unit, London.

H. W. Mayer (1976) 'The BIS Concept of the Eurocurrency Market', *Euromoney*, May, pp.60–6

H. W. Mayer (1979a) 'The BIS Statistics on International Banking' Paper presented to the *International Association for Research in Income and Wealth General Conference*, Portschack, Austria.

H. W. Mayer (1979b) 'Credit and Liquidity Creation in the International Banking Sector', *BIS Economic Paper*, No.1, November.

M. S. Mendelsohn (1979) 'That Sinking Feeling', *The Banker*, January, pp.57–9.

R. H. Mills Jr. and E. D. Short (1979) 'US Banks and the North American Eurocurrency Market', *Federal Reserve Board International Finance Discussion Paper*, No. 134, April, Washington DC.

Morgan Guaranty (1976) 'Estimating external debt', *World Financial Markets*, December, pp.4–8.

Morgan Guaranty (1977) 'Notes on statistics on international lending', *World Financial Markets*, May, pp.5–7.

Morgan Guaranty (1981) 'International banking facilities' *World Financial Markets*, November, pp.6–11.

Morgan Guaranty (1983) 'Global debt: assessment and prescriptions', *World Financial Markets*, February, pp.1–14.

P. Nagy (1979) *Country Risk — how to assess, quantify and monitor it*, Euromoney Publications Ltd., London.

P. Neuhaus (1982) 'Floating interest rates and developing country debt' *Finance and Development*, December, pp.37–8.

J. Niehans and J. Hewson (1976) 'The Euro-Dollar Market and Monetary Theory', *Journal of Money, Credit and Banking*, February, pp.1–27.

B. Nowzad (1981) 'The IMF and its Critics', *Princeton Essays in International Finance*, No. 146, December.

B. Nowzad (1982) 'Debt in developing countries: some issues for the 1980's', *Finance and Development*, March, pp.13–16.

J. C. O'Connor (1980) 'IFS Data on Deposit Banks' Foreign Accounts', *IMF Papers on International Financial Statistics (PIFS) Series*, 1980/3.

OECD (1974) 'Debt Problems of Developing Countries', Paris.

OECD (1982a) 'External Debt of Developing Countries: 1982 Survey', Paris.

OECD (1982b) 'Geographical distribution of financial flows to developing countries, 1978/1981', Paris.

OECD (1982c) 'The Medium-Term Euro-credit Market in 1978–81', *Financial Market Trends*, March, pp.1–35.

T. M. Reichmann and R. T. Stillson (1978) 'Experience with Programs of Balance of Payments Adjustments in the Higher Credit Tranches, 1963–73', *IMF Staff Papers*, June, pp. 293–309.

D. Roberts (1981) 'The LDC Debt Burden' *Federal Reserve Bank of New York Quarterly Review*, Spring, pp.33–41.

K. Saini and P. Bates (1978) 'Statistical techniques for determining debt — servicing capacity for developing countries: Analytical review of the Literature and further empirical results', *Federal Reserve Bank of New York Research Paper*, No. 7818, September.

H. Sandeman (1979) 'How much risk are Eurobanks taking?' *The Banker*, January, pp.71–7.

J. W. Saxe (1979) 'External Debt and Capital Flows: A Review of Reports of the World Bank on the External Debt of Developing Countries'. Paper presented to the *International Association for Research in Income and Wealth General Conference*, Portschack, Austria.

E. D. Short and B. B. White (1978) 'International Bank Lending: A Guided Tour through the Data', *Federal Reserve Bank of New York Quarterly*

Review, Autumn, pp.39–46.

R. Solomon (1977) 'A Perspective on the Debt of Developing Countries', *Brookings Papers on Economic Activity,* No.2, pp.479–510.

R. Solomon (1981) 'The Debt of Developing Countries: Another Look' *Brookings Papers on Economic Activity,* No. 2, pp.593–606.

B. Stein (1980) 'Statistics of resource flows to developing countries'. Updated version of paper presented to the *International Association for Research in Income and Wealth General Conference,* Portschack, Austria.

J. Sterling (1980a) 'How big is the international lending market?', *The Banker,* January, pp.77–87.

J. Sterling (1980b) 'Competitive Advantage in Bank Eurocurrency Lending' *Unpublished PhD thesis,* Johns Hopkins University, Baltimore.

J. S. Thornton (1980) 'Liquidity Creation in the Euromarkets', *Business Economist,* Summer, pp.40–6.

J. Walmsley (1982) 'International Banking Facilities — we have lift-off', *The Banker,* February, pp.91–6.

R. J. Walton (1981) 'Foreign Transactor Breakdown for International Financial Statistics (IFS) data on Deposit Banks' Foreign Accounts', *IMF Papers on International Financial Statistics (PIFS) Series,* 1981/2.

J. H. Williamson (1982) 'The Lending Policies of the International Monetary Fund', *Policy Analyses in International Economics,* Institute for International Economics, August.

Statistical Sources

Bank For International Settlements:

Annual Report
Press Release — 'International banking developments'
Press Release — 'The maturity distribution of international bank lending'

Bank of England:

Quarterly Bulletin

International Bank for Reconstruction and Development (World Bank):

Borrowing in International Capital Markets (EC–181)
World Debt Tables (EC–167)

International Monetary Fund:

International Financial Statistics
Survey

Morgan Guaranty Trust Company:

World Financial Markets

Organisation for Economic Cooperation and Development:
Development Cooperation: efforts and policies of the Development Assistance Committee
Financial Market Trends
Financial Statistics

Index